THE RELUCTANT KING

BY MICHAEL ROSS

THE RELUCTANT KING

JOSEPH BONAPARTE
KING OF THE TWO SICILIES AND SPAIN

 MASON / CHARTER   NEW YORK 1977

Library of Congress Cataloging in Publication Data

Ross, Michael, 1905-
    The reluctant king.

    Bibliography: p.
    Includes index.
        1. Joseph Bonaparte, King of Spain, 1768-1844.
2. Statesman—France—Biography. I. Title.
DC216.5.R67 1977   946'.06'0924 [B]   76-51395
ISBN 0-88405-493-4

Contents

Illustrations

Author's Foreword

Some years ago while browsing in a secondhand book shop I came across two volumes published by John Murray in 1855 bearing the title: *The Confidential Correspondence of Napoleon Bonaparte with his brother Joseph, sometime King of Spain*, with the subtitle: *Selected and translated from the Mémoires du roi Joseph*. I soon found myself engrossed in this correspondence and increasingly curious to learn something more concerning the 'sometime King of Spain' of whom I confess I knew practically nothing. From my school days I remembered that he had been decisively defeated at Vitoria, leaving behind him on the field of battle the royal treasure and the royal chamber-pot. And that was about all.

The anonymous translator of the *Confidential Correspondence* mentioned above had chosen to select many more letters from Napoleon to his brother than letters from Joseph himself. Determined to remedy this omission I sought out Du Casse's unabridged *Mémoires et Correspondance* in the library of the Institut français and from these there emerged a clearer picture of the *roi philosophe*. The more I read the more I felt in sympathy with this elder brother of the great Napoleon. However, it was not until I read Christopher Herold's *Mistress to an Age*, the life story of Madame de Staël, in which Joseph appears as a cultivated, liberal minded and charming man, that my first impressions of him were confirmed and that the idea of writing his biography began to formulate in my mind. First, however, it was necessary to find out whether other writers had already published a comprehensive biography. To my surprise, with the exception of *The Gentle Bonaparte* by Owen Connolly and two comparatively recent French works I could find none, though there were a number of works by Spanish, French, Italian and American authors devoted to certain periods of Joseph's long life (cf Bibliography).

7

Author's Foreword

In this biography I make no claims to original research; my story has been pieced together from a number of sources, some familiar, others less well known. I am particularly indebted to Bernard Nabonne's *Joseph Bonaparte, le roi philosophe* and perhaps even more to Gabriel Girod de l'Ain's *Joseph Bonaparte, le roi malgré lui*, to which I owe most of the information concerning Joseph's love affairs; for Napoleon's military campaigns I have relied on various sources, but for the Peninsular War I have depended almost entirely on Sir Arthur Bryant's *The Great Duke*. To the best of my ability I have acknowledged these and all other sources in my notes.

I have one other confession to make. It is some three years since I completed the first draft of this book. It proved to be far too long, and at my publisher's request I deleted some 20,000 words, including many notes. These I have now been asked to reinsert. Unfortunately my original typescript has been destroyed, and with it many of the notes. Thus, in the present volume, although I am able to supply sources, I cannot always give page numbers of the volumes to which I refer. To do so would entail rereading countless books in the British Museum and elsewhere, a task which I find altogether too daunting and which I have firmly declined.

In conclusion I wish to express my gratitude to all historians and memorialists, past and present, who have helped me to compile this biography, and to many friends in both England and France who have encouraged me in my work.

Barnes 1975   MICHAEL ROSS

'Joseph was born to be loved.'
TALLEYRAND

I

Childhood and Youth

1767–1793

Joseph-Napoleon Bonaparte, the eldest brother of the great Napoleon, was born in Corsica on 7 January 1767. If he is remembered at all, it is as an unsuccessful King of Naples and later of Spain; a dilettante man of letters, extravagant, pleasure-loving, amorous and lazy, who left no mark on the pages of history. His image is quite overshadowed by that of the Man of Destiny. The ten volumes of his *Mémoires et correspondance*, so carefully compiled and edited by the Baron du Casse, are almost forgotten; the works of his memorialists, Miot, Comte de Melito, General Bigarré, Abel Hugo and many others are long out of print. Yet Frédéric Masson, the Napoleonic historian, in whose eyes his idol could make no mistakes and who has rarely a good word to say of his brothers and sisters, writes of Joseph:

> Of all Napoleon's family, Joseph deserves a place apart . . . Joseph, who has never been accorded the merit he deserves, was of all the Bonapartes the most level-headed. His intentions, which more often than not he was unable to implement, both in Naples and Madrid, deserve to be studied in relation to his character and show that perhaps, of all Napoleon's brothers, he alone deserved to be worthy of a Kingdom.[1]

It is only recently that a complete biography of Joseph has appeared in France, *Joseph Bonaparte, le roi philosophe*, written by Bernard Nabonne, published in 1949, but this too is out of print. In 1970 there appeared another and more comprehensive life to fill the lacuna by Gabriel Girod de l'Ain, *Joseph Bonaparte, le roi malgré lui*. In English, apart from *The Gentle Bonaparte* by the American historian, Owen Connolly, published in 1968, there seems to be no

11

work exclusively devoted to Joseph's chequered seventy-six years of life.

To explain Joseph's character and his relations with his brother it must never be forgotten that the Bonapartes were Corsicans. It is their Corsican heritage which accounts for the very close ties that linked the family despite great differences of opinion and temperament. Notwithstanding a vein of Catholicism, like all Corsicans they were pagan at heart, unaffected by Christian precepts of original sin and damnation. Frédéric Masson in his *Napoléon et sa famille* says of the Bonapartes:

> They believed in Luck, Destiny and Fate far more than in the God of Christians. They placed their faith in the blind and deaf divinity who haunted the imagination of the ancients. Had this belief in destiny been replaced by Catholic precepts of self-discipline, sacrifice, abnegation and renunciation, they would have lost their self-confidence.[2]

Like all islanders, the Corsicans resented intruders. Much as they had hated the invasions and depredations of the Barbary corsairs, they still found the presence of their Genoese protectors intolerable. In 1764, when the struggle for Corsican independence under the leadership of Pasquale Paoli was at its height, the bankrupt Genoese Republic, unable to continue a costly and ineffective war, sold the island to France. Charles Bonaparte, a penniless law student of eighteen, and his child wife, Letizia, four years his junior,[3] were among Paoli's most fervent followers. Charles's family was reputedly of noble Florentine origin, from the town of Sarzane in Tuscany. In the first half of the sixteenth century, one Francesco Buona-Parte had left his native land to settle in the Genoese dependency of Corsica. For many years Francesco's descendants occupied important positions in Ajaccio, and allied themselves with the local nobility. Little by little, however, they were reduced by penury to more humble roles; not one seems to have thought of seeking fortune further afield. But noble birth counted for nothing; under the domination of the Republic of Genoa, titles of nobility were not recognized by law; landed property alone gave a man status and qualified him for a seat on the Council of Elders or to become a member of the Cathedral Chapter. But on 15 August 1764, when Corsica became officially French, the picture changed. The very few Corsicans who could claim noble lineage were now entitled to many of the same privileges as their peers in France; they were exempt from certain taxes; well-paid sinecures were open to them; their elder children were admitted gratis to

12

French colleges and military and naval academies. For the penurious Charles Bonaparte, with no land to call his own but the possessor of an aristocratic pedigree (if only it could be found), this was an opportunity which it would have been foolish to miss. But Charles did not turn coat immediately.

To most islanders, Charles included, the French occupation was scarcely less odious than that of the Genoese. For three years the French were harassed by Corsican nationalists – *maquisards* – who, under Pasquale Paoli, still fought for independence. Charles and his young wife were as fervent nationalists as any and shared all the rigours of partisan warfare. Volatile and flippant as Charles might have been, he remained a loyal Paolist until 1767. By this time the French were firmly established on the island. Paoli fled to London. Charles Bonaparte, the former fighter for the cause of independence, a lawyer with no practice and a growing family, finally decided to take French nationality. He solicited (and gained) the patronage of Louis XV's representative, the Comte de Marbeuf, Governor of the island, and now went to extraordinary lengths to establish his titles of nobility, which had long fallen into desuetude – if they had ever existed. Thirty years later, his son Joseph wrote : 'My father became a good Frenchman once he realized the immense advantages his country would obtain by a union with France.' It would have been more honest to have substituted the word 'himself' for 'his country'. During the Revolution his children conveniently forgot his claim to the title of Count which, after the Eighteenth Brumaire, Napoleon preferred to treat as a joke.

Charles Bonaparte was an attractive-looking young man. He was wilful, extravagant, constantly in debt and an inveterate borrower, but from all accounts he was a delightful companion and possessed all the famous Bonaparte charm, which he passed on to his children (Louis excepted). Despite Charles's faults, the Comte de Marbeuf seems to have genuinely liked him, while his family treated him with tolerant affection. His wife was made of sterner stuff.

Letizia Ramolino was undoubtedly descended from a noble Lombard family, the Counts of Coll'Alto, one of whom had been awarded lands in the neighbourhood of Ajaccio by the Doge of Genoa in 1490. Letizia's mother, after two years of widowhood, had married a Genoese officer of Swiss extraction, by the name of Francesco Fesch, to whom she bore a child, the future Cardinal Joseph Fesch, who was to play an important part in the lives of the Bonapartes. Uncle Fesch was born in 1763 and was thus only five years senior to his nephew Joseph and almost twenty years younger

13

than his half-sister Letizia. On her marriage to Charles Bonaparte, Letizia's modest dowry consisted of a small estate valued at 7,000 livres; nevertheless, she managed her little property with the greatest care and for years was the mainstay of her family.

When Joseph was born, the young couple were still fervent Corsican patriots, living the hard and dangerous life of partisans. At the close of 1766, Paoli had summoned them to the citadel of Corte, and it was here that Letizia gave birth to the future king on 7 January 1767. On the very next day, the child was baptized in the Church of the Most Blessed Annunciation and received the names Joseph-Napoleon. The baptismal register was inscribed in Latin – *cui impositum fuit nomen Joseph Nabolion.* As a child, however, Joseph was always known by the Italian form, Giuseppe, while Letizia invariably referred to Napoleon as 'Nabulio'. Just as there had always been Josephs in the Bonaparte family, so there had been other Napoleons, but the imperial myth has perpetuated the notion that the future emperor was the first of that name, a legend which he himself encouraged. Apart from Joseph-Napoleon himself, there were among his immediate relatives an uncle Napoleon and a cousin of the same name who was killed on the field of Ponte-Nuove, fighting in the final battle against the new French masters of the island. The name, which was that of an obscure ninth-century Greek saint, was translated by General Bonaparte when in Egypt to mean 'Lion of the Desert'.

Despite Charles's straitened circumstances, aggravated by a long residence in Pisa, where he studied for the Bar, and the expenses he incurred in his search for a genealogical tree, without which there was no future for him, the Bonaparte family continued to grow in number. The future emperor was born in 1769; Luciano (Lucien) six years later; Maria-Anna-Eliza (the future Élise) in 1777; Louis in 1778; Paoletta (Pauline) in 1780; Maria Annunziada (Caroline) in 1782; and lastly Jerome in 1784.

There were thus only nineteen months separating the two elder brothers, while Lucien, seven years younger, was to remain, next to Joseph, the closest in the Emperor's affections until his misalliance with Christine Boyer, the sister of an innkeeper with whom he was lodging. It was this proximity of age which accounted for the intimacy which, despite incompatibility of temperament and differences of opinion, united the two elder brothers in what today is called a love-hate relationship, which lasted all their lives. 'There are only three people I have ever loved,' Napoleon was to tell Daunou, the organizer of the *Institut* and official archivist under the Empire, 'my mother, Joseph and my wife [Josephine].'

14

Joseph's childhood was without incident. He and Napoleon were inseparable companions and shared together their childish escapades. The boys attended the same dame-school in Ajaccio, where they learnt to read and write. Later they both went to the same boys' school, under an excellent Jesuit teacher, the Abbé Recco, an enthusiastic classical historian, who first gave Napoleon his abiding taste for history. But even at this early age Napoleon had, as he admitted to Las Cases in St Helena, complete ascendancy over Joseph.

By 1771, Charles Bonaparte had at last managed to establish his titles of nobility, at least to the Comte de Marbeuf's satisfaction, but not without very considerable expense and the connivance of an accommodating genealogist. Although he deluded himself into the belief that he was entitled to call himself 'Count', real proof was still lacking, as his eldest son well knew. In the same year, thanks to Marbeuf, Charles had the gratification of being chosen to represent one of the four hundred families selected by Louis XV to form a Corsican nobility.[4] In 1773, he was appointed Royal Councillor and Assessor of the town and province of Ajaccio. In 1777, he visited Paris as a member of the deputation of Corsican nobles to the Court of Versailles. In the following year he returned to France accompanied by a youthful cousin, Aurèle Varèse, and young 'Uncle' Fesch, who was to attend the seminary at Aix, and his two sons, Joseph and Napoleon, aged eleven and nine years respectively.

On 15 December the party embarked for Marseilles. Leaving Fesch at Aix, they continued up the Rhône Valley to Autun, the episcopal see of Monsignor Marbeuf. While Charles continued on his way to Paris and Versailles to solicit the state grants for his children's education, to which, as a member of the *noblesse*, he was now ostensibly entitled, the boys remained behind in the care of the bishop. It had already been decided that Joseph was to make the Church his career; Napoleon, who at the age of nine had already made up his mind that only the army or navy would satisfy his youthful ambition, waited impatiently to hear if his father had been successful in obtaining his admission to the Military Academy of Brienne.

It was not only the Bishop of Autun's intention that Joseph should become a priest, but also that of Charles de Buonaparte, as he now styled himself. This was most unusual. Among the French aristocracy it was almost invariably the eldest son who was destined for a military or naval career, thus leaving him free to marry and perpetuate the family line, while the younger entered the Church. There was, of course, never any question of Joseph having a 'vocation'. In the

15

eighteenth century a young gentleman entered the Church to serve God, just as another would join the army to serve his king. In reversing the usual practice, Charles had perhaps already noticed the fundamental difference in the character of the two boys.

In the meantime, the Bishop arranged that both Joseph and Napoleon should attend school in Autun, under the tutelage of the Abbé Chardon, whose teaching was put to such good effect that by the following April, the two boys, who hitherto had spoken almost nothing but Italian, were fluent in French. Joseph was the more adept of the two and learnt to speak without an accent, though his spelling was frequently faulty. Napoleon, on the other hand, was never to be mistaken for other than a *méridional*. Both boys were precocious. Thirty years later Joseph wrote of his ten-year-old brother: 'Napoleon shared his reading of ancient and modern history with me; I also gave him an account of mine, which was less serious.'

On 21 April the two boys were parted for the first time in their lives. Charles's mission had proved successful: Napoleon was entered for Brienne with a bursary; and his sister Élise, thanks to the patronage of the Comte de Marbeuf, was to be granted a place in the Maison Royale de Saint-Cyr, the élite school for daughters of the nobility. 'I have never forgotten the moment of our separation,' wrote Joseph in years to come. 'I was in floods of tears; Napoleon shed but one, which he was at pains to hide. The Abbé Simon, our vice-principal, who was a witness to our farewell, said to me after his departure: "He may have shed only one tear, but that tear expressed as much sorrow at leaving you as all yours." '5

Joseph continued with his studies at Autun, where he was to be joined presently by his brother Lucien. While Napoleon, at Brienne, found it difficult to accustom himself to live without his 'whipping boy' (his *souffre douleur*, to use his own phrase), Joseph seems to have settled down quite happily on his own. Unfortunately we know very little of his life at this time. We know that he was popular with his fellow students and was full of mischief, and that his childish scrapes (perhaps not always so childish) were to earn him the censure of Monsignor Marbeuf, the Bishop, with whom he spent his holidays. Although he was lazy, his natural gifts brought him scholastic success, including a first prize in French with an essay on a tragedy by Corneille, not a set piece, but one which he had read for his private enjoyment. He himself admitted that he owed his success to the fact that he read novels and plays secretly during his recreation hours. His 'less serious reading which was never out of my hands' included *Télémaque* by Fénelon and *Les Saisons* by Saint-Lambert (which he

16

received as prizes); at school he also played the leading comic role of Dorante in Molière's comedy *Les Fâcheux*. When the Governor of Burgundy, the Prince de Condé, on his way to Dijon (where he was to preside at a meeting of the *États*) graciously broke his journey at Autun to attend the school prizegiving, it was Joseph who was chosen to compose and recite the panegyric in his honour. One is reminded of another schoolboy student of rhetoric, Maximilien Robespierre, who was called on to write and deliver a similar address on the occasion of Louis XVI's visit to the college of Saint-Louis-le-Grand. The ceremonies completed, *Monsieur le Prince* asked young Joseph what was his chosen career. Before he had time to reply, Monsignor Marbeuf broke in. 'The Church', he said. 'Unable to hide my resentment,' Joseph wrote in his memoirs, 'I hastened to answer "I wish to serve my King." The next day I wrote to my brother Napoleon to tell him that I had decided to join the artillery provided he gave up his intention of joining the navy.'[6] It was this circumstance that determined Napoleon to join the Artillery Corps.

Joseph's decision to renounce the Church horrified his family and prompted an indignant letter from Napoleon, to which his brother paid no attention. Napoleon therefore appealed to his uncle Nicolo Paravicini, his father's brother-in-law (not Fesch, as Jung and Nabonne state), to use his influence in deflecting Joseph from his rash resolve.

In a long letter he points out why Joseph was unsuited to a military career. 'He lacks the necessary boldness [*hardiesse*] to face the perils of battle,' he wrote, 'and his feeble health could never sustain the rigours of a campaign.' He then goes on to say that his ignorance of mathematics would preclude him from entering either the artillery or the corps of engineers, or from becoming a naval officer: 'For such careers require four years of hard work, but I don't think that to spend every day working is compatible with his frivolous character and extravagant habits . . .' In conclusion, Napoleon adds: 'We must make a final effort to turn him into an ecclesiastic . . . [and] hope that Joseph, with his education and talents, will see reason and *become the support of the family*, for Monsignor the Bishop of Autun is bound to provide him with an excellent benefice and he will certainly eventually become a bishop.'

This letter, running to several pages, one of the first of Napoleon's vast correspondence, is a remarkable achievement for a boy of fourteen. He was even then 'seizing the power' which he was to exercise over his family after the 13 Vendémiaire. He was sweeping under the carpet all Corsican traditions by assuming the place of his father

17

(already suffering from the illness from which he was to die seven months later) and usurping the place of his elder brother as head of the clan. True, he was willing that Joseph should be the 'support of the family', but not by any particular effort on his part, but thanks to episcopal benefices, like his great-uncle the Archdeacon, who always 'had a few louis tucked away in his mattress' to eke out Charles's and Letizia's income.

Unfortunately, Napoleon's opinions of people, even those expressed at an early age, have only too frequently been accepted as valid. There was undoubtedly some justification in his criticism of Joseph; he was certainly inclined to be frivolous and extravagant, but a boy who read Corneille and Fénelon's attack on the policy of Louis XIV for pleasure was surely not altogether frivolous. True, he was never cut out to be a soldier; but it was not true to say that Joseph lacked courage, nor was it true to say that he had feeble health. On the contrary, he was remarkably robust and, except for the last few days of his long life, he never had a serious illness. On the contrary, it was Napoleon (who always equated frenzied activity with good health and passivity with some form of physical debility) who had a morbid fear that his father's illness was hereditary, who suffered from kidney and bladder disorders and skin troubles, who bolted his food and had chronic indigestion. Despite all Joseph's efforts in the future to execute the missions entrusted to him, many of which he carried out brilliantly and with admirable common sense, he was always to be regarded by Napoleon as *frivole et léger*.

We do not know whether Uncle Paravicini tried to use his influence to change Joseph's mind or not, but at all events the young man remained adamant.

In June, Charles decided to visit France again. His decision was not dictated solely by Joseph's choice of profession, but also because he was anxious to consult Lasonne, the Queen's physician and an old acquaintance, and to escort Élise to school at Saint-Cyr. He also wished to remove young Lucien from Autun and place him in Brienne at the same time as Joseph, should the latter still be determined on a military career. On 18 July 1784 he wrote from Paris to the Marquis de Ségur, the Minister of War, soliciting places for his two boys. Ségur referred him to the Marquis de Timbrune, Inspector General of military schools. No opposition was placed in the way of Joseph's entry either to Brienne or to the school of military engineering and artillery at Metz. All that was required of him were four quarterings of nobility and a certificate of education. The former was obligingly vouched for on the authority of M. de Marbeuf; the latter was already provided by the Abbé Chardon. No state grant, however, was available for a third son, and Charles was obliged to pay 600 louis to obtain Lucien's admission. Philosophically, he agreed, although he was already heavily in debt and had been obliged to borrow 25 louis to help defray the expenses of his journey.[7]

Very much the poorer, both in pocket and health, Charles returned to Corsica, accompanied by Joseph, who was happy to spend his last holidays as a civilian with his mother, whom he had not seen for five years. Even Napoleon seems to have become reconciled to the idea of Joseph's change of career. In his memoirs Joseph writes:

> In 1784, once again in my native country, I found myself a complete stranger, due to my utter ignorance of my mother tongue which separated me from my compatriots.
> . . . Although my father told me that I was at perfect liberty to choose my own career, he made it clear that he would have preferred me to stay in Corsica where one day I would have a seat on the *Conseil Superieur* . . . I still insisted on my decision to pursue a military career in the artillery, which would take me back to France and allow me to rejoin the friend of my childhood. During the short time I spent in Corsica, I continued reading Bezout's *Cours de Mathématique* to help me pass my exams.[8]

Soon, however, the principal reason which attracted Joseph to Brienne was removed when Napoleon was transferred to the École Militaire de Paris on 22 October 1784. Nevertheless, once again Charles decided to visit France with Joseph. His presence was required over a lawsuit which he had brought against a Jesuit foundation, which he claimed had defrauded him of property rightfully his; secondly, his health had much deteriorated and he was anxious to have another consultation with Lasonne. He was in constant pain and subject to violent attacks of vomiting; he was obviously a very sick man.

The passage of father and son to Marseilles could not have been more unfavourable. Buffeted by storms, they were first driven back to Calvi and then on to the shores of Provence. When finally they disembarked, Charles was too weak to stand. Instead of proceeding to Paris, Charles was hurried to Aix, where a Corsican friend, Dr Tournatori, advised him to go to Montpellier, where the medical faculty had a reputation second to none. The doctors diagnosed his ailment as cancer of the stomach (though modern medical knowledge attributes it to a perforated ulcer) and were unable to do anything for the wretched man.

Fortunately for Joseph, he was not alone during these trying times.

19

Uncle Fesch, who had now completed his studies at the seminary at Aix, came to join him, and there were many other expatriate Corsicans who extended him a welcome hand, not least an old friend of Letizia's, Madame Permon, *née* Comnène (who claimed descent from the emperors of Byzantium), the wife of a wealthy army contractor. It must be recollected that the seventeen-year-old Joseph, apart from these friends, was entirely on his own, without the support of his brothers and sisters.

Joseph wrote later:

After a period of three months, [my father] expired in our arms at the age of thirty-nine. In his last moments he received the formal promise which he demanded of me to renounce the profession of arms and return to Corsica where his still young wife and seven children of tender age had need of my care. Napoleon, at the age of fifteen was the only one to have emerged from childhood . . .

I spent the first few weeks, after the death of my father, in Aix, where I was cordially received by friends of the family. I always retain the warmest recollections of their kindness which I have tried to repay whenever possible.[9]

To give Joseph his due, he was always a loyal friend – a more loyal friend, perhaps, than lover.

Although Joseph does not seem to have been deeply disturbed emotionally by his father's death – after all, he had seen so little of him – the consequences of his early decease must have been intimidating for a seventeen-year-old boy. He had solemnly sworn to renounce a military career and return to Corsica to provide for his mother and young sisters and brothers. He was faced with an accumulation of debts, an unsettled lawsuit, the necessity of putting his little property in order and of finding means sufficient with which to study for the Bar now that he had decided to follow in his father's footsteps. It is hardly surprising that he showed no hurry to face his new responsibilities and that he remained to enjoy a few more days and weeks of freedom under the hospitable roof of Madame Permon in Montpellier and with the friends of his father in Aix. But they were not unprofitable weeks. He made arrangements to enrol in the law school at some future date, and it was thanks to the generosity of these friends that he was able to return to Corsica with a little money in his pocket.

Once back in Ajaccio, he quickly adapted himself to his new role of Count Joseph de Buonaparte, head of the family. He familiarized himself again with the people, their language and their customs. He developed a liking and aptitude for farming which he retained all his life. Friends and relatives were eager to help. Great-uncle Lucien, the Archdeacon, who had never failed to help Letizia in the past, once more drew on his precious savings to help the boy. Uncle Fesch, impecunious as Joseph, was always ready with good advice. Uncle Nicolo Paravacini also came to the rescue, while his Aunt Gertrude, Nicolo's young and sentimental wife, who was a little in love with her handsome young nephew, accompanied the young farmer everywhere on horseback, and it was largely thanks to her that Joseph once again picked up the ways of his native land. Throughout his life, Joseph retained the tenderest memories of Gertrude; she is the only woman of whom he makes any mention during this period of his adolescence. Other friends, including the young lawyer Pozzo di Borgo, the Bonapartes' top-floor neighbour (who later, when Napoleon crowned himself Emperor, became the implacable enemy of the family and gave his services to the Tsar), all rallied round to provide moral support and indispensable legal advice. It is difficult to reconcile Joseph's reputation as a 'dull plodder'[10] or lazy ne'er-do-well with his activities at this time. He personally supervised the family olive groves, vineyards, nursery gardens and mulberry plantation, and took a professional interest in the livestock of the little estate.

In the midst of all these activities he was not unconcerned for his own future as a lawyer, but, as yet, there was no question of starting his studies. The family was still obliged to live with the greatest economy. But although Joseph could not yet afford to pursue his legal studies, he took a paternal interest in his brothers and sisters. All business and family correspondence devolved on him. It was he who kept in touch with Napoleon, Lucien and Élise in France. He wrote to solicit a state grant for his brother Louis to enter Brienne, for family plans had now been changed again – Lucien was to give up a military career for the Church and attend the seminary at Aix, where Joseph obtained for him a bursary. It was essential that there should be one churchman in the family. Joseph, as long as he was not called upon to fill the role, saw the advantages of that.

On 29 May 1786, the nineteen-year-old Joseph wrote to his sister Élise at Saint-Cyr. After giving her the family news, he went on to say :

> . . . Your uncle the Archdeacon is still suffering from gout. He remembers you in his prayers and mama never ceases to remind you of your religious duties and to impress on you the importance of fulfilling the obligations due to your position.
>
> I am, my dear sister,
> your most affectionate eldest brother
> de Buonaparte

This letter, concluding with 'your eldest brother' and signed 'de Buonaparte', just as his father had done, leaves no doubt that Joseph regarded himself very much as head of the family. His ascendancy was soon to be put to the test. On 15 September 1786, after just over eight years of absence, the seventeen-year-old Napoleon, a second lieutenant of eight months' seniority in the artillery *Régiment de la Fère*, returned to Corsica on an extended furlough to share Joseph's responsibilities.

In 1787, taking advantage of Napoleon's presence in Ajaccio, Joseph, with financial help from his great-uncle the Archdeacon, left for Pisa (not Aix as originally intended) to pursue his legal studies. His choice of Pisa was not only dictated by the fact that his father had studied there, but also because at that time it was the intellectual centre most frequented by expatriate Corsicans. 'I had,' he wrote, 'the triple intention of perfecting my Italian, of studying law and of learning the condition of my family interests which had been abandoned since the death of my father.'

Joseph was enrolled in Professor Lampredi's class (international law), but it seems that he did not apply himself with great diligence to his studies, and it was largely thanks to his remarkable memory that he eventually passed his examinations. At the beginning of 1788 the Archdeacon sent him 80 écus on condition that his young nephew should write a thesis and pass his doctorate examinations. His mother also wrote him an urgent letter (in Italian) in which she said:

> From your uncle's letter you will learn what you must do. He wants you to obtain your doctorate. You know the state of the family, and it is unnecessary for me to tell you to be as economical as possible. We have no servant, so do what you can to bring one back with you . . .

Madame Bonaparte goes on to say:

> This servant must not be too young, somewhere in her forties.

Perhaps Letizia was thinking of the peccadilloes committed by her husband when he was a student at Pisa University, of which her indignant grandfather Pietra-Santa had not hesitated to keep her informed.

Joseph's year at the university was passed agreeably enough. He spent nearly all his evenings with his exiled Corsican compatriots, principally at the home of Clemente Paoli, the elder brother of

Pasquale, at whose house he met many friends of the latter. Many of his father's friends came to these gatherings, including Antoine Saliceti.

Saliceti, ten years Joseph's senior, was also studying law. Their friendship was reciprocal, a friendship which in the years to come always remained constant, and which had an influence on the destiny of the Bonapartes often underestimated by historians. Saliceti's patriotic sentiments fired Joseph to write a pamphlet entitled *Lettre de Pascal Paoli à ses compatriotes* with the subtitle : *An appeal to regenerate Corsica in conformity with the improvements which are being prepared by all the provinces of France.*

Joseph's law studies, in fact, left him a great deal of leisure and gave him the opportunity of entering into correspondence with a notary by the name of Giovanni-Antonio Vivaldi who lived in the little town of Sarzane. The proofs of the Bonapartes' titles to nobility, which had so haunted his father Charles, and on which the fortunes of his family might still depend, were said to be found in Sarzane. He also wrote a letter to Ferdinand, Grand Duke of Tuscany, soliciting him to acknowledge officially the Florentine origin of his family, but apparently he received no more than a formal acknowledgement to his letter.

On 1 May 1788 Joseph, who had now run out of funds, left Pisa for Bastia after passing all his examinations and receiving the degree of doctor (*introque jure*) in civil and canon law. In Ajaccio he just had time to embrace Napoleon again at the termination of the latter's extended furlough, which had commenced at the end of the summer of 1786.

Joseph was delighted to see his brother again, but their reunion was short-lived. On 15 June, after almost two years' furlough, Napoleon was obliged to return to his regiment, now stationed at Auxonne. In the following month, Joseph was officially nominated *avocat du Conseil supérieur de la Corse* at Bastia. Joseph writes in his memoirs :

I pleaded on only one, unique [*sic*] occasion in Ajaccio; I had however the satisfaction of absolving and procuring the liberty of a young man accused of murder committed in self-defence. But later, I was constantly elected by popular vote to occupy public positions.[11]

Joseph, writing forty-one years after the events recorded above, often confuses dates and omits (conveniently) certain episodes in his life. His statement that later 'I was constantly elected . . . to occupy public positions' requires some qualification. Though this statement is true enough, it was not until the following year that he occupied any

23

important position. In fact, in 1789, on the eve of the convocation of the States General in France, Joseph decided to resign his post with the *Conseil supérieur* and return once more to Italy to establish once and for all his titles of nobility.

While Napoleon had long shown his Republican sympathies, Joseph seems to have been quite unmoved by the stirrings that were about to deprive the nobility of their privileges and topple Louis XVI from his throne. But to be fair to Joseph it must be remembered that communications between Paris and Corsica were slow, and even in France itself there were many intelligent people who still did not realize the true significance of what was happening.

Napoleon, on the other hand, even before the convocation of the States General on 4 May, had realized that tremendous changes were about to take place, and further that Corsica, as a province or part of France, would be affected. Although a dedicated opponent of the *ancien régime* – he had already written in the previous year in a pamphlet entitled *Dissertation sur l'autorité royale*, 'There are very few kings who do not deserve to lose their thrones' – he had no longer any reason to oppose a France advocating the Rights of Man which promised the liberty of the individual and people, which to his mind was synonymous with the liberation of Corsica. In September 1789, news from his homeland convinced him that he should return there without delay. Paoli, to whom Mirabeau had granted an amnesty with other patriot émigrés, was expected to return from his enforced exile in London. Napoleon had no doubt that he would gain the confidence of the old soldier and become his right-hand man and eventual successor when age and fatigue should force 'il Babbo'[12] to retire. At twenty years of age, this little artillery officer had no other ambition. He applied for six months' leave and immediately set out for his beloved homeland.

Joseph seized the occasion to revisit Italy. This time he was able to meet the Grand Duke of Tuscany, thanks to the good offices of Cardinal Loménie de Brienne, at that time French Minister to the Duchy of Tuscany. He once again visited Sarzane, where he re-engaged the services of the notary Vivaldi to continue with his enquiries. Vivaldi promised to obtain the proofs of nobility thanks to the scholarship and savoir-faire of an archivist of his acquaintance. On 21 April Joseph returned to Pisa, where he continued to badger Vivaldi to lose no time in confirming that the Bonapartes of Sarzane were of Florentine origin (*come é certissimo*) and that relative documents existed to prove that the family could trace its descent from the year 1245.[13] What is truly extraordinary is that in not one of the

24

eleven letters written by Joseph to Vivaldi between 21 April and 14 August does he give the slightest hint of any interest in events taking place in France.[14]

According to Colonna de Cesare Rocca in his *La Vérité sur les Bonapartes avant Napoléon* (published in 1899), Joseph's researches proved fruitless, and the genealogical tree which was later drawn up on the orders of Napoleon III was completely false.[15]

On his return to Ajaccio Joseph could no longer ignore events in France. The two young Bonapartes, once more united, found themselves torn by conflicting sentiments. They had to reconcile their Corsican patriotism with their French culture and personal ambitions. We are not concerned here with Napoleon's participation in events between 1789 and 1793, except in so far as they concern Joseph. The latter, as a qualified doctor of law, was soon to find employment again. He was appointed secretary to General Rossi, the president of a *Comité général des trois ordres* which had been constituted in Ajaccio to establish peace in a country torn by various factions. Next, he obtained an honorary position on the municipal council

and, for the first time was able to keep in touch with everything that was happening in Paris. Since I was the only member of the municipality with a perfect knowledge of French, it was thanks to me that the municipality received details of the new laws which in future we were to enact and which filled us with enthusiasm.[16]

On 30 November 1789, on the recommendation of Saliceti, the Constituent Assembly rejected Genoese proposals to reoccupy Corsica and reaffirmed the integration of the island with France. It was not until 4 December that Napoleon's hopes were realized. Mirabeau introduced a motion, which was passed by the *Assemblée*, authorizing all Corsicans who had been expatriated for fighting for independence to return to their country. Paoli returned from London to be given a warm welcome by Louis XVI, Mirabeau, La Fayette and members of the Constituent Assembly.

Joseph, lately appointed to the *Directoire* of the district of Ajaccio, was chosen, together with Pozzo di Borgo, to meet il Babbo at Lyons and escort him home. Unfortunately the delegation from Bastia was more persuasive than that of Ajaccio, and it was at Macinagio, north of Bastia, that Paoli landed on 14 July 1790. Nevertheless, Joseph had had the pleasure of Paoli's company on his journey from Lyons to Marseilles and did his best to obliterate from the great man's mind his father's collaboration with Marbeuf, though apparently not as successfully as Joseph would have us believe from his memoirs. From subsequent events it would appear, however, that Paoli had found the young man's company agreeable.

Napoleon received his brother coldly on his return. He did not trust Joseph's protestations that Paoli had forgiven the Bonaparte family. His dreams of becoming il Babbo's right-hand man and eventual successor were fading.

On 9 September 1790, at Orezza, Paoli convened a meeting to select the heads of districts. Although officially too young (twenty-five years was the prescribed age) Joseph was chosen to represent the district of Ajaccio. Napoleon, harbouring as ever his opinion of Joseph as *frivole et léger*, insisted on accompanying him. He still believed that he was better qualified to gain the confidence of the great patriot than his brother. The two young men travelled slowly on horseback from Ajaccio to Orezza. Joseph, in his memoirs, gives an enlightening account of this autumnal journey.

> . . . [Napoleon] was constantly engrossed with trying to guess the positions taken up by the troops of the various nations which, during the course of so many years, had fought over this little island. My dreams were of quite a different nature; the strangeness and beauty of the landscape interested me much more.[17]

The difference in character of the two brothers could scarcely be put more succinctly.

The *Consulta*, as the former sovereign revolutionary committees were known in Corsica, was held at Orezza from 9 to 27 September. Paoli was elected (unconstitutionally) both President of the Directory of Corsica and Commander-in-Chief of the newly-formed National Guard. In fact he was virtually viceroy to a king in faraway France, whose powers were being increasingly sapped by the National Assembly and revolutionary factions.

Paoli's welcome to the Bonaparte brothers confirmed Napoleon's opinion that the hero of the Resistance was not favourably inclined to these 'sons of Charles', the former partisan who had not only turned collaborator, but had sent his boys to French colleges. He was particularly irritated by Napoleon, this young whippersnapper of a lieutenant who pestered him with questions and told him that he was proposing to write a history of Corsica. Il Babbo cut him short by replying: 'History, Monsieur, is not written in the years of one's youth'.[18]

The meeting at Orezza brought no benefits to the Bonapartes.

Paoli accepted in his government only his old companions who had remained anti-French. Joseph, who had entertained hopes of being chosen as one of the four members of the Directoire, was obliged to content himself with a minor position in Ajaccio.

Disappointed and slightly apprehensive because he had overstayed his furlough by six months, Napoleon left for Auxonne on 11 February 1791, taking his brother Louis with him, promising Letizia that he would take care of him. But he was not long absent from home. Eight months later he was back again in Ajaccio, where he found Joseph much more favourably placed than when he had left him. He was now a member of the central Directoire with a salary of 1,600 livres a year. On 11 October the old Archdeacon, who had been such a prop to Charles and Letizia in their hours of need, died, leaving all his carefully hoarded economies to the young Bonapartes. Napoleon (or Las Cases) claims in the *Mémorial de Sainte-Hélène*[19] that on his deathbed the old Archdeacon prophesied that Napoleon would be *a great man*. Joseph, in a letter dated 1 August 1824, wrote protesting to Las Cases :

> My mother, Cardinal Fesch and most of my brothers and sisters who were present at my great-uncle's last moments, could have told you in the interests of truth, that before prophesying that Napoleon 'would be a great man', [the Archdeacon] had said . . . 'I die content, because I foresee the *eldest* of my nephew's sons not only in a position to succeed me as head of our family, but also I see him one day as head of the administration of our country.'[20]

This, at the time, was certainly optimistic thinking. Joseph had stood for election for the Legislative Assembly, but had been defeated by 398 votes to 64, a fact which he conveniently omitted from his memoirs : on the other hand, he had the satisfactory of being appointed *juge du tribunal*. With his great-uncle's inheritance he bought some property, a profitable speculation on behalf of his family which is almost invariably attributed to Napoleon. Neither of these facts seem to be consistent with his reputation as *un homme frivole et léger*. Lieutenant Napoleon Bonaparte, on the other hand, had ambitions of a different sort. With a little money in his pocket, he canvassed for the post of second-in-command of the battalion of the Civil Guard of Ajaccio, sometimes known as the *Bataillon volontaire*, with the rank of brevet lieutenant-colonel. He was duly elected by a small majority on 31 March 1792. In parenthesis it might be mentioned that the Deputy Muratti, the scrutineer of the polls, was mysteriously abducted during the count. There seems no doubt that the election was rigged. Mathieu Pozzo di Borgo, Paolist candidate for the post, was defeated. It is hardly surprising that the breach between the old patriot and the Bonapartes was still further widened. Of the two brothers, it was Napoleon who showed a complete lack of responsibility, for on 5 April 1792, in an insane moment, he ordered out the volunteers to attack the citadel of Ajaccio, garrisoned by French regular soldiers loyal to the old administration. It was an action which pleased no one. Strong representations were made to the Legislative Assembly which had now superseded the Constituent Assembly as the Government in Paris. Lucien, with Jacobin sympathies, who was already forging himself a political career, wrote to Joseph from Toulon :

> I must tell you in all truth, that I believe Napoleon, with such lack of principles, is a dangerous man. I believe his inclination is that of a tyrant, and in the event of a counter-revolution, he is quite capable of becoming a turn-coat.

For a self-professed Paolist, Corsican Nationalist, ardent Republican and an officer wearing what was still officially the King's uniform, Napoleon's conduct can only be attributed to the fact that he was already a megalomaniac in search of self-aggrandisement, who, if unable to become Paoli's legitimate successor, was determined to become master of the island by a military coup. In the event, the coup failed with some loss of life. Not only had he committed a criminal act, but he had overstayed his leave by four months. It was high time that he returned to his regiment. In May he took ship for France. Incredibly, he was not arrested and court-martialled. He did not even report to his regiment. Instead, he took modest lodgings in Paris. Here, thanks to influential Corsican friends with strong Republican views, he was reinstated in his regiment and even promoted to the rank of captain on 10 July. He seemed to have had no regimental duties, for he was still in the capital on the fatal 10 August when he watched the mob storm the Tuileries and saw the King and his family taken to the Manège under the protection of the Assemblée. On 21 September, the National Assembly dissolved itself, to be replaced by the National Convention. France was proclaimed a Republic.

Napoleon once again asked for leave to return to Corsica on the pretext of escorting home his sister Élise from the former aristocratic school of Saint-Cyr which had now been closed. His request was granted. The number and length of Napoleon's furloughs between the time he was first gazetted second lieutenant on 1 January 1786 until he finally left the shores of Corsica for good, on 11 April 1793, seems incredible by any standards. In the course of seven years, he was absent from his regiment for more than forty-two months.

This fifth and last visit (on 15 October 1792) to his native land was to prove disastrous to his Corsican ambitions.

Paoli was master of the island. Despite the fact that the old patriot was more separatist and anti-French than ever, his appointment as Governor of the island had been confirmed by the Convention. But the excesses committed in the name of the Republic and the execution of the King had disgusted him. Napoleon, on the other hand, had been able to reconcile his Corsican patriotism with his loyalty to the new regime in France. The first successes of the French armies had filled him with enthusiasm. For him, the fate of Corsica was linked with that of France and he openly allied himself with Saliceti's Jacobin party. Paoli's hostility to Napoleon and the whole Bonaparte clan was greater than ever.

In these circumstances, what future was there for Captain Bonaparte, once again a lieutenant-colonel in the Ajaccio volunteers? In January 1793, an opportunity to further his ambitions seemed to present itself. The Convention had ordered an invasion of Sardinia. The first expeditionary force under Admiral Truguet had been intercepted by the British fleet and forced to withdraw. On 23 February, a second attack, commanded by Paoli's nephew, Colonel Cesare Colonna, was launched. Napoleon obtained for himself the command of the artillery which was to bombard La Maddalena from the little island of San Stefano. But no sooner had he received his baptism of fire, than the invading forces were ordered to re-embark for Corsica. Paoli had betrayed them. He was accused of selling his country to the English to provide a naval base for an attack on Toulon.

Earlier, on 30 January, the Convention, by no means fully assured of Paoli's loyalty, had already decided to send three *commissaires*, including Saliceti, to Corsica to report on the political situation. On 2 February, shortly after Colonna's failure to capture La Maddalena, they arrived in Marseilles. A week later they were in Bastia, where after stormy meetings with the Directoire, they were left in no doubt of the anti-French and separatist sentiments of the majority of the islanders.

Saliceti ordered that Paoli should be divested of his rank and privileges and that the pro-French Casabianca, an old friend of Joseph's from Pisa, be appointed in his place. Casabianca promptly issued a warrant for the arrest of his predecessor but, as Paoli had foreseen, the municipality of Corte refused to take any action and allowed the old man to seek the safety of the maquis.

The eighteen-year-old Lucien, still in Toulon, earning himself the reputation as an ardent Jacobin and already gaining a name for himself among the revolutionary clubs as an orator, wrote an indiscreet letter to his brother in which he denounced il Babbo as an enemy of the Republic. 'Didn't you anticipate it?' he wrote. 'A warrant for the arrest of Paoli and Pozzo di Borgo has been issued and our fortune is made.' The letter was intercepted by Paolist nationalists. From now on, the Bonapartes were branded as traitors to their country and deserving of death.

Joseph, to some extent, seems to have escaped the general opprobrium and had remained in Corte, the Paolist stronghold, where for some time he had been attempting to reconcile the various factions in the Consulta. Napoleon, on the other hand, was so hated that even his life was threatened. It was no longer safe for him to remain in Ajaccio. He fled across the mountains to Bastia to seek the protection of Saliceti. On his first attempt he was captured by Paolist partisans, but managed to escape. When he finally reached Bastia, he was able to persuade the *conventionnels*, but only with great difficulty, to mount a military expedition against the Paolist rebels in Ajaccio (30 May). The expedition proved a failure, but it sealed the fate of Napoleon and his family. While the Convention was preparing to declare Paoli an outlaw, il Babbo and his followers condemned the whole of the Bonaparte family to 'perpetual execration and deprived them of all rights of citizenship [*les avez condamnés à une perpetuelle exécration et infamie*]'.[21]

Not only Napoleon but his mother, brothers and sisters were now also in danger. He lost no time in sending a message warning Letizia to make ready to escape. '*Preparavi, questo paese nonje per noi.*'[22] On 3 June, shortly before the Bonaparte house was sacked by angry citizens of Ajaccio, Letizia, accompanied by Élise, Louis, Pauline, Caroline and Jerome, met Napoleon by prearrangement at Aspretto, whence they embarked for Calvi. Here they were given shelter by Letizia's cousin, Lorenzo Ciuberta. A few days later they were joined by Joseph and Uncle Fesch. On 11 June 1793 they embarked secretly for Toulon, where they were given an enthusiastic welcome by Lucien. Joseph and the whole family, to Lucien's surprise, were horrified and frightened by the excesses committed by the Revolutionary Tribunals. 'The air was literally unbreathable,' Joseph wrote later. They could scarcely wait to obtain passports to leave the town for the healthier atmosphere of La Valette, a few miles distant, where Lucien had obtained lodgings for them. A chapter in the life of the two brothers was now closed. Strangely enough it was Joseph's destiny to fulfil his great-uncle's prophecy; he was to become, in all but name, head of the Corsican administration, if only temporarily. Napoleon, instead of becoming ruler of the maquis, was to be crowned Emperor of the French and the despot of Europe. He was never to set foot in Corsica again.

Questo paese non e per noi

II

Marriage and Napoleon's
Rise to Power

1793–1796

The family was not to remain long in La Valette. Aware that the Girondist faction, sickened by the atrocities committed by the Jacobins, were preparing to cede Toulon to the English, Joseph arranged for Letizia and the children to move to Le Beausset on the road to Marseilles, before Admiral Hood's squadron supported by Royalist forces sailed into the port. Napoleon in the meantime left for Nice to rejoin his regiment (now known as the 4th Artillery), which formed part of the Army of Italy. Joseph, very conscious of his responsibilities, departed for Paris to seek assistance from the Government, not only for his own family, but for other expatriate Republican Corsicans who had been forced to leave the island once Paoli had placed it under the protection of the English.

Joseph, aged twenty-four, moved with perfect ease in a society and city entirely new to him. He possessed to a very high degree the faculty of adaptation and self-assurance, very different from the over-weaning presumption of the rest of his family. He quickly made contact with Saliceti, who also had been forced to leave the island, and other Corsican deputies of the Convention who obtained for him interviews with important personages in the administration. To these he explained with verve the situation in Corsica and was successful in presenting an extremely well-composed petition in which he solicited (and was granted) a relief fund of 600,000 livres for 'patriot' refugees. He also urged the Government to send an expeditionary force, to be raised from the Army of Italy, to drive the English from his homeland.

Joseph Bonaparte, *c.* 1806

Letizia Bonaparte,
Joseph's mother

Charles Bonaparte,
Joseph's father

Three commissioners – Albitte, Chauvet and Saliceti – together with Joseph, who acted as secretary to the last, were sent to the Midi to make the necessary arrangements. Corsica was still Joseph's main preoccupation. Despite his disgust with what he had seen in Toulon, he makes no mention in his memoirs of events in Paris, which Marat and Robespierre had turned into a bloodbath. France was not only at war with the Coalition, but was herself in the throes of internecine strife between the ultra-Jacobin party and the moderate Girondists. Civil war was raging throughout the south; Toulon, as Joseph knew, was about to be occupied by the English fleet; the Marseillais were ready to support the Spanish (who were already in occupation of the province of Roussillon) and had besieged Avignon; Lyons, too, had risen in revolt and was invested by the troops of General Kellermann – the Vendée had declared war on the Convention 'in the name of God and the King'; in Brittany, the Chouan leaders, Jean Cottereau and Georges Cadoudal, had raised the white banner of the Bourbons. In Normandy, where many Girondins had taken refuge, the Marquis de Frotté was already supporting a federalist movement. The Reign of Terror had spread from Paris to the provinces. *Représentants en mission*, under orders from the newly-formed Committee of Public Safety, were everywhere scouring the country accompanied by the guillotine.

Joseph's only mention of these events are incidental. In his *Mémoires* he writes :

> I was in Paris at the time of the murder of Marat and the death of Charlotte Corday [on 11 and 13 July respectively]. The barriers were closed by order of the Committee of Public Safety and it was only thanks to the protection of our deputies that I was able to leave the city with our *représentants en mission*.[1]

The mission encountered further difficulties at Lyons and Avignon and was obliged to make detours. But by the time Joseph reached Marseilles, the city had already been subdued by the *sans-culotte* ex-housepainter General Carteaux.

With Marseilles once again in the hands of the Convention and peace restored to the town (but not before the guillotine had exacted a further hideous toll of heads), Joseph sent for his family, and now that there was no immediate possibility of sending an expeditionary force to Corsica, he remained with the army of Italy besieging Toulon.[2] On 4 September, thanks to Saliceti, with whom his ties of friendship, first established in Pisa, had been greatly strengthened during their journey from Paris, he obtained the post of *Commissaire des guerres* (First Class), assistant to Chauvet, the *Commissaire ordinateur* (Intendant-General of Supplies).

Joseph's appointment was highly irregular; only senior officers were eligible for this post, but Joseph overcame the difficulty by calmly appropriating Napoleon's brevet lieutenant-colonelcy in the Ajaccio Volunteers, to which he maintained he was legally entitled. Of course, nothing could be further from the truth, and well Joseph knew it.³ The benefits of his new post were considerable; apart from his salary of 6,000 livres, he received allowances for lodging and all official expenses, and free forage for his saddle horses.

Although he could never condone the atrocities perpetrated in the name of Liberty, Equality and Fraternity, Joseph had now become an ardent Republican and conveniently forgot that he had ever claimed to have been Comte de Buonaparte.

He took his duties very seriously and, from his headquarters at Ollioules, he took ruthless measures to ensure that the army was properly fed. For example, on 22 September he issued orders that any soldiers 'discovering' wheat in the fields would receive half the market value of what they brought in. But although he worked hard, he never forgot Corsica, where he still believed he had an important role to play.

On 19 September 1793 he was elected commissary of the executive council of the Council of Corsica. He combined his new duties, which to begin with were honorary, with those of war commissary, but he was allowed to draw 2,400 livres for out-of-pocket expenses for his mission, which he devoted to the relief of his family, whom he now installed in a requisitioned private house in Marseilles, formerly the property of an émigré, M. de Cypières. Lucien had also obtained a post with the commissariat in charge of military food supplies and forage (*garde magazin*) at Saint-Maximin (Var) at a salary of 100 francs per month. Unsubstantiated stories recount that Letizia and the youthful Pauline and Élise further contributed to the family budget by taking in laundry. Napoleon, on his army pay, could contribute little or nothing at this time to assist his family. Despite popular legend, it was Joseph, not Napoleon, who was still the main support of the Bonaparte clan.

It was during this month of September 1793 that two events of great importance occurred in Joseph's life. On 8 September, sponsored by Chauvet and Saliceti, recently elected Freemasons, he too was initiated as a member of the brotherhood. To be a Freemason in Revolutionary France at this time had enormous advantages. Many

34

senior military officers and politicians belonged to lodges and were naturally inclined to help fellow members of the fraternity. The advantages were almost comparable with those belonging to the *noblesse* under the old régime, a fact of which Joseph was well aware.

The second event of importance occurred on 18 or 19 September, when during a short visit to Marseilles he met Désirée Clary. The repressive measures taken by the representatives of the Convention against the notabilities of Marseilles were particularly severe, as they provided a simple means of filling the coffers of the Republic, by confiscating the property of the condemned. Among the prominent wealthy citizens of Marseilles was the sixty-eight-year-old François Clary, shipping merchant and underwriter, who, with his son Nicolas and son-in-law Antoine, conducted a profitable business with the Levant, where in exchange for cloth he imported cereals, coffee, spices and dyes. Despite the fact that in 1789 François Clary had enthusiastically welcomed the new régime, he was among those whom the Convention now proscribed as anti-Revolutionary and was temporarily remanded, together with his family. Étienne, his eldest son by his first marriage,[4] however, was not so lucky. On the flimsiest of excuses he was arrested and thrown into prison. The Representatives of the People were certain that they would soon find a pretext to send him to the guillotine and confiscate his property. Marcelle, Étienne's wife, 'one of those Marseillaises with a sonorous voice whom nothing could daunt',[5] hurried to the municipal headquarters, to seek an interview with the Representative Albitte to plead for her husband's release. With her she took her husband's lovely sixteen-year-old step-sister, Désirée, François Clary's youngest daughter by his second marriage. Albitte, like so many parvenu bureaucrats, kept his suppliants waiting in the crowded ante-chamber. The day was warm; Désirée fell asleep and when she awoke late in the evening, it was to find herself alone in an empty room. Marcelle, favourably received by Albitte, had hurried to the gaol where her husband was imprisoned to inform him that there was every reason to hope for his early release, leaving Désirée to find her own way home. But it was already dark when Désirée awoke. A charming young man, emerging from Albitte's room, told her that the streets of Marseilles were unsafe for a *'petite demoiselle'* and offered to escort her to her parents' house. Désirée accepted his offer with pleasure and together they walked home chatting like old friends. The young man's name was Joseph Bonaparte. Politely he asked permission of Désirée to pay his respects to her parents on the following morning, as he was due to leave for Ollioules almost immediately.

Such is the version which Désirée herself gave many years later when, as Queen of Sweden, she told the story to her chamberlain, Baron Hochschild. Her uncle Victor Somis,[6] a lieutenant-colonel in the Corps of Engineers and an 'avowed aristocrat', gives a slightly different account in a memoir he wrote for his nephew Nicolas in 1815, now in the possession of M. Girod de l'Ain. Somis recounts that it was not to Chauvet that Marcelle addressed herself, but to Joseph, who was gaining great influence in the Revolutionary Tribunal, at that time presided over by a certain Citizen Maillet, a man of comparatively moderate views and a Freemason. The question always remains – why should Joseph, now a fervent Republican, have interested himself in the fate of Étienne? Cynical historians have maintained that he was only interested in ingratiating himself with the Clary family so that he might find an opportunity of paying court to either one or the other of the two daughters, both of whom possessed considerable dowries. However, knowing Joseph's character, a kinder interpretation would be that his action was dictated entirely by his natural goodness of heart. Although Étienne escaped the guillotine, it was some time before he was released from prison. He was luckier than many other members of the Clary-Somis family who lost their lives when the more indulgent Maillet was replaced by Barras and Fréron, who introduced the terrible Law of Suspects, by which, on the unsubstantiated word of an informer alone, a man might be arrested and executed within twenty-four hours. Nearly all those whom Maillet had spared were rearrested and guillotined; their properties were confiscated, bringing millions of francs into the Conventional Government coffers.

Old François Clary would almost certainly have been executed had he not died in his bed before Barras and Fréron started on their programme of wholesale murder. Étienne on his release from prison took refuge in Genoa, but his half-brother Nicolas, more astutely, professed his loyalty to the new régime and was sent officially to Italy on the pretext of buying corn for the armies of the south. Fortunately for the two half-brothers, a large proportion of the Clary fortune was invested in Italy. Nicolas, who was shortly to be joined by his brother-in-law Antoine in his business enterprises (with great success), first installed himself at Leghorn and was later appointed French Consul in Naples.

In Marseilles, there now remained only Madame Clary and her two daughters, Désirée and Julie. Naturally Joseph, after his intervention on behalf of Étienne, was a very welcome guest at their house in the rue de Rome. For a rich, bourgeois family which had constantly been threatened with death, it is easy to imagine Madame Clary's satisfaction in counting among her friends this handsome young man who was on the best of terms with the powerful Saliceti and the Revolutionary Tribunal.

Baron Hochschild, paraphrasing Désirée in later years, wrote :

Joseph Bonaparte became attached to his little protégée, who, for her part, was not insensible to his attentions. Soon he became an intimate friend of the Clary household, and after a few weeks asked Désirée's hand in marriage as soon as she had reached the age of sixteen [Hochschild is wrong : Désirée was seventeen when he proposed].

Joseph often talked . . . of one of his brothers, an officer in the artillery, who had distinguished himself during the siege of Toulon. While his brother was on a short visit to Marseilles, Joseph introduced him to the Clary family.

The description which Queen Désirée gave me of Napoleon at this time does not correspond at all with the idea which I had formed from his portraits. These seem to represent a grave and severe man, almost taciturn, while according to the Queen, who now met him for the first time, this young man, to whom Joseph introduced her, was full of fun and a thoroughly good fellow. 'His arrival [said the Queen] soon led to a change of plans for our future. We had not known him long before he said, "In a happy household, one of the two partners must be prepared to give way to the other. You, Joseph, can never make up your mind [*tu es d'un caractère indécis*]; the same thing applies to Désirée; it would, therefore, be much better if you were to marry Julie. As for Désirée," he said, taking her on his knees, "it is you who will be my wife." '[7]

The Duchess of Abrantès (the wife of Marshal Junot) in her memoirs presents Napoleon in a much less flattering light. She describes him as 'skinny, with a sickly yellow complexion, with long, uncombed hair which fell on either side of his face like dog's ears'. She describes his hands (of which, later, he was so proud) as small, thin and 'black'. His dress, she says, was always untidy and his boots unpolished. 'All he had to recommend him was his glance and smile which were always admirable.'[8] Nevertheless, he seems to have fascinated Désirée, the beauty of the family, who appears to have had no objection to exchanging places with Julie; indeed she was beginning to find Joseph a little too serious-minded for her taste, while Julie, who was madly in love with Joseph, was only too delighted. Certainly, Joseph could not have been seriously in love with either of the two girls, for he accepted the arrangement with complete equanimity – after all, although Julie was much the plainer of the two sisters, their dowries were identical. Napoleon, on the other hand, entertained a genuine affection for Désirée – until he met Josephine de Beauharnais.

Despite the atmosphere of mourning and terror by which they were surrounded in this spring of 1794, the two young Demoiselles Clary continued to indulge in romantic dreams and plans for the future. As in all times of trouble, death, which at other times would have caused the profoundest grief, had become almost commonplace. The constant danger in which people were living added a spice to life. The emigration of so many men gave women a greater independence; deep-rooted conventions were forgotten. People's sensibilities had been dulled by events; they were no longer surprised or shocked by what was happening around them. Joseph himself, who had been so appalled by what he saw when he first arrived in Toulon, now seems to have accepted the Terror almost as a matter of course. It is quite apparent from the many letters and documents that have come down to us, that the Revolution, which from many aspects seems to us to have been an intolerable nightmare, was for a great number of people a period of extraordinary exaltation, when love, heroism and ambition blossomed as never before. The fact remains that, despite Fréron's bloody rule, the young couples enjoyed an idyllic courtship, apparently little concerned by the horrors committed almost on their doorstep. In May, the two brothers were obliged to return to their respective duties, but without as yet declaring their intentions to Madame Clary. Napoleon rejoined the headquarters of the Army of Italy at Nice, but was able to spend much of his time with his mother and younger brothers and sisters, now comfortably accommodated in the pretentiously named 'Château de Sallé', near Antibes, while Joseph went to Toulon to help prepare the long-postponed expedition to Corsica, which was shortly to become a reality, and which he himself was to accompany.

In June, fourteen men o' war and four frigates, under the command of Admiral Martin, set sail 'to clear the seas of the English to allow the military transports a safe passage to the island'. The French, however, on sighting the British squadron, under the command of Sir Henry Hotham, Vice-Admiral of the Blue, found themselves so outnumbered that, after 'honourably keeping the sea for a week', they put back to the safety of Golfe Juan. Joseph, a disappointed man, returned to Toulon. Temporarily abandoning his dreams of carving out a brilliant future for himself in Corsica, his thoughts now turned to entering into a business partnership with Nicolas. But for this he would need capital. The sooner he could touch Julie's dowry the

better. In July he officially asked for her hand in marriage. Madame
Clary was only too delighted to have this charming young man, a
ci-devant count, as her future son-in-law; he was so much more level-
headed, so much better equipped to deal with business matters than
his younger brother, whom she regarded as altogether too volatile
and whose future, despite his brilliant success at Toulon and his rapid
promotion to the rank of brigadier-general, still seemed far from
secure.

On 7 Thermidor (29 July), two days before the fall of Robespierre,
the marriage banns were published in Marseilles. On 1 August the
civil wedding was performed before the mayor of the neighbouring
village of Cuges, where the Clarys possessed a farm. The only witnesses were two *assesseurs municipaux* (probably town clerks), a wig-
maker and Madame Clary, her stepdaughter Honorine Blait,[9] and
Désirée. Letizia, who had become on friendly terms with Marcelle
Clary during her stay in Marseilles, contented herself with sending an
affectionate message to the young couple. Napoleon, who had only
returned to Nice on 27 July from a military mission to Genoa,
whither he had been sent by Augustin Robespierre, the younger
brother of Maximilien,[10] thought it unnecessary to attend the wedding
as he knew that Joseph and Julie were to spend their honeymoon at
the Château de Sallé, bringing Désirée with them.

In future years, Joseph always attributed his vast fortune to Julie's
dowry. Regrettably, he was lying. Most of his wealth was accumulated
in a much more unethical manner, but it was only as recently at 1948
that M. Gabriel Girod de l'Ain discovered, in the departmental
archives of Bouches-du-Rhône, the exact amount of Julie's dowry.
This came in all to 81,718 livres, nothing like enough to meet Joseph's
extravagant expenditure during the years 1797–8, but in 1794
representing a very considerable sum to an impoverished Corsican.

Napoleon, in fact, was to see very little of Désirée at the Château de
Sallé, but long enough to revive his tender feelings for her and decide
him to make her his wife as soon as circumstances permitted – but
at the moment, the future remained extremely uncertain. The
9th Thermidor (27 July 1794), which announced the fall of the
Robespierre dictatorship, threatened the Bonaparte family with
disaster. Napoleon had made no secret of his admiration for
Maximilien ('Marat and Robespierre are my saints,' he had written
in a recent pamphlet, *Le Souper de Beaucaire*[11]) and of his friendship
with Augustin, who had offered him the command of the National

Guard of Paris in place of the incompetent drunken General Henriot, an offer, however, which Napoleon had prudently declined. 'It is not so easy to keep one's head on one's shoulders in Paris as it is in Saint-Maximin,' he told his family. 'Young Robespierre is a good fellow, but his brother is not to be treated lightly . . . I would never consent to be the lackey of such a man . . . Today, the only honourable place for me is with the army. Have patience; one day I will command Paris.'[12]

But his constant changes of political adherence and his recent friendship with ultra-Jacobins had lost him the confidence of the newly-elected members of the Committee of Public Safety, who stigmatized him as 'the personification of intrigue and deceit'. He was ordered to Paris to face a court of enquiry. Saliceti, however, had already anticipated the Committee's order and had had him arrested and imprisoned at Fort Carré near Antibes.

There are historians who maintain that Saliceti, recently appointed Representative to the Army of the Alps, and now an ardent Thermidorian, had Napoleon imprisoned because he was jealous of his young compatriot's growing influence with the Army of Italy. In fact, by arresting him, Saliceti was doing Napoleon a favour and probably saved him from what might have been a worse fate in Paris. Napoleon's imprisonment, in any case, lasted only ten days. Despite the odium in which he was held in Paris, Napoleon was soon restored to his command, thanks to the petticoat intervention of the *'adorable Félicité'*, the wife of General Turreau (the Butcher of the Vendée), who was spending a honeymoon furlough with her husband on the Côte d'Azur. Napoleon was not the only one to benefit by her intervention: Louis, aged sixteen, was appointed (quite irregularly) a brevet lieutenant of artillery.

After Napoleon's release, the Bonapartes returned from Antibes to stay with the Clary family in Marseilles. Letizia was happy that Napoleon was once again courting the rich Désirée; Madame Clary, however, was not so pleased. 'One Bonaparte in the family is quite sufficient,' she declared. But his visit to Marseilles was of only short duration. In February we find him in Savona and later in Toulon, helping to organize the second expedition against Corsica, which Joseph was once again to accompany.

This second expedition, once more under the command of Admiral Martin, was to have put to sea on 11 February, but the weather proved so foul that it was not until 2 March that the French fleet was able to leave the shelter of Toulon harbour. Joseph wrote of Martin: 'Beneath the somewhat crusty exterior of a Republican sailor, this officer had one of the kindest hearts I have ever known; he even went so far as to give up his berth to me.'[13] A likely story! The expedition started off well with the capture of a British ship but, off Cap Noli, Martin ran into Hotham's Anglo-Neapolitan squadron. Although this time the fleets were equally matched in numbers, Martin's crews, three-quarters of whom had had no training and were at sea for the first time, were no match for the English sailors. After losing two of his ships, Martin disengaged from the battle. On 12 March, the two fleets were again within sight of each other. Martin tried to avoid action, but the wind and various accidents during the night retarded his retreat. A partial and very straggling encounter followed, which was renewed again on 14 March, when two of the French ships were captured. The rest escaped, for the British fleet was scattered and Hotham failed to follow up his success, despite the remonstrances of Nelson, who at the time of the engagement was commanding *Agamemnon*. To Nelson's disgust, the battle was regarded in England as a great victory and Hotham was treated as a hero.

On 19 March, Joseph, thoroughly disheartened, disembarked at Toulon, where he was to meet with yet another disappointment. Despite the fact that he had married into a devout Catholic family and was a good Republican bourgeois (although at one time, in a moment of folly, he had adopted a Roman name, as was fashionable among members of the Jacobin clubs, and had signed himself Scævola-Joseph), he had been accused in his absence of extreme Jacobin sympathies and dismissed from his post as *commissaire des guerres*. Even the deputy Chiappe, his compatriot and family friend, had been unsuccessful in having him reinstated, and for the time being Joseph had to be contented with the subordinate position of Inspector of Hospitals. His thoughts turned more and more towards a business partnership with his successful merchant brother-in-law Nicolas in Italy, where perhaps, with the help of Chiappe and Saliceti, he might even obtain a consular post in Genoa[14] or Leghorn.

Lucien, with more reason, had been dismissed from his post at Saint-Maximin, and was only too pleased to have found employment in the more humble role of 'Inspector of Military Transport' (i.e. wagons and mules) at Cette. Here the self-styled *sans-culotte* Lucien Brutus was tracked down by the Royalist *Compagnons de Jehu* and would probably have lost his life but for the intervention of two Conventional *représentants en mission* who, though they rescued him from the 'White Terror', nevertheless imprisoned him in Aix as a suspected terrorist involved in the attempted coup of 1 Prairial.

41

Letizia moved heaven and earth to obtain his release. Finally, it was Chiappe who persuaded Barras to have him set free. On 5 August, after three weeks of confinement, Lucien, leaving his wife Christine Boyer and baby daughter in Saint-Maximin, joined *Madame mére*, Jerome and Pauline in Marseilles.

Almost four months previously, on 16 April, Napoleon had received orders from the Committee of Public Safety appointing him to the Army of the West as Commander-in-Chief of artillery. Napoleon, reluctant to leave Désirée, postponed his departure until 8 May, when, accompanied by young Louis and his two aides-de-camp, Lieutenant Junot and Major Marmont (whose services he had enlisted without even asking permission of his superiors), he set out on a leisurely journey to Paris. He was certainly in no hurry to assume his new command and disliked intensely the idea of serving in the Army of the West, which after an uneasy truce was once more engaged in fighting the heroic peasant armies of Charette and Stofflet in the Vendée, and the Chouans in Brittany, under the leadership of the Cottereau brothers and the great Georges Cadoudal. During the past three years, Republican general after general had lost his reputation (and sometimes his head) in one of the most terrible civil wars ever fought.[15] Napoleon had no desire to be counted among their number. Furthermore, his entire interest lay with the Army of Italy.

It was not until 16 May that Napoleon reported to Aubry, in charge of postings, a Girondist twenty years Napoleon's senior who was also an artillery officer but more of a politician than a soldier. He considered the promotion of this young Corsican protégé of Robespierre to have been altogether too rapid, and maintained that he was not equipped to command such an élite corps as the artillery. In view of the reputation that Napoleon had already earned as a planner, Aubry must have known that this was absolute nonsense, for it was Napoleon who had actually planned two of the offensive actions, namely the capture of the Piedmontese port of Oneglia and Dego, the strategic key to the plains of Piedmont, which had been carried out successfully by General Dumberion in the previous April and September. All this and more must have been known to Aubry, but the older man was understandably angry that this impudent twenty-six-year-old general should have taken more than a month to report for duty. Overruling the orders of the Committee of Public Safety, he posted him to the infantry. Napoleon was furious; he protested that, as a gunnery officer, he was unsuited to command infantry troops. When this failed to move Aubry, he pleaded ill-health. This could not have been a premeditated decision, for he had already sent Junot ahead to Nantes where the Army of the West had its headquarters, with his horses and luggage. Aubry, exasperated, curtly dismissed him. Napoleon was demoted to the rank of *chef de bataillon* (major) on the reserve with half pay, with no official duties.

Probably out of pride, Napoleon was not prepared to admit the truth to Joseph. On 23 June he wrote to him : 'I am employed as a general of brigade with the Army of the West, but not in the artillery. I am ill, which forces me to take a furlough of two or three months.' Again, as late as 25 July, he wrote : 'I am appointed as a general of the Army of the West, but my illness [unspecified] keeps me here.'

There are so many contradictory stories concerning Napoleon at this time, that it is difficult to arrive at the truth. Barras claims in his memoirs that the young general was so poor and out at elbow, that he felt obliged to fit him out with decent clothing. The Duchess of Abrantès also describes him as incredibly shabby, wearing civilian clothes with a top hat 'which either completely concealed his features, or which he wore on the back of his head'. We know that Napoleon was never particularly tidy in his dress and only rarely indulged in the ostentatious sartorial extravagances so favoured by officers of the Revolutionary army. Could it not be simply that, having forwarded all his luggage and horses to Nantes, he was reduced to wearing the clothes in which he had travelled from Marseilles? Joseph in his memoirs makes a very definite point that his brother was certainly not living a life of penury. Unfortunately none of Joseph's letters written to his brother at this time have survived, whereas practically every letter written by Napoleon to Joseph and Désirée is still extant. From these, it would appear, even allowing for certain exaggerations and omissions, that during his period of more or less self-chosen unemployment, he was far from idle. He still had influential friends among the Corsican and Southern deputies of the Convention, including the powerful Sieyès and Pontécoulant, the new Minister of War, who obtained for him some vague staff appointment until his health should be restored. He tried to find a situation for Lucien (in this he was not immediately successful); he obtained a place for little Jerome in a boarding school, and although unable to obtain a regular commission for Louis in an artillery regiment, he was able to send him to Châlons, 'where', as he wrote to Joseph, 'he will pass his examinations and become an officer in a year's time'. He continued to write affectionate letters to Désirée, who, although she replied less and less frequently, asked him to send her his portrait. 'I am going to have it painted if she still wishes it,' he wrote to Joseph.

> If not, keep it for yourself. In whatever circumstances you may be placed, you know well, my friend, that you cannot have a better or dearer friend than myself. If you are going away for some time, send me your own portrait. We have lived together for so many years, so closely united, that our hearts have become one, and you know how entirely mine belongs to you.

Although Napoleon would have preferred his brother to stay close to him in France, Joseph had already decided that there was no future for him there and was determined to settle in Genoa with his wife and Désirée and invest Julie's dowry in his brother-in-law's prosperous mercantile business. It was Napoleon who obtained for him his passports and an introduction from the Committee of Foreign Affairs to the French Minister in Genoa, without which papers Joseph would have been proscribed as an *émigré*.

One of the strangest phenomena of the French Revolution was that even when the country was torn between various factions and civil war, even at the height of the Terror, when the streets of Paris literally ran with blood, people still thronged the theatres, Mesdames Tallien, de Staël and Récamier still held their salons, and a febrile gaiety seemed to infect the people of Paris. Despite Napoleon's assertion in one of his many letters to Joseph at this time, that 'luxury, pleasure and the arts are reviving here in a wonderful manner', and that 'life here is much happier than in Genoa', the capital during the last days of the Convention was in a constant state of turmoil. The first sight that met the eyes of Benjamin Constant when he arrived in Paris from Switzerland on 15 May 1794 was cartloads of 'Robespierrot' gendarmes being led off to execution.

Everywhere slogans were to be seen reading: 'People of France! Return to your Church and King, only then will you have bread.' The abolition of the *Loi du Maximum* and the soaring price of bread had plunged the country in misery. The people were hungry. On 12 Germinal (1 April) the women of Paris forced their way into the Assembly demanding bread and the restitution of the Constitution of 1793. On 1 Prairial (20 May) the Chamber was again invaded, this time by workmen from the suburbs of Antoine and Marceau. After killing Féraud, one of the deputies, they had presented his head

44

impaled on a pike to Boissy d'Anglas, who imperturbably saluted it. For three whole days the rioters fought the National Guard and troops commanded by Pichegru, and withdrew only when the Convention threatened to bombard the Faubourg Antoine. Seventeen members of the former Jacobin government who had sided with the rioters were arrested.

Up to the very last, the Convention had certainly had a disturbed existence. The tide had turned against mob law. The new Constitution of the Year III took effect on 9 October 1795 with the formation of an Executive Directory. The Legislature was divided into two chambers (*conseils*) – the *Anciens* and the *Conseil de cinq cents*, the Five Hundred. The fear, however, of reaction, whether revolutionary or royalist, taking effect at the coming (restricted) elections, inspired further modifications – in the first instance, that two-thirds of the deputies of the Council of Five Hundred must be chosen from the members of the Convention itself.

The claim that the structure of the old Assembly was still preserved in the new constitution failed to convince many Parisians, including former constituents, members of the legal profession, the bourgeois and working classes. Exploiting this discontent, the Royalists united in opposing the new decrees. The main centres of resistance were the Odéon and the Le Pelletier *sections*. At a plenary session, the Convention ordered General Menou to disarm the *sections* and to take command of the little troop defending the Tuileries.

In the evening of 12 Vendémiaire (5 October) Bonaparte hastened to the Assembly, which was in all-night session, where he heard his own name proposed among others considered as replacements for Menou, whose conduct of the operations was considered altogether too weak.

The rest of the story is too well known to repeat in detail. In brief, it was Napoleon whom Barras chose to replace Menou. On the following day Napoleon, who had been authorized to use force if necessary, sent a cavalry officer, none other than Joachim Murat, to collect some guns from the nearest depot, and posted them to command the approaches to the Tuileries in which the Government had barricaded themselves. As the mob approached the barricades of the rue Saint-Honoré, Napoleon opened fire with his well-known 'whiff of grape shot' and dispersed the rioters. This was the famous 13 Vendemiaire which was to set Napoleon on his path to glory and to allow the gentle Joseph to become twice a king.

In a letter to Joseph, written at two o'clock in the morning, Napoleon recounted the events of that famous day.

45

At last all is over. My first task is to give you the news. Everyday the Royalists were becoming increasingly bolder. The Convention ordered the *section* of Le Pelletier to be disarmed; the troops sent against it were repulsed. Menou was forthwith deprived of his command. The Convention next appointed Barras to command the armed forces; the Committee appointed me as second-in-command. We deployed our troops; the enemy attacked; a great many were killed. We disarmed the *sections*. Fortune is on my side.

P.S.   My fond regards to Julie and Eugénie.[16]

What Napoleon did not tell his brother was that, just before being summoned by Barras, he had said to Junot: 'Ah, if only the *sections* would put me at their head, I would guarantee to have them in the Tuileries within two hours and drive out all those miserable *conventionnels* . . .'

On 30 October the Convention was dissolved, to be replaced by the Directoire. The new constitution, however, was far from satisfactory; a fatal antagonism was to be created between the legislative and executive Assemblies and there was to be frequent disagreement between the five Directors.[17]

On 9 October Napoleon was appointed second-in-command of the Army of the Interior (that is to say, all troops not at the front) under the (theoretical) orders of Barras. On 1 November Barras resigned his military duties and appointed Napoleon to replace him as Commander-in-Chief. On 4 Ventôse, Year IV (25 February 1796), just over four and a half months since Napoleon had suppressed the revolt which he had been prepared to abet, he was given command of the Army of Italy. In the words of Marmont, 'The doors of immortality were opened'.

III

Napoleon's Marriage :
First Italian Campaign

1796–1797

As soon as Napoleon was appointed to the command of the Army of the Interior his first thoughts were for his family. He obtained an appointment for Lucien as commissary with the Army of the Rhine; he chose Uncle Fesch as his secretary and Louis as his aide-de-camp. On 17 November, he wrote to Joseph :

> The family [his mother and sisters in Marseilles] is in want of nothing. I have sent them money, assignats etc. I received 400,000 francs for you only a few days ago . . . Adieu, my dear Joseph; the only want I feel is your society . . .

Joseph was of course delighted with his brother's success, but he had no particular wish to visit Paris. Genoa was a charming town with a mild winter climate, business was prospering : moreover Julie was expecting her first child. He continued to write to his brother asking him to use his influence to procure him a consulship, somewhere on the Italian riviera if possible, but now, all of a sudden, apart from six short letters, Napoleon ceased to write. To begin with, he had excused himself on the grounds that he was too busy. For three months Joseph scarcely received any direct news from the young general. But the real reason for Napoleon's silence was not because he was too busy, but because he had fallen madly in love with Josephine Tascher de la Pagerie, widow of the *ci-devant* Vicomte de Beauharnais and ex-mistress of Barras, and was reluctant – even ashamed – to announce to his family and Désirée that he intended to marry this beautiful Creole.

47

It was not until 31 December that he once again resumed his correspondence with Joseph, who had reproached him with his silence.

In a few days you will have letters of marque. You will soon be a consul. Don't be uneasy. If you are tired of Genoa, I see no objection to your coming to Paris. I can give you an apartment, a table and a carriage . . . If you do not wish for a consulship, come here. Adieu, my dear Joseph; you would wrong me if you thought I could be indifferent to you for one instant, or to anything that concerns you. Be of good cheer, and, if you are tired, come to Paris and amuse yourself until I find something suitable for you to do.

The letters of marque to which Napoleon refers authorized Joseph to arm two privateers, licensed to engage in 'piracy' against ships under the British flag trading in the Mediterranean. How Joseph managed to raise the money to acquire and arm these privateers is still a mystery. Perhaps Nicolas and Antoine had invested capital in this venture. But more mysterious is how Napoleon raised the 400,000 francs which he placed to Joseph's credit in November. All that is known is that Joseph had taken an interest in a coral fishery, but this would hardly account for his sudden access to riches. It is quite clear that Napoleon regarded family and public interests as almost synonymous.

On 27 February he was told that he was appointed to command the Army in Italy in place of Scherer, and Saliceti had been nominated *Commissaire du Directoire* to the Army. The latter's appointment could hardly have been more beneficial to the Bonaparte brothers. For Napoleon, Saliceti's appointment was of prime importance, for he knew that in this compatriot he had a friend on whose loyalty he could depend entirely. Too many generals had lost their heads or reputations because of mere whisper of suspicion that they were lacking in *civisme* (revolutionary zeal). Commissaires were to be feared almost more than the enemy. So long as Saliceti remained the political representative of the Directoire, Napoleon had nothing to fear on this score.

But the appointments of Saliceti and Napoleon were by no means universally popular. The economist and ex-Conventionnel Du Pont de Nemours wrote to Rewbell, one of the five members[1] of the Directoire :

My dear Colleague, – I am told you[2] have entrusted the Army of Italy – our last hope if the war is to continue – to two Corsicans,

Buonaparte and Saliceti. I find it difficult to believe that you have made such a mistake. Don't you know what these Corsicans are like? For two thousand years, nobody has been able to trust them. They are fickle by nature and all have their fortunes to make. Pitt can give them more guineas than we can mint ha'pence. Such men must always be kept under, even if they should have merit. The best thing to do, would be to make peace. If you insist on making war, at least don't entrust its conduct to Corsicans, particularly in Italy. Are there no Frenchmen?

I salute you, embrace you and commiserate with you.

Du Pont de Nemours need not have worried. Napoleon certainly justified the Directoire's choice. In a succession of incredibly rapid encircling movements over very difficult terrain, Napoleon inflicted a series of crushing defeats on the enemy. On 26 April he issued the following order of the day:

Soldiers! In fifteen days you have won six victories, captured twenty-one colours, fifty guns, several fortresses and conquered the richest part of Piedmont; you have taken fifteen thousand prisoners, killed or wounded more than ten thousand men.

The Austrians had been forced back to the north-east to defend the line of the Po; the Piedmontese, to the north-west to cover Turin. Vittorio-Amadeo III, King of Sardinia and Piedmont, seeing that his country was practically indefensible, sent plenipotentiaries to meet Napoleon at Cherasco, thirty-three miles south of Turin. Here, on 28 April, an armistice was signed. Piedmont was no longer a member of the Coalition.

Three weeks before his lightning conquest of Piedmont, Napoleon had sent his aide-de-camp Captain Junot to invite Joseph to visit him at his headquarters at Albenga, a little port eighty-five kilometres west of Genoa. Leaving Julie, who had just given birth to a daughter (who was to die a few days later), Joseph hastened to join his brother. They were reunited on 7 April.

It was some little while before Napoleon had dared to inform his family that he had been secretly wedded to Josephine on 9 March. He had so feared the reaction of his family to the news that he had taken as his wife a woman not only considerably older than himself, but who, apart from Barras, was well known to have had numerous lovers, that he wanted none of his family to be in Paris at the time of his wedding. He had therefore hastened Lucien's departure to the Army of the Rhine and had sent Louis, an aide-de-camp, to Marmont's father at Châtillon on the pretext of obtaining horses and

49

wagons for his army. It was only now that Joseph was angry and disappointed. Ever since Napoleon's future had seemed assured, he had hoped that he would make Désirée his wife. Désirée herself, although informed by gossips of Napoleon's courtship of the beautiful Creole, had refused to believe that her former lover could have been so unfaithful to her. Lucien and Louis were horrified when they learnt that their brother had married 'this woman old enough to be their grandmother'. Only Jerome, who had been at school with Josephine's son, Eugène de Beauharnais, remained indifferent.

It was not until 22 March, almost a fortnight after his marriage, that Napoleon, during an overnight visit to Marseilles on his way to join his army, had plucked up enough courage to face his mother and sisters. After a painful nine hours, he had persuaded Letizia to write a letter to Josephine, a letter which she first submitted to Joseph, in Genoa, for his approval.

During Joseph's visit to Albenga, he too had been persuaded to write to Josephine: 'Madame, I learnt with the greatest interest of your marriage with my brother. The friendship which unites me to him, cannot make me insensible to the happiness he will find with you . . .' Joseph ends this extremely curt letter in the most formal and almost business-like manner: '*Agréez, je vous prie, l'assurance fraternelle avec laquelle je suis votre beau-frère.*'

Despite the coldness of this note, Napoleon was grateful to his elder brother; he begged him to remain at his side. Joseph, who was becoming thoroughly irritated by Nicolas's miserly attitude and constant criticism (although later he was to appreciate his brother-in-law's business acumen), was only too pleased to find an excuse to leave Genoa and readily agreed to accompany his brother on his forthcoming campaign.

Fourteen days later Piedmont was conquered and the armistice, which virtually made that state a vassal of France and no longer a member of the Coalition, was signed. According to Joseph

It was at Cherasco on 5 Floréal [24 April] that Napoleon entrusted me with the task of informing the Directoire of his decision to make peace [with Sardinia] as soon as possible, in order to isolate the Austrians in Italy. His aide-de-camp, Junot, was charged with the presentation of the captured standards. We left together in the same post-chaise and arrived in Paris twenty hours after our departure from Nice. It would be difficult to give an adequate idea of the enthusiasm shown by the people. In view of our rapid progress, a courier preceded us to give the people time to assemble and come out to welcome us.

In Paris the demonstrations were just as enthusiastic. The members of the Directoire vied with each other to express their satisfaction.³

The Directoire gave its approval to the armistice; Charles Delacroix, Minister of Foreign Affairs, offered Joseph the post of Minister to the Court of Turin as soon as peace was signed. Joseph, according to his memoirs, vehemently protested, for although ambitious to embark on a diplomatic career, he 'had no wish to start at the top' (*sans prétendre d'emblée au premier poste*).

Joseph's visit to Paris, however, was not confined entirely to official business; he also had private affairs to attend to. Napoleon had asked him to keep an eye on Josephine, provide her with money if necessary and deliver a letter in which he begged her to join him in Italy. Joseph was furnished with an introduction which read:

> My brother will hand you this letter. I have the greatest affection for him. I hope he will have yours; he deserves it. Nature has endowed him with a gentle and loyal heart. *He overflows with good qualities.* I have written asking Barras to find him a consulship in some port in Italy. *He is anxious to live with his little wife far from storm and strife and the great affairs of this world.*

There was no sympathy between Joseph and his sister-in-law at their first meeting. As neither of them was in a hurry to leave for Italy, Joseph decided it was more profitable for him to remain in Paris and cultivate the society of men in power, and enjoy the pleasures of the capital. He accepted, almost as his due, but always with modesty, the compliments lavished on him. No one seemed to question his right 'to wear the laurels conferred on his brother' or ask what part he had actually played in Napoleon's victories. His name alone was sufficient to place him in the limelight, while poor brave Junot remained in the shade.

Joseph's other private business took the form of a very astute financial transaction. This consisted of taking advantage of a troop of cavalry on its way to Paris from Nice, to protect a consignment of 1,000 *louis d'or*,⁴ which he had obtained from a M. Collot, an immensely wealthy army contractor, against a letter of credit drawn on Nicolas. Joseph's pretext was that there would be nothing to be gained in Genoa once peace had been signed, while, on the contrary, in France, ten per cent could be obtained from investment in property. But the real reason for this transaction was that Joseph was anxious to have access to his wife's dowry, hitherto entirely in the hands of Nicolas, who had placed it in the form of *assignats* (whose value was

51

rapidly falling) in his business, over which Joseph apparently had little or no control.

Nicolas, tempted by the ten per cent profit, took the bait and honoured the letter of credit, but rushed to Paris to see that the 'good for nothing' Joseph invested the 1,000 *louis* wisely. Joseph in his memoirs tells us that he used the money to acquire property of 'little importance' in the Département of La Marne.

His other 'business', that which concerned Josephine, was far less agreeable. His initial dislike of his sister-in-law had turned to positive horror when he realized that only a few weeks subsequent to her marriage with his beloved brother, she was already conducting a passionate love affair with a charming handsome young cavalry officer named Hippolyte Charles. Nor was Charles the only young man to enjoy her favours. Among others was the dashing young Gascon Joachim Murat, whom Napoleon had also entrusted with a mission to Paris and a letter of introduction to the châtelaine of the house in the rue Chantereine, which had been a present from Barras to Josephine while still his mistress, and which Napoleon had made his home. It was impossible for Joseph to tell his brother the truth; he would never have believed him. Madly in love, Napoleon was prepared to believe any excuse offered by Josephine for not joining him, even when she wrote claiming that she was pregnant.

Joseph was placed in the most invidious position. His brother wrote him letter after letter begging him to use all his influence to persuade Josephine to return to his side. In one such letter Napoleon wrote:

> Since from our childhood we have been united by ties of blood and the tenderest affection, I implore you to do for her what I would glory to do myself. Only you can take my place. After her, after my Josephine, I have no concern for anyone but you.

Certainly this letter, ambiguous as it is, does not have the connotations it seems to imply. Although Josephine lavished all her feminine charms on Joseph, he did not avail himself of the opportunities she afforded to Murat. On the contrary, perhaps because of the presence of Nicolas in Paris, there is every reason to suppose that Joseph's life in the capital, although surrounded by temptations, was nothing but exemplary.

Josephine's 'affairs', in particular her liaison with Hippolyte Charles (her little '*polichinelle*', as she called him), and her repeated refusals to join her husband in Italy, had become a public scandal. Barras, who naturally felt a certain responsibility for Napoleon's marriage, decided that Charles must be posted to Italy. Only then would Josephine renounce the pleasures of the capital. His plan was successful. On 24 June, Josephine set out for Italy accompanied by Hippolyte, Junot, Nicolas and Joseph, together with a retinue of servants, including her personal maid, with whom Junot was soon on the most intimate terms, and to whom she naturally revealed all her mistress's secrets.

The journey proved to be much more pleasant than Joseph had anticipated. On their way through Savoy and Piedmont, the travellers stopped at every town which offered diversion. While crossing the Alps, Joseph made the acquaintance of a young wounded soldier who told him the story of his life, a story which so moved him that he was prompted, there and then, to begin writing a romance, subsequently to be published under the title of *Moïna, ou la villageoise de Mont-Cenis*, a sentimental novel of no merit.

After a brief visit to the King of Sardinia in Turin, the travellers resumed their journey to Milan, where they arrived on 9 July 1796, to be greeted by an impatient and long-suffering Napoleon. The young and very much in love Commander-in-Chief had been awaiting the arrival of his wife ever since 15 May, when he had made his triumphal entry into the Lombard capital after his spectacular victory at Lodi, where he had reputedly led the famous charge over the bridge spanning the river Addi. In fact it was the devoted ugly little Berthier (who was to become Napoleon's invaluable logistic expert) and the indomitable heroic Lannes who led the charge; Napoleon followed. There is, however, no doubt that Napoleon showed the greatest courage during the action. Never had his prestige been so high with the rank and file of the army. Although the storming of the bridge had no real strategic influence on the campaign, 'it had produced a profound psychological effect on the troops taking part and also on Napoleon himself. For the first time he had fought in the front line with his men and they now hailed him as *le petit caporal*. It certainly fortified his own feeling of self-confidence.'[5] Years later, he confided to Las Cases in St Helena : 'It was only after Lodi that I got the idea that, after all, I might play a decisive role on our political stage. It was then that the first spark of my high ambition was born.' When Las Cases asked him if it was he who had led the charge, Napoleon, unblushingly, replied 'yes'.[6]

A short while later, Joseph and Nicolas also left Milan to return to Genoa.

By the end of June Napoleon had wrested the whole of Lombardy from the Austrian yoke. He spent only a fortnight in Milan, just long enough to re-equip his tattered troops at the expense of the inhabitants whom he had come to liberate, and from whom he extracted not only the enormous sum of the equivalent of £800,000, but from whom he also stole works of art, regarded as national treasures. In consequence, there were serious risings in the province, particularly in Pavia, which were ruthlessly crushed, always, of course, in the name of *Liberté, Égalité et Fraternité.*

Infringing the neutrality of the Republic of Venezia, Napoleon established his forward outposts on the line of the river Adige in Venetian territory, leaving Mantua in his rear to be invested by Sérurier. Only then, in obedience to directives he had received from the Convention in May, did he send Murat with a flying column to assert French authority over Genoa while Augereau was ordered to Bologna, which formed one of the Papal States. Napoleon himself followed Augereau with a third column which he threatened to use against Rome unless his territorial demands were met. His blackmail was effective. On 23 June the delegates of a terrified Pope Pius VI signed an armistice with Napoleon, by which France was ceded the territories of Bologna, Ferrara and Ancona, and was paid a vast indemnity (though protection money would be a more appropriate term), together with a precious contribution of art treasures from the Vatican collections. Next, Napoleon made a lightning dash across the Appenines to Pistoja, Leghorn and Florence and forced the Grand Duke of Tuscany into submission. By July he was back in Milan, the richer by millions, awaiting the arrival of Josephine.

On 29 July the Austrian army, now under the command of Field-Marshal Count von Wurmser, opened its expected counter-attack.

The campaign of August–December 1796 was hotly contested. In August the French were forced to abandon their forward position on the Adige, which they had occupied since May, and were driven back more than thirty miles to the west bank of the Mincio. Their position was extremely insecure. The Austrians had succeeded in penetrating the French centre and had driven a deep wedge down the Mincio valley. Had he not lost contact with his right flank, Wurmser could have rolled up the dispersed French divisions separately, one after the other. But Napoleon, in one of his most brilliant defensive battles (Castiglione, 5 August), regained the initiative and forced Wurmser to retire. Determined to give the enemy no respite, he forced his tired troops to follow up their victory. In this he was completely successful. By the beginning of September the French were on the upper reaches of the Adige and by the 5th had occupied Trento. So confident was Napoleon now of effecting his great pincer movement on Austria, in collaboration with the Armies of the Rhine under Moreau, that he had already sent a coded message to the latter advising him to advance up the Danube while he continued to push forward through the mountains to Bolzano and thence, over the Brenner Pass, to Innsbruck.

But the plan failed when a fresh Austrian army of 40,000 men, under the command of the veteran Hungarian Field-Marshal Allvintzy, advancing from the Piave, threatened the French rear. To counter this new move, Napoleon was forced to withdraw to the south, following the right bank of the Adige. Despite his recent optimism, Napoleon was in fact in an extremely weak position. He could expect no reinforcements; Moreau had been held up; 18,000 of Napoleon's men were sick or wounded in hospital, including a number of senior officers; 9,000 men under Sérurier (himself suffering from a severe attack of malaria) were tied up blockading von Wurmser in Mantua. Napoleon had only 11,000 men of Augereau's and Masséna's divisions with which to oppose Allvintzy.

On 15 November Augereau's division, after crossing the Adige by a pontoon bridge, made contact with Allvintzy's outposts at Arcola, a small village on the left bank.[7] Although the first attack on Arcola proved unsuccessful, Napoleon, after withdrawing his troops to the right bank under cover of night, secretly constructed another pontoon bridge to the south. On the 16th, Masséna's and Augereau's divisions once again crossed the Adige. A turning movement from the new bridge on Allvintzy's right forced him to retreat to Vincenza with the loss of 6,000 men. Another resounding name could now be added to the regimental banners of the Republican armies – Arcola.

The campaign of 1796 ended with the French once again holding the line of the Adige, with a strong foothold in the province of Venezia, but still with an Austrian corps locked up in Mantua behind their lines. But in mid-January 1797 the fortunes of war were definitely in favour of the French. In an attempt to relieve Mantua, Allvintzy was decisively defeated in the battle of Rivoli (14 January). A further attempt to relieve the garrison by General Provera, Allvintzy's second-in-command, was foiled at the battle of La Favorita two days later. On 2 February the garrison of Mantua, on the point of starvation and decimated by malaria, capitulated. The road to Austria lay open.

IV

Corsican Deputy and
Ambassador to Rome

1797–1798

The whole of Lombardy, Mantua included, was now under French domination. On the pretext that the Venetian Republic had assisted the Austrian forces during the 1796 campaign, Napoleon now treated this province as enemy country. By the spring of 1797, he was in possession of all Venetian territories, including part of the Dalmatian coast, the Ionian islands and Corfu. He had extracted vast sums from the Venetian treasury and had robbed the city of Venice itself of some of its most priceless art treasures. Now once again he turned his attention to Rome and terrified the Pope into further concessions, arguing that His Holiness had been dilatory in honouring the armistice terms signed at Bologna in the previous year. Under the Treaty of Tolentino, which he signed with the papal delegates in February 1797, he levied, or more accurately, robbed the Holy See of a further three million francs and additional works of art, and successfully bullied the delegates into ceding to France the papal fiefs of Avignon and Comtant (part of the Provençal department of Vaucluse) together with Ancona, Ferrara and Bologna. As though this was not enough, on his own initiative he ejected the Duke of Modena from his duchy and constructed the Cispadane Republic out of the ducal territories, and the already ceded Papal States of Romagna; to this he now added, under the name of the Cisalpine Republic (again without authority from his masters in Paris), the conquered districts of Lombardy.

With the defeat of Allvintzy at Arcola and the capitulation of Mantua and with the whole of north and central Italy under French domination, the fate of Austria was a foregone conclusion. By 4 April,

56

after forcing the passes of the Carnic Alps and the Tyrol, Masséna and Joubert, now reinforced by Bernadotte and divisions loaned by Kléber from the Army of Sambre-et-Meuse, were within ninety miles of Vienna. On the 7th, Austrian plenipotentiaries met Napoleon at Judenberg, where an armistice was agreed. On the 18th, a preliminary peace treaty was signed at Schloss Egenwald, near Leoben, between Napoleon on behalf of the Directoire and Count Cobenzl on behalf of the Austrian Empire.

With the signing of peace with Rome and Naples, and the occupation of Leghorn by the French, the position of the British in Corsica, always precarious, was made even more difficult. The directive issued to Napoleon by the Executive Council in May had specified among other objectives, the 'liberation' of Corsica. Napoleon, however, had neither the troops nor ships available for an invasion of the island. He therefore turned to Joseph, to whom he entrusted the task of raising an expeditionary force composed of Corsican émigrés and several hundred Corsican soldiers already enrolled in his Army of Italy. Miot, the French Minister to the Court of Tuscany and old friend of Joseph, was appointed *Commissaire général* to be in charge of the administration of the island, and General Gentili, a former comrade of Paoli, was given the command of the expeditionary force, which was to embark at Leghorn for Bastia.

Corsican officers had already preceded the expedition with consignments of arms for partisans, and had already fomented risings against the British occupying forces. Few in number, and already faced by a hostile population, the British did not wait for the forthcoming invasion, but evacuated the island without a fight. By the time Joseph landed on his native shores at the end of October 1796, the tricolor flag was already flying above the citadel of Ajaccio. Four years had elapsed since the day when, as a young man, with no money and no future, Joseph had fled from the island he so loved, 'condemned to perpetual execration and deprived of all rights of citizenship'. The same people who had cursed him, together with the whole Buonaparte family, and who had sacked the family home in 1793, now gave him an enthusiastic welcome. The whole of Ajaccio turned out to meet him. He was escorted in triumph to the fine Ornan house, where he was to reside until the Casa Buonaparte was once again restored, refurnished and recarpeted. Joseph wrote to Napoleon on 10 December : 'Come what may, I want to see [our home] in good condition, worthy to be lived in'. *Come what may* : perhaps Joseph himself was

57

scarcely able to believe in the extraordinary changes of fortune experienced by himself and his family in four short years, and had asked himself 'Can this last?', or as his mother had already begun to say in her vile French accent : *'Pourvou que ça doure.'*

In all but name, Joseph was governor of Corsica. He immediately proposed a number of reforms which his friend Miot ratified. The island was divided into two departments – Liamone and Gollo, with Ajaccio as administrative capital of the former (for the Buonapartes) and Bastia as capital of the latter (for Saliceti). With Miot's unquestioning approval, he appointed friends and members of his family to all important administrative posts and dismissed all those who had ever shown hostility to the Buonapartes. Lucien, who had arrived in Bastia in February 1797, was given the rank of *Commissaire ordonnateur.*

'Don't mix yourself up in Corsican affairs,' Joseph wrote to Napoleon. On 11 April 1797 he was elected deputy for Liamone by the Council of Five Hundred with a total of 103 votes out of 104. Only then did he return to Italy to assume his appointment as Minister to Parma (with a salary of 18,000 francs per annum) which Charles Delacroix had promised him as soon as peace with the Infante Ferdinand, Duke of Parma, had been ratified by Spain (as it was on 18 December 1796). His appointment had been approved by the Duke on 1 March 1797 but, curiously enough, Joseph tells us in his memoirs that he only learned of his appointment 'indirectly' from his brother when he visited him at Judenberg on 8 April, shortly before the signing of the preliminary peace treaty of Leoben. He had been received in audience by the Duke on 29 March, but only presented his credentials on 6 May – which shows how little knowledge he had of diplomatic protocol. His duties, however, were purely nominal.

He only just had time to get to know the Duke, a pupil of the philosopher Condillac, and his Duchess, a sister of Marie-Antoinette, both of whom he liked, before he received two official communiqués from the Directoire, dated 6 and 15 May respectively, the first appointing him Minister Plenipotentiary to the Holy See, the second promoting him to ambassadorial status with a salary of 60,000 francs per annum in specie.[1] Delacroix wrote an accompanying flattering letter :

> The *Directoire executif* has decided, Citizen, that you would be of greater service to the Republic in a more eminent post than that to which it first assigned you. It has taken the first opportunity to make use of your talents and provide you with the just recompense which your previous service merits.

On 18 May, Napoleon had signed the preliminary peace treaty of Leoben; Joseph was appointed to Rome nineteen days later. It needs no great stretch of the imagination to connect the two events.

Before assuming his new post Joseph, accompanied by Julie, spent some little while at the Castel Mombello, the magnificent residence near Milan where Napoleon had established his 'court'. Here the whole family, with the exception of Lucien (still in disgrace since his marriage to Christine Boyer, the innkeeper's sister), were united to celebrate the wedding of the silly, giddy Pauline to a young general of brigade, Victor Leclerc, and to ratify the civil marriage of poor plain Élise to Captain Félix Bacciochi (a thoroughly stupid man, fifteen years her senior) which had taken place in Marseilles on 1 May with Letizia's blessing but without Napoleon's knowledge or consent. Not content with a civil ceremony alone, Napoleon insisted that both couples should now receive the blessing of the Church. On 14 June, by special dispensation from the Bishop of Milan, the double church wedding was solemnized behind closed doors in the private chapel of Mombello.

This reunion of the Bonaparte family had not been a happy one. With the exception of Joseph, all felt awkward in the brilliant company of the Italian poets, artists and savants whom Napoleon had gathered around him. Madame mère, in particular, felt out of place; furthermore she detested Josephine. Pauline, who had been more or less forced into marriage with Leclerc, behaved like the impossible child she was and embarrassed all concerned with her stupid, inane prattle. She too disliked Josephine and was to incur her lasting hostility when a little later she revealed to Napoleon Josephine's liaison with Hippolyte Charles.

The family soon dispersed. Madame mère, whose only thought was to return to Ajaccio, now that Corsica had been liberated, embarked in July with Élise and Bacciochi for Bastia, where they were greeted by Lucien. In the same month Pauline and Leclerc, after a honeymoon on Lake Como, left for Milan and thence for Paris. Jerome was packed off to school; Louis, relieved of his post as aide-de-camp to his brother, was posted with the rank of captain to a cavalry regiment.[2] A little later Joseph and Julie, accompanied by Caroline, then fifteen years of age, left for Rome.[3] They arrived in the capital on 31 August and took up residence in the hotel of a Signor Pio on the via Condotti, near the Piazza d'Espagna. This, however, was only a temporary arrangement, for within a few days Joseph rented as his embassy the Palazzo Orsini 'alla Longhara' in the Trastevere quarter of Rome, far from other diplomatic missions. Why he should have decided to establish his mission in such a humble quarter, reputedly one of the poorest in Rome (although the Orsini Palace itself was a magnificent building and had once been the residence of Queen Christine of Sweden) has always been a matter of speculation. Frédéric Masson, if not one of the greatest authorities on the Bonaparte family certainly one of the most prolific, puts forward the assumption 'that the under-privileged Trasteverini were Republican in sympathy and friends of the French Revolution, and that the new ambassador established himself here with the intention of playing the demagogue. Joseph, however, was the last person in the world to wish to stir up a revolt, and little credence can be given to Masson's contention.

The new ambassador was in no hurry to present his credentials to the Pope. It was not until 4 November 1797 that Joseph wrote to Talleyrand (who had now replaced Delacroix as Minister of Foreign Affairs):

> On 6 Brumaire [27 October] I presented my credentials to the Pope, with whom I had an interview lasting more than an hour . . . The Pontiff has entirely regained his health. Every day he takes a drive of eight or nine miles in his carriage. He has all the freshness and gaiety of youth.

As far as Joseph's diplomatic mission was concerned, it was more or less one of courtesy, all the disagreeable roles devolving on the 'infamous and terrible' Haller, the treasurer of the Army of Italy, who was entrusted with the collection of the tributes levied on the Papal States, and on the erudite mathematician Gaspard Monge, whose task it was to select five hundred of the most rare and precious manuscripts from the Vatican library, and finally on Napoleon himself, who was given almost plenipotentiary powers. On 1 October Talleyrand wrote to Joseph: 'In all circumstances you will take directions from your brother, the Commander-in-Chief, to whom the Directoire, by the decree of 7 Prairial [26 May 1797], has given full authority to take whatever action the situation and events call for in the interests of the Republic'.

During Joseph's first months in Rome all went more or less smoothly. Even before he had presented his credentials, the Pope sent him a present of six horses from his own stables as a welcoming gift. Prince Chigi sent him four more, and the Secretary of State Cardinal Doria made up the round dozen by the present of an additional two. On 17 October, on the same day as he presented his letters of credence,[4] he gave a magnificent reception for the Sacred College, the Diplomatic Corps and the Roman nobility, where Constanza Braschi, a niece of the Pope, presented the ladies to Julie. Joseph's charm, his perfect command of Italian, his ability to quote Dante and Petrarch, produced the most favourable impression. Even shy little Julie overcame her natural timidity. When in Genoa, she had learnt to speak Italian fluently 'and as a good Provençal felt quite at home among the pines and cypress trees of the Eternal City.'[5] Cardinal Doria, in particular, took a liking to Joseph, who on his own initiative effected with him a territorial exchange favourable to the Duke of Parma, whose interests as Infante of Spain (with which country France was now allied) Joseph was anxious to promote. The Cardinal, impressed by Joseph's statesmanship, said of him publicly, 'Not all the Mazarins are dead'.

Almost every day the Ambassador received tokens of his popularity. He was overwhelmed with gifts; magnificent receptions were given in his honour; men of letters dedicated their works to Julie and Caroline. These tokens of esteem for the ambassador of an avowedly anti-clerical state, which was robbing the papal dominions of their treasures, were dictated not only by a desire by curry favour with the representative of a conquering nation (though even Joseph's greatest admirers must admit that there was a degree of sycophancy) but by the belief that in Joseph there was to be found a kind, gentle and cultivated man, who earnestly believed in peace on earth and good-will towards man, who would act as a buffer between Rome and his rapacious brother.

On 23 December Madame François Clary, with her daughter Désirée and her son Nicolas, arrived from Genoa on a visit. But there also arrived other and less welcome guests, sent to Joseph by Napoleon. The first to arrive was Eugène de Beauharnais; next came Adjutant-General Sherlock, who had been on Napoleon's staff at the time of Vendémiaire; and then in mid-November came Duphot, a twenty-seven-year-old general of brigade, who brought with him verbal instructions and a letter from Napoleon. What the verbal instructions were, we can only guess, but the contents of the letter are known :

> General of Brigade Duphot will hand you this letter. I recommend him to you. He will speak to you of the marriage he wishes to contract with your sister-in-law. I believe that this alliance will be to our advantage.

Napoleon was anxious to see Désirée married. He had always had a slightly guilty conscience where his ex-fiancée was concerned. She had loved him, and had still believed in him even when Saliceti first confirmed the news to a horrified Joseph that his brother was paying court to Josephine. As late as January 1796 Napoleon had not revealed his real reasons for breaking off his (unofficial) engagement, but had excused himself to Désirée by saying that if she could not obtain the consent of her mother and brother to their marriage, it would perhaps be better to break off all liaison (*rompre toute liaison*).

Duphot was both brave and intelligent and had made a certain name for himself in literary circles with his '*Ode to the shades of heroes killed in the name of Liberty*'. He had made the acquaintance of Désirée at the residence of the French Minister to Genoa, but she always vehemently denied that they were ever engaged.

With the arrival of this young general, the calm life of the Palazzo Orsini was shattered. Napoleon and Talleyrand had had no immediate wish to quarrel with the Pope, but none the less Napoleon was determined to show who was master. His letters to Joseph quoted below are a fair example of his attitude:

> 2 September 1797
>
> You will find, Citizen Ambassador, with this letter a despatch of the Roman Minister at Milan intercepted by us. I request you make known to His Holiness that I am dissatisfied with this Minister and that I wish the Court of Rome to remove him.

In another letter of the same date, Napoleon writes:

> Citizen Ambassador, I request you to make the Court of Rome explain itself and recognize the Cisalpine Republic as the King of Sardinia and the Republics of Genoa and Venice have done.

> 29 September 1797
>
> I have received, Citizen Ambassador, your letter of 3 Vendémiaire [24 September]. You will make known immediately to the Court of Rome that if General Provera[6] is not immediately sent away from Rome, the French Republic will consider his presence there as an act of hostility on the part of His Holiness. Explain how indecent it is, when the fate of Rome depended on us, when she owes her very existence to our generosity, to see the Pope renewing his intrigues. You may say in your conversations with the Secretary of State, and even in your note, if necessary, that *the French Republic was generous at Talento [sic]. She will not be so again under similar circumstances. . . .* Should the Pope die *you will do all that you possibly can to prevent him having a successor and to bring about a Revolution*. The King

of Naples will keep quiet. Should he move after the Revolution has been made and the people have seized power, you will tell him that the people of Rome are under the protection of the French Republic. If on the Pope's death there is no insurrection in Rome, and there are no means of preventing the election of a new Pope, do not suffer Cardinal Albani to be named. You will not only use your right [!] of pronouncing an exclusion, but you will alarm the Cardinals by threatening that *in that event, I shall instantly march on Rome.*

Apparently Napoleon's threats concerning Provera were disregarded. The Austrian general was still in Rome in command of the papal troops in December, for in an undated letter written in that month from Milan (presumably before the 5th, since on that date Napoleon was already in Paris) he wrote :

You may declare positively to the Court of Rome that if the Pope receives in his service any officer known to have been in the service of the Emperor, all good understanding ceases between France and Rome. We shall take it as a declaration of war.

Although it would appear from these letters that Duphot was not sent to Rome to stir up the populace except in the event of the Pope's death (which did not occur until 1799), as subsequent events show, the contrary might well have been the case. The Pope was certainly apprehensive. Joseph had demanded the release of all political prisoners, but not all had been given their freedom; those whom the Roman Court regarded as the most dangerous were still in confinement. In the same letter quoted above, Napoleon wrote :

You will make known to the Secretary of State that, if His Holiness should attempt to execute any of the prisoners whose freedom you have demanded, the French Republic will retaliate by arresting all the relatives of Cardinal Rusca and of the other Cardinals who mislead the Court of Rome. *Let the style of your notes be concise and firm. If necessary, leave Rome and go to Florence or to Ancona.*
You will not fail to let His Holiness and the Secretary of State understand that as soon as you cross the Roman frontier, you will declare the annexation of Ancona to the Cisalpine Republic. This, of course, is to be spoken, not to be written.

On 27 December, at a Republican banquet at which Duphot took the chair, the young general promised that all political prisoners released from the papal prisons would have the support of France. Taking this promise literally, former prisoners and a crowd of sympathizers hurried to the French Embassy and were only dispersed with difficulty. On the following day, a crowd of Revolutionaries, led by a sculptor named Ceracchi,[7] assembled in front of the Palazzo Orsini, brandishing tricolor cockades and shouting 'Long live the Roman people! Long live the Republic!'

Papal troops were sent to disperse the crowd, which took refuge within the railings guarding the palace. The soldiers unfortunately pursued the mob into what was extra-territorial property under the jurisdiction of France. Joseph immediately donned his diplomatic uniform and, accompanied by his staff, placed himself between the frightened crowd and the soldiers, whom he ordered to withdraw immediately. To add more weight to his words, he drew his sword, an example which was followed by Duphot and his other officers. As the papal troops began to withdraw, the crowd surged forward, with Joseph willy-nilly at their head. Once outside the gates of the palace, the Ambassador and his officers would have done well to beat a retreat, but the impetuous Duphot, brandishing his sword, continued to advance. In Joseph's account of the affair, written three days later to Talleyrand, he wrote:

> The over-courageous Duphot, accustomed to conquer, dashed forward and within minutes was surrounded by the bayonets of the soldiers. General Sherlock and I, instinctively, out of feelings of patriotism, followed him. Duphot's misguided courage brought him to the Porta Smettimania. I saw a soldier discharge his musket and shoot him in the chest. A second shot stretched him lifeless in the road. A further fifty shots were fired into his inanimate body. All the firing was then directed at us. Sherlock pointed out a side road which led us back to the gardens of the palace . . .
>
> My wife and her sister, who was to have become the wife of the brave Duphot on the following day, had just been forcibly carried into the palace by my secretaries and two young artists. . . . The steps of the Embassy were covered in blood and strewn with dead and groaning wounded. We managed to close the three doors of the façade opening on to the street. The lamentations of Duphot's beloved, the absence of her mother and brother, who had previously left the palace on a sightseeing tour of the monuments of Rome, and the fusillade which still continued in the streets, made this one of the most heart-rending scenes imaginable . . .

Further in his report to Talleyrand, Joseph accuses 'spies well known to the Government' of 'inciting the crowd by shouting "*Vive le peuple romain! Vive la République!*" louder than others'. He then

The Bonapartes' house
at Ajaccio

Désirée Clary

A portrait of Julie Bonaparte when she was Queen of Spain, with her
eldest daughter Zenaïde

goes on to accuse 'the cowardly and undisciplined Roman soldiery' of deliberately assassinating Duphot. But there is no evidence that the crowd was incited by 'spies well known to the Government'. This is a very enigmatic sentence. What spies and on whose behalf were they working? One is left wondering to what government Joseph is referring. Surely the papal authorities would not have provoked such a disturbance except perhaps as a pretext to rearrest dangerous liberated prisoners. This however seems highly improbable. The papal authorities would never have gone out of their way to antagonize the French; nor would they have deliberately assassinated a French general. Duphot's death was caused by his own foolhardy behaviour. Unless it was Joseph's deliberate intention to find an excuse to quarrel with the papal court, he and his officers would have been better advised not to interfere and to have remained within the Embassy confines rather than expose themselves to bullets not intended for them.

Thirty-two years later, Joseph, on rereading his report, asserted that there was not a single word which he would wish to change, but either he was deluding himself or hiding the truth. Also many years later, Baron Hochschild, chamberlain to Désirée when she was Queen of Sweden, was to read the report to his Queen. At one point in his narration she interrupted him: 'Oh! But that's not true. I would never have married Duphot who didn't please me in the least. Joseph just wanted to turn a happy phrase.'[8]

Was this Joseph's only departure from the truth? What were Napoleon's verbal instructions which Duphot had transmitted to him in September? Napoleon was constantly threatening the Pope either with the invasion of Rome or with the annexation of Ancona. The Directoire had never really approved the Peace of Tolentino. After the subjugation of Lombardy and the creation of the Cisalpine Republic, Rewbell, La Révellière and Barras had expected Napoleon to overthrow the Papacy immediately. Although the peace treaty had brought enormous financial and territorial advantages to France, the 'torch of fanaticism' demanded by the anti-clerical Jacobins had not been extinguished. So relieved was the Pope not to be ousted from the Vatican and still be allowed to preserve the essentials, that he wrote to Napoleon assuring him of 'his greatest esteem' and gave him his 'paternal and apostolic blessing', to which Napoleon replied: 'All Europe knows the pacific and conciliatory virtues of Your Holiness. The French Republic will, I hope, be one of Rome's truest friends. . . .'

When news of this friendly exchange of correspondence became known in Paris there was widespread indignation among sincere Republicans and the *parti philosophe*. Only Talleyrand openly expressed his approval of the manner in which the young general had handled the situation. By signing the Peace of Tolentino Napoleon had not only gained financial and territorial advantages for France, but had also gained valuable time in which to recoup his tattered and war-weary armies. It is obvious that the Peace of Tolentino was an act of sheer hypocrisy. Once his armies were re-equipped and rested, Napoleon sought every excuse, even the flimsiest (as we can see from his letters to Joseph), to make war. Weeks before the Duphot affair thirty thousand troops were massed outside Ancona, and only a few days before the incident, Napoleon had written to his brother: 'If necessary leave Rome . . . You will not fail to let both His Holiness and the Secretary of State understand that as soon as you cross the Roman frontier, you will declare the annexation of Ancona to the Cisalpine Republic . . .' How is it possible in the circumstances to believe that the 'invasion' of the Embassy was not premeditated? Duphot's death was of course unfortunate, but served conveniently as an added excuse for a declaration of war.

As soon as Joseph and his staff had regained the safety of the Embassy, he despatched a message to the papal Secretary of State Cardinal Doria to inform him of what had happened, but the only persons to come to his aid were Angelini and Azara, the Ministers of Tuscany and Spain, who alone were quite incapable of dispersing the demonstrators gathered for refuge in the gardens and courtyard of the Embassy and who had no authority to order the withdrawal of the Vatican troops surrounding the palazzo. 'In view of the unwillingness of the Papal Court to fulfil its obligations', Joseph decided at two o'clock in the morning to demand his passports. A little later, Cardinal Doria remitted these to him 'with great mortification', at the same time informing Joseph that because of the Pope's 'delicate state of health', he had been unable to inform His Holiness of what had taken place, but promised to afford the French Republic every satisfaction it should require.

Before dawn on 28 December Joseph, with his family and the entire personnel of the Embassy, left for Florence.

The version of the events of these momentous days provided by Joseph is generally accepted as true, particularly in view of his report to Talleyrand. Why should he lie to Talleyrand? On the other hand, surely it would have been impossible to evacuate not only his family, but all the embassy personnel, complete with baggage and presumably diplomatic files and papers, all within the space of a few hours. All circumstantial evidence points to the fact that the Ambassador had either been previously ordered to find an excuse to leave Rome or that he himself had decided to do so. One further detail casts doubt on the truth of his report, a detail which he omits from his memoirs. Shortly before leaving Rome he had chartered a Genoese vessel at Cività Vecchia to carry his personal effects to France. The ship was intercepted by Barbary pirates and subsequently wrecked, minus its cargo, off the coast of Corsica. As soon as Joseph learnt of its loss, he requested Talleyrand to order all French consuls in North Africa to institute immediate proceedings for the restitution of his stolen property. This seems natural enough, but what seems strange is that when M. Guillet, the French consul in Tangier, asked for a manifest of the cargo, Joseph hurriedly called off all enquiries. This gave rise to rumours (though none was ever substantiated) that the cargo consisted at least in part of works of art, gold and jewels dishonestly acquired as 'tribute' from the Papal States by Haller, which, with Joseph's connivance, he was discreetly shipping home to France under diplomatic cover, for which service, it was claimed, Joseph was to have received a share of the spoils. No evidence has ever been produced to confirm that Joseph was an accessory to theft but, if the story is true, he was soon consoled for his loss, for Napoleon, before leaving for Egypt in the following May, entrusted to his care millions of lire which he had brought back from Italy, which, originally intended for the Directoire, he had finally kept for himself.[9] Part of this money was to provide for Josephine's personal expenses, but Joseph, whose invidious task it was to act as her trustee during his brother's absence and generally act as watch-dog, was powerless to control her extravagance or her love affairs. In fact, he saw as little of her as possible but kept himself well informed of all her movements. Josephine bitterly complained to Barras that Joseph persistently kept her short of cash and had appropriated thirty million francs of her allowance for himself.[10]

In the meantime the murder of Duphot had provided the Directoire with the long-awaited excuse to invade Rome. On 5 December Berthier, who had replaced Napoleon as Commander-in-Chief of the Army of Italy, was ordered to march on the Eternal City. On 15 February 1798 Rome was declared a Republic.

V

Joseph, Député, Philosophe, and Man of the World

1798–1800

On his return to Paris on 25 January 1798, Joseph was again able to bask in the reflected glory of his brother, who, since the signing of the Peace of Campo Formio, was the hero of all France. Never had any French general been overwhelmed with such honours. The peace with Austria had ceded Belgium to France and had ratified her frontiers on the left bank of the Rhine; Italy was at her feet. After five years of war, the Republic now seemed firmly entrenched on the continent of Europe.

Joseph's first concern was to rent a modest house in the rue de Saints-Pères. Although no longer in receipt of his diplomatic salary, he was nevertheless a rich man.[1] He claimed and was awarded arrears of pay in addition to 50,000 francs for travelling expenses. He was offered (or so he maintained later) the post of Ambassador to Berlin in place of Sieyès, but refused the appointment. Instead, remembering that he was the elected deputy of the Corsican department of Liamone, he took his seat in the Council of Five Hundred. He also played a small part in the preparations for his brother's Egyptian campaign, but as he was always more interested in diplomacy and politics than in military campaigns, this was a venture in which he never showed any real interest.

Since his house in the rue des Saints-Pères was quite inadequate for a man of his social position, he now cast around for a suitable residence in which to entertain his many friends and notabilities of all shades of political opinion. His choice fell on a magnificent mansion in the rue des Errancis (on the site of what is now 61 rue du Rocher) in the quartier d'Europe. This mansion, built by Jacques-Ange Gabriel, architect of many famous buildings including the Hôtel Crillon (Place de la Concorde) and the Petit Trianon at Versailles, was surrounded by extensive grounds, beyond which stretched market gardens, and overlooked by what is today the Parc Monceau and the plain of Villiers. It seemed more like a country château than a Parisian town house and far removed from the fashionable aristocratic Faubourg Saint-Germain or the newly-acquired houses of the *nouveaux riches* on the right bank. Exclusive of furnishing, Joseph paid 60,000 francs for his new residence.

This new house was soon the scene of some of the most brilliant receptions held in Paris, already famous for its salons, to which liberals, former émigrés, the *directeurs* and their opponents, and not least, Madame de Staël, were happy to be invited.

Joseph's intimate friendship with Bernadotte dates from this period. It is not known when the two men first met – probably at the house of their mutual friend Madame de Staël, with whom both Joseph and Bernadotte were always to remain on the most friendly terms, but whom Napoleon detested. Fifteen months previously, when Bernadotte first arrived in Italy with 20,000 reinforcements from the Rhine Army of Sambre-et-Meuse, he had been filled with admiration for Napoleon, but the continual pinpricks he received at the hands of his youthful commander-in-chief and the open hostility shown to him and his officers by Napoleon's chief of staff Berthier (who so exasperated him that on three occasions he challenged him to a duel) rapidly modified his first enthusiasm for the great Bonaparte.[2]

The truth of the matter was that although Napoleon had welcomed the reinforcements as far as campaigning was concerned, he found them in every other way a perfect nuisance, for the arrival of this splendid division, strong, disciplined and well-equipped, was the cause of endless friction between the ragged rascals of the citizens' army and the smart men of what Napoleon disparagingly called the 'gentlemen's army'. Moreover, almost from the start, Bernadotte, a Jacobin at heart, had doubts concerning Napoleon's fidelity to the ideals of the Republic.[3] He did not believe that the little Corsican had come to Italy to liberate a down-trodden people from the imperial yoke of Austria, but to seek self-aggrandizement and, above all, loot. The Army of the Rhine, on the other hand, under Joubert and Moreau had always remained true to the highest ideals of the Revolution; looting was forbidden and *Liberté, Égalité et Fraternité* was not just an empty slogan but was extended to the peoples of the conquered provinces. It is not surprising that there was no love lost between the two men. Bernadotte was therefore all the more surprised and pleased to find in the elder Bonaparte a kindred spirit who offered him the hand of friendship and made him a welcome and honoured guest in his house. The two men had indeed much in common. Bernadotte had been obliged to leave his post as Ambassador to Vienna in circumstances very similar to those which had forced Joseph to quit Rome; both were southerners (Bernadotte was from Béarn); both were the sons of impoverished lawyers (though Bernadotte could claim no pretensions to nobility); both had acquired their not inconsiderable knowledge of the humanities, not so much from school (Bernadotte had only attended a village school) but by personal inclination. Moreover, Bernadotte knew Corsica, where he had served as a private soldier in the *Régiment Royal de Marine* from 1780 to 1782, and was also familiar with Marseilles, where he had served as a sergeant from June 1789 to May 1790.[4]

Bernadotte was an exceptionally handsome man (as a sergeant he had earned the nickname of *Belle Jambe*); he was courteous, affable and good company, and like Joseph was very adaptable and moved with ease in any society; in short, very different from the *sans-culotte* generals like Carteaux or Rossignol, or the other former sergeants such as the vulgar Augereau, Davout, or the roly-poly stupid Victor.

Within a fortnight of meeting Désirée, Bernadotte had asked Joseph for her hand in marriage. It was eagerly accorded. Joseph had no doubt that Madame Clary and Nicolas, who should have been the first to be consulted, would agree. He was right. No sooner had he written to Madame Clary than she answered by return of courier giving her blessing to the union. Since neither she nor Nicolas had ever met Bernadotte and only had Joseph's word that he was a suitable match, it is clear that Joseph had greatly risen in the esteem of the Clary family since the days when he had lived with them in Genoa. Now, as the brother of the conqueror of Italy and hero of France, and himself an ex-ambassador who had treated with the Pope, whatever Joseph said must be right. Madame Clary was a snob. Joseph was no longer *ce coquin-là*, as Nicolas had so recently called him; he was now rich and influential.

The marriage took place on 17 August 1798 at Sceaux, where Bernadotte had rented a modest house. Those present were Joseph and Julie, Lucien and his wife Christine, and Victor Somis, Désirée's maternal uncle.

In an (undated) letter from Cairo, Napoleon wrote to Joseph: 'I wish Désirée all happiness if she marries Bernadotte. She deserves it.' There is no evidence, other than Las Cases's word, to support Frédéric Masson's assertion that he wrote a furious letter to Joseph accusing him of the most infamous conduct in 'procuring' Désirée for Bernadotte. On the contrary, in a long letter dated 25 July, he expresses the warmest regard for his brother. 'I have many domestic worries; *the veil has been completely torn from my eyes.*[5] *You alone of all people in this world remain to me.*' In the *Mémorial de Sainte-Hélène*, Las Cases quotes this letter but suppresses the italicized words.

It seems strange that Joseph, who had so discouraged Napoleon's engagement to Désirée, should have acquiesced so willingly in her marriage to Bernadotte. Various explanations have been put forward to explain his motives. Although Joseph was devoted to Napoleon in many ways, it has been suggested that he much preferred that, as his wife's sister, Désirée should marry a man who shared his own liberal and humanist views, rather than an *arriviste* like Napoleon, who almost from the outset had given ample proof that his soaring ambition was leading him further and further from the ideals he had entertained as a youth in 1789, and that his main preoccupation was personal power. Another, and cynical, reason propounded by Frédéric Masson, is that Bernadotte, a brilliant soldier and leader of men, who had shown himself 'quite capable of standing up to Napoleon', himself aspired to become military dictator, and that Joseph entertained ambitions of becoming his political adviser. What better means to achieve this goal than by allying himself to Bernadotte by family ties?[6] Another reason put forward is that by accepting Bernadotte into the Corsican clan, he was neutralizing a possible rival to his brother. This theory is much more plausible. In those troubled times, popularity and success were ephemeral. Although on his return to Paris from Italy Napoleon had been hailed as the hero of all France, it was not long since that the fortunes of the victor of Arcola and Rivoli had been seriously imperilled. Following the Royalist successes in the elections of May 1797, there had appeared a proliferation of newspapers, 'moderate' and even Royalist, hostile both to the Republic and to Napoleon, whose measures in Italy they violently attacked. Pichegru, the newly-elected president of the Council of Five Hundred, who had been suspected of engaging in treasonable intrigues with the Bourbons at the time of Dumouriez's defection, made no secret of his dislike for the young commander-in-chief. When Napoleon occupied the Venetian Republic, the newly-formed Royalist Clichy Club demanded his immediate dismissal and arrest. He was accused not only of violating the neutrality of a sovereign state, but of robbing it of millions for his own benefit. Even the Republican Directors, Barras, Rewbell and La Révellière, though grateful for the vast fortunes in specie and works of art which Napoleon sent home from Italy, viewed with mounting apprehension his high-handed and lofty disregard for their directives, and did not hesitate to remind him of his duties; there was even talk of replacing him by Kellermann. Under these attacks, Napoleon redoubled his efforts to prove his Republican zeal and loyalty to the Constitution. He warned Barras of the danger of a counter-revolution. 'Arrest all émigrés,' he wrote; 'if you have need of force, summon the armies.' But it was only when the treasonable activities of Pichegru were confirmed by documents which had fallen into Napoleon's hands and which he had hastened to send to Barras by the hand of Augereau that Barras was able to convince Rewbell and La Révellière of the danger threatening the Republic. Immediate action was necessary. The two other Directors, Barthélémy and Carnot, were both under suspicion; Carnot, in fact, had made no attempt to conceal his Royalist sympathies. But only by unconstitutional methods, in other words, a military coup d'état, could Carnot and Barthélémy be disposed of and the freely elected anti-Republican deputies be hounded out of the Assemblies.

On 17 Fructidor (2 September) rumours were deliberately circulated of a hypothetical plot to restore the Bourbons to the throne. On the following day the Tuileries, the seat of the two Assemblies, was surrounded by troops of the Paris garrison under the command of Augereau. Barthélémy and Pichegru – once hailed as 'the Saviour of the Country' – and a dozen deputies were arrested, Carnot, the veteran 'Organizer of Victories', managed to escape and fled to Switzerland. On the orders of the new Triumvirate – Barras, Rewbell and La Révellière – the Republican minority of the two Assemblies annulled elections in forty-nine departments, suspended the freedom of the press and 'eliminated' seventy suspected deputies, sixty-five of whom were deported to the penal colony of Guiana, a sentence tantamount to death. Pichegru, who was among the condemned, managed to escape and find asylum in England. In the following days pitiless measures, reminiscent of the Terror, were taken against returned émigrés and non-juring priests, over a thousand of whom, under sentence of deportation, remained forgotten in the stinking prison hulks of Oléron and Ré.

Despite Napoleon's efforts to convince Barras of his undying loyalty and that although he was the conqueror of Italy he was still at heart the General of Vendémiaire, it was not he but Hoche whom the Triumvirate first approached to carry out their military coup. Hoche, however, had refused to act unconstitutionally, and so, almost by accident, it fell to Napoleon's lieutenant Augereau 'to restore the Republic'. But it was no wonder that Napoleon had been uneasy; there would have been little chance of his survival or of that of his family had the partisans of Louis XVIII been triumphant.

If it should fall to Napoleon to save the Republic, either on the order of the Directoire or on his own initiative, Bernadotte, as a member of the 'Corsican clan', would not stand in his way. Indeed, as we shall see, when on 18 Brumaire 1799 Napoleon overthrew the Directoire to become First Consul, Bernadotte, who might well have led the opposition, remained strictly neutral.

Many other suggestions have been made to explain Joseph's acquiescence in Bernadotte's marriage, many of which are palpably absurd, such as Barras's contention that Joseph, envisaging that one day Bernadotte might wish to usurp the dictatorial powers that Napoleon was already planning for himself, planted Désirée as a spy (*'l'inclination de Mme Bernadotte pour les Corses était une véritable dépendance, qui l'entraînait à un abandon dangereux de tous les détails personnels des intimités de son mari'*).[7] But at the time of his marriage Bernadotte had no more reason to suspect, any more than Joseph, that Napoleon in faraway Egypt was planning to assume absolute power. On the contrary, far from meditating any ambitious plans, Napoleon, thoroughly disillusioned with life, had written to Joseph on 25 July :

> . . . I may be back in France in two months . . . Let me have on my arrival a villa near Paris or in Burgundy; I intend to shut myself up for the winter. I am tired of human nature. I want solitude and isolation. Greatness fatigues me; feeling is dried up. At 29, glory has become flat . . . Adieu my only friend, I have never been unjust to you, as you must admit . . . You understand me . . .

Admittedly, this letter was written in a moment of despondency after Napoleon had learnt of Josephine's continued infidelities, and no doubt Joseph accepted the sentiments expressed therein with a pinch of salt. On the other hand, what powers could Napoleon assume? Because of his age, he was not eligible to become a Director and under the present Constitution there seemed to be no great political opportunities open to him. It was only after his return to France, when he sized up the political situation, that his ambition once more took wing.

On 28 October 1798 Joseph acquired his second residence, the château and vast ground of Mortefontaine on the edge of the forest of Ermenonville, forty-seven kilometres north-east of Paris. The château, built in the style of Louis XIII, consisted of a central building, two storeys high, flanked at either end by taller, three-storeyed wings; the whole was surmounted by high steep-pitched mansard roofs. The enormous estate of 589 hectares comprised agricultural and

73

grazing land, woods, rough shooting, a little hamlet of eight houses (Charlepont), two windmills and a splendid park. The château and estate were valued at 258,000 francs, exclusive of a yearly leasehold of 5,000 francs. When Joseph acquired this magnificent property it had been untenanted ever since the Revolution; the gardens were choked with weeds, the paths and alleys were overgrown with grass, the fishponds were unstocked and stagnant.

For fifteen years Mortefontaine was to be one of Joseph's favourite distractions and the haven of peace for which he hankered during his troubled life as King of Spain. He spent vast sums of money on improvements and on enlarging the property, to the great benefit of the local people, for whom these were lean years. Throughout his life he had a passion for landscape gardening. He constructed grottoes and 'Roman' ruins, and diverted a river through the grounds. An artificial island and a grassy mound, surmounted by clumps of trees, were added to give a 'romantic' touch to the scene. He planted vineyards and embellished the grounds with already fully grown beech trees. He also built a theatre, a chapel and orangeries. He was to add continually to his estate and in 1803 bought the neighbouring property of Survilliers, the name which he was to adopt when an exile in the United States.

When not superintending his estate, Joseph continued to play an active but discreet role behind the scenes of the political stage. Five months after his acquisition of Mortefontaine, he resigned his seat on the Council of Five Hundred, to which Lucien, with whom he was now on the most intimate terms, succeeded him as Corsican deputy for Liamone in April 1799.[8] Lucien, the former ultra-Jacobin, the fiery demagogue of the revolutionary clubs of Toulon and Saint-Maximim, had, in the last few years, considerably modified his views, and now used his very considerable talents as an orator in support of the moderate party of the Assembly. If by disposing of Carnot and Pichegru and the pro-Royalist and right-wing elements in the Assembly, the coup d'état of Fructidor had saved the Republic from a Royalist counter-revolution, it had entirely failed to establish a stable government in place of the old. Politically and morally, France was not only rotten but bankrupt. A police report, quoted by M. André Castelot,[9] states : 'Moral perversion is extreme in Paris. The practice of sodomy and lesbianism is as brazen-faced as prostitution, and continues to grow.' Corruption was universal and cynically flaunted. The profiteers of the Revolution, scandalously enriched, insulted the poverty of the masses with their ostentatious display of wealth. The situation in the provinces was not much better. According to Mon-

74

signor Le Coz, a constitutional bishop, 'Fornication, adultery, incest, poison and murder are prevalent even in country districts. Such are the terrible fruits of *philosophisme*.'[10] The unfortunate *encyclopédistes* and *philosophes* seem to have been the scapegoats for every ill.

These were the days of the extravagantly dressed *'Incroyables'* and *'Merveilleuses'*, when women wore transparent dresses *à la Grecque*, when every other house in the Palais Royal was a brothel where every vice was catered for.

The general malaise extended to the Government. The Directoire was thoroughly discredited. Its policy of annexation and extortion had resulted in the formation of a second Coalition in March 1799. Russia had joined forces with the Austrians. In the next few months, disaster was to follow disaster. Jourdan, advancing towards Vienna, was driven back over the Rhine by the Archduke Charles; Schérer was defeated at Magnano and was replaced by Moreau, who was recalled from disgrace. Masséna, who had begun to advance on Vienna from Switzerland (which had been annexed and was now known as the Helvetian Republic), was pinned down in Zurich by the Russian General Korsakoff. Souvoroff out-manoeuvred Moreau on the Trebbia and annihilated Macdonald's smaller force from the south, which was attempting to effect a junction with Moreau, who was obliged to fall back on Genoa. Souvoroff, to his disgust, was ordered to remain in Italy, instead of pressing on into France, while the Austrians re-established themselves in Lombardy. Joubert re-appeared on the scene with a fresh army, but was defeated and himself killed at Novi by a combined Russian and Austrian army. Despite what Napoleon had written to Joseph in 1797, the King of Naples had not remained quiet. The newly-formed Parthenopean Republic of the Two Sicilies was easily overthrown and the Bourbons were restored to the throne to wreak a terrible vengeance on their revolutionary subjects (in which Nelson was to play his own discreditable part). With the exception of Genoa, the whole of Italy was lost to France, while in Flanders a combined Russian and English force was threatening her northern frontiers.[11]

These repeated defeats, which completely nullified Napoleon's brilliant conquests, can be explained by the fact that, for one reason or another, France had been deprived of her best generals. The traitor Pichegru was in exile; Hoche, after an abortive invasion of Ireland, had mysteriously died of poison; at the beginning of 1799, Moreau was in temporary disgrace; Bernadotte had resigned from the *Armée d'Observation*; Championnet, the hero of Fleurus who had helped to found the Parthenopean Republic, had been dismissed for attempting to put a brake on the rapacity of the Directoire's agents. The brave and honest Joubert, who had been dismissed for trying to establish a wise, libertarian government in Italy 'which would have cemented the links between two nations with a common destiny',[12] was only reinstated when the situation seemed really desperate. Napoleon was far away, lost in the sands of Africa.

Hitherto France had either conquered or had at least held her ground. Now she was threatened on all sides. Defeated and bankrupt, France longed for a change of government. Every Frenchman knew a change must come, but how and when, no one knew.

The coup d'état of Fructidor had not solved France's problems. The Directors, consisting of the 'Triumvirate' of la Révellière, Rewbell, Barras and the newly-elected Merlin de Douai and Treilhard, who had replaced Pichegru and Carnot, were in constant disagreement among themselves. The restrictive measures, reminiscent of 1793, which the 'Triumvirate' had reintroduced—the proscription of priests, the hunting down and execution of hundreds of returned émigrés, whether guilty or not, the strict censorship of the press, and even of theatres and private correspondence – had alienated public opinion. In the elections of 1798, a number of Jacobins had succeeded in becoming elected to the Conseils, but the Directoire, seeing in them a danger no less great than that which the Royalists had presented in 1797, persuaded the docile Conseils to invalidate one hundred and six of them. By the decree of 12 Floréal, Year VI (11 May 1798) the executive deprived eight departments of popular representation and, to all intents and purposes, hand-picked their own candidates. Popular franchise had become a farce. Although the financial policies introduced since Fructidor had successfully lowered food prices, they had at the same time ruined peasant producers and rendered *rentiers* bankrupt. Commerce was stagnant. General discontent with the Government was further enhanced by the military defeats and brought to a head by the disastrous Russo-Austrian victory over Joubert at Novi.

Republican activity was now concentrated in the Army. Policies were no longer in the hands of the people. The desire for a change of government was almost universal.

Fouché claims that it was he who was responsible for persuading Barras to get rid of Rewbell, but that it was in fact Fouché who engineered Rewbell's elimination is doubtful. Merlin and Treilhard themselves forced him to retire, using him as the scapegoat for all the evils that had befallen France. The question remained, who was to replace him? Merlin and Treilhard 'and their pot-bellied acolytes' decided to substitute him by Duval, 'a mediocrity of a man' who at that time was Minister of Police,[13] but the moderates and intellectuals of the *parti philosophique* had long had their eyes on the ex-Abbé Sieyès, a member of the *Institut* and Ambassador to Berlin.[14] For ten years Sieyès had been working on the 'perfect constitution', but although full details of his great work had not yet been divulged, he had earned a reputation as a wise and astute politician. Mirabeau had had the greatest admiration for him and always addressed him as '*Mon maître*', and Madame de Staël had declared : 'The writings and opinions of the Abbé Sieyès will establish a new era in politics, just as the works of Newton have done in physics.'

Fouché says of him :

I was aware that he was developing some strong and truly Revolutionary ideas; but I also knew him to be obstinate and cunning; moreover, I believed him to have at the back of his mind, ideas which were incompatible with our fundamental liberties and institutions. Although I was not for him, I belonged to the côterie which suddenly favoured him, though what impelled me to do so, I don't know. It was alleged that it was important to have at the head of affairs the man who, above all others, was the best equipped to persuade Prussia, in her own interests, to remain neutral . . . We were assured that he was an astute politician, inasmuch as he had been the first to alert us of the formation of this new and scandalous [*sic*] Coalition. . . .

Then came the elections. I still laugh at the disappointment of the subtle Merlin and of his creature, the worthy Duval, when they first learnt that a number of their supporters had defected. Neither Merlin nor Duval could understand how an assured majority could all of a sudden become a minority. But we, who knew how such things were manipulated, laughed heartily over some excellent dinners, in the course of which we had carefully sifted the political ground. Merlin saw in Sieyès a dangerous rival, and from that moment withdrew into a sullen silence.[15]

To begin with, no one was more active than Lucien in support of Sieyès. In later years, Fouché was to write of him :

. . . I developed such a high esteem for him, that I believed that if only such a man could persuade his colleagues to follow in his footsteps, the future safety of the Republic and better legislation were assured. After several conversations with him, I was entirely on his side. Under the Constitution of Year III, the power of the Executive and Legislative Assemblies were ill-balanced. Between the two Assemblies there had been no balance, with the result that one coup d'état followed another. All that was required to win through and

77

establish a lasting Republic was a level-headed man at the helm, armed with powers to keep the excesses of both the Government and the Chamber of Representatives under control.[16]

Sieyès's first concern was to reconstitute the Directoire by the so-called *coup de Prairial* (18 June). He got rid of Treilhard on a point of order, with the intention of substituting him by Roger-Ducos, his own devoted follower. But in this his plan misfired. Gohier, a Jacobin, unsympathetic to Sieyès, was elected in Ducos's place and nominated president. Soon Merlin and La Révellière were forced to retire when threatened with exposure of their malversation and replaced by Sieyès's candidates, Roger-Ducos and General Moulin, a choice which both he and Lucien, who had been active in their support, were soon to regret. Lucien described them as 'men whose private lives were above reproach, but who in public showed a complete lack of intelligence, but worse still, after we had elected them, in the hopes of forming a better government, showed no inclination to support Sieyès.[17]

Barras, while supporting Sieyès, was careful not to compromise himself too far, and gave a friendly warning to Joseph and Lucien that Sieyès's position was far from secure and advised them not to commit themselves too deeply on his side. Indeed, there was no more agreement in the new Directoire than in the old. Pandemonium disrupted the meetings of the Councils. The former Jacobin club, reconstituted under the name of 'The Society of Friends of Liberty and Equality', was now installed in the famous *Manège*. Here, among scenes of wild disorder, the most extravagant measures were voted. Sieyès's moderate policies were violently attacked, but he remained steadfast to his friends. He even went so far as to proclaim publicly that the Terrorists were an even greater danger to the Republic than any Royalist movement. In the Council of Five Hundred he knew he had the support of Talleyrand, Roederer, Cambacérès and the *parti philosophique.*

Fouché, appointed to the Ministry of Police in place of Duval, was authorized to suppress the extremists of both Left and Right. The Society of Friends of Liberty and Equality was disbanded. Jourdan, Joseph's friend, one of its leading members, approached Bernadotte with a plan to arrest Barras and Sieyès and establish with him, Jourdan, a new government based on the lines of the old Constitutional Committee of Public Safety. Bernadotte would have nothing to do with this. Jourdan, in a speech delivered from the Tribune of the Council of Five Hundred on 27 Fructidor, advocated that parliamentary rule should be temporarily abolished and the Constitution forgotten. The wildest confusion followed this speech. Deputies fought among themselves on the floor of the Assembly. Paris was paralysed with fear – fear that a reign of terror, worse than that of 1793, would be restored. Guards were placed round the Luxembourg, the seat of the Directoire. The fear spread to the provinces. The Law of Hostages, which had been passed in August, had revived the fighting spirit of the Royalist partisans in the west. Whole villages were abandoned; it was better to risk one's life fighting in the ranks of the Chouans or Vendéens than face deportation. Conscription had the same effect; young recruits deserted in large numbers, often to join the countless bands of brigands roaming the highways and terrorizing all rural France.[18]

Without yet another coup d'état, Sieyès seemed incapable of achieving a stable government. 'What is needed', he said to Fouché, 'is not only a head, but a sword.'[19] His first choice of a 'sword' had fallen on the once discredited, honest Republican Joubert, but Joubert had been killed by a sniper's bullet on 15 August in the disastrous battle of Novi. Bernadotte seemed a possible alternative. Invalided home from the Army of the Rhine ten months previously, he had been appointed Minister of War. As Barras later admitted : 'Never had there been a more efficient or more diligent minister than he'. Bernadotte, with the army behind him, would have proved a useful ally, but he resolutely refused to involve himself in the overthrow of a political party by unconstitutional means. Fouché, in his *Mémoires*, tells us that Barras had first tried to persuade the General that a coup d'état to save the country was an essential, but temporary, expedient. When Bernadotte still refused to co-operate Barras, in a final attempt to gain his support, promised him the part of commander-in-chief, just as Jourdan had proposed. Bernadotte, however, was not to be bought; he was already working himself to the bone as Minister of War, keeping the armies in the field supplied and building up reserves. Exasperated by Barras's attitude Bernadotte, in an acrimonious dispute, threatened to resign his ministry. Barras, who chose to attribute Bernadotte's lack of co-operation to personal ambition, and seeing in him a possible political rival, hurried off to inform Sieyès and Roger-Ducos (though not Moulins and Gohier) that Bernadotte had voluntarily resigned. Bernadotte, who had never believed for a moment that his rash words would be taken at their face value, was furious when he received a letter from Sieyès accepting his resignation. In reply he wrote : 'Citizen President, I acknowledge your official communication of yesterday's date and your accompanying obliging letter and note that you accept my resignation which I never tendered . . .'

Of the other generals available, Augereau and Jourdan, the ultra-Jacobins, were naturally out of the question; Masséna, the only reliable commander to achieve success in the campaign against the second Coalition, was too busy holding off the Archduke Charles and Souvoroff in the passes of Switzerland.[20] The incompetent Brune, although lucky in Flanders, was hardly a man to be relied on, while the inept Lefebvre, the military governor of Paris, could be dismissed from Sieyès's mind immediately—'he had been a sergeant-major, and a sergeant-major he remained to the end of his days.' Napoleon was far away, but in any case, even if Sieyès was successful in establishing a new Constitution, with himself as head of government, he had no wish to share his power with a man as ambitious as the Little General of Vendémiaire. There only remained the honest, politically unambitious, staunch Republican Moreau. But at the back of almost everybody's mind was the name of Bonaparte, the conquering hero of Italy and negotiator of the Peace of Campo Formio. Details of his distant campaign in Egypt and Syria and the destruction of the French fleet in the battle of the Nile were not generally known to the French public. On the other hand, his defeat of the Mamelukes in the Battle of the Pyramids had raised him once more to the pinnacle of fame and popularity. His disastrous policy with the Sublime Porte, which had thrown his would-be allies, the Turks, into an alliance with their hereditary enemies the Russians; the loss of Corfu and the Ionian islands – these were events which were not reported in the French press, nor was there any mention of his failure to seize Acre or of the subsequent retreat of his plague-stricken army across the sands of Sinai. These unpalatable truths were either unknown or kept discreetly hidden. Napoleon's own despatches to the Directoire were extremely mendacious; he refers, for example, to the 'glorious events accomplished during the last three months in Syria', explaining that his reason for not allowing his troops to enter Acre was only because of the plague raging there. In the minds of the majority of French people Napoleon was still the invincible general, the man of destiny who would restore France to her former glory and bring peace and prosperity to a divided nation.

It was against this turbulent background that Joseph established his 'court' at Mortefontaine. Joseph was, of course, a profiteer who had 'scandalously enriched himself at the expense of the Republic', but it would have been strange if he had not done so, when every government official, and with few exceptions every general, was doing, or had done, the same. At least Joseph had not made his fortune as an army commissary supplying shoddy goods to the forces, nor had his personal ambition or desire for wealth ever conflicted with his fundamental Republican and liberal ideals. Nevertheless, he was astute enough not to compromise himself with any particular party and invited men and women of every political shade of opinion to his receptions at Mortefontaine. Although like Lucien he believed in Sieyès, he was at pains to keep on good terms with Gohier and Moulins, against whom his younger brother was employing his most bitter invective in the Council of Five Hundred. Roederer and Talleyrand, who were to prove useful future allies, were also frequent visitors to his home, but of all the numerous guests to Mortefontaine, his favourites were the intellectuals – Boulay de la Meurthe, who was so largely instrumental in drawing up the famous Code, to which Napoleon gave his name; Cabanis, the philosopher-doctor and pupil of Condillac, whose ideas on the care of the mentally and physically sick, especially among the poor, were a hundred years or more before their time; his old friend Miot, lately Ambassador to the Court of Tuscany; the former *Conventionnel* Andrieux, dramatist and lawyer, former vice-president of the Court of Appeal and member of the *Institut*; Bernadin de Saint-Pierre, the author of *Paul et Virginie*; Jean Debry, who had stood by Napoleon when the latter had been threatened with court martial; Moreau and his friend Volney, the philosopher, traveller and author, whom he had known in his youth in Corsica; Benjamin Constant; and, of course, the egregious Germaine de Staël – in short, almost every member of that brilliant and enlightened set who had gathered round old Madame Helvétius in Auteuil or who met weekly at the Club de Salm, or at the famous *Diners du tridi*, where some of the most brilliant intellects in Europe gathered together.

In his memoirs Joseph makes little mention of his activities during the period covering Napoleon's absence in Egypt and Syria. He seems to have shown remarkably little interest in his brother's military campaign. When, on 26 December 1798, Bernadotte wrote from Mainz, where he was then divisional commander of the Army of the Rhine, to tell him that 'I have no hesitation in declaring that the army in Egypt will succumb unless it receives help from Metropolitan France' and begging him to use his influence with Barras, Rewbell, Talleyrand and Admiral Bruix to send reinforcements and supplies to the Army of the Orient, Joseph did nothing. The only member of the Bonaparte family to have shown any concern for Napoleon's welfare while in Egypt was Louis. Joseph was fully aware, however, that popular opinion was demanding the return of his brother. In his memoirs, he writes :

The reverses suffered by our armies in Italy, the open dissensions between the Directoire and the two Councils; the legislative measures, such as the use of force and the law of hostages, and the declaration that the country was in danger, were creating a general feeling of discontent throughout the country. Everyone, at this time, was regretting the absence of General Bonaparte and wished with all their hearts for his recall. . . . It was in these circumstances that I sent to Egypt Bourbakis, a Greek, the father of two sons educated at the French Military Academy.[21]

What Joseph did not know was that, secretly, Barras, Rewbell and La Révellière had already written to Napoleon urging him to return, 'either with, or without his army'. In the event, Napoleon was never to receive Barras's message or Bourbakis's mission. It was only during an exchange of prisoners, after the battle of Abu Qir, that Napoleon learnt from English newspapers sent to him by Commodore Sir Sidney Smith that in France things were going badly. *'La Patrie est en danger!'* Jourdan had fulminated from the Tribune of the Five Hundred. What a splendid excuse for Napoleon to desert his army and return home!

On 18 August Napoleon left Cairo stealthily at night, on the pretence that he was going to Upper Egypt to the assistance of the brave Desaix. On the 22nd he reached Alexandria, where, accompanied by Generals Marmont, Lannes, Murat, Berthier and Andréossy, and the scholars Berthollet and Monge, he embarked in the frigate *Muriot* for France, leaving behind a letter for Kléber, ordering him to assume command of the *Armée de l'Orient*.

There is little evidence to suggest that Napoleon's return was immediately prompted either by Joseph or Barras; the Director's despatch and Bourbakis's mission only arrived in Cairo after his departure. His Egyptian adventure had proved a failure; let others take the blame. Always the opportunist, Napoleon, on learning the true state of affairs at home, had jumped at the chance of redeeming his mistakes by appearing in France just at the moment when a soldier-politician was most needed. He could not have planned his 'miraculous' return at a more opportune moment. Five days after his arrival at Fréjus (where, contrary to all quarantine regulations, he disembarked on 18 Vendémaire – always an auspicious date for Napoleon) the news of his splendid victory at Abu Qir (when Murat at the head of a cavalry brigade had charged and broken through the Turkish lines, personally wounding and capturing the Turkish commander-in-chief) had just been announced to a jubilant Paris.

The Turks had been driven into the sea to be drowned or killed. The French casualties amounted to no more than a thousand. The disasters of Acre and Jaffa and the destruction of the French fleet were ignored or remained unknown. The invincible Bonaparte had returned as the Messiah. There are writers who maintain that it was Joseph who had prepared public opinion for his brother's reappearance; there are others who maintain, on the contrary, that Joseph was disappointed at Napoleon's unexpected premature arrival; it has been alleged that he himself was preparing a coup d'état with the help of Sieyès and Moreau. Such a supposition is so foreign to Joseph's character that it can be dismissed without further comment. The first indication Joseph had of his brother's return came from Gohier, who sent his secretary to Mortefontaine in the middle of the night to inform him of Bonaparte's arrival at Fréjus.[22] On the following morning Joseph left Paris with Lucien, Louis and Leclerc to meet his brother and tell him all the latest political news and of Josephine's follies.

Sieyès was dining with Moreau in the Luxembourg when the news of Napoleon's return arrived, and it was Moreau who said: 'There's your man. He will carry out your coup d'état much better than I could ever do.'[23] Details of the famous coup d'état of 18 Brumaire are too well known to recount here. Lucien, who had been elected President of the Five Hundred shortly after his brother's arrival in France, was active in Napoleon's support, but Sieyès still had to be won over. Sieyès, who, as already mentioned, did not trust Napoleon, was now even more strongly opposed to him. This key figure of the Directoire, whom Napoleon had been so tactless as to offend by his deliberate rudeness at a dinner given in his honour, openly expressed the opinion that 'this conceited young general, who had abandoned his army without authorization, deserved to be shot'.[24] Napoleon riposted by spreading rumours that Sieyès was in the pay of Prussia and intrigued to have him removed from office; Barras was to assume the highest executive position, while he, Napoleon, would be appointed military commander-in-chief. When Barras refused to fall in with these plans, Napoleon had no alternative but to climb down and seek a reconciliation with Sieyès. Joseph persuaded his friend Cabanis to bring about this tricky rapprochement. In his memoirs, he writes:

. . . I saw Monsieur Cabanis, who was still a member of the Five Hundred and on intimate terms, as I knew, with Director Sieyès, with whom we were to dine the following day. Cabanis had prepared him for my visit and after our dinner Sieyès took me aside and said: 'I want to go along with General Bonaparte, since there is no one in the whole army who is more Republican at heart than he. All the same, I know what to expect. As soon as he has succeeded, he will leave his two colleagues behind him – *like this*!' With these words he suddenly thrust himself behind Cabanis and came between us, flinging out his arms, pushing us backwards against the chimney piece, so that he was left standing alone in the middle of the room – much to the astonishment of those guests unused to his outbursts of Provençal temperament. When I described this scene to Napoleon he laughed heartily, exclaiming, '*Vive les gens d'esprit!* This is an excellent omen.'[25]

Sieyès had found his 'sword', though not the 'sword' he wanted.

The coup d'état was accomplished almost without bloodshed or reprisals. After ten years of violent upheavals the nation could scarcely fail to respond to the promise of a general reconciliation. Napoleon seemed to many to be the *deus ex machina*. However, it must not be thought that Napoleon assumed dictatorial powers immediately. It was essential that everything should appear to be done legally. Everyone demanded a new Republican constitution. Sieyès, as all knew, had been elaborating his 'pyramidal' constitution for years. The essence of his plan was such that any move in the direction of autocracy would be doomed to failure. It was a constitution of the most extraordinary complexity. Most of Sieyès's suggested reforms were tacitly approved by Napoleon, but the first clash occurred when the question arose of who should assume the highest executive power. Sieyès's idea had been to elect a Grand Elector on the lines of the President of the United States of America – Sieyès himself, naturally – with a senate consisting of sixty-two members and a tripartite legislature, consisting of a Council of State (fifty members), a Tribunate (one hundred members) and a *Législatif* (fifty members).

The concept of a Grand Elector was laughed to scorn by Napoleon. Boulay de la Meurthe, the friend of Joseph, put forward a compromise whereby a Grand Elector would be replaced by a First Consul – Napoleon – assisted in a purely advisory capacity by two other Consuls – Sieyès and Roger-Ducos. In a travesty of a vote, Napoleon was elected First Consul with almost plenipotentiary powers. Sieyès was quietly bought off with a pension and an estate in the country to be replaced by the more accommodating Cambacérès; Ducos was replaced by Lebrun. The country as a whole remained unmoved by the fact that France was now ruled by a dictator in all but name. The people remained in almost complete ignorance of what a momentous event had just occurred.

Joseph's role in the coup d'état remained throughout extremely discreet. It was Napoleon himself who had seized the initiative by taking command of the Paris garrison troops with the assent of Lefebvre and the willing help of Murat, Berthier and Savary. It was Lucien who, with the support of Sieyès, Roger-Ducos and Fouché, made himself responsible for 'manipulating' the recalcitrant members of the Councils. Joseph's role was that of public relations officer. On 29 October it was he who had given a dinner party at Mortefontaine so that Bernadotte, Roederer, Regnault de Saint Jean-d'Angely and other influential persons could meet Napoleon. It was he who brought Bernadotte in the early morning of 18 Brumaire to the rue de Victoire, where Napoleon, with a mixture of threats and cajolery, attempted in vain to win him over to his side; it was Joseph who then inveigled Bernadotte out of Paris to a lunch in the country lest he should decide to interfere with Napoleon's military 'assault' on the Orangerie. It was Joseph who, after the coup, advised his brother and wooed the minority of the Councils and, as he put it, 'legalized' the new regime. According to Miot :

> We hesitated which side to take until Joseph had the idea of summoning what remained of the Five Hundred, all of whom were prepared to vote for what we had intended to accomplish in the morning with the concurrence of the whole Assembly. It was these remaining deputies who voted the decrees suppressing the Councils, abolishing the Directoire and creating the three Consuls.[26]

But credit for the success of the coup must be given to Lucien – and to Sieyès – who kept their heads when Napoleon had made his humiliating exit from the Chamber with blood streaming down his cheeks – not from the daggers of the angry deputies, as he maintained, but because in his nervous excitement, after an almost incoherent speech (which Lucien had wisely interrupted), he had scratched the pustules on his face with which at that time he was afflicted.

It was Sieyès who rallied the distraught Napoleon as he nervously paced the room above the chamber awaiting the result of the deputies' vote and who, on receipt of the news that the young general had been outlawed, exclaimed : 'By outlawing you, they have outlawed themselves.' It was only then that Napoleon, recovering his presence of mind, rushed to the window overlooking the courtyard where Murat and his troops were drawn up, and sword in hand, shouted : '*Aux armes!*'

Although Bernadotte had not actively opposed the coup, he had made it quite clear that he was unsympathetic to the overthrow of a

government by force. Joseph, in his memoirs, is at pains to explain
that Bernadotte was not an enemy of the family, but of the arbitrary
methods employed by Napoleon to achieve power. The recent oppres-
sions, following the coup d'état of Fructidor, was still very much in
the minds of the people and, once the present coup had been achieved,
Bernadotte wisely left Paris with Désirée, disguised as a boy, to seek
asylum in the country home of General Sarazin, an old comrade in
arms. 'A few days later', Joseph wrote, 'I was successful in having
the names of Jourdan, Saliceti and Bernadotte deleted from the list
drawn up by Fouché of those condemned to be deported . . .'[27]
Bernadotte was allowed to return to his home at 291 rue Cisalpine
(today 34 rue Monceau).

Joseph was elected a member of the *Corps legislatif* and, a little
later, was appointed to the Council of State.

> I refused to become a member of the Ministry because I preferred to
> live quietly at Mortefontaine; however, because I felt it was necessary
> to be of some service to my country and my brother, I promised to
> sacrifice for ever the pleasures of domestic bliss and a country life in
> exchange for what I believed to be my duty by accepting missions for
> which I considered myself to be suited.

After explaining the reasons for Napoleon's choice of Talleyrand
and Fouché as ministers, Joseph continues:

> At that period of our history, I believe that I rendered my country
> some service. For Napoleon, nothing else counted provided that his
> government represented the best interests of the nation; his main
> preoccupation was to keep himself informed of public opinion . . . I,
> more than anyone, was qualified to enlighten him . . . I saw a great
> many people both in towns and in the country and unflaggingly
> *observed and probed* into what were the true wishes and needs of the
> different classes of society. How many times have I discussed some
> administrative or legislative measure in order to learn the opinion of
> such and such enlightened person, or of a member of such and such
> a class of society, whether in Paris, Lyons or Marseilles. So much so,
> indeed, that the English police at that time nicknamed me 'Joseph
> the Influential'.[28]

Busy as Joseph was sounding public opinion on behalf of his
brother, he still found time to look after his own financial interests
and to keep a brotherly eye on the younger members of his family.
Caroline had fallen in love with the dashing Joachim Murat, to

whom, with Napoleon's consent, she was married in a civil ceremony at Mortefontaine on 20 January 1800, with Bernadotte, Leclerc and Louis acting as witnesses. Nor did he forget his friends. Thanks to Joseph, Bernadotte was restored to favour and was appointed to the Council of State; Benjamin Constant was elected a member of the Tribune; but, try as he might, he was unable to bring about a rapprochement between Napoleon and Madame de Staël. The greater the power assumed by Napoleon, the more the First Consul came to despise the *'idéologues'*, a word which he claimed to have invented, but which was originally coined by the *ci-devant* aristocrat and soldier-philosopher Destutt de Tracy. In Napoleon's language *'idéologue'*, like *'métaphysicien'*, connoted an intellectual dreamer, opposed to everything he stood for.[29] In fact, the very men he had courted so assiduously on his first return from Italy and subsequently from Egypt, and who had helped him to his present position, were those whom he now castigated the most violently.

VI

The Peacemaker

1800–1802

Among the useful services rendered by Joseph to his country were the negotiations of treaties with other states, a task for which he was admirably qualified. He had a natural flair for diplomacy, which he regarded as a far more efficacious weapon than the sword and much more profitable.

Joseph's first official mission was to re-establish friendly relations with the United States. Franco-American relations had been most harmonious in 1781, when Lord Cornwallis and his British Army had surrendered to American and French forces at Yorktown, but, incredible as it may seem, by 1799 the two Republics were perilously close to war. Now that America had achieved independence, she could not ignore the realities of necessary contacts, political and economic, with both Britain and France. It was, however, difficult to steer a middle course. There was still a strong feeling of kinship with Britain, coupled with the need for friendly relations with the world's foremost sea power. On the other hand, it had been France who had sent the troops, guns and ships that had helped the Americans to gain their independence. The pro-British faction won the day, despite the fact that the Royal Navy had seized American vessels carrying cargo to the West Indies. Washington, still President, sought accommodation rather than retaliation. The American mission sent to London was, to its surprise, cordially received. Since the British seemed anxious to heal wounds and differences with the Americans, the mission was authorized to negotiate a treaty, which was ratified in 1796. The Directoire regarded this as a calculated insult to France. In a series of devious and complicated negotiations Talleyrand, as Minister for Foreign Affairs, attempted to patch up the quarrel to his own financial advantage. In effect, what he said was that unless America was prepared to buy peace, the French Government must consider the United States as enemies. The Americans refused to pay. Talleyrand wanted money, not war, but he had succeeded far better than Britain had ever done in alienating America from France.

When negotiations were reopened, the Directoire had vanished and Bonaparte had been declared First Consul. In order to show his friendship for the United States, one of Napoleon's first acts was to order his army to wear mourning on the occasion of Washington's death. He next appointed a commission consisting of Joseph, Monsieur de Fleury (former Minister of Marine) and Roederer to enter into negotiations with the American representatives whom he had invited to France. Thanks to Talleyrand's chicanery, the Americans were somewhat suspicious. Discussions dragged on. The U.S. representatives had no authority to make any decision without reference to their federal government, which, of course, in the days of sail, took an interminable time. Joseph took the opportunity of joining Napoleon in Italy.

To explain the First Consul's presence in Italy, we must parenthetically leave Joseph and return to Napoleon's foreign policy in Europe.

Having put his house in some semblance of order, with the help of Joseph, to whom historians, as a whole, give little or no credit, Napoleon's next step as First Consul was to reorganize the army on the eastern frontier with a view to resuming the offensive against Austria. Masséna was transferred from Switzerland to command the Army of Italy; the Armies of the Rhine and Danube were merged into one under Moreau on 24 November 1800. With a complete disregard for diplomatic protocol, the First Consul wrote personal letters on 24 December to George III and to the Emperor Francis of Austria, suggesting that the time was now ripe for the peaceful settlement of all outstanding questions on the basis of the status quo. He hinted to Austria that this would mean a withdrawal from Lombardy to the Adige line, a hypocritical gesture, for on the very same day he issued a proclamation to the French Army: 'Soldiers! It is no longer your frontiers that you are called to defend : *We must invade the countries of our enemies.*'

He appointed Lucien Minister of the Interior, so that he could keep his eye on the police, internal security and censorship, though in reality it was Fouché, Minister of Police, who had his finger on the pulse of the nation. In January he instructed Talleyrand, Minister of

Foreign Affairs, to raise a loan of eight or nine million francs from Portugal and ordered Marmont to raise a further fifteen millions from Holland and Hamburg. By early spring, he had scraped together sufficient funds to form a fourth new Army of Reserve and partially re-equip his existing forces.[1] Under Sieyès's new Constitution, the First Consul was officially precluded from command of the armies, but a trifle like this was not one to stand in the way of Napoleon. In April he issued a new Consular Decree: 'General Berthier, Minister of War, is appointed Commander-in-Chief of the Reserve Army. Citizen Carnot is appointed Minister of War.' To quote General Sir James Marshall-Cornwall: 'Bonaparte thus avoided the constitutional brake on his military activities and outwitted his political rivals by putting his own yes-men in nominal command; this devolution of command proved to be a complete farce.'[2]

The campaign of 1800, with the famous crossing of the Saint Bernard Pass, culminating in the decisive battle of Marengo, has been described in detail by many writers, mostly glorifying Napoleon. The boldness of the overall design, the formation of the Army of Reserve (assembled at Dijon in circumstances of the utmost secrecy), the speed with which Napoleon improvised new tactical moves as needs demanded (e.g. his change of route across the Alps), have almost invariably been described as the work of a commander of genius. Only when these factors are analysed by such great military historians as the late Sir Basil Liddell Hart and Sir James Marshall-Cornwall do we realize that Napoleon was far from infallible. In fact, the crossing of the Alps was badly planned and Napoleon made one tactical mistake after another, though in extenuation it must be admitted that these mistakes were largely due to the inefficiency of his intelligence service:

> On the day before the decsive battle of Marengo, Bonaparte was rash enough to send away his ablest corps commander, Desaix, and one of his strongest divisions on a wild goose-chase to the south, based on the wrong guess as to Melas's [the Austrian Commander-in-Chief's] intentions; on the very day of the battle, he despatched another division, 3,500 strong, in the opposite direction. Consequently, at noon on the day of the crucial battle, he had left himself with no reserves and would have been defeated, if Desaix had not arrived in the nick of time.[3]

Apart from depriving himself of infantry reserves, Napoleon had failed to supply himself with adequate artillery support – inexcusable in a gunnery officer. By four o'clock, the battle was already lost to the French; only Desaix's timely arrival turned certain defeat into victory. Desaix was killed in action. Napoleon, in his official bulletin, naturally made no mention of Desaix's decisive role and claimed for himself all credit for 'his' victory.

Napoleon's departure in May to take command of the army in the field had been viewed with considerable misgiving by many of his supporters, not least by Joseph. Napoleon had arrived in France to restore order out of chaos, but in days when a general officer in the field was often subject to the same dangers as the lowest of his subordinates, who was to replace the First Consul, should he be killed? Moreover, despite his (and Joseph's) attempts to reconcile all political factions, Napoleon's seat in the saddle was by no means secure. Before he had left for Italy in May, there had already been attempts on his life. Both Jacobins and Royalists were opposed to the consular régime, which had assumed what was almost a regal aspect; the first, because the new régime represented an almost complete repudiation of Republican principles; the second, because with the establishment of almost monarchical rule, the restoration of the Bourbons seemed more distant than ever.

Joseph, although he could never be accused of personal political ambition, never forgot his Corsican origins and that he was still head of the Bonaparte clan; he desired at all costs that his family, now raised from poverty to power and riches, should retain their prestige. Even before Napoleon was officially appointed First Consul for life, Joseph was demanding that his brother should appoint him as his successor, particularly as it was generally assumed that Napoleon would never have an heir – at least not by his legitimate wife. Lest it be thought that Joseph was entirely motivated by personal consider-ations, it should be remembered that all Frenchmen educated in religious or royal colleges before the Revolution believed in hereditary assumption of rank by primogeniture or direct collateral relationship. This was regarded as a sacred and indisputable principle. Now that a quasi-monarchial institution had already been established, Joseph's pretensions were regarded as only right and proper. Among his many friends who visited him at Mortefontaine were the *ci-devant* noblemen the Marquis de Jaucourt and the Marquis Stanislas de Girardin, both staunch Republicans who were among the first to draw his attention to the necessity for Napoleon to nominate him as his successor. This was one of the reasons for Joseph's visit to Italy.

Napoleon, however, had no wish to name his heir and refused to discuss the matter. Scarcely had Joseph arrived in Milan than

Napoleon packed him off with Generals Lannes and Victor on a visit to Lake Maggiore, while he left for Paris to reap the laurels of 'his' victory at Marengo. Joseph returned to the capital a few days later, on 4 July 1800.

The convention with the American representatives was finally signed on 3 October. Joseph celebrated the occasion by holding a magnificent reception at Mortefontaine, attended by the three Consuls, all senior ministers, the *corps diplomatique* and two of the great French protagonists of the American War of Independence, La Fayette and La Rochefoucauld-Liancourt. There was a gala concert, illuminations and fireworks, and a play, for which the most famous actors and actresses were engaged. Frédéric Masson, always ready to criticize the brothers of his idol, recounts that the fête was a disaster: it rained in buckets. Not only did Joseph's *maître d'hôtel* forget to supply the guests with knives for the banquet; both he and his staff were drunk.

True or not, the successful conclusion of the negotiations represented a minor triumph for Joseph – a minor triumph, because already the new American republic was fundamentally well disposed towards Revolutionary France, based as they both were on the Rights of Man. It had only been the greed of the diplomatic representatives of the Directoire and Talleyrand which had caused friction between the two republics.

Much more important was Joseph's second diplomatic mission when he negotiated the Treaty of Lunéville with the Austrian plenipotentiary Count Ludwig von Cobenzl, the same who had been a signatory to the Treaty of Campo Formio. Although the victory of Marengo had been decisive inasmuch as it had forced the Austrians to withdraw behind the line of the Adige in accordance with terms of the convention of Alessandria, this did not apply to the German theatre of war, where Moreau's Army of the Rhine was still engaged fighting the Austrians under the Archduke Charles and General Kray in the Black Forest. Only after Moreau had crossed the Danube at Hochstädt after smashing Kray's army and had occupied Augsburg and Munich were hostilities temporarily brought to an end by the Convention of Parsdorf (15 July). Britain, however, was still undefeated and, as Austria was pledged not to make a separate peace before February 1801, the political situation was complicated and the preliminary peace negotiations, started at Lunéville in November, dragged on. Meanwhile, the military situation in Egypt had deteriorated since the assassination of Kléber on 14 June (the same day as the victory of Marengo). Communications with the Army of the Orient had been made more difficult by Admiral Lord Keith's capture of Malta at the beginning of September. Exasperated by these setbacks and delays, Napoleon ordered his army commanders to break the armistices on both German and Italian fronts. Hostilities were resumed on 5 November. On the German front, the war was brought to an end by Moreau's crushing victory over the Archduke John at Hohenlinden on 3 December, resulting in the Armistice of Steyr three weeks later, and, on the Italian front, with the signing of the Convention of Trentino on 9 February after Macdonald had forced the Splügen Pass in the depths of winter and pushed forward through the Trentino to Bolzano.

Peace negotiations were now resumed at Lunéville. Relations between Joseph and Count Cobenzl seem to have been of the most cordial, despite the rupture of the armistices. 'Count Cobenzl', Joseph tells us, 'was a most agreeable man, who expressed himself admirably in French, having been educated in France. He had lived for a long while at the court of the Empress Catherine of Russia, of whom he delighted to talk . . . During the course of the negotiations, I had the pleasure of obtaining the cession of Mantua, which under the terms of the armistice concluded in Italy, had remained in the hands of the Austrians . . .'[4] The cession of Mantua prompted Moreau to send Joseph a despatch which read : 'Citizen Minister, accept my compliments for the manner in which you besieged and captured Mantua without leaving Lunéville.'

The negotiations were protracted and were only concluded on 9 February 1801. Every night Joseph and the Austrian Minister dined alternately at the other's residence. Napoleon did not share his brother's liking for Cobenzl, whom he accused of having unnecessarily dragged out negotiations but, once peace was signed, he wrote to his brother : 'You can tell him [Cobenzl] that if he had not had the good sense to remain in Lunéville, we should have imposed harder conditions on Austria. I have but one more word to say : *The Nation is satisfied with the Treaty and I am particularly satisfied with it.*'

Joseph, in his memoirs, is a little over-modest. In fact the Peace of Lunéville effectively brought an end to the second Coalition. The territorial settlements were approximately the same as those enacted by the Treaty of Campo Formio in 1797. France retained Belgium and the left bank of the Rhine; in Italy, Austria was given in compensation the territory of Venezia as far west as the Adige. Lombardy, including the Duchies of Parma, Modena and Tuscany, was recognized as the Cisalpine Republic. The Batavian (Dutch), Helvetian (Geneva and part of Switzerland), Italian and Ligurian (Genoese)

Republics were recognized as nominally independent states, but were in reality under French domination. Only Britain now remained to be contended with. Napoleon and his generals might win battles on land, but at sea the British fleet still ruled supreme. Abercromby's victory at Alexandria (28 March) had finally forced the French to evacuate Egypt and shattered Napoleon's hopes of Oriental expansion; the assassination of Tsar Paul on 23 March and Admiral Hyde Parker's destruction of the Danish fleet at the battle of Copenhagen on 2 April (largely with the help of Nelson) had combined to a large degree to prevent Napoleon's scheme for a confederation of northern states by which he had hoped to cripple British trade. Despite the fact that on the continent of Europe he had regained all the territorial advantages which had been lost by France under the Directoire, his position at home was by no means secure. While Joseph was negotiating peace terms at Lunéville, there had been another attempt on the First Consul's life. On Christmas Eve, when driving through the rue Saint-Nicaise on his way to hear a performance of Haydn's *Creation*, a carefully prepared plot to blow up his carriage with a time bomb concealed in a covered waggon blocking the street only failed in its purpose by the mistiming of a few seconds. Napoleon was convinced that this plot had been hatched by 'Jacobins, Terrorists and Anarchists', all of whom he lumped together under one label. Fouché, however, knew better. He had already established the fact that this was the work of Royalists. In an extraordinary display of temper, Napoleon refused to believe him. 'I don't have to rely on you,' he shouted at his Minister of Police, 'I have my own police.' When Fouché remained silent, Napoleon stormed at him: 'Well, d'you still insist that this was the work of Royalists?' To which Fouché replied: 'Undoubtedly, and what's more, within a week I will prove it.'[5]

Napoleon had no intention of waiting that long to punish his would-be assassins. Talleyrand, remembering Fouché's own terrible record during the Terror in Lyons, suspected him of shielding old friends and advised the First Consul to have him shot!

Dubois, the Prefect of Police for the Seine, who was ostensibly under the orders of Fouché, but who now only took his orders from the First Consul himself, was instructed to draw up a list of suspects. In a travesty of a trial, one hundred and sixty persons whose names were to be found on Dubois's list were condemned to be deported to penal colonies.

In the meantime, Fouché had established beyond any shadow of doubt that the real culprits were Royalist Chouans. This made not the slightest difference to Napoleon, who insisted that even if not guilty

94

of this particular attempt on his life the 'terrorists' named by Dubois were nevertheless enemies of the nation and potential murderers who deserved their fate. Other arrests followed; those who were not deported to die in Cayenne or in the Seychelles, or left to rot in the hulks of Oléron or the Ile de Ré, were executed.

Joseph and many of his friends of the *parti philosophique*, although fundamentally opposed to the act passed by the Chambers which legalized these sentences (the first of the decrees of the *senatus consultum*, which were gradually to become substitutes for genuine laws), abstained from voting in the ballot which declared these measures constitutional (5 January 1801). Special courts, very much on the lines of military courts martial, were set up throughout France, ostensibly to rid the country of the many bandits infesting the roads.[6] Although entirely contrary to the democratic spirit of the Republic, these courts were welcomed generally by the people, who were tired of terrorism in any form and saw in Napoleon not a tyrant but a saviour.

Although the terrorist threat had now been effectively eliminated, there still remained a very real threat from the Royalists. In order to guarantee internal peace, and, in particular, to pacify the west, it was considered essential to restore freedom of religion to the country. To all intents and purposes, the Revolution was over. A new era had begun and it was time to establish a Concordat with Rome.

The First Consul showed characteristic astuteness in his choice of representatives for the negotiations with the Holy See. The principals were the Abbé Bernier, sometime curé of Saint-Laud, who had played a pre-eminent role with the counter-revolutionary Vendéen armies in the terrible civil war of 1793, and M. Cretet, who had replaced Lucien (now Ambassador in Madrid) as Minister of the Interior. Joseph, though he took no active part in drawing up the articles, was appointed to hold a watching brief, firstly because, to quote his brother's own words: 'It is essential that you efface the memory of the harm you [!] have done the Papacy', and, secondly, because Napoleon wished to have a Bonaparte as a signatory. Cardinals Consalvi, Spira and Caselli represented Pope Pius VII.

The negotiations were in fact a continuation of the demands and concessions which had already been discussed between Napoleon and the Holy See. The Concordat, however, was not achieved without difficulty. There were still many liberals, especially in the Tribunate, who were strongly opposed to what amounted to the reintroduction of Catholicism as the state religion, but by a special decree of the *senatus consultum* and considerable legal chicanery, the Assemblies were 'purged' of the most dissident members. Criticism from the Left was effectively gagged; the ratification of the Concordat, it was thought, could now proceed without opposition. Certain articles were added which deprived the papacy of some of its privileges and marked a return to the Gallican Church of 1682. *The Régime of the Catholic Church in its relation with the Rights and Policy of the State* provided that there should be one liturgy and one catechism for all Catholic churches in France (Article 39).

Deaf to the protests of the Cardinal Legate Consalvi, the First Consul, moreover, insisted on the inclusion of the twelve already existing constitutional bishops in the episcopal body. Finally, the Protestant religion was officially recognized and endowed. This tolerant measure, inspired by Joseph, Talleyrand and Fouché, would in their opinion overcome the last parliamentary resistance to the signing of the Convention. But even after the 'purging', there was still opposition in the Tribunal, which was summoned to an extraordinary session on 5 April, when seven out of eighty-five deputies voted against the Concordat and Articles, while in the *Corps législatif*, which at this juncture had merely been 'renewed', only two hundred and twenty-eight out of three hundred members voted in favour, twenty-one voting against and fifty-one abstaining.

The Concordat was finally signed at two o'clock in the morning of 21 June in Joseph's town residence in the rue du Faubourg Saint-Honoré, which he had recently acquired in place of the mansion in the rue d'Errancis, which he now considered too modest for his present exalted position.

Joseph's new *hôtel particulier* had been built in 1725 for Louis Blouin, Chancellor to Louis XV. When Joseph bought this mansion, it was known as the Hôtel Marbeuf after its previous owner, Ange-Jacques, Marquis de Marbeuf, none other than the nephew of the Governor of Corsica, who had befriended the Bonaparte family and to whose kindness both Joseph and his brothers owed their education. Like all Joseph's residences, the Hôtel Marbeuf was magnificent. It possessed large grounds adjacent to the leafy Champs Élysées, and its high-ceilinged rooms still possessed the original Louis XV gilded panelling and glass cabinets, filled with a splendid collection of Chinese porcelain.

Little Julie must have seemed dwarfed by her new magnificent surroundings, but she was happy there, for her mother and her brother Nicolas and her sister Honorine (now Madame de Villeneufve)

Zenaïde and Charlotte,
Joseph and Julie's two
daughters

Marshal Soult

Goya's 'Con razon ó sinella', from his 'Desastros de la guerra' series

King Joseph's second entry into Madrid

lived close by in the rue d'Augesseau. It was in this mansion in the rue du Faubourg Saint-Honoré that, on 8 July 1801, Julie gave birth to a daughter, to be named Zenaïde-Charlotte-Julie. Her first child, born in Genoa, had died a few days after birth; another daughter, born in the previous year, had survived only a few hours. Joseph in his memoirs confuses dates and writes of his third daughter Charlotte being born 'on the same day and at the same hour as the signing of the Concordat'.

The Hôtel Marbeuf was to be the scene of receptions equalling in splendour those given by Joseph at Mortefontaine. Among his most honoured guests was Lord Cornwallis, the British Ambassador, who arrived in Paris in the early winter of 1801 to discuss peace terms with France and her allies Spain and Holland. The importance of establishing lasting peace with Great Britain was appreciated by all, none more so than Napoleon himself. 'One Treaty signed with the consent of the Court of Saint James is worth ten signed with the House of Austria.' In his memoirs, Joseph writes :

An initial armistice had already been signed in London [1 October 1801]. On his arrival in Paris, Lord Cornwallis was suitably received by the First Consul. I gave a dinner in his honour, to which I invited several distinguished Englishmen who had already arrived in Paris together with a number of Frenchmen whom I considered proper for him to meet. I remember, as we left the table, he said to me : 'I know that M. de La Fayette is one of your friends; I would have been happy to have seen him here. I am not complaining, however, of your diplomatic discretion : I suppose you thought it would embarrass me to meet the General of Georgetown.[7] I am grateful to you for your tactful consideration; but I hope when we know each other better you will discard all reserve, so that we can stop acting like diplomats, but like men who sincerely wish to accomplish what our governments demand of us, and arrive promptly at a solid peace.'[8]

All the diplomatic protocol, so carefully prepared by the Ministry of Foreign Affairs, had been dissipated in a moment by Joseph's charm. The official meeting between the plenipotentiaries at Amiens a few days later was no less cordial. The Spanish representative Azara was, of course, an old friend of Joseph's from the days when the two had served together in Rome. Schimmelpenninck, the Dutch envoy, was no less cordial. There is no doubt that Joseph and his two aides Jaucourt and Girardin made a most favourable impression. The Peace was signed on 27 March 1802, and to all appearances it would have seemed that Joseph had achieved the impossible and that the disputes between Britain, France, Spain and Holland had been settled. Britain retained possession of Trinidad and Ceylon (disputed respectively by the Spanish and French) and gained an open port at the Cape of Good Hope; the Republic of the Ionian Islands (Venetian) was recognized; Malta was restored to the Knights of Saint John; Spain and Holland regained their colonies, with the exception of New Orleans, which had been ceded to the French under the Treaty of Ildefonso negotiated by Lucien while ambassador in Madrid, but which, however, Napoleon was to sell, together with the whole of Louisiana, to the United States in May of the following year. The French were to quit Rome and Naples; Turkey was restored to its integrity. It was agreed that Lombardy, or rather what was now called the Cisalpine Republic, should remain under French domination; Napoleon had 'accepted' its presidency by the *senatus consultum* of Lyons in January.

But such favourable peace terms had not been won by charm alone. Joseph had shown throughout remarkably sound sense. On 17 March he wrote to his brother:

> I do not doubt of success, but we need a few more days of patience and firmness. These fellows [the British] can only be defeated with their own weapons – imperturbability and phlegm. Where former treaties were concerned, they always got their own way because of what they call French impatience. From now on, we can show them that their hopes are ill-founded. Given a little time, we can gain another point every day.

The peace treaty was regarded as a magnificent triumph by all France. 'When I arrived in Paris', writes Joseph in his memoirs, 'the First Consul was at the Opera. He had me come to his box and presenting me to the audience, announced the declaration of peace. It is easy to guess what passed through both our hearts at that moment!'[9]

VII

Imperial Highness,
Heir Presumptive, and Colonel
of the 4th Regiment of the Line

1802–1805

Joseph's part in the Treaty of Lunéville, however, was little appreciated outside his own circle of friends. Madame de Staël wrote to him enthusiastically from Coppet, calling him the 'peacemaker', and Talleyrand wrote him a personal letter of congratulation. But the world as a whole only learnt the details of the peace terms from the columns of the official consular organ, the *Moniteur*, in which all credit for success was naturally attributed to Napoleon himself.

For the first time in ten years, France knew peace. It was common knowledge that Napoleon, now at the height of his popularity, was aiming at absolute rule. The Bonaparte clan was more than ever anxious that he should appoint a successor. Among his family there seems to have been a general consensus of opinion that his luck would not last, or that he would be assassinated. Joseph, as head of the family, naturally thought that he should be nominated his heir, but, as we have already seen, this was a subject which Napoleon had refused to discuss with him. Lucien, who had been so largely instrumental in bringing about the successful conclusion to the coup d'état of Brumaire, also entertained hopes of being the chosen 'Dauphin', since, as he said, Joseph was not a true Republican and 'his indolence and dilettantism precluded him from high office'.[1]

It was now clear that Josephine would never provide Napoleon with an heir; but it was equally clear that Napoleon was quite adamant that none of his brothers was worthy to succeed him. The alternative was either to adopt an heir or choose another wife. Josephine, to consolidate her position, worked hard to effect a marriage between young Louis Bonaparte and her daughter Hortense de Beauharnais. Napoleon himself saw this as an admirable solution to the question of heritage. 'Perhaps we will have no children,' he said to Josephine. 'I brought up Louis, whom I regard as a son. You love your daughter more than anyone in the world. Their children will be ours. We will adopt them and this adoption will console us for having none. But the young people must find our plan a happy one.'[2]

The 'young people' did not find the plan a happy one. Louis grudgingly agreed; as a brave and loyal soldier and a devoted brother he found it difficult to refuse Napoleon anything; Hortense, equally devoted to her mother, and anxious to save her from the ignominy of divorce, nevertheless viewed the prospect of marriage with Louis with misgiving, for her bridegroom-to-be, once so gay and charming, had developed into a morose hypochondriac. The truth of the matter was that this brave young soldier, although 'he had escaped the bullets of the enemy, had been struck down by the darts of Venus'. In plain words, he had contracted syphilis and for the rest of his life was in almost constant pain and suffered from partial paralysis of the hands and forearms (diagnosed as rheumatism). Despite the young couple's mutual lack of sympathy, they were married in Paris on 4 January 1802 by the mayor of the *Ire arrondissement.* The civil ceremony was immediately followed by a religious service, an occasion which gave Murat and Caroline the opportunity of having their own civil wedding blessed *in facie Ecclesiae.*

Just over eight months later, Hortense gave birth to a boy, to be named Napoleon-Charles. Now, at last, the First Consul could adopt an heir who was not only a Bonaparte but a de Beauharnais. The birth of this boy child gave pleasure to no one, excepting Napoleon and Josephine. Louis himself had doubts regarding the legitimacy of his son. The very idea that his own putative offspring might one day be the ruler of France, to whom he would have to bow down, disgusted him. Little Napoleon-Charles, however, died in 1807 and Louis was saved this possible humiliation. His third son, Charles Louis-Napoleon (born 1808, later Napoleon III, and whose legitimacy he had even greater reason to suspect[3]) only became Emperor of the French in 1852, six years after Louis's death and twenty-six years after he had already abdicated his throne of Holland.

Relations between Napoleon and Joseph after the Treaty of Lunéville became extremely strained, not only because Napoleon refused to recognize him as his heir, but because Joseph insisted on remaining on friendly terms with members of the liberal opposition and even with those generals who openly disapproved of the First Consul's policies. The Concordat (ratified on 15 April), in which Joseph was recognized to have played a merely passive role, had been severely criticized both by members of the Tribunate and especially by the army – Moreau's Army of the Rhine in particular. These soldiers of the Revolution, who had fought against kings and priests, were only too ready to denounce a policy which, in the parlance of the day, 'threatened to make monks of them all'. Bernadotte, Moreau, Brune, Lannes, Macdonald and many others openly expressed their disgust. The Army of the Rhine, not yet disbanded, represented a real threat. It would have been difficult for Napoleon to have attacked Moreau, the hero of Hohenlinden, and one of the most popular men in France. On the other hand, it was not impossible to trump up an excuse to send his army overseas, for example to send it to San Domingo (Haiti) 'to overthrow the black government of the Negro Toussaint l'Ouverture'.

Although slavery had been abolished by the Convention and Toussaint had been officially appointed Commander-in-Chief of the island, Napoleon, in one of the most double-faced dealings of his whole career, chose to see in the black republic a threat to West Indian trade. In fact, Toussaint, a loyal subject of the French Republic, had effectively driven the English and Spanish from the island. On 9 May 1801 he had sent a copy of his new constitution to Napoleon for his approval; the First Consul had graciously replied, 'If the flag of France flies over San Domingo, it is thanks to you and your brave blacks.' True, he criticized the fact that the constitution smacked a little too much of autonomy, but this was something that could be amicably settled. But only a few days later, on instructions from the First Consul, the *Corps législatif* passed a resolution re-establishing slavery in all colonies. An expeditionary force, consisting almost entirely of the Army of the Rhine, under the command of Leclerc, was sent to San Domingo to suppress the anticipated revolt. None of the soldiers realized that they were being sent to restore slavery.

Napoleon could have found no better way of ridding himself of a dissident army. Although Toussaint was captured and conveyed to France where he died in prison without trial, protesting to the last that he was a 'son of the one and indivisible Republic', war continued. Of the French army of 33,000 men, only a few thousand returned. Leclerc died of yellow fever, no white colonists remained and the Negro and mulatto population was decimated. France had lost her richest colony and her bravest soldiers. In the *Mémorial de Sainte Hélène*, Napoleon had the grace to admit that he had made a mistake.

In the circumstances it is hardly surprising that Joseph's friend Moreau detested the First Consul and that gentle Joseph himself regarded the whole episode as utterly discreditable. Now under the command of Bernadotte, the Army of the West, which had effectively subdued the Chouans, was showing signs of mutiny. A plot, known as the *Complot de libels*, in which twelve senior offices were involved, calling on all officers loyal to the Republic to overthrow the tyrant, was uncovered; Bernadotte was said to be implicated.[4] Julie and Joseph both defended their brother-in-law. Napoleon is said to have told Joseph: 'You had better realize that if your wretched southern hot-head continues to find fault with any acts of government, I'll have him shot in the Place du Carrousel . . .'[5]

Napoleon, however, eventually contented himself with depriving Bernadotte of his command and disbanding the dissident garrison of Rennes (which also happened to be Moreau's home town), but could not stop Bernadotte from frequenting the salons of Madame de Staël and Madame Récamier, the meeting-places for liberals, *idéologues*, Royalists and all who felt themselves betrayed by the man on whom they had once pinned their hopes. Joseph seems to have come in for little criticism for his part in the signing of the Concordat, and together with Lucien remained a welcome guest at these gatherings, especially at the house of Germaine de Staël, the 'hospital for defeated parties', as she called it.

That Joseph was often extremely critical of Napoleon was common knowledge. Although Lucien's memoirs are far from reliable, the sidelights he throws on Joseph's character in this respect can be accepted as truth. For example, Lucien reiterates the fact that although Napoleon frequently lost his temper with Joseph, whose criticisms exasperated him, these quarrels never lasted long, 'because fundamentally, he knew that Joseph loved and admired him far more than he was prepared to admit . . . He never failed to show the greatest devotion to the Emperor in his hours of misfortune, and always retained the most tender and compassionate memories of him.' As Napoleon's power increased, so he became more and more autocratic and would only accept men around him who would obey without discussion. 'Joseph alone,' wrote Lucien, 'although nearly always finally acceding to Napoleon's wishes, invariably retained the right to speak his own mind.'[6]

Nevertheless there were times when Joseph absolutely refused to comply with his brother's demands. In 1803, for example, Napoleon wrote to Joseph : 'I assure you that it is for the good of the State and for myself that you should accept the post of Chancellor of the Senate if it is offered to you. I will judge of your attachment to me by your conduct in this matter.'

Despite this appeal to his brotherly affection, Joseph absolutely refused to become a member of the Ministry – just as he had refused to join the Ministry after the coup d'état of Brumaire – and preferred his life as a country gentleman at Mortefontaine. Lucien, rather maliciously, attributes Joseph's refusal 'to the obstinacy of a weak man, who wishes to show that he has a mind of his own', and points out that formerly he had had no scruples in accepting a seat in the Senate at a salary of 120,000 francs a year. Lucien goes on to say :

Napoleon showed his displeasure at Joseph's attitude in his usual fashion, that is to say by scarcely speaking to him, or by not speaking to him at all, or even by refusing to receive him when he called. On these occasions Joseph happily consoled himself by retiring to his well-loved Mortefontaine while awaiting the inevitable recall to favour. Napoleon always showed the greatest *indulgence* and even *deference* to Joseph, which could be traced back to the fact that he was the elder.

Lucien further relates that Joseph 'was invariably affable in his conversation; only to Napoleon did he fail to show the same amiability'. Sometimes, we are told, the conversations between the two brothers degenerated into the most puerile quarrels, almost as though 'they were acting out a *commedia dell'arte*, where the actors, after indulging in the most violent abuse in public, end by embracing each other in the wings'.[7]

There is no doubt that, however much Joseph may have loved his brother, his dreamy and romantic temperament more often than not clashed violently with that of his despotic soldier brother. He disliked the regal pomp and etiquette with which Napoleon was now beginning to surround himself. On 18 April 1802 (Easter Day), when a grand ceremony was held at Nôtre-Dame to celebrate the re-establishment of the Church (when four battalions of infantry lined up in the Cathedral presented arms at the moment of the elevation of the Host!), Joseph refused to take his place at his brother's side. On 15 August, a fortnight after Napoleon had been nominated First Consul for life, when another equally grand ceremony was held to celebrate the ratification of the Concordat, Joseph refused to be driven to Nôtre-Dame in a coach drawn by eight horses, as the new consular protocol demanded, but drove humbly in a hired carriage like those used by the other government officials present. On the other hand, together with Lucien, he accepted to sit on the committee which inaugurated the establishment of the order of the Légion d'Honneur (19 May 1802), which by constituting a *corps d'élite*, was considered by many to be at variance with true Republican traditions and to be equivalent to the formation of a new aristocracy. Moreau tied the ribbon to the tail of his horse and nominated his chef a member of the 'Légion de Casserole'.

The more the First Consul surrounded himself with pomp and ceremony, the more glittering displays of military glory he held in the Champs de Mars, the more Joseph affected the style of a private country gentleman – though admittedly a gentleman of wealth, like one of the great English milords. His old friend Miot, after two years' absence in Corsica, was greatly struck by the change of atmosphere when he now attended Joseph's receptions at Mortefontaine or at the Hôtel Marbeuf: 'No more top boots, no more trousers, no more cockades. Instead there were silk stockings, buckled shoes, parade swords and *chapeaux sous le bras.*'[8]

Not representative of the Republican ideals of Year III, perhaps, but deliberately anti-militaristic. The days of the *sans-culottes* were long over. In 1802 the accumulation of riches in no way conflicted with the ideals of even the most devoted Republicans. Moreau, than whom there was no more dedicated Republican, kept court on a scale almost equal to that of Joseph. Lucien, who still claimed to be a Jacobin at heart, had no compunction in amassing millions. What the Republicans of 1801–2 demanded was not an equal distribution of wealth but the abolition of aristocratic privilege, the institution of popular franchise and freedom of the press – in short, a constitution based on the American or even English model. This was something which Napoleon could never accept. He believed that the whole safety and future of France depended on an autocratic dictatorship.

Lucien tells us in his memoirs that Napoleon even carried his regal pretensions within the family circle; for example, when at a dinner party given at Mortefontaine he made an absurd scene about the question of precedence of seating arrangements at table.

Although Napoleon still claimed to hold his mother in the greatest esteem, he was now, nevertheless, ashamed of what he regarded as her peasant ways, of her inability to speak French correctly, or even Italian, which she still spoke mixed with Corsican patois. When Joseph and Lucien protested, Napoleon, the former great Corsican patriot, accused them of not being proper Frenchmen! Indignantly, Joseph asked him if he imagined that Marie de Medici spoke French impeccably, or that Henry of Navarre – '*eung de nos meilleurrs rrrois*', as he mimicked – spoke with anything but the strongest meridional accent. Each of the brothers, as Roederer recounts in his journal, reacted in his own way against Napoleon's pretensions and his insistence on etiquette : Louis, grudgingly, like a schoolboy before his headmaster; Lucien always insisting on being treated as a brother and not as some junior official; Joseph, though more outspokenly critical than the other, usually finally acceding to his brother's wishes.[9]

When on 2 August 1802 Napoleon was proclaimed Consul for Life and empowered by the Senate to appoint his own successor, the thorny question of a 'dauphin' became even more accentuated. Julie was once again expecting a child and the whole Bonaparte clan awaited with impatience to learn whether this time she would give birth to a boy or a girl. If Joseph, the eldest of the family, was to have a son, surely Napoleon would recognize him as his heir instead of the little Charles-Napoleon, the son of Louis and Hortense? The question, however, did not arise. On 31 October Julie gave birth to her fourth daughter, Charlotte. Napoleon, well aware of Joseph's hopes, wrote to him maliciously : 'My congratulations to Madame Joseph. She makes such beautiful girls that it will recompense her for not having a son.' Considering that two of 'the beautiful girls' had died in infancy, the letter was less than kind.

For the Bonaparte clan, the following year 1803 was one of marriages, thwarted ambitions and continual bickerings. There was no longer the slightest doubt that the Consulate would soon be trans-formed into an hereditary monarchy. Royalists who had once enter-tained hopes that it was Napoleon's intention to restore the Bourbons, as General Monck had once restored Charles II to the throne of England, had long since been undeceived. If Napoleon, however, was bent on establishing a hereditary monarchy, then what more natural than to appoint one of his family as heir apparent? Joseph became obsessed with the question of succession. He certainly had no wish to become an emperor or a king – this is clear from his subsequent behaviour – but should Napoleon die or be assassinated without appointing an heir, it would almost certainly lead to a restoration of the Bourbons, or at the worst a return to Jacobin rule and the Terror, and the end of the Bonaparte family. Joseph now began hinting that it was high time for Napoleon to divorce Josephine, a view which was shared by most of the family.

Joseph's obsession with Napoleon's refusal to name an heir was not his only worry at this time. Pauline, or Paulette as the family usually called her, the prettiest and most frivolous of his sisters, had come to live with him at the Hôtel Marbeuf on her return from San Domingo, where her unfortunate husband Leclerc had died a few months previously. Paulette, as Joseph soon realized, was becoming increasingly bored with her status as a sorrowing widow. Already there was talk of various lovers. Before she could compromise her family too far, it was essential to find her a suitable husband. Fortunately a certain Florentine diplomat, the Cavaliere Angiolini, whom Joseph had known in Rome, was at this time visiting Paris in the entourage of the immensely wealthy Prince Camillo Borghese. Don Camillo, Prince of Sulmona, Rossaro, Vivaro, Duce de Ceri, Poggio Nativo, Baron Crapolatri, etc., etc., commended himself to Joseph as a highly desirable brother-in-law, not only because he was the richest man in Italy, but also because he was an avowed Jacobin who had fought alongside Championnet when the latter had liberated the Kingdom of the Two Sicilies to form the Parthenopian Republic. Angiolini promised to act as marriage broker. The Prince, far from raising any objections to the match, was overwhelmed with the honour of being invited to become the brother-in-law of the First Consul, and almost from the first meeting with Paulette was head over heels in love with her. Paulette for her part had no objection to marrying this wealthy and handsome prince; indeed, the sooner the better.

The marriage was celebrated in the chapel of Mortefontaine on 28 August. Although Napoleon was happy to have a 'real prince' in the family, he was angry with Joseph for arranging this precipitate marriage, which contravened Article 228 of the Civil Code stipulating that a widow might only contract a second marriage nine months after the death of her first husband; also because the wedding had been celebrated almost clandestinely while he was absent on a military tour of inspection in Holland and Belgium. Napoleon, however, soon forgave Joseph, and after a civil wedding held on 5 November the young couple left for Rome. Napoleon wrote to Paulette from Boulogne: 'Love your husband, bring happiness to your house and, above all, don't be frivolous or capricious . . . I love you and will always be glad to hear that you are happy.'

Alas, Pauline lived up to none of these precepts and within a year was complaining that she would sooner be the 'widow of General Leclerc with a pension of 20,000 livres than be the wife of a eunuch'. Though he dearly loved Paulette, Napoleon indulged in one of his famous rages when he learnt that she wished to return to Paris without Camillo. 'As far as Paris is concerned,' he wrote, 'I assure you will find no support here and I will never receive you without your husband . . . If you quarrel with your husband, it is entirely your own fault, and France will be forbidden to you.' Neither Joseph nor Letizia could reconcile the unhappy couple.

A much more serious family quarrel was that which followed the news of Lucien's clandestine marriage to his mistress Alexandrine Jouberthon, the widow of a bankrupt financier, who too had died from cholera during the disastrous expedition to San Domingo. Lucien first met Alexandrine in 1802, two years after the death of his wife Christine from puerperal poisoning. On 24 May 1803 Alexandrine bore Lucien a child, Jules-Laurence-Julien, but the marriage was not celebrated until 26 October. Napoleon's relations with Lucien had been constantly strained ever since the latter had been nominated Minister of the Interior, when he had deliberately allowed the premature circulation of a so-called anonymous pamphlet (written by Fontanes with Napoleon's full knowledge) which, in no uncertain terms, called on the First Consul to assume dictatorial powers.

It has been suggested that Lucien, the ardent Republican, deliberately allowed the premature promulgation of this pamphlet to discredit his brother. If this was his intention, he was certainly successful. Its publication roused all true Republicans to fury, and nowhere was resentment greater than in the army. Officers openly plotted in taverns and drank to the downfall of the tyrant. Appalled by the reaction this pamphlet had caused, Napoleon disclaimed any previous knowledge of its existence and told Fouché that he should have had Lucien shot for allowing its circulation. Lucien, however, was let off lightly. Although dismissed from his Ministry, he was appointed Ambassador to Madrid, where he did exceptionally well, both politically and financially; though most of the personal fortune which he brought back from his diplomatic mission, was, to his chagrin, promptly appropriated by Napoleon. Lucien's greatest achievement as Ambassador was the negotiation of the secret Treaty of San' Ildefonso, whereby Spain ceded part of Louisiana to France. When in 1803 Napoleon sold the whole of the territory to the United States for 70 million francs, Lucien was incensed. Relations between the two brothers remained extremely cool. Napoleon had never been able to forgive him for marrying Alexandrine Jouberthon, whom he refused to recognize. Lucien replied that he did not care one way or another whether his brother recognized his wife or not, and, in reference to Barras's part in Napoleon's own marriage, remarked that Alexandrine had neither brought him command of an army nor a dowry.

To Napoleon's fury, both Letizia and Joseph took the part of Lucien. Joseph was once more in disgrace and for months the two elder brothers were scarcely on speaking terms, while Lucien and his family, accompanied by Madame mère, retired into voluntary exile in Italy.

When, on 28 March 1804, Napoleon was proclaimed Emperor, Lucien was summoned to Saint-Cloud. Napoleon told him that he was prepared to accept him as his successor provided he renounced his son's right of primogeniture. Lucien categorically refused. 'My wife, myself and my son, are as one,' he exclaimed angrily. 'You too married a widow, but mine is neither old nor does she stink . . . It is more honourable to marry one's own mistress than marry the mistress of another . . . You want to destroy the Republic; so be it. Raise yourself up on its corpse . . . But the Empire which you wish to uphold by violence, will itself be destroyed by violence.'[10] Prophetic words!

The breach between the two brothers was not healed for another eleven years.

Immediately following the Peace of Amiens, Napoleon's popularity had never been higher, but now his increasing ambition had swung popular opinion in the opposite direction. With the muzzling of the press and universal censorship, overt criticism was impossible. Miot, Comte de Melito, writes in his memoirs:

> The return of a monarchy was distasteful to everybody, but the proposal to establish an hereditary line, was regarded in quite a different light, and I must admit, that on the whole, it seemed more reassuring than alarming. NOT THAT ANY PERSONAL AFFECTION TOWARDS THE FIRST CONSUL disposed the people to look favourably on this fresh accession of greatness to himself or his family, FOR NEVER HAD HE BEEN MORE DISLIKED [*Miot's capitals*]. There was such pressing need for stability and peace, the future looked so gloomy, the general apprehension so great, the return of the Bourbons with so many injuries to avenge was so dreaded, that the Senate and Tribunate eagerly strove to avert the danger against which they themselves felt defenceless.[11]

The return of the Bourbons was obviously something that all Republicans feared. Napoleon's abduction and brutal murder of the Duc d'Enghien on 21 March 1804 produced no popular outburst of indignation comparable to the Dreyfus affair many years later.

The Peace of Amiens was not to last long. In 1802 Napoleon had incorporated Piedmont into France without compensating the King of Sardinia as had been promised, and had annexed the island of Elba. He had particularly irritated the English by refusing to evacuate Holland and, with tactics reminiscent of Hitler, had intervened in the constitution of Switzerland. On the pretext of terminating internal Swiss feuds, he had threatened to send in General Ney, with fourteen battalions, to keep internal order. Under the threat of invasion, Switzerland virtually became a French dependency. There are many French historians who claim that the rupture of the Treaty of Amiens is to be blamed on Pitt. Under the treaty, the British were obliged to evacuate Malta and hand the island back to the Knights of Saint John. This, however, Pitt refused to do so long as France's expansion beyond her natural borders continued. On 11 March 1803 Napoleon wrote to the Tsar of Russia and the King of Prussia seeking their support to oust the British from the island. On the same day, he ordered the French fleet to be assembled at Dunkirk and Cherbourg in preparation for an invasion of England and Ireland. On 13 March he had a violent altercation with Lord Whitworth, the British Ambassador, who left Paris on 12 May. On the 16th Britain declared war.

Throughout the year 1803 France was fully occupied in planning the invasion of England. Napoleon's frame of mind was well described by the French historian Thiers : 'Now all of a sudden he was mastered by a patriotic and at the same time personal wrath, and from now on to conquer, humiliate, trample down and annihilate England became the passion of his life.'[12]

In June, Mortier occupied Hanover and disarmed the Hanoverian army. In the same month five assembly camps were formed for the invasion of England and Ireland; in August the main invasion camps were formed at Saint-Omer and Bruges, and flotillas were concentrated at Ambleteuse, Wimereux, Boulogne and Étaples.

Joseph continued to pester his brother concerning his succession. He had refused to accept the title of Prince of Piedmont and would be content with nothing less than to be proclaimed officially his brother's heir. In 1804 there were more Royalist plots against Napoleon's life. Cadoudal, 'le Grand Georges', leader of the Breton Royalists, Pichegru and Moreau were all implicated; Cadoudal was executed, Pichegru died in prison under the most suspicious circumstances (it was said that he had committed suicide, but he was almost certainly strangled); Moreau, who was accused of plotting to kidnap Napoleon, was brought to trial. However, such were the demonstrations in Moreau's favour, that, guilty or not – his guilt was never satisfactorily established – it would have been impossible to have had him condemned to the scaffold; instead, he was banished to America on 24 June.

These plots against Napoleon's life emphasized more than ever the very real need for the appointment of a successor. Joseph redoubled his efforts to persuade his brother to name him as his heir.

The detractors of the Bonaparte family had no need to point out the obvious anomaly of the situation: here was the eldest brother, the head of the Bonaparte family, soliciting his junior to provide him with the rights of succession. Although Joseph had no political ambitions, he was still titular head of the Bonaparte clan and, unless his brother produced a son and heir, it was only right that should Napoleon predecease him, he should assume his mantle. In his own mind, he was quite convinced that Napoleon would never father a son so long as Josephine was his wife. When Napoleon was proclaimed Emperor, Joseph told him categorically that he would never assume the title of Prince unless he was declared his heir and would forbid Julie to bear the train of the Empress at the forthcoming coronation.

Napoleon was deeply wounded. Unable to overcome his brother's obstinacy, he appealed to Roederer, one of Joseph's most devoted friends, to bring about a reconciliation. Roederer's attempts to patch up the quarrel were unsuccessful. In his memoirs he writes that Joseph was so infuriated by Napoleon's policies, that, unlike his usual gentle self, he was apt to fly into the most violent rages. 'I want Napoleon to realize', Joseph shouted, 'that there are some people who are not prepared to surrender to his caprices. If he should once more plunge Europe into a bloody war which he could well avoid, I will reunite all Frenchmen who still remain friends of liberty to prevent such tyranny.'[13]

On one occasion Joseph seized a pistol and fired it at a full-length portrait of his brother, shouting abuse at the image of the 'tyrant'. Napoleon was astute enough to realize that although Joseph could still be a formidable opponent of his own ambitions and that his influence in the Senate was considerable, he was nevertheless susceptible to flattery. He therefore sought a means of ridding himself, at least temporarily, of his tiresome elder brother who 'talks of nothing but my death'.

In the Organic Articles drawn up by the Senate, Joseph was declared the Emperor's heir, but this was completely nullified by an additional clause which stipulated that the Emperor could adopt as his successor one of his brother's sons. To Joseph, Napoleon made it quite clear that a new dynasty could only be founded on 'military glory', and that if Joseph still wished to lay claim to the succession he could only do so by learning how to command an army – something which could only be achieved by experience and not from textbooks. 'With some naïvety,' writes Girod de l'Ain, 'Joseph allowed himself to be convinced', and thus, on 18 April 1804 (i.e. a month before Napoleon was officially proclaimed Emperor), the *Senat Conservateur* received a letter from the First Consul in which he wrote :

> Senator Joseph Bonaparte, Grand Officer of the Legion of Honour, has expressed to me his wish to share in the dangers of the army encamped on the shores of Boulogne so that he can participate in its glory . . .
>
> Having already served under my own eyes during the first campaigns of the war and having given proof of his courage and ability in the art of war as a *chef de bataillon*, I have nominated him *Colonel Commandant* of the 4th Regiment of the Line, one of the most distinguished corps of the army, which can be counted among those which, always placed in the most dangerous positions, has never lost one of its standards and has often retrieved or decided a victory.
>
> In consequence, I desire that the Senate agrees to the demand made by Senator Joseph Bonaparte to absent himself from all deliberations of the Senate while his military service retains him in the army.[14]

Could the Senate really believe in 'the proofs of courage' shown by Joseph at Toulon, or assume that the heroic conduct of the 4th Regiment of the Line in days past reflected any credit on its new colonel, or that this newly-appointed colonel was about to face the 'dangers' of the army encamped at Boulogne?

The reply of the Senate to the First Consul was a model of grandiloquence and flattery: 'Like all France, the whole of Europe views with joy that your family is following in the footsteps of your glorious career and is summoned today to mould the destiny of the world.'

An order of the day, signed by Soult, Commander-in-Chief of the Army of Boulogne, dated 10 Floréal, Year XII (30 April 1804), announced that Citizen Joseph Bonaparte had arrived on the previous evening at Pont de Briques.

> *The highest honours* due to his rank as brother of the First Consul, and as senator and Grand officer of the Legion of Honour were accorded to him . . . The Army will appreciate the *honour* which the Government has bestowed on it by appointing one of the most important personages of the state to command one of its most distinguished corps . . .

So long as the problem of the succession was not yet settled, Joseph continued to be obsessed by the subject of inheritance. There was a strange dichotomy in Joseph's character. Fundamentally he was an honest democrat; although he despised his brother for his imperial pretensions, he certainly enjoyed all the advantages and riches which Napoleon's position brought to him. However much he might insist to his 'philosophic' and liberal friends that he despised titles and honours, and that he was a true Republican at heart, and although continually complaining of Napoleon and his policies, he accepted from him not only the sinecure appointment of Grand Elector at a salary of 333,333 francs per annum, with a sumptuous apartment in the Luxembourg, but also that of *Senatorerie de Bruxelles* with a palace and an honorarium of 24,727 francs and a further 200,000 francs as Grand Officer of the Legion of Honour.

As though this was not enough, Joseph wrote to Julie on 14 May:

If my brother does not do for me what he promised when I agreed to leave for the army, which my confidence and affection merit; if there are any concessions or restrictions to be made, then I think, *ma chère amie*, we ought not to sacrifice our happiness and that of our children. The simplest thing would be to return to Mortefontaine and our friends, or, should this prove impossible, to live elsewhere. To sacrifice one's tastes and affections in return for nothing, in exchange for eventual power and the consequent annoyance resulting from disappointed hopes, is to behave like a fool or an intrigant. Nature has endowed me with no ambition.[15]

It is difficult to understand what Joseph implies by 'sacrifice'. It was scarcely a sacrifice to be named his brother's heir presumptive, since this was something that he had been demanding for months; and what can he mean by the 'annoyances resulting from disappointed hopes'?

This letter was obviously meant to be seen by Napoleon – not that it would have made the slightest difference. During Joseph's absence in Boulogne the *senatus consultum* had already added the fatal clause allowing Napoleon to appoint one of his brother's sons as his heir. Still in Joseph's absence, Napoleon was proclaimed Emperor of the French on 18 May, but it was not until 22 November that Joseph, with a fine pretence of reluctance, accepted the title of Serene Imperial Highness, Prince Joseph-Napoleon, with an additional allowance of 350,000 francs a year. All in all, he had not done too badly.

Joseph in his memoirs, written thirty years later, says little about his military service at Boulogne :

> I was nearly forty years of age at the time. All my life had been spent in civil functions, except for a few months during the first Italian campaign. I felt certain repugnance at being made a colonel, but once I had arrived at the camp, I soon felt at home. I appreciated the importance of learning details of the service from veteran colonels with experience and whose reputation was already established. The First Consul spent some time at the camp. I was not long in following him to Paris, where he awaited the results of the continual renascent machinations of the enemies of the Revolution, both within and without France.[16]

Joseph then goes on to recount at length the plots of Pichegru, Moreau and the murder of the Duc d'Enghien. He attributes the abduction and execution of the latter to a mistake on the part of the Comte Réal, though at the time he and the whole Bonaparte family were horrified by Napoleon's action, for which his mother never forgave him.

Joseph's short term of military service in Boulogne, according to General Bigarré, was by no means inactive. He took part in embarkation exercises and was present at an exchange of fire between British frigates and French gunboats. Joseph appears to have been popular with the men and to have been instrumental, at least in part, in establishing good relations between soldiers and sailors, previously very strained.

He refused to be accommodated in a special house which had been built and furnished for him, but shared quarters similar to those of other officers. Since wives and mistresses were not admitted to the camp, it was in the hospitable houses of Boulogne, Dunkirk and neighbouring villages that the military, when not engaged on exercises, found distraction. Joseph, who on this occasion was not accompanied by Julie, soon found consolation in the arms of 'a charming lady from Dunkirk, named Madame F . . ., an excellent musician, full of gaiety, grace and youth', according to Constant, Napoleon's *valet de chambre.* The name of this lady was Fagan; she was known to have already seduced Soult, the Commander-in-Chief, Generals Saint-Hilary and Andréossy and several other important persons, but of these, writes Constant, she loved only two – Soult and Joseph . . .

> . . . but this rivalry was in no way prejudicial to Madame F . . . A clever tactician, she adroitly provoked the jealousy of her two lovers,

by accepting turn and turn about, compliments and bouquets of roses (or sometimes something even better) from each in turn. One evening when Madame F . . . was holding her usual court on the first floor of her house in the rue des Minimes, where people were gaily chatting and gaming, two bourgeois, wearing wigs and spectacles, were introduced to the mistress of the house by a certain Commissaire-ordinateur named Arcambal, as two war commissaries. After mixing with the guests and engaging in polite conversation, they were about to take their leave, when Madame F . . . begged the two 'commissaries' to stay, telling them that there was to be dancing and some innocent childish games. Having lost one such game, one of the 'commissaries' was obliged to pay a forfeit by acting as 'door-keeper' while the winner retired to Madame F . . .'s room for *'un voyage à Cythère'*. When the lovers returned, apparently highly satisfied with each other, the 'door-keeper' asked permission to leave with his friend. A few moments later, the artisan who lived on the ground floor brought Madam F . . . a note, which made her blush with pleasure :

> Thank you, Madame, for the kind reception which you accorded me. If one day you would like to visit my humble quarters [*baraque*], I will once again act as a door-keeper should you think fit, but this time I won't allow anyone else to accompany you on the *voyage à Cythère*.
>
> (Signed) BONAPARTE

Without disclosing the contents of this note, Madame F . . . could not resist revealing the true identity of the so-called commissary to her guests.[17]

One wonders how Constant had access to this note. Girod de l'Ain writes in his recent biography of Joseph :

> If this flattering conquest was no more than a passing *affaire* as far as Joseph was concerned, this is not to say that it did not have far-reaching and aggravating consequences in time to come. Is it not possible that Marshal Soult's attitude to Joseph in Andalusia in the summer of 1812, was the revengeful act of a jealous lover who had been made a cuckold?[18]

Madame Fagan was by no means the only woman whose favours Joseph was to enjoy while in Boulogne. There was Madame Regnault de Saint-Jean-d'Angely, the wife of his friend, the *ci-devant* Comte and man of letters, and Mademoiselle Le Gros of the Théâtre Français; there was also a certain 'Adèle', whose identity remains a mystery. All we know from her letters is that she was the wife of a junior officer. There was also another woman, a certain 'V . . . s', about whom we know nothing. It is only recently that knowledge of Joseph's love life in Boulogne has come to light. Throughout his life, Joseph seldom destroyed correspondence, even though this was often of the most compromising nature.

When on 21 July 1813 Joseph, King of Spain, was forced to flee from the battlefield of Vitoria on horseback, abandoning his private coach and wagons to the English, he left behind, not only the treasure of the royal palaces of Madrid, but also his personal possessions. The Duke of Wellington restored everything to the Spanish, with the exception of the paintings now gracing Apsley House, which the grateful Ferdinand VII presented to him as a gift. The Duke, however, did retain for himself as a souvenir a case, of not very great value as he imagined, which he believed to contain pistols, but which in fact contained hundreds of letters, mostly from Julie, some from other members of his family and others from his mistresses. Forgotten for years in an attic, these were found by the seventh Duke, who on the advice of the French ambassador at the time, Monsieur Massigli, generously presented them to the Institut de France in 1954. It is thanks to M. Girod de l'Ain, who has had access to these letters, that we now know so much of Joseph's amorous intrigues.

Joseph could never resist a pretty woman, and very few pretty women seemed to have been able to resist Joseph. Napoleon, who was kept constantly informed of Joseph's every action, often reprimanded him for his infidelities to Julie, but since the First Consul's own affairs at this time with Madame Duchâtel, the young wife of an elderly Councillor of State, with Eleanore de la Plaigne and other young charmers, were no secret, he was scarcely in a position to criticize his elder brother's moral behaviour.

Once Napolean had instituted what he called the 'System', he insisted that his family should only consort with the nobility.[19] That Louis should marry Hortense was perfectly in order : she was, after all, his own stepchild and the daughter of a count; but, as we have seen, he was furious when Lucien married the bourgeoise Madame Jouberthon, and wished him to obtain a divorce and marry Marie-Louise, Queen Regent of Etruria, the widow of Ludovico I; he insisted that the marriage of his youngest brother Jerome, the nineteen-year-old midshipman, to the Boston beauty Miss Paterson should be annulled so that he could marry Princess Catherine of Württemberg. Joseph, despite his constant infidelities, would never discard Julie, whom he truly loved.

Having at last agreed to accept the title of Prince, Joseph left Boulogne for Paris on 8 August for his official investiture. As his apartments in the Luxembourg were not yet prepared for him, the representatives of the Senate, *Corps legislatif* and the Tribune came to pay their respects to the Grand Elector, His Imperial Highness Prince Joseph-Napoleon Bonaparte at the Hôtel Marbeuf.

François de Neufchâteau, a former member of the Directoire, acted as spokesman for the Senate: 'We all know His Royal Highness's love of simplicity . . . For him true grandeur consists in being useful to his fellow men and the most flattering tribute we can bestow on him is to recognize the good that he does.' Fontanes now in turn spoke for the *Corps legislatif*: 'How could the French people have done other than place at their head a family in which are combined the art of conquest and the art of government, a talent for negotiation, eloquence, heroism, grace, wit and charm . . .'

Napoleon, to whom these speeches were reported, was none too pleased to be placed in the same category as a mere diplomat. He was also unreasonably irritated that Joseph failed to appreciate the court costume he was obliged to wear, which he had had designed by David, and which consisted of a white silk tunic embroidered and fringed with gold lace and a flame-coloured[20] cloak reaching to the ground, lined with ermine. The *petite-tenue*, so called, consisted of an embroidered velvet tunic over which was worn a gold baldric with dress sword and a shorter cloak, also flame-coloured, embroidered with gold bees, and a lace cravat. In both cases the costume was completed by a hat with a turned-up brim, *à la Henri Quatre*, secured by a jewelled clasp surmounted by white ostrich plumes.

Although Joseph had now accepted the title of Imperial Royal Highness for life and on official occasions wore what he regarded as ridiculous fancy costume, he made no secret of the fact that he regarded the whole situation as absurd – except that his emoluments were enormous. The creation of all these new Imperial titles struck him as utterly ridiculous. Louis a Grand Constable indeed! Cambacérès, Arch-Chancellor; Lebrun, Arch-Treasurer! And in addition there was a Grand Almoner, a Grand Marshal of the Palace, a Grand Master of the Hunt, a Grand Master of Ceremonies and a Grand Chamberlain (Talleyrand) together with Chamberlains and Almoners-in-ordinary (including two bishops), two masters of horse, with the medieval titles of *Écuyers cavalcadours*, pages and heralds at arms, etc., etc. Perhaps, of all, the most absurd was the title of Grand Admiral bestowed on the cavalry general Murat.

Napoleon insisted that his family should maintain households on an equally royal scale to that of his own. In one of his perpetual quarrels with Joseph, he had said: 'My household is yours. It should only be filled with soldiers and former noblemen. There are still enough fine names around to fill your needs.' Joseph, as usual, made pretence of falling in with his brother's requirements, but nevertheless filled his 'court' with people of his own choice. For example, as lady-in-waiting to Julie he appointed Madame Louis de Girardin, a divorcee and woman of advanced liberal ideals – in short, the sort of woman Napoleon detested most – and, as maids of honour, he appointed Mmes Miot, Bolgarde and Dessoles, all of whom were of the bourgeoisie. His first chamberlain was his old friend Jaucourt, who, although a real marquis of the *vieille noblesse*, was a former Jacobin, a Protestant who had recently married his ex-mistress, the Duchesse de la Châtre. His second chamberlain was another old friend, General Mathieu Dumas, well known for his liberal views and a former Councillor of State and ex-member of the Legislature. As equerries he chose his devoted friend Stanislas de Girardin, once a rabid Jacobin, who had joined the army as a captain to be at Joseph's side while he was in Boulogne, and two well-known liberals, Colonels Cavaignac and Lafon-Blaniac, both Gascons, recommended by Murat. As his chaplain he chose another notorious liberal, an ex-constituent abbé named Villaret, now Bishop of Casal.

These appointments provoked another quarrel between the brothers even more violent than usual. So bitter was the row this time, that Joseph threatened to resign from all his functions and retire to Germany. Napoleon, it is said, was so upset that he could not sleep for six days, but as usual the quarrel was patched up. Nevertheless, the Emperor was determined to wean Joseph away from his liberal views and somehow convert him to the Imperial System. He had already won over many adherents from among his critics by creating them members of the Legion of Honour and had placated his generals by instituting the marshalship. Since all else had failed with Joseph, he would have to make him a king.

Plans in the meantime were going ahead for the *Sacre* and Coronation. Joseph was persuaded to return to Paris on 5 Frimaire (27 November) for a dinner at Fontainebleau held in honour of the Pope on the day following the arrival of His Holiness. Julie and Uncle Fesch were also present at this banquet, which was followed by a concert which the Pope declined to attend. His Holiness in fact was deeply offended, not merely because of the astonishing reception he had received, in which the mere honours due to a temporal sovereign had been paid, to the exclusion of all recognition of him as the Supreme Pontiff and head of the Catholic Church, but because every breach of papal etiquette and protocol had been committed.

Joseph was involved in another farce on 1 December, on the eve of the Consecration, when as Grand Elector he ushered the Senate in a body into the Throne Room. The purpose of this was to announce the result of the plebiscite, something which could have been done in a few words, since the Imperial Government had already been in existence for six months. François de Neufchâteau, who presided, reaffirmed in a long and wordy speech that the Emperor held his position only from the sovereign power of the people. He proclaimed that the object of the plebiscite had been 'to introduce into the government by a single man, principles which would safeguard the interests of all, and give to the Republic the strength of the Republic'. Napoleon, by an extraordinary anomaly, was *de facto*, if not *de jure* Emperor of a Republic. Right up to 1807, Imperial decrees bore the formula : 'Napoleon by the grace of God and the *Constitution of the Republic, etc.*' It was only after 1807 that the word 'Republic' disappeared from the coinage, at the same time as the Republican calendar was abolished.

The Coronation, which for theatrical flummery could not be paralleled, duly took place on 2 December. Madame mère and Lucien refused to attend. Jerome was serving at sea.[21] Joseph and Louis, in their absurd costumes, drove to Notre-Dame in the same coach as Napoleon and Josephine, a coach which had never been equalled in magnificence and ostentation.[22]

Joseph had finally agreed to allow Julie to act as train-bearer to Josephine, together with Hortense, Élise, Caroline and Pauline, who performed their duties as perfunctorily as possible. The mass concluded, the Pope, the cardinals and the priests of his train retired to the vestry. Here the Grand Almoner, standing beside the Emperor, held open the Gospels. In the presence of the *Corps legislatif* and Council of State, Joseph unrolled the text of the oath before the Emperor. With one hand on the Gospels, Napoleon repeated the oath in a low voice :

I swear to maintain the territory of the *Republic* in its integrity; to respect and enforce the laws of the Concordat and Freedom of Worship; to respect and enforce Equality before the Law, political and civil liberty and the irreversibility of the sales of National Property; to impose no duty or tax except according to law; and to govern only in accordance with the interests, happiness and glory of the French people.

Joseph in his memoirs tells us nothing of what he thought of all this, but it is not difficult to guess. 'If only our father could have seen us,' Napoleon whispered to him during the ceremony. Although Joseph had fulfilled his duties as Grand Elector and had conformed to all his brother's wishes during the coronation ceremonies, as indeed had the former Jacobin marshals who carried the imperial regalia, he continued to irritate his brother by mixing with the liberal opposition.

At the time of the Coronation the Cisalpine Republic of north Italy was declared a monarchy. There was not even the pretence that the newly-conquered territory was to remain a republic. Reluctantly Count Melzi, Vice-President of the Republic, came to Paris to ask Napoleon to appoint a king. Who more suitable than Joseph? But as soon as Joseph learnt that to accept the crown of Lombardy meant renouncing any claims to become Napoleon's heir, he declined. In vain Napoleon tried to bribe him with a gift of 200,000 francs. Joseph pocketed the money but refused the throne. Not unnaturally there were further quarrels. Napoleon then turned to Louis. He proposed that Louis's son, the infant Napoleon-Charles, should be proclaimed King and that Louis should act as regent until the boy became of age. But Louis refused to act as second fiddle to his son, whose parentage he again disputed. Lucien and Jerome were both still in disgrace, the former for marrying Madame Jouberthon, the latter for marrying Betty Paterson, whose marriage was not yet annulled. Both were therefore ineligible. Caroline was naturally anxious that her husband Murat should be chosen – he was after all one of the family. It was he who had borne the crown on its cushion during the ceremony of the *Sacre*. Napoleon indeed considered this possibility but, after discussions with Count Melzi and other Italian statesmen, it was decided that the dashing Gascon had made too many enemies in Italy to be acceptable. There was nothing left except to crown himself King of Italy with the iron crown of Lombardy and appoint his stepson, young Eugène de Beauharnais, as Viceroy.

The incorporation of northern Italy under the direct rule of the Emperor led to immediate political repercussions. Perhaps Austria would have accepted Joseph as King, but Napoleon never. A new Austro-Russian coalition was formed: war was inevitable.

Before setting out for Milan, accompanied by Josephine, for the coronation ceremonies, Napoleon had a further interview with Joseph. On 31 March 1805 the two brothers met at Fontainebleau, where again their differences were patched up. Bored with camp life in Boulogne, Joseph requested to be relieved of his duties. Napoleon, anxious to placate him, authorized him to make a tour of inspection

119

of the frontier fortresses of Belgium and the Rhine. Joseph was delighted with the prospect of change from regular military duties. On 14 April he arrived at Brussels, where he was received with all due pomp and ceremony in his new rank of Imperial Highness. He took the opportunity of taking possession of his *senatorerie*, and, in his capacity of Grand Elector, presided over the Electoral College of the Dijl. On the 29th he was in Dunkirk. From here he wrote to his brother describing the pomp with which he had been greeted. 'Almost a thousand horsemen, consisting of mayors and notabilities of all sorts, came out from miles around to meet me . . . Ghent, Bruges and Ostend and this town [Dunkirk] all seemed to show the same warmth of heart as I remarked among the inhabitants of Brussels and Antwerp.'[23]

Once his triumphal progress had been accomplished, Joseph returned to the camp of Boulogne, where he was received with all the ceremony due to a Prince of the Blood (though this was a title he never assumed) and where he distributed largesse to the troops, an act which considerably annoyed Napoleon.

After spending almost a fortnight at the camp of Boulogne, he left again on 11 May for Saint-Omer, Arras, Douai, Lille, Mainz, Hüningen, Neu-Brisbach and Strasbourg. He often made these last visits incognito, so that he could inspect these frontier strongposts of the Empire objectively. Murat had also been sent on a similar mission to the Black Forest, also incognito. How either could have passed for other than what they were, is impossible to imagine, especially the flamboyant Gascon. On 30 May Joseph was joined at Nancy by Julie and Désirée who had just spent their annual cure at the waters of Plombières. Although Joseph's commission as Colonel of the 4th Regiment of the Line had never in effect been officially revoked, he decided he had now had enough of military life and, without asking leave of anyone, left for Mortefontaine. His commanding officer, the thirty-two-year-old General Salligny, was scarcely in a position to reprimand His Serene Imperial Highness for dereliction of duty, especially since Joseph gave one of his famous receptions in honour of the general's marriage to Julie's niece.

Although Napoleon, on his return from his coronation at Milan, was none too pleased with Joseph's behaviour, he as usual soon forgave his brother. He even forgave Pauline, who despite his orders had returned to France and was staying with Joseph. Her husband the Prince Borghese, from whom she was only too pleased to be separated, was appointed to the Army at Boulogne.

On 30 August 1805 this magnificent army, which for two years had been training for the invasion of England, was now to be withdrawn to face the new menace formed by the Austro-Russian coalition in the east.

Joseph was the first to be informed of this change of plans. He was utterly opposed to another Continental war and did not hesitate to air his views. Napoleon, however, was determined on war and appointed Joseph his Regent while he took command of the armies, but entrusted Cambacérès with the administration of the country in his absence. Joseph's views however were sufficiently well known for Lucchiesi, the Prussian Minister in Paris, to write to his government: '*Les amis de l'ordre et des idées sages, croiraient trouver le complement des bienfaits de la Providence si la mort de Napoléon pouvait mettre le Prince Joseph à sa place.*' In other words, all sane thinking Frenchmen would be happy if a merciful providence would remove Napoleon from the scene so that Joseph could take his place.

VIII

King of the Two Sicilies

1805–1808

Once Napoleon had left for Germany at the head of his armies, Joseph took up residence in the now refurbished Luxembourg, very different in style from the Republican austerity which had characterized the palace during its occupation by the Directoire. Receptions, ballets and concerts were the order of the day. Although France was suffering from severe economic depression, Joseph's apologists explain his prodigality by the fact that he was determined to divert public attention from the real situation affecting the country. Certainly Cambacérès did nothing to dissuade him from setting an example to Paris of luxury and lavish expenditure. Although it was Cambacérès who assumed the main political responsibilities, it was Joseph who acted as 'public relations officer'; it was he who was responsible for recruitment and for issuing the almost daily bulletins announcing victories to the sound of salvos of artillery and the peal of church bells. But even these reassuring bulletins were insufficient to prevent a run on the banks. On one occasion as many as two thousand persons queued up at the Banque de France to change their paper money (in which they had lost all confidence) against gold. The defeat of the Franco-Spanish fleet on 21 October at Trafalgar had thoroughly alarmed the nation.

Fortunately on 12 December Colonel Lebrun, A.D.C. to the Emperor, brought news of the victory of Austerlitz (2 December) to Joseph as he sat with his family in his box at the Théâtre Français. He announced the news to a joyous audience. Confidence was almost immediately restored. Peace seemed imminent. Joseph himself authorized the *Moniteur* and the *Journal de Paris* to publish articles stating that Austrian plenipotentiaries were ready to discuss terms. On 13 December Napoleon wrote an angry letter to Joseph:

> You need not have announced so pompously that the enemy have sent plenipotentiaries . . . I did not think it worth putting into a bulletin, still less did it deserve to be mentioned in the theatres. The mere word *peace* means nothing; what we need is a *glorious* peace. Nothing could be more ill-conceived or more unpolitic than what [you] have just done in Paris.

Two days later, after Napoleon had received a letter from Joseph, dated 7 December, in which he told him that the people of Paris were clamouring for peace, the Emperor wrote again: 'I am not accustomed to let my policy be governed by the gossip of Paris and I am sorry that you attach so much importance to it.' Peace was signed at Presburg on 27 December, but on the very same day Napoleon issued a grandiloquently worded bulletin to the Army of Italy announcing his intention of reoccupying the Kingdom of the Two Sicilies:

> Soldiers! March; throw into the waves, if they wait for you, the weak battalions of the Tyrant of the Seas. Show the world how we punish treachery. Let me hear without delay that all Italy is subject to my authority or to that of my allies: that the finest of countries is relieved from the yoke of the most faithless of men: that the sacredness of treaties has been avenged: and that my brave soldiers, massacred in the ports of Sicily on their return from Egypt, after having escaped from the desert and a hundred battles, are at length avenged.
>
> Soldiers, my brother marches at your head. He knows my plans, he possesses my authority and my confidence. Give him yours.

At the same time he wrote again to Joseph: 'I shall remain here a few days to receive the ratification of the Treaty and to give the army its last orders . . .' and then, almost casually, in the next paragraph he continues:

> I intend to take possession of the Kingdom of Naples. Marshal Masséna and General Saint-Cyr are marching on that Kingdom with two *corps d'armée*. I have named you my Lieutenant, commander-in-chief of the Army of Naples.
>
> I wish you to set off for Rome forty hours after receipt of this letter and let your first despatch inform me that you have entered Naples, driven out the treacherous court and subjected that part of Italy to our authority . . . Your title as my Lieutenant gives you authority over the marshals . . . Do not tell anyone where you are going, except the Arch-Chancellor [Cambacérès].

Joseph was not altogether surprised. The treaty of neutrality signed between Naples and France on 8 October had been flagrantly violated. No sooner had the French troops occupying the Kingdom of the Two Sicilies been withdrawn, than a mixed force of 12,000 Montenegrins (for the purpose named 'Russians'), 8,000 British and a handful of Paolist Corsicans and French émigrés landed at Naples at the invitation of Queen Marie-Caroline, the true ruler of the Two Sicilies. After the shattering victory over the Austro-Russian army at Austerlitz, the 'Russians' withdrew to the Ionian islands while the British retreated across the straits of Messina to Sicily. But as long as British and Russian forces remained in the heel of Italy, they represented a serious threat. The conquest of the Two Sicilies was essential to Napoleon's policy if the British were to be prevented from completely dominating the Mediterranean.

For once, Joseph had no hesitation in obeying his brother's imperious orders. Talleyrand, who of course was in the secret (indeed, was there any time when the wily ex-bishop was not *au fait* with Napoleon's plans?), had warned Joseph that this time the Emperor would never forgive him, would even exile him if he refused to comply with his demands. On 19 January the Emperor wrote to Joseph from Stuttgart :

> I wish you to enter the Kingdom of Naples in the first days of February . . . You will make no truce, you will hear of no capitulation. My will is that the Bourbons shall have ceased to reign at Naples. I intend to seat on that throne a Prince of my own House – first of all you, if not, another . . .

Joseph set out for Rome immediately, leaving Julie, who was ill, at Mortefontaine. He would have liked her to accompany him to share in his new-found glory. But Julie, who unlike her Bonaparte sisters-in-law hated pomp and ceremony and who took her husband's tirades against titles and honours seriously, was relieved to have an excuse to remain at home. Napoleon was full of gratitude to his brother for obeying him so promptly. On his return to Paris on 27 January the Emperor wrote :

> My brother, – I reached Paris yesterday evening . . . I am delighted with everything that you did while you were at Paris. Receive my best thanks, and, as a proof of how well I am pleased, I shall send you by the first messenger my portrait on a snuff-box.
>   Hold a proper tone towards the army. Suffer no peculation. I hope that you are pleased with Masséna; if not, send him back. It seems

that the Queen of Naples has been trying to bribe him. Let nothing affect your plans. I reckon on your entering the kingdom of Naples the first week in February.

Today the Princess Julie and her children dine with me . . .

I hear that the court of Naples sends Cardinal Ruffo to me with propositions of peace. My orders are that he be not allowed to come to Paris. You must immediately commence hostilities, and make all your arrangements for taking immediate possession of the Kingdom of Naples without listening to any propositions of peace, armistice or suspension of arms – reject them all indiscriminately.

He also told Joseph that he had arranged an advantageous marriage for his eldest daughter, aged three, 'with a little prince who will one day be a great prince' (i.e. Charles-Napoleon, son of Louis and Hortense).

Delayed by snow on the Mont Cenis pass, Joseph only arrived in Turin on 18 January and reached Rome on the 23rd. He was received in audience by the Pope, with whom he signed a treaty whereby the Papal States were to provide him with supplies for the army. After three days in Rome he took nominal command of his troops – in fact commanded by Masséna – and left for the south. General Gouvion Saint-Cyr, the ice-cold calculating ex-artist, perhaps the strangest of all the Emperor's generals,[1] who had been in command of the French garrison of Naples for two years, furious at being superseded by Masséna, left in a huff for Paris. Masséna himself was displeased to be under the orders of Joseph, but was somewhat placated when Joseph constantly deferred to him and took his advice. The army consisted of three corps: 16,000 French troops under the direct command of Masséna, 13,000 under General Reynier and 7,000 Italian and 3,000 Poles under General Lechi.

On 8 and 9 February these three corps invaded the Kingdom of Naples. In vain Queen Caroline had begged the Emperor to show mercy, but nothing would deflect him from his purpose. '*Châtiez cette coquine*', he wrote to Joseph. The three corps continued their advance; the first towards Capua via Monte Cassino; the second by the Via Appiano along the coast; the third through the Abruzzi towards Aquila and the Adriatic. There was scarcely any resistance. The 30,000 Neapolitan regulars retreated into Calabria, and the 'masses', whom Queen Caroline had armed, made no attempt to rise in revolt.

On 12 February, the important fortress of Capua fired three rounds of cannon, for which on the following morning the governor made '*des excuses multipliées et très sérieuses*', as Joseph reported. Only

Gaeta, situated on the tip of a peninsula on the west coast, refused to surrender. Gaeta had the advantage of being supplied from the sea by the English fleet and commanded by Prince von Hesse-Philipstadt, a brave and stubborn German, and held out for six months before capitulating to Masséna with the honours of war.

It was at Gaeta that the French suffered the only two officially reported casualties during the course of their advance: General Brigny, whose head was blown off while he was making a reconnaissance, and a Captain Lamy, A.D.C. to General Reynier, who was shot by mistake when, under a flag of truce, he was sent to parley with the enemy, an action for which Prince von Hesse-Philipstadt apologized profusely.

Joseph was at Capua when he learnt that his advance guard had already occupied Naples without firing a shot. The Bourbons had fled across the straits of Messina to Palermo.

On 15 February Joseph, the lieutenant of the Emperor (for he was not yet proclaimed King), made his solemn entrance, under a hastily constructed triumphal arch, into his new capital to the sound of military bands, the peal of bells and salutes of cannon. The Senate presented him with the keys of the city. The crowds that turned out to watch this triumphal entry were curious rather than hostile. The *lazzarone*, whom Queen Caroline had armed, staged no demonstration; but if Joseph had expected to find a magnificent palace awaiting him he was to be disappointed. Queen Marie-Caroline had denuded the place of everything movable. All the furniture, even window frames, even the stores of wood for heating purposes, had been removed to Sicily with the aid of British ships, although a few of these were blown back by storms and fell into the hands of the French. Later it was discovered that even livestock from royal farms had been removed and that the arsenal was empty, as were the banks, from which almost all private funds had been removed.

On the 16th, the day after his arrival, Joseph wrote to Napoleon:

This Sunday morning I went to mass, which was celebrated by Cardinal Ruffo, archbishop of this city; I made a fine present to Saint Janvier [Januario]. There was a considerable crowd present who were unable to contain their joy when I placed a diamond necklace around the image of the Saint.

This way of gaining the esteem of his future subjects naturally seemed absurd to Napoleon. On 8 March he wrote to Joseph: 'It is not by flattering the people that you gain their sympathy.' Almost

126

every day Joseph was to receive letters from his brother in the same vein.

What neither Napoleon nor Joseph seemed to have realized was that the Kingdom of the Two Sicilies was an impoverished country and that the Emperor's system of levying taxes on the peoples of conquered territories was here quite impracticable. Joseph honestly did his best for his new subjects. On 29 March 1806 he wrote to his brother :

> I neglect no means to carry out your Majesty's orders, and if you allow me to continue in my own way, I hope to fulfil your intentions perfectly and arrive at the same ends though perhaps a little more slowly, but I will eventually get there with no difficulties and without the people grumbling at the methods I employ.

Joseph's optimism was unfounded. He discovered on his tours of Calabria and the Abruzzi, a land which instead of flowing with milk and honey, as poets had led him to believe, was a savage mountainous country unsuitable for agriculture, icy cold in winter and torrid in summer, populated by a people as savage in character as the landscape which surrounded them. Although at Casenza, the capital of Calabria, where he first learnt that Napoleon had proclaimed him King of the Two Sicilies (11 March 1806), 'he was greeted with extraordinary enthusiasm',[2] the peasantry were in fact already in revolt. Just as in Spain, later, the presence of Imperial troops brought insurrection.

Joseph, at the time, does not seem to have realized in the least what formidable opposition there was and in what danger he was placed. The military escort which preceded him along the coast road to Cosenza was not only harassed by partisans but came under fire from British warships stationed offshore.

However, during the first months of Joseph's reign, he did his utmost for his country. He suppressed feudalism, dissolved the all-too-powerful convents, sold crown lands, began to organize primary schools, founded universities, divided the kingdom into provinces administered on similar lines to those of French departments; he created a *corps législatif* and courts 'independent of the wishes of the Prince'. He was greatly helped in this work by those of his friends who had accompanied him from France : Miot, whom he appointed Minister of War; Roederer, Minister of Finance; and especially Saliceti, whom he made Minister of Police. He also did his best to create in Naples a centre of the arts and to make his theatre a rival to the Opéra of Paris. He built a triumphal road from Naples to Capodimonte which he named the Corso Napoleone and built the charming *Logetta a Mare*; he built viaducts and roads, and ordered a statue of the poet Torquato Tasso to be erected at Sorrento.

He was living in a cloud-cuckoo-land, as he was to do later in Spain. Even the capture of Capri by Sir Sidney Smith[3] on the day he was proclaimed King did not dishearten him too much. His budget on 26 February showed a deficit of 1,500,000 francs per month, which he naïvely thought Napoleon would adjust for him. Needless to say, Napoleon did nothing of the sort. The Emperor replied that he could expect no money from France and advised his brother to clap a tax of 30 millions on the wretched Neapolitans. On 31 May 1806 Napoleon wrote to him:

> My brother: I repeat that you must not trust these Neapolitans, especially in respect of your kitchen staff and personal guard, otherwise you run the risk of being poisoned or assassinated . . . Your *valet de chambre*, your cooks, the guards who sleep in your apartments, those who wake you in the middle of the night to bring you despatches, must all be French . . . Your door must be closed from the inside and you must not open it to your aide-de-camp until you are sure that you recognize his voice. These precautions are important. The character of the Neapolitans has been known ever since time immemorial and you have to deal with a woman who is crime personified.

In Naples itself all seemed quiet, but in the provinces, especially in Calabria, where Gaeta was still holding out against Masséna, there was revolt. On 1 July, a British force under General Stuart landed in the bay of Sant' Euphoria, better known to English readers as Maida Vale. Two days later, for the first time, a British force was confronted by the so far invincible veteran Napoleonic troops, commanded by General Reynier. The cliché of the 'thin red line', or in this case 'the two thin red lines', is no exaggeration. Thanks to the wonderful discipline of the British and their superior fire power, Stuart's troops achieved an overwhelming victory, a victory which might have been even more decisive had they had cavalry to follow up the routed enemy.

The battle of Maida, though a comparatively minor affair as far as numbers were concerned, had immense psychological repercussions. In England, this first victory over veteran troops of the Revolution was hailed with the utmost enthusiasm. How many Englishmen realize today that a whole district of London, Maida Vale, is named after General Stuart's victory? The new British military tactics gave

A portrait of
Marshal Bernadotte
by J. J. de Lose, 1805

An engraving
depicting a scene during
'el dos de Mayo', 1808

The flight of King Joseph
from Vitoria, 1813

A view of the
Palace of the Luxembourg
from the gardens

the army a fresh confidence which stood them in good stead later in Portugal, Spain, and at Waterloo. At the same time, Reynier's veteran troops – French, Swiss and Poles – were completely demoralized by their defeat, in which they lost 1,405 killed, 2,732 prisoners and 3,000 more sick, who had contracted malaria or dysentery during their month-long retreat to Naples. The Calabrian peasants, who hitherto had believed the French to be invincible, now took new heart and murdered every French soldier to fall into their hands.

This battle and the subsequent revolt in Calabria at last opened Joseph's eyes to the seriousness of his own position. Although affecting the greatest calm, he moved his court to Capodimonte, fearing that the English might make a landing in the Bay of Naples itself. Capri, only a few miles distant, was already in their hands, and it was only lack of cavalry that prevented a large-scale invasion. In his letters to the Emperor, Joseph played down Reynier's defeat. It was fortunate that Gaeta at last surrendered to Masséna three weeks after this débâcle. Napoleon was still convinced that an invasion of the island of Sicily was a possibility. Calabria had, of course, to be subdued first, but despite Joseph's demands the Emperor refused to send more troops to his aid, writing on 13 July :

> Grant no pardons, execute at least 600 rebels for they have murdered a greater number of my soldiers. Let the houses of at least 30 of the principal heads of villages be burnt and distribute their property among the troops. Disarm all the inhabitants and pillage five or six of the larger villages which have behaved worst . . . Confiscate the public property of the rebellious villages and give it to the army. Above all disarm vigorously, etc., etc.

Napoleon continued to write almost daily to Joseph. Indeed his correspondence with Joseph runs into hundreds of letters. His knowledge of troop movements in South Italy, though obviously out of date, was quite phenomenal. Far from supplying Joseph with troops, in many of his letters he demanded that Joseph should send back to him his much-needed cavalry. He filled his letters with the most detailed military advice, always admonishing Joseph for being too kind-hearted; '*Votre coeur est trop bon*' was the leitmotiv of all his letters of July and August of 1806. (The last letter in which he had *tutoyé* his brother was written from Boulogne in 1803.)

Before the battle of Maida, all had been calm in Naples. The Bourbons had never been popular and Joseph's court, in his hastily refurnished palace, was to all appearances one of contentment. Although he wrote to Julie expressing his desire that she should rejoin him and how much he wished to embrace Zenaïde and his darling little Lotte again, one wonders how sincere he was, since he was now conducting an affair with a French lady named 'Eliza' (her correspondence with the King is among the letters captured at Vitoria), who was probably none other than the widow of the unfortunate Captain Lamy, killed at Gaeta. But the affair was decidedly one-sided, and it was not long before Joseph packed her off to Paris 'to improve her education' with a pension. On the other hand he was shortly to become involved in a love affair of a much more serious nature with the young and beautiful twenty-one-year-old Duchessa Maria-Giulia Colonna, wife of the Duce d'Atri – perhaps the greatest love of his life. To be fair to Joseph, he had once more asked Julie to join him, or rather, he had asked permission of the Emperor, after the latter's victory of Jena, to invite her to join him in Naples. At that time Napoleon, without actually forbidding the reunion, discouraged it. From Posen, where he was preparing for the Russian campaign, he wrote :

> You are master and can do what you like about this; but truth to tell as Julie is so content in Paris and it so revolts me to think of women and children in the midst of sedition and rebellions, I don't see why she should not put off her journey for a little longer. I have written to tell her that you have asked for her, but I think she should spend some of the winter in Paris.

This letter must have come as a relief to Joseph. From the very many daily, sometimes twice-daily letters which Giulia wrote to the King and which fell into Wellington's hands, we can see that this love affair was no passing fancy, although, according to Stendhal, Joseph was also at the time having a passing affair with a Mlle Miller, about whom nothing is known, though it is assumed that she was an actress. General Bigarré writes in his memoirs :

> The Sovereign has often been reproached for having loved women too well and to have spent time in their company which would have been better employed in improving the lot of his people. It is true that King Joseph possessed all the gallantry of a Henri IV, but it is incorrect to assume that he wasted one single hour in the delights of the fair sex which might have been spent with his Council of State or Council of Ministers.[4]

Girod de l'Ain writes :

We get the impression that if he told his mistresses that he was only too glad to escape the affairs of state in their embraces, he was equally glad to escape from these same embraces, their tears and the 'mewling' of his illegitimate children,[5] by making long journeys through his territories.[6]

Certainly during 1807 Joseph, with considerable courage, toured his domains. After a long journey in the spring along the Adriatic coast and through Apulia as far as Taranto, he made a difficult and dangerous journey through the Abruzzi. In the last weeks of September, ten days after the Duchessa d'Atri had given birth, after a difficult accouchement, to his son Giulio, he stayed at Venafro, north of Capua, and thence journeyed eastwards to Campobasso and returned by Morcone to Santa Lucia.

His journeys made him realize that lasting peace in his own kingdom could only be achieved if peace was restored throughout Europe. On 29 March he had written to his brother:

Sire, I am in that frame of mind which Your Majesty knows well: I want to be quite frank. Very well then! *Your Majesty must make peace at all costs.* Your Majesty is victorious everywhere. You must refrain from shedding any more of the blood of your people: it is for a prince to remain a hero. One stretch of territory more or less should not matter to you. Any concessions you make will be glorious, because they will be beneficial to your people . . . Sire, you should not hazard the greatest monument raised to the grandeur of the human race, by which I mean the unbelievable glory which you have accumulated in the past ten years of your life . . .

This letter, written a few days after the bloody battle of Eylau, failed to move Napoleon in any way. It was only after his victory at Friedland, three months later, that he agreed to sign the armistice of Tilsit.

In October 1807 Joseph asked the Emperor's permission to visit Paris because his wife's ill health prevented her from coming to Naples. Napoleon refused permission, but arranged to meet his brother in Venice on 3 December. Their conversations, which lasted several days, were held in secret, and turned mainly on the fate of Spain, where the quarrels between the weak King Charles and his son the Infante Ferdinand and Godoy, the Queen's young lover, now virtual autocrat of Spain, Prime Minister and commander of her armies, made a good excuse for French intervention.

The Empire of Charles Quint was a tempting prize for the

ambitious megalomaniac Napoleon. If we are to believe Joseph's friend Miot, who was in a favourable position to know the facts, it was at Venice that Napoleon suggested to Joseph that he should exchange the throne of Naples for that of Madrid. Joseph, horrified at the thought of yet another war, suggested a peaceful means of attaching the kingdom of Spain to France – by proclaiming Ferdinand King and arranging a marriage between him and one of the young Bonapartes, for example the daughter of Lucien. Napoleon saw in this a splendid solution of reconciling himself with his young brother. Joseph offered to act as mediator and to arrange a meeting between the two brothers.

On 8 December Napoleon and Joseph left together for Mantua. On the 11th they parted company and in the evening of the same day Joseph met Lucien at Modena. Lucien agreed to meet Napoleon in Mantua while Joseph returned south, highly satisfied that he had effected what he believed to have been an excellent reconciliation and that the future of the Bonaparte dynasty was assured. But he soon learnt that his efforts had been in vain. Napoleon, who had always disapproved of Lucien's second marriage to Madame Jouberthon, insisted that he should divorce. When Lucien refused, Napoleon inevitably burst into one of his famous rages. In his memoirs Lucien states that Napoleon told him : 'If you divorce you won't be the only one, for I will too, and Joseph will do the same.' This was quite untrue; Joseph had no intention of divorcing Julie. Lucien and Napoleon parted irreconcilable for almost another seven years.

The Emperor's mind was now turned more and more towards Spain, which he did not wish to leave in the hands of the Bourbons. Once again he offered the crown to Joseph, who once again refused to accept it. Next he approached Louis and Hortense, who had spent the summer of 1807 in the Pyrenees, where Louis's health had much improved, but Louis, much as he disliked the crown of Holland, had the good sense to prefer The Hague, despite its fogs and bitter winters, to the insecurity of Madrid. For the second time Napoleon approached Joseph, who had returned to Naples.

Calabria had now been more or less subdued, and his kingdom was enjoying a period of comparative tranquillity. Although he was still obliged to maintain almost 40,000 troops to secure peace, Joseph was now realizing two of his greatest ambitions : the creation of an order of chivalry and the conquest of Sicily. Napoleon thoroughly disapproved of the first. He was jealous of his own Legion of Honour and put all manner of obstacles in Joseph's way, but finally Joseph overcame all his objections and instituted the Order of the Two

Sicilies – a five-pointed star, enamelled in red, suspended from an eagle attached by a blue ribbon, 'the colour of the monarchy founded by the Normans'; in the centre of the star were the arms of the city of Naples and on the reverse those of Sicily. Joseph would have preferred to have had a representation of his own head instead of the latter, but this Napoleon absolutely refused to allow. Nevertheless, Joseph was delighted and drew up a list of five hundred Knights of the Silver Star, one hundred commanders of the Golden Star, and fifty members of the *Grand Cordon*, to whom pensions according to their rank were to be granted.

Anxious as Napoleon was to conquer Sicily and drive the house of Bourbon-Parma out of Palermo and to occupy Corfu, he was now equally interested in extending his Imperial dominions to include the Iberian peninsula. Once Sicily was conquered, he was determined to remove Joseph from Naples and place him on the throne of Spain. He was, however, well aware that Joseph would not willingly agree to renounce the throne of the Two Sicilies while he enjoyed the *dolce vita* of Naples in the embraces of the beautiful Duchessa d'Atri. Napoleon was determined that this liaison should be terminated and now, changing his mind, decided that Julie, who hated the thought of playing the part of Queen, should join her husband. Julie had constantly pleaded ill health, while Joseph had hypocritically written to her begging her to make her home in Naples. To keep up the pretence of marital fidelity Joseph had from time to time prepared royal apartments for Julie and had constantly dispatched aides-de-camp to Mortefontaine with the ostensible purpose of escorting her back to Naples; but each time an aide-de-camp returned it was to inform Joseph that his wife was too ill to travel. This comedy was to come to an end when in November 1807 Julie took it into her head to visit Napoleon at Fontainebleau. The Emperor, indignant at finding this sweet, gentle creature in the best of health, made a scene which she was never to forget. Straightaway he wrote to Joseph : 'Your wife came to see me yesterday. I found her in perfect health and was shocked that she had not left to join you. I told her so, because I am accustomed to seeing wives with their husbands . . .'

This time it was impossible to dissimulate further. Joseph, pretending to conform to his brother's wishes, sent his friend Roederer to Bologna with orders to await the arrival of Queen Julie, who in fact had no intention of leaving France to assume her royal duties which so terrified her. When the Queen failed to arrive at Bologna, instead

133

of returning to Naples, Roederer crossed the Alps and journeyed to Paris and thence to Mortefontaine. When Julie heard that a minister had come all the way from Naples to escort her back to her husband, she fell in a dead faint.[7] However, this time there could be no more procrastination. On 18 March 1808 she left Mortefontaine with Zenaïde, Charlotte and her niece, Rosine Salligny. After a comfortable passage across the Saint-Bernard, she arrived in Naples on 3 April. Her fears proved groundless. At Joseph's court there was none of the strict protocol on which Napoleon insisted, and she was immediately made to feel at home.

The arrival of Julie was naturally a terrible trial for the Duchessa d'Atri, who was once again three months with child by her royal lover. The letters she wrote to Joseph at this time show a remarkable unselfishness; she thinks of nothing but his welfare. 'I could never allow you to fail in your duties,' she writes. 'I hold your welfare too much at heart . . .' Then again, falling into the romantic style of the novelists of the period, she writes:

> My heart is too deeply wounded, *bon, bon ami,* to be easily healed . . . But you must think only of taking care of yourself for the sake of your family's happiness. Because I am unhappy, my state of health deserves compassion, but do not imagine that I am afraid of death; on the contrary, I desire it, because I am persuaded that it is essential for your happiness . . .

In a long letter written on 29 April, she writes: 'I love you. If I told you that I wished to abandon you, it was only for the sake of your family. You saw my tears, so you saw how much this cost me. But then, are you not the father of Giulio? Ah! This is enough for me to adore you for ever!'

Naturally, Julie's presence obliged Joseph to change his way of life; his meetings with the Duchessa became less and less frequent. Stanislas de Girardin, in his *Journal*,[8] gives an interesting picture of the Neapolitan court at this time:

> Nothing could have been more agreeable than our intimate soirées. The King likes literature; he has summoned the poet Monti, who gives us the most interesting readings. The Queen takes the greatest interest in the latest novels . . .
>
> The Queen likes her villa at Santa Lucia, but the house is so small that she cannot receive many visitors. This is a shame; one would like to know her better and she would only benefit by showing herself more. Perhaps she would do better not to live in such retirement. From

time to time, Her Majesty makes little excursions . . . In the evenings, to amuse the young Princesses, a sort of hunt is arranged, called a *diluvio*, which consists of catching birds in nets strung between orange trees . . .[8]

Miot, in his memoirs, writes:

The Queen's presence had a very happy influence on public opinion. Moreover, the Queen, by her considerate conduct, by her tact and by the kindly welcome she gave to ladies of the highest rank who solicited the honour of being received at Court, won the affection and esteem of all.[9]

Despite several plots to assassinate the King, Julie remained calm and always appeared to be unworried. Naples reminded her of her native Marseilles and its climate had beneficial effects on her health. Although the royal palace was uncomfortable, and the almost non-existent gardens were sunk below road level, the view from the terrace across the bay was magnificent, and the Union Jack flying insolently over the island of Capri was scarcely visible.

Among the subjects discussed between Napoleon and Joseph at their meeting in Venice in the previous December were the conquest of Sicily (occupied by the English since Trafalgar) and the occupation of Corfu (vacated by the Russians after the Treaty of Tilsit). On 25 January 1808 the Emperor wrote a five-thousand-word letter to Joseph giving him the fullest details, down to the last minutiae, of how the invasion of Sicily should be conducted. Admiral Ganteaume's fleet, however, which had sailed from Rochefort on 17 January to join the Toulon squadron (destined to protect the Straits of Messina and ferry the Imperial troops across to the island) and which was planned to reach Naples between 10 and 15 February, failed to arrive. The element of surprise on which Napoleon had counted was lost. All the Emperor's plans went awry. Ganteaume's fleet, delayed by storms, only arrived at its destination at the end of April; the invasion of Sicily was now out of the question. Instead, Ganteaume was ordered to the Ionian islands to prevent the British from forming bases and to reinforce the slender French garrison already established in Corfu.

By March, then, the Emperor had abandoned all thought of the immediate conquest of Sicily; his plans were now entirely centred on the Iberian peninsula. On 5 March he had already written to Joseph:

'It is possible that within a week I shall be in Spain.' Joseph had paid scant attention to this letter; he was too busy distributing his new order of chivalry and installing Julie in the magnificent palace of Caserta, but on 28 April he was shaken out of his complacency by another letter from the Emperor which read:

> It is not impossible that within five or six days I will be writing to order you to come to Bayonne. You will leave the command of your troops to General Jourdan and the regency of our Kingdom to whom you please. Your wife will remain in Naples. Relays along the road will be prepared for you . . . However, for the moment all is uncertain.

To explain Napoleon's policy in the Iberian peninsula we must return to the year 1807. Trafalgar had not entirely destroyed Napoleon's Navy. His Brest fleet was still intact and he had created a new fleet in Toulon. Following the Treaty of Tilsit, Napoleon not only had sixty-two French, Spanish and Dutch ships at his disposal but also twenty-five Russian men o' war plus, he hoped, nine Portuguese. He only had to secure Sweden's eleven and Denmark's eighteen battleships to have one hundred and twenty-five ships of the line, enough to break Britain's maritime superiority. The British Government, sensing the danger, although not at war with Denmark, ordered Admiral James Gambier with a flotilla of twenty-five ships to Copenhagen. After five days of intermittent bombardment the Danes surrendered their entire fleet.

On reception of this news Napoleon gave vent to one of his famous displays of temper. At a diplomatic reception held at Fontainebleau he declared that he would no longer tolerate an English ambassador on European soil. 'The English declare they will no longer respect neutrals on the high seas; I will no longer respect them on land.' Then, turning to the Portuguese Ambassador, he shouted: 'If Portugal does not do as I wish, in two months' time the House of Braganza will cease to exist in Europe.' He was determined, now that the rest of Europe was at peace, to concentrate his whole force against the last corner of the Continent where the English merchant still had a foothold.[10]

Early in October it was learnt that an army of 30,000 men under Junot had assembled at Bayonne and was about to cross the Bidassoa and march on Lisbon. Foiled in his attempt to seize the ships of the Danish navy, Napoleon was determined to seize the Portuguese fleet lying in the Tagus. By virtue of a secret treaty signed at Fontainebleau, he had obtained permission from the Spanish King Carlos IV and his corrupt minister Godoy to occupy the principal towns of Biscaya and Navarre and for French troops to have free access to Spanish territory for the invasion of Portugal. Junot was ordered to make all possible speed and press over the mountains of Galicia by almost impassable roads under pouring rain to reach Lisbon before the British had time to remove the Portuguese warships. On the last day of November, after covering three hundred miles in a fortnight, Junot's army straggled into the Portuguese capital with less than 2,000 of its original 30,000 men, only to find that the court and fleet had already sailed away across the Atlantic to Rio de Janeiro under British escort.

The bid to seize the Portuguese fleet having failed, Napoleon now resorted to still more drastic measures to 'break the stranglehold of Britain's naval blockade and destroy the stubborn will of the nation still resisting his bid for universal hegemony'.[11] In December 1807, in a series of decrees issued from Milan, he outlawed all neutral vessels which submitted to British search or touched at British ports. Although he now controlled the whole coastline of Europe from Kronstadt to Trieste, there were still loopholes admitting British trade; smuggling had become a major industry and, since his commercial decrees were not always enforced with the rigidity he desired, he substituted annexation for control in all possible cases. Spain, officially France's ally, must be occupied and the British driven out of Gibraltar; moreover, by virtually incorporating Spain within his dominions, he would have complete control of her fleet and colonies. With this extra naval strength and the elimination of Gibraltar he hoped to make the Mediterranean a French lake – the scheme of 1798 revived.

There is nothing in Napoleon's correspondence in the early months of 1808 to suggest that he expected any opposition from the Spanish people. He believed that they would welcome a Bonaparte on the throne in place of the effete Bourbons. The reign of Carlos III (1754–88), the third of the Spanish Bourbon kings, had been one of subservience to France but, despite Carlos III's religious bigotry, Spain under his rule had seldom been more successful economically. Although nearly all his ministers had been *afrancesados*, their reforms were based rather on the theory of the *encyclopédistes* than on the reality of conditions still existing in Spain. There still remained a wide gulf between the body of the nation and the educated classes.

Carlos III's successor to the throne in 1788, Carlos IV, a man of the most mediocre intelligence, was completely under the thumb of his Queen, Marie-Louise of Parma (also a Bourbon). He retained for only a short while his father's enlightened ministers, who were soon replaced by Godoy, his wife's lover, whose unbounded influence both over the King and the Queen and whose limitless greed and shameless subservience to France brought the nation to the verge of ruin. Godoy not only assumed almost all political offices in his own person, but secretly schemed with Napoleon to obtain half of Portugal as an independent kingdom for himself.

Although at the outbreak of the French Revolution Carlos IV, horrified by the execution of Louis XVI, had declared war against the new Republic and had actively collaborated with the Coalition, only two years later, in 1795, Godoy was to earn for himself the title of 'Prince of Peace' by negotiating the Treaty of Bâle, which ultimately resulted in the Treaty of San' Ildefonso, which in turn bound Spain to an offensive and defensive alliance against England. The results of Godoy's policies were devastating to Spain. In 1797 the Spanish Navy was defeated by Admiral Jervis in the battle of Cape St Vincent; Trinidad was captured and henceforth all commercial communications between Spain and her colonies were almost hopelessly destroyed as the British Royal Navy sank her treasure ships and blockaded her ports.

Godoy and his royal master and mistress were blamed for all the ills that had befallen Spain. The Infante Ferdinand, Prince of the Asturias, jealous of Godoy's increasing influence, stirred up revolt against his own father. The subsequent rising of Aranjuez, which overthrew both Godoy and the King, was not the work of informed 'liberals' (as both Joseph and Napoleon believed) but was engineered by a group of malcontent nobles in alliance with the Prince of the Asturias, using as instruments army officers and the mob. An attempt by King Carlos, his Queen and Godoy to escape to Buenos Aires was foiled. Carlos was forced to resign the throne and Ferdinand was proclaimed King. The moment was now ripe for Napoleon to intervene. He played off the resentment of the 'old court' and their frantic appeals to the French to save Godoy from the vengeance of his enemies against Ferdinand's craving for French support. Thus the Emperor could settle the dynastic question by enticing Ferdinand with specious promises to meet him at Bayonne and there forcing both him and his father to abdicate the throne in favour of Joseph.

So long as Napoleon appeared to endorse Ferdinand against Godoy, Spain 'awaited its fate from the Emperor'. Up to the time of the Bayonne meeting, despite the fact that French troops had infiltrated into key points in Spain (Burgos, Pamplona and Barcelona were all occupied by Imperial troops by the end of February 1808), the people remained passive. It was the virtual kidnapping of the Prince of the

Asturias and Murat's subsequent occupation of Madrid that provoked the spontaneous and unexpected rising. The rising, to quote Professor Felix Markham,[12] was thus in part 'a revolution of disappointed hopes'.

On 6 May, the Emperor wrote to Joseph :

My Brother – You will find annexed a pamphlet which will acquaint you with the affairs in Spain. The conclusion is approaching. King Charles has yielded to me his right to the throne and is about to retire to Compiègne with the Queen and some of the children. A few days before this treaty was signed, the Prince of the Asturias abdicated . . . The Grand Duke of Berg [Murat] has been appointed lieutenant of the Kingdom and President of all the Councils.

There was a great insurrection in Madrid on 2 May; between 30,000 and 40,000 persons gathered in the streets and houses and fired from the windows. Two battalions of my guards and four or five hundred of my cavalry brought them to their senses. More than two thousand of the populace were killed. I had sixty thousand men in Madrid who could do nothing. We have taken advantage of this occurrence to disarm the city.

This was the massacre made famous by Goya's paintings and etchings,[13] yet Napoleon utters no word of regret. A mere two thousand or so Spanish patriots killed by the sabres of his Mamelukes, but what were two thousand dead to this Man of Destiny? And for what? Merely to satisfy the uninhibited ambition of a megalomaniac.

Joseph did not learn until five days later that his brother had officially chosen him to become ruler of Spain. In a further and more explicit letter from Bayonne, dated 11 May 1808, Napoleon wrote :

. . . I wish you, therefore, immediately after the receipt of this letter, to appoint whom you please Regent, and to come to Bayonne by way of Turin, Mont Cenis and Lyons. You will receive this letter on the 19th, you will start on the 20th, and you will be here on the 1st of June. Before you go, leave instructions with Marshal Jourdan as to the disposition of your troops, and make arrangements as if you were to be absent only to the 1st of July. Be secret, however; your journey will probably excite only too much suspicion, but you will say that you are going to the North of Italy to confer with me on important matters.

Having decided to obey his brother and believing that he could retain the crown of both Naples and Spain – and why not since Charles III had been King not only of Spain but also of the Two

Sicilies? – Joseph took the road for Bayonne on 23 May. He appointed no regent, but allowed his Neapolitan subjects to believe that he would shortly return. At Bologna he visited Lucien, who was intending to leave for America[14] and whose reminiscences of his period as Ambassador in Madrid and accounts of the Spanish people did nothing to inspire Joseph with confidence.

On leaving Lucien he visited Turin, where the Prince Camillo Borghese had been installed as Governor-General. Here he found his sister Pauline living apart from her husband, whom she now detested. She persuaded her brother to take her back to France. Contrary to all Napoleon's orders, Joseph took it on himself to authorize Pauline to return to Paris. Knowing that such was Napoleon's need of him, he considered it improbable that he would be reprimanded. Joseph continued his journey to Bayonne by easy stages, in no hurry to accept the new burdens that were to be imposed upon him. On his way he received many letters from Julie and also from the Duchessa. The latter seems to have remained on good terms with Julie, but whether the Queen was aware of her liaison with her husband is not apparent. It seems highly improbable that Julie was so innocent as to be unaware of the passionate love affair that her husband had been conducting with the beautiful Duchessa during her absence. But if she was aware, she gives no hint of the fact in her letters; there is no word of reproach : on the contrary, they are filled with terms of affection. After only three months and four days as Queen, Julie left Naples for ever, to the regret of her subjects. A popular song of the time runs as follows :

> *Lo Re e' venuto da regnante*
> *E' partito da brigante*
> *La Regina*
> *E' venuta da mappina*
> *E' partita da regina.*[15]

There is no doubt that Joseph's almost clandestine departure had thoroughly alarmed the Neapolitan court, especially the French whom he left behind, who feared an English invasion and the return of the Bourbons. It was no use, as Napoleon had advised in his letter of 11 May, that he should pretend that he was merely visiting northern Italy to confer with the Emperor on important matters, for it was already an open secret that the Emperor intended to make him King of Spain. It must not be forgotten that ties of friendship existed among officers which had been forged during their campaigns and

140

that they learnt a great deal more from gossip and their personal correspondence than from the newspapers, which were always extremely guarded in their comments on political events. The aides-de-camp acting as couriers were also an invaluable source of information. The daily regularity and speed with which these couriers covered the thirteen hundred miles between Naples and Bayonne was nothing less than miraculous.

IX

From Naples to Madrid

1808

On 6 June 1808, even before Joseph arrived at Bayonne and even before Napoleon had officially informed his brother that it was his irrevocable decision to place him on the throne,[1] the Emperor had already issued the following proclamation:

> The Junta of State, the Council of Castile etc., having already made known to us that it was their wish that the interregnum should be brought to an end immediately, we proclaim our well-beloved brother Joseph-Napoleon, at present King of Naples and Sicily, as King of Spain and the Indies. We guarantee to the King of Spain the independence and integrity of his States, be they in Europe, America, the Indies or elsewhere.[2]

The Junta of State and Council of Castile had of course been handpicked by Napoleon himself, although only ninety-one deputies out of one hundred and fifty made their appearance. On 8 June, when news was received that Joseph's travelling berline was approaching Bayonne, Napoleon went out to meet his brother and greeted him as one sovereign to another. Joseph's own account of his meeting with his brother is misleading. He states that it was not until he had reached Bayonne that he knew for certain of the Emperor's plans for him, and that it was only now that he was 'talked into accepting the crown'.[3] This is obviously untrue. Be that as it may, the welcome given to him by the Junta of State and Council of Castile was enough, we are told, to persuade him that the people of Spain were awaiting his arrival with pleasurable anticipation. But can this be true? He already knew that Murat had suppressed a revolt in Madrid and had been told that the last of the rebels had been eliminated.

But how could he be unaware that not only Madrid but the whole of Spain was in a state of ferment? Even before his arrival in Bayonne the Revolutionary Junta of Seville had requested Sir Hew Dalrymple, Governor of Gibraltar, to supply money and arms with which to combat the Imperial forces now swarming across the Peninsula. A few days later, on 30 May, the gentry and clergy of the Asturias, under the Duke of Santa Cruz, had met in conclave at Oviedo and decided to appeal to London for help. The Asturian delegation, which landed at Falmouth on 6 June after a hazardous journey, had been given an enthusiastic welcome. 'In their excitement and anger, the Spanish people appeared to have forgotten that they were at war with the island state which had stopped their trade, sunk their treasure ships and blockaded their ports; they only thought of England now as a common enemy of the hated oppressor.'[4]

The British, too, forgot the long war with Spain. By the beginning of July peace was declared between the two nations and preliminaries for a formal alliance entered into. The flame of insurrection in the meantime had spread from Spain to Portugal, where the Bishop of Oporto had led a successful rising against the pro-French governor. Within a matter of days Junot's hold on the country had been limited to little more than Lisbon and surrounding districts and the principal fortresses. The way lay open for British invasion of the Peninsula. This was a threat which Napoleon took lightly, since initially the Spanish were not anxious to have another foreign army fighting on their soil. Money and arms, as the Spanish had explained to Wellesley when he landed at Corunna on 19 July, were all they needed; fighting men they had in plenty; the British would be better employed in Portugal. Remembering what they suffered at the hands of their French allies and all they had suffered from the British at sea, the Spanish attitude was perhaps excusable, but it bore no relation to the facts. True, fighting men they did have in plenty, but these were ill trained and, with few exceptions, their regular officers were unbelievably incompetent. Only a week before Wellesley's arrival at Corunna, Marshal Bessières had won an overwhelming victory at Medina del Río Seco over the combined armies of Galicia and Leon, commanded by the elderly and almost senile General Cuesta and the almost equally incompetent Blake, a Spanish general of Irish descent. Dupont, marching southwards on Andalusia with 15,000 troops, mostly raw and ill-disciplined conscripts, had captured and sacked Córdoba, Moncey had gained another victory over Cuesta at Cabezón and had occupied Valladolid. The British, discouraged by their own allies from invading Spain, were safely out of the way in Portugal; the little army of redcoats could be dealt with later.

These victories might have been encouraging to Napoleon, but it must have been clear to Joseph that a whole nation which had spontaneously risen in arms against the French was not going to welcome a Bonaparte on the throne. However irrational the Spanish people's enthusiasm for the banished Ferdinand might have been, this proud race was bound to resent a foreign usurper as their king. On 7 July, shortly before setting out for Madrid, Joseph wrote to the Duchessa d'Atri (his first letter since February):

I received your letter of the 22nd. I am very touched by all you tell me. I know I would feel the same if I were in your place. Here, it is only with the greatest difficulty that I prevent myself from constantly thinking of you, but I force myself to deal with my affairs of State. You must believe me when I tell you that I love you very much; I am sure you will be convinced of this when I make the following confession : Never has anyone been placed in such a bizarre position as that in which I find myself. Although devoid of all ambition and having no wish to achieve the honours so universally coveted by others . . . and obliged to leave behind me those by whom I am wanted and by whom I am loved, nevertheless *I find myself crowned King of a people who seem to reject me.* But although I am quite well aware of all this, I still have to behave as though I think otherwise; but the fact remains that *I would much prefer to lead the private life to which I was born than to be a king* . . . If I behave like an ambitious man, it is only due to force of circumstances. But, *ma chère amie,* I cannot change the circumstances in which I live . . . *I am not afraid, because I have a clear conscience.* I could not put up with my position, which I dislike intensely, if my conscience were uneasy. I will sacrifice everything to my honour because my honour lies in my conscience.

What will come of all this? How can I find happiness when my position is quite incompatible with my character; when I have to use all my courage and reason to reconcile the two . . . I am like a lost voyager, out of sight of land, carried away by irresistible currents on a distant sea. Whatever moments of happiness I have had, my dearest angel, have only been those spent with you . . . but such thoughts only add to the regret that I cannot consecrate my future to a quiet life and a state of permanent tranquillity.

I believe in what I have to do and in what I am doing. But I bitterly regret that I am forced to do what I would prefer not to to do . . . Adieu, my dear Giulia, I embrace you and little Jules. Adieu my poor little angels, but I will see you again. Yes! Courage, *mon amie, I will see you again.*

This letter, found among Joseph's correspondence after the rout of

Vitoria, may never have been sent. It may have been a rough draft or a copy. But as Girod de l'Ain writes in his biography of Joseph:

> We find here all the signs of Joseph's weakness of character; his wavering between his public and his private life; his ambition but lack of will; allowing himself to be controlled by events, instead of controlling events himself; always laying stress on his conscience and honour, but forgetting both when it suited him; always unhappy, because dividing his life between remorse and regrets, he lived in a perpetual state of imbalance and compromise.[5]

There can be no doubt that had Joseph been willingly accepted as King of Spain, he would have been a far better king than Ferdinand VII. There is no reason to doubt that when he wrote 'I believe in what I have to do and in what I am doing' he was anything but sincere. He knew the Spanish government to have been utterly corrupt and honestly wished, with the aid of enlightened Spanish ministers, to introduce practical reforms in the social and economic life of the country. He wished to be accepted as a Spanish king, and to the end of his days denied absolutely that he was aware of Napoleon's intentions to annex Spain as part of his policy of world hegemony.

During the month Joseph spent in Bayonne before entering his new kingdom he spent his time learning Spanish and preparing a draft constitution for his new subjects on which Murat and his advisers had already been working. This draft constitution, which was unanimously approved by the Junta of Bayonne on 7 July, was in many ways admirable and a great improvement on any enjoyed by the Spanish under the Bourbons. But it must be remembered that this was merely a draft constitution and could not become law until Joseph was officially proclaimed King and approved by the *Cortes* (which was to consist of twenty-four members, to be nominated by Joseph himself, and a chamber of 162 deputies, representing the three estates, to be elected by suffrage).

It was also during this month that Joseph took the opportunity of rewarding his friends in Naples with the honours and riches of the kingdom which he was about to abdicate. It is easy to criticize him for generosity which in fact cost him nothing. Among the principal beneficiaries were the Marquis de Gallo, former Neapolitan Ambassador to France, who had quickly changed his allegiance when his Bourbon masters fled to Palermo and later became Joseph's devoted servant; and Jourdan, the one-time rabid Jacobin, who to his disappointment had never received a title from Napoleon (punishment for not collaborating in the *coup de Brumaire* – he had expected to be made the Comte de Fleurus); naturally, among others rewarded for 'services rendered' were the Duchessa d'Atri and her father, Andrea Colonna, Prince of Stigliano, whom Joseph had appointed 'Grand Chamberlain' (and to whom Julie was wont to refer as *'le Grand Imbecile'*). According to Murat, the total value of the gifts both in cash and lands amounted to two and a half million ducats, which left a deep hole in his exchequer when he assumed the crown of Naples.

Towards the end of June, Joseph wrote to Julie advising her to leave Naples, but without giving her specific instructions whether she should proceed to Paris or Madrid. On 1 July, Julie wrote to her husband : 'I received your letter of the 22nd. I have already given orders that nothing should be removed from here so that we cannot be reproached for having devastated our country.' However, the linen and silver which had been sent from the Hôtel Marbeuf were returned to Paris. Joseph's carriage and horses, estimated to be worth more than a million francs, were to be sent to Madrid, together with his library and personal papers. On the receipt of another letter, dated 27 June, Julie decided to leave Naples on 7 July. Just before her departure, she wrote again to Joseph :

> Like you, I think it would be better if I went directly to Madrid. The troubles and miseries of Spain do not disturb me. So long as I can be with you, I will be content. Your children are very happy at the thought of seeing you again . . . Everyone expresses the greatest regret at seeing me leave. Judging by the demonstrations of affection I have received during my short stay in this country, I believe I would have been greatly loved . . .

Julie was not unhappy to leave. The weather had turned unbearably hot that summer and the children had been ill. They were forced to travel by night to avoid the heat and dust of the day. Julie broke her journey at Stupinghi to spend two days with Camillo Borghese (Pauline, profiting by Joseph's permission to leave for France, was already in Paris); on 17 July, she crossed the Mont Cenis Pass and two days later arrived in Lyons to await further instructions from her husband. On 28 July Joseph, without mentioning the real reason why he did not wish her to proceed to Madrid, advised her, on Napoleon's recommendation, to return to Mortefontaine, at least for the time being.

On 9 July, Don José Primero, King of Spain, with an imposing escort of 1,500 dragoons and accompanied by some sixty coaches containing chamberlains, equerries, Spanish grandees and personal domestic staff, left for his new kingdom. Napoleon drove with him as far as the frontier of the Bidassoa. Among Joseph's entourage were several old friends, including Stanislas de Girardin, whom Napoleon had recently created Count of the Empire, and Generals Salligny and Matthieu. Among the Spanish grandees were the Duque del Parque, his newly-appointed Captain of the Guard, the Duque de l'Infantado (both of whom almost immediately defected), the Duque de Frias, who was particularly devoted to Joseph, and other distinguished noblemen and generals.

The Emperor continued to remain optimistic and congratulated himself on receiving the Tsar's approbation of his political moves at Bayonne. 'They know all about the Spanish affair,' he wrote to Joseph, 'and approve of it.' This statement lends credence to du Casse's theory[6] that by virtue of a secret clause of the Treaty of Tilsit, the world had been divided into two zones of influence. The one reserved to Russia included Turkey and Asia; the one reserved to France included Egypt, the whole of North Africa, Malta, Spain and Portugal, where the Bourbons and the House of Braganza were to cede their thrones to two princes of the Bonaparte family.

In spite of the imposing entourage of francophile Spanish grandees who accompanied Joseph on his setting out for Madrid, and even the fact that the Prince of the Asturias, who had been banished to the Château of Valençay,[7] had sent him a congratulatory letter, concluding with the words 'I beg Your Catholic Majesty to accept the oath of loyalty which I owe to you, together with all the Spaniards who are with me', we know now, from his letter to Giulia d'Atri, that he was most certainly not without apprehension, which was fully justified as soon as he had crossed the frontier. On 10 July, once he had passed San Sebastian, he was well aware of the looks of terror and hatred on the faces of the inhabitants whom he encountered at each stage of his journey. On 12 July he wrote to Napoleon from Vitoria :

No one so far has told Your Majesty the truth. The fact is that there is not a single Spaniard who shows himself to be favourable to me except the small number of persons travelling in my company. The others, who came here and from other towns and villages before my arrival, have now gone into hiding, panic-stricken by the unanimous opinion of their compatriots.

If your Majesty is not engaged in another Continental War, you must give serious consideration to sending as many troops and as much money as possible to Spain.

Napoleon replied:

> I received your letter at three o'clock this morning. I am sorry to see
> that your courage seems to fail you; it is the only misfortune which
> I feared. Troops are continuously pouring into Spain from all quarters
> . . . I enclose a list of troops already in Spain . . .

The Emperor then gives a detailed list of the various corps distributed
over the Peninsula, amounting in all to 116,000 men under arms.
'You talk of Continental war,' he concludes. 'I thought I had already
told you that our relations with Russia were good. With regard to
Austria, the fuss she is making is only due to panic. It is all unimpor-
tant.' But Napoleon was quite wrong. Within nine months he was at
war with Austria.

Joseph was not satisfied with his reply. Again he wrote complaining that no one had told the Emperor the real truth. 'If I am to live
without the shame of failure I must be supplied with vast resources
of men and money.' He further complained that the generals were
acting independently without consulting him. 'The command cannot
be divided,' he wrote. *'At my age and in my position* I may have
advisers but no masters in Spain. Your Majesty can do what he likes,
but the storm is too violent for me to perish because of ill considered
measures . . .'

A week later Napoleon replied:

> My Brother – It is you who command; I have already told you so;
> I will say so in my general orders. Savary acknowledges it in his
> general reports to the Chief of Staff when he says that he shall not
> move without your orders. You might therefore have spared yourself
> a page of twaddle . . .

Nevertheless the generals continued to act independently and were
even encouraged to do so by the Emperor. The withdrawal of
Gobert's division from Dupont's army advancing into Andalusia on
Savary's orders, contrary to Joseph's specific instructions, resulted in
an overwhelming defeat of the French. As Dupont continued his
southward march after the sack of Córdoba, a grimly angry countryside rose in his rear while, at the same time, the Army of Andalusia
under the command of Spain's ablest general, Don Fernando-Xavier
Castaños, advanced to bar his way to Seville, supported by an
English force from Gibraltar. Never had a French army met with
such open hatred on all sides. Dupont lost his nerve and fell back on

the bleak highlands of the Sierra Morena. But in this stark country there was no food to support an army of fifteen thousand men. On 23 July, Castaños and the partisans closed in on Dupont. Faced by famine and almost certain annihilation, he capitulated at Baylen. The fifteen thousand men laid down their arms. Never had Napoleon's armies suffered such a defeat.

On 20 July, at seven o'clock in the evening, Joseph made his entry into Madrid. Although Savary had made careful preparations for the King's arrival and had ordered all church bells to be rung and cannons to fire salutes, and had given instructions that drapery and tapestries should be hung from windows along the processional routes, the houses remained obstinately shuttered and the medals bearing the head of Don José Primero, destined to be thrown to a cheering crowd, fell on empty streets. The fine tapestries and carpets which Spaniards are accustomed to hang from their windows on the occasion of fiestas were often derisively replaced by rags. Nearly all the notabilities had fled or were in hiding. Joseph, heartbroken, compared their emigration to that which had deprived France of her élite in 1789. Generals Merlin and Franchesci-Delonne and his aide-de-camp Clermont-Tonnerre rode on horseback beside His Majesty's coach. The second coach was occupied by General Salligny and his *chambellan de service*; the third coach was empty. This was all that was left of the magnificent cortège that had left Bayonne only eleven days previously. The King drove to the royal palace by way of the Calle Alcale, the Puerto del Sol and the Calle del Arsenal, through a city of the dead.

General Salligny and Stanislas de Girardin both confirm that when the Council of Castile accepted the new draft constitution presented to them in Bayonne on 7 July Joseph announced that he wished none but Spaniards to be in his government. As de Girardin wrote: 'He believed that he could quietly step into the shoes of Charles IV.'[8] But he was soon disillusioned, and realized that only with the help of the French armies could he hope to rule Spain. The Council of Castile, summoned to ratify the constitution, reneged on the grounds that the Junta of Bayonne had been forced into acceptance under duress.

But even when Joseph informed his brother of the fact, Napoleon treated the affair lightly. 'You have a large number of partisans in Spain,' he wrote,

but they are intimidated. You have all honest people on your side but they fear to come forward. I don't deny that you have a serious

149

task before you, but it is a great and glorious task. Marshal Bessières's victory entirely defeating Cuesta and the Army of the Line in Galicia has greatly improved the state of affairs . . . You ought not to be surprised at having to conquer your kingdom. Philip V and Henry IV were forced to conquer theirs. Be happy; don't allow yourself to be so easily affected and don't doubt for an instant that everything will end sooner and more happily than you think.

Joseph hastened to reply: 'No Sire, you are deceived: the honest people are as little on my side as the rogues. *Your glory will be wrecked in Spain.* My tomb will be a monument to your want of power to support me.'

Napoleon continued to write letter after letter, all in the same optimistic vein, but the courier service in Spain was nothing like so safe and efficient as that between Naples and Bayonne, and the Emperor was almost invariably sadly out of touch with current events. For example, on 30 July he wrote: 'It is inconceivable that after reaching San Clemente, Marshal Moncey should have retired from Aragon on Ocaña,' but in fact had Moncey not retreated towards Madrid he would almost certainly have suffered the same fate as Dupont at Baylen. As late as 30 July, that is to say, eleven days after Dupont's surrender, Napoleon was still writing: 'General Dupont has already 20,000 men; if he has committed no mistake with such a force, he has nothing to fear.' Throughout the whole of the Peninsular campaign, the Emperor remained consistently out of touch with events and the generals more and more took the initiative into their own hands.

Despite the formidable obstacles confronting Joseph, he was determined to carry out his duties as king. His first consideration was to attempt to put a stop to the pillage and atrocities committed by the Imperial troops. He had been appalled to learn that at Medina del Río Seco nearly every woman, from the youngest to the oldest, had been raped under the eyes of their fathers and husbands and that at Cuenca the monasteries and churches had been stripped of their plate and sacred ornaments with the connivance of the French generals and put up for sale in the capital.

Joseph chose 25 July, the feast day of Santiago de Compostela, patron saint of Spain, the day on which to proclaim himself officially king and receive the oath of allegiance from his subjects. Only very few notabilities came to pay their homage. On the 26th, Joseph summoned all the high-ranking clergy to the palace and delivered a carefully prepared speech: 'God's will alone reigns on earth. This is a truth that cannot be denied. It is the duty of every good Catholic to submit to His will . . . If my dynasty has succeeded that of the Bourbons, it is by God's permission. To disobey me, is to disobey God . . .'9

Although no more of a believer than Napoleon, Joseph entered into his role so well that both Stanislas de Girardin and the Comte de la Forest (whom Napoleon had appointed Ambassador to the Court of Madrid and who disliked Joseph) both reported that Joseph's audience was greatly moved by his address. But since at the time Joseph did not speak Castilian as well as he was to later, only his opening sentences were more or less intelligible. The remainder of his discourse was made in a mixture of French and Italian and was largely incomprehensible to his listeners. But the monks and priests appeared to pay the greatest attention to his homily, which he delivered with such *singulière onction* (as La Forest wrote to Talleyrand), that Joseph was convinced he had made a great impression on his ecclesiastical congregation.

At the time when he was pronouncing this discourse, he had no idea that the British fleet had just captured five French ships of the line and a frigate off Cadiz; nor had he heard of the much more serious disaster suffered by Dupont at Baylen. Rumours of this great victory, however, had already spread among the Madrileños, who made no secret of their joy and hailed it as the greatest Spanish triumph over French arms since the capture of Francis I at the battle of Pavia in 1524.

Dupont's defeat gave fresh heart to the Spanish people. They boasted that they, and they alone, had been able to defeat the soldiers of Austerlitz. But in fact Dupont's troops were not veterans; on the contrary, they were an ill-disciplined hotch-potch of conscripts, many from Napoleon's vassal countries, whose defeat was not only due to what Napoleon described as Dupont's 'horrible generalship', but additionally to their reluctance to part with the vast wagonloads of booty pillaged from Córdoba which seriously hampered their movements. Never again was a Spanish army to win a pitched battle in the field. Napoleon summed up his opinion of the Spanish regular army as the worst in Europe, while Wellington's judgement (though not in reference to the *guerilleros*) was: 'I have never known the Spaniards do anything, much less anything well.'10 This was due neither to lack of courage nor entirely to bad generalship (though, goodness knows, with few exceptions their professional officers were a sorry lot), but to the fact that the armies were regarded as provincial forces not to be sacrificed to neighbouring provinces, not even to the nation. Indeed at one time the Junta of Seville almost declared war on Granada and refused to send the Andalusian Army to defend the critical Ebro front when the French, after the first panic caused by Dupont's defeat, were massing for a counter-offensive. Although the situation was to improve later, in 1808 each province and almost every big city had its own Junta which pursued its own policy, political and military. The Central Junta of Government, which Ferdinand had left in Madrid to govern during his absence, had been ordered to cultivate French friendship at all costs, and since the Councils, of which Murat had been made President, were not modified until after the popular rising, it meant that official Spain could not take the leadership of the instinctive movement against France. The situation in Spain was therefore extremely complicated, and it is hardly surprising that from the very start Napoleon misread the temper of the Spanish people. Because the Council of Madrid, the bourgeoisie and nobles had been fearful that the rising of 2 May, so pitilessly suppressed by Murat, might have been the preliminary to a reign of terror similar to that in France in 1793, the Emperor imagined that the educated classes would recognize him as their saviour and the regenerator of their country. Of course it was true that there were many educated Spaniards who feared mob rule, but it was for this very reason that men like the enlightened *philosophe*, author and lawyer Jovellanos, who for his radical views and attacks on the Church had been banished to Majorca during the rule of Carlos IV,[11] and that great aristocrat, Don José de Palafox, Duque de Saragossa, and the Duque de Santa Cruz in Oviedo, both of whom believed in a liberal constitutional monarchy, took the side of the masses, and channelled what might have developed into a class revolution into a national rising against the foreign invader, fought under the banner of Ferdinand, the so-called 'Desired One', whom they despised, but whose rule was preferable to that of Revolutionary France. It was the sequestration of the crown by a foreigner that touched the pride and very existence of the Spanish people, who forgot that only a century earlier Louis XIV had presented his grandson Philippe, Duc d'Anjou, to his court as the new King of Spain, and that their monarchy was Bourbon.

On 29 July, a tired and dusty French officer, released on parole by Castaños, rode into Madrid to break the news of Dupont's surrender. Gobert's corps had also been routed and Gobert himself killed. With the exception of Moncey's corps there now remained few effective troops between Castaños's army and the capital. The garrison of

Madrid itself only amounted to a few thousand men, a large proportion of whom were non-combatants engaged on administrative duties. The army which remained to Joseph, with the exception of some of the old regiments of the guard belonging to Moncey's corps, probably constituted some of the worst troops in the whole of the Imperial Army; nearly all of them were conscripts who had had no training whatsoever and whose officers were little better.

To Joseph's credit, he did not lose his head. He was not only concerned with the evacuation of his army, but also with the two thousand French civilians (this is the figure supplied by La Forest[12]) who were employed in various capacities and who, because of the excesses committed by the Imperial troops, would have certainly fallen victims to Spanish reprisals. It was not until he had seen the last of his compatriots safely out of the capital that he himself left Madrid, leaving the palace just as he had found it.

At five o'clock on the morning of 31 July, after having spent only eight days in his capital, Joseph, accompanied by Moncey and his staff, left the city on horseback for the north. There is absolutely no evidence to support the claims made by some historians that 'the King lost his nerve and bolted out of Madrid across the passes into Old Castile and that all his court bolted with him',[13] or that Moncey escorted them in as dignified a way as the courtiers' hurry permitted. On the contrary, Joseph remained extremely level-headed. Despite Napoleon's later criticism that he should never have left Madrid, he could not have held his capital with the troops at his disposal. It was far better to retire to Burgos to join up with Bessières's corps and hold the Ebro-Douro line.

Joseph's Imperial troops proved almost more of a menace than the Spanish themselves. On 3 August, on reaching Buitrago, he found that his baggage train had been looted by his own men; that his advance guard, in a drunken frolic, had set fire to the castle where he had proposed to spend the night and had wantonly destroyed all the neighbouring crops; and that the whole village had been deserted by the terrified inhabitants.

Immediately after his arrival at Burgos on the 9th, Joseph, thoroughly disgusted with his army, with Spain and his crown, wrote twice to the Emperor seeking his permission to abdicate. He expressed his conviction that the Spaniards would never be reconciled to his rule or forgive the injuries inflicted on them by France. If Napoleon insisted on ruling Spain, he wrote, he should appoint himself King, just as he had done in Lombardy, and appoint whomsoever he wished as viceroy, while he, Joseph, returned to Naples. It was too late. Although Murat did not take up residence in Naples until 6 September, he had been proclaimed King of the Two Sicilies on 15 July at Bayonne, and Napoleon had no intention of reversing his decision.

While Joseph was writing to his brother in this pessimistic vein, the Emperor was more concerned with the rise of nationalism in Germany, where a threatened coalition of Prussia, the Confederation of the German States and Austria (where the war party was representing itself again in the ascendant) was menacing his world dominion. The matter of first importance was to overawe Europe by a fresh demonstration of the amity between himself and the Tsar. It was for this reason that he summoned the conference of Erfurt, to be held in October, where the courts of Russia, Prussia, Austria and all the vassal princes were to be represented. While fully aware that the suppression of Spain would require large forces, he could not possibly release his armies from the Elbe and the Rhine until, with the aid of Russia, he had cowed Austria and Prussia into subjection. It is this consideration which explains his letter to Joseph and the accompanying despatch from Berthier to Savary, written on 9 August shortly after he had learnt of Dupont's disastrous defeat at Baylen.

> My Brother – you cannot imagine what pain it gives me to think of you struggling with events which are as much above what you are accustomed to, as they are beneath your natural character. Dupont has dishonoured our flag. What incapacity, what cowardice! I feel really grieved that I cannot be with you and my soldiers at this juncture. I have ordered Ney to join you . . .

At the same time, he ordered Berthier to write to Savary:

> If Castaños advances and you fight him, the best may be hoped; but the manner in which he moved towards Dupont leads us to expect from him great caution.
>
> Perhaps, by means of a flag of truce, a suspension of hostilities might be agreed on, without the King's apparent interference, terminable on eight days' notice by either party, giving to the French the line of the Douro, and then, passing by Almazan, the Ebro. The insurgents might think such an armistice desirable, as it could enable them to organize themselves in Madrid, and it might not be unfavourable to us, as it would enable us to see what that organization would be, and to ascertain what the Nation really wishes.

This proposal for an armistice, surrendering to the insurgents all

Spain south of the Ebro and Douro, that is to say four-fifths of the country, for the avowed purpose of allowing them to organize themselves in Madrid and of ascertaining the wishes of the Spanish nation, contrasts strangely with the general tone of Napoleon's correspondence. It seems to show that he did not really feel the confidence of success which he expressed in his letters to Joseph. He was biding his time until he could release the Grande Armée. In the event, the armistice was never signed. After a few days in Burgos, Joseph retired first to Miranda and then to Vitoria, where he was joined by Ney and Jourdan, whom he appointed Chief of Staff. His confidence was greatly restored by the presence of Bessières's corps and the arrival from Naples of his old friends Generals Dumas, Stroltz, Ferri-Pisani, Bigarré and Hugo, who had brought with them his magnificent coach and horses. With efficient generals and an army of 65,000 men he felt fully justified in launching a counter-offensive and re-establishing himself as King in Madrid. Ney, the toughest and most resolute of all the Emperor's fighting men, who arrived in Spain on 30 August, and Jourdan, who had arrived a few days earlier, both supported Joseph's plan. The Emperor, however, was completely opposed to it. In two extremely long and detailed letters, dated 15 and 16 September, he points out all the risks inherent in such an action. He writes: 'The position of the Army of Spain for purposes of offence is essentially bad . . . To change one's line of operations is *something which only a man of genius ought to attempt* . . .' The towns of Tudelo, on the Ebro, and Burgos are the two key points which Napoleon insists Joseph should never surrender.

'I know nothing of what you have done', he wrote later to Joseph on his return to Paris from Erfurt, 'except that it is bad . . . At present the enemy's presumption is so great that I am inclined to think that he will remain where he is, the nearer to us the better. A well arranged manoeuvre could terminate the war by a single blow; but for this, *my presence is necessary.*'

Poor Joseph, who had thought to win a wonderful victory and re-install himself on the throne of Spain – and why not, since not only Ney, a far from stupid general, but Jourdan and other generals supported him? – was treated by his younger brother as though he was an ignorant schoolboy. One is left with the impression that Napoleon, and only Napoleon, wished to have the glory of restoring Joseph to the throne of Spain.

But by this time, Joseph himself had already relinquished the idea of reoccupying Madrid on his own initiative. He was now solely interested in consolidating his line behind the Ebro and the Douro while awaiting the arrival of his formidable brother and further reinforcements from Germany. Napoleon had paid no attention to his pleas to be allowed to abdicate; he had merely contented himself with acknowledging receipt of his brother's letters, telling him that the northern courts had now recognized him as King and ordering him to appoint ambassadors to the courts of Russia and Austria and to send a minister to Copenhagen. 'By the end of January,' he wrote, 'you will have 100,000 men and there will not be in all Spain one village in insurrection . . . Do not be in the least uneasy.'

It was all very well for Napoleon to write 'do not be in the least uneasy', but ever since the battle of Baylen the partisans had become increasingly active. In the autumn of 1808 they were reinforced by a formidable ally in the person of the Marqués de la Romana. In 1807, when Spain had been the nominal ally of France, Napoleon had insisted on removing the pick of the Spanish army under the command of Romana to reinforce Bernadotte in Hanover. On the Emperor's orders Romana's forces had been moved from Hamburg to the north of Copenhagen and distributed throughout the Danish islands to prevent organized disaffection. When in 1808 news filtered through from Spain, and particularly from Bayonne and Baylen, Romana found himself serving not allies but the oppressors of his country. The Spaniards longed to return home, but escape by land was impossible. Escape by sea was far more promising: the Baltic swarmed with British warships. By means of a series of picaresque plots, involving a Scottish priest from Regensburg disguised as an itinerant commercial traveller in chocolate and cigars, Romana succeeded in making contact with the British and was so successful in organizing his escape and that of his troops that by the time Bernadotte realized that something was afoot it was too late; on 21 August 1808 Admiral Keates had arrived with troop ships and an escorting squadron, and the Spanish army was safely embarked. On 11 October, Romana and his 9,000 men were landed at Santander in the north of Spain. But worse still was the news that Sir Arthur Wellesley had landed in Portugal on 1 August. Napoleon affected to make light of this. A week later he wrote to Joseph: 'You must try to preserve the line of the Douro, to keep up communications with Portugal. The English are of little importance . . . Lord Wellesley [sic] has not more than 4,000 men.' He was to change his tune, however, when he learnt on the 21st that Wellesley had decisively defeated Junot at Vimiero and had occupied Lisbon.

By the evacuation of Junot's army from Portugal under the unfortunate terms of the convention of Cintra and Romana's arrival at

Santander, the way was laid open for a British landing in Galicia, which unless effectively intercepted could cut the French lifeline between Bayonne and Madrid.

Although Junot's defeat at Vimiero had greatly encouraged Spanish resistance, Napoleon found one consolation in the arrival of British troops in the Peninsula. In the words of A. G. Macdonnell: 'The leopards had come ashore after all these years from their floating fortresses and were now within range.'[14] After Erfurt, where in appearance, at least, the conference was successful, and the immediate danger of war with Prussia and Austria had been averted, the Emperor was free to intervene personally in Spain. He withdrew three whole corps from his veteran armies of the Rhine and Elbe and two divisions of cuirassiers and the entire Imperial Guard stationed in Paris. With these mighty forces he had no doubt whatsoever that he could re-establish Joseph on his throne, subdue all Spain and drive the miserable little English army back into the sea.

X

King of Spain and
the Indies

1808–1809

Joseph had already left Burgos for Calahorra on the Ebro on his way
to Miranda, where he intended to establish his headquarters, when
the news of Junot's defeat at Vimiero first reached him. This fact
would scarcely be worth mentioning, except that it was at Calahorra
that he was to earn a reputation which took him a long time to live
down. He and his staff were lodged in the mansion of a local grandee
who possessed a famous cellar. Perhaps it was the news of Junot's
capitulation and the consequent desertion of many of Joseph's troops,
including officers, who, with or without permission, left for France,
that prompted Joseph's headquarters staff to forget their sorrows in
over-indulgence. Joseph, who throughout his life was known for his
sober habits, may or may not have been guilty of helping to empty
his host's cellar, but nevertheless no sooner had he left Calahorra than
the news rapidly spread that in the course of a single night he and
his companions had drunk the place dry. Henceforth Joseph's reputation as a drunkard rapidly spread through Spain. Caricaturists
represented him as red nosed and squint-eyed, usually clutching a
bottle in each hand. During his absence from Madrid, a satirical play
was produced entitled *Don Pepé Botella* (Don Pepé the Bottle) in
which the King was represented as a hideous deformed drunkard.
For a long while this undeserved nickname of *Don Pepe Botella* stuck
to the unfortunate handsome Joseph. The ignorant peasants firmly
believed in this false image and fought for princes whose appearance,
had they but seen Goya's court portraits, would no doubt have
horrified them. Strangely enough, although there was every reason

158

to criticize Joseph for his 'predilection for the fair sex of Spain', to quote from General Hugo's memoirs, 'this was a weakness which never earned him the same opprobrium as his supposed addiction to the bottle'.[1]

All unaware of the reputation he had earned in a single night, he left Calahorra to establish his headquarters at Miranda, which he was obliged to leave in a hurry when, on 22 September, Stanislas de Girardin suddenly kicked open the door of his room and informed him that Spanish sharpshooters had already infiltrated thus far north and were attacking the French outposts. Joseph lost no time in ordering his staff to evacuate the town and gain the safety of Vitoria. Here there was less danger of a surprise attack and moreover it had the advantage of easy communication with the French frontier.

It was here that Joseph received Napoleon's lengthy observations on his proposed plans to march on Madrid. He decided, therefore, to remain in Vitoria and await the arrival of his brother with reinforcements. In the meantime, Joseph could do little. He had ordered Moncey to hold the line at Tudela; Palafox, against all odds, was still holding out against the French in Saragossa, and until artillery reinforcements were received there was nothing Joseph could do to force the surrender of this capital of Aragon.

Both Joseph and Napoleon had exaggerated when the king had written that he had 'not a single partisan', and when the Emperor had written : 'All honest men are on your side, but are frightened to come forward'. Both, to some extent, were right. There were certainly many *liberales*, who like the Whigs in England saw in Napoleonic rule the salvation of Europe from feudal domination, the establishment of an efficient Civil Code and (in Spain) an end to the Inquisition. Among such liberal thinkers was the Marquis of Montehermoso, who owned a villa near Vitoria. He was only too pleased to put his mansion at Joseph's disposal and move into a house opposite.

It had been exactly four months since Joseph had left Naples and the Duchessa d'Atri, who was expecting another child by him and was just as much in love as ever. During these months Joseph had remained faithful to her; to salve his conscience he had settled a generous pension on her and had accepted her brother Antonio Colonna as his equerry; from time to time he still wrote to her affectionate letters. But Joseph was incapable of remaining faithful for long. At Vitoria, the opportunity to take Napoleon's advice to 'be gay' now presented itself so conveniently that Joseph was incapable of resisting temptation. The consequence of what Joseph thought was to be a little passing love affair turned out to be of great importance in his life. Stanislas de Girardin tells the story in his memoirs (published in 1829); it was copied almost word for word in an article by General Abel Hugo which appeared in the *Revue des Deux Mondes* of 15 April 1833. Both therefore appeared during the lifetime of Joseph, who made no attempt to deny the truth of their contents, contrary to his repudiation of the *Mémoires* of Bourienne.[2]

The following account is textually that given by Girardin :

Don José Primero was installed in the finest house of the city, modelled on those little mansions in the Chaussée d'Antin built in the eighteenth century. It contained a well-furnished library and an agreeable garden, two things which were rare in Spain. Its proprietors, the Marques and Marquesa del Montehermoso, had placed it at the disposal of the King and were themselves lodged in a house which they owned on the opposite side of the road. Thus it was that, looking out of the window of his room, Joseph observed a very attractive, dark-haired Spanish girl of eighteen or perhaps a little more. Having confided to his faithful servant Christophe that she greatly pleased him and that he would willingly give her two hundred Napoleons [equivalent to 13,000 francs, a very considerable sum] if she would consent to spend the night with him, the valet, dressed in his best embroidered coat, with sword at side and hat under arm, knocked on the door opposite. Announcing himself as coming on behalf of Don José Primero, he was immediately introduced into the room which faced the window of the King : it was the child's nursery and the young nursemaid was indeed there. Christophe, without beating about the bush, explained the purpose of his mission. The embarrassment of the little Spanish maid was not caused so much by the advantageous and flattering proposition made to her, as by the presence in the room of her mistress. A smiling glance from the latter seemed to convey her permission and allowed Christophe to assure the King that 'all conditions of the Treaty had been agreed and it now only remained for him to ratify them'.

[On the following morning, those invited to the King's levee were obliged to wait in vain. It was not until very late, that the King summoned Girardin to ask him the latest news. Girardin replied:] 'A very strange anecdote is being circulated of which Your Majesty is the principal hero. It is said that Your Majesty made propositions to a young Spanish soubrette and that the mistress of the latter, the Marquesa del Montehermoso the owner of your house, knew of it and has spoken of it in society. She expressed her surprise that a man as

160

agreeable as Your Majesty should not have addressed himself to persons of higher social rank, and that she was sure that in the best society of Vitoria there were ladies who would be infinitely flattered to be the object of your attentions. Madame de Montehermoso said this in the presence of people whom she believed to be in a position to repeat her words to you.'

'Did she say this in your presence?' asked Joseph.

'No, Sire, I have not the honour of knowing her, nor of having ever seen her.'[3]

On the following day, the King invited Girardin to dine with him. There were only two other guests – the Marques and Marquesa del Montehermoso. 'It was easy for me to see', Girardin continues, 'that the Marquesa was already something more than just the mistress of the house in which we were.' Girardin describes the Marquesa as elegant and with a fine figure, a fluent linguist speaking Italian and French perfectly; he tells us that she also sang agreeably to the accompaniment of the guitar and was a sufficiently good miniature painter to make an excellent likeness of the King. Although Girardin says that she was no longer in her first youth, she was probably no more than twenty-five.

As for the Marques, her husband, Girardin describes him as 'a tall, eccentric man, very pleased with himself, a decided enemy of monks, priests and the Inquisition, who seemed not at all put out by Joseph's relations with his wife'. The King showed his gratitude to him for his complacency by appointing him his chamberlain and officially naming him a grandee of Spain and by purchasing his house at three times its value (1 million francs at present value – 1974). 'I am persuaded that this acquisition will impress the Army, France and Europe,' Joseph told Girardin. 'It will be said that unless I was convinced that I would recover Spain, I would never have acquired this property.' 'I don't know what France and Europe will say,' Girardin claims to have replied, 'but I do know that your military staff may well claim that your Marquise is not worth 300,000 francs.'[4]

Joseph was not at all pleased with this answer. Girardin claims that Joseph, like his brother Napoleon, could not stand anyone who opposed his wishes. As soon as the King could find a pretext to get rid of the man who had been one of his most faithful and intimate friends, he did so. He authorized Girardin – and this was equivalent to an order – to return to Paris, where Stanislas's father had just died after a long illness. On 3 October, the one-time friends parted and, although they were to meet again, their relations were never the same.

While Joseph was enjoying the favours of the delightful Marquesa he still remained in constant correspondence with his brother and incessantly, but unsuccessfully, tried to exercise his authority over his generals and endeavoured to persuade both them and Napoleon that only a policy of magnanimity would bring peace to Spain. He again exhorted the Emperor to give him sole command of the armies, at least until he, the Emperor, personally took charge.

Napoleon, however, paid no attention either to his brother or to the Pope, who had now added to the fanaticism of the Spanish by showing his sympathy to their cause and excommunicating the Emperor. Napoleon had only one solution – force. A huge deployment of troops in the Peninsula would solve every difficulty; only by spreading terror throughout the country could he subdue the insurgents and allow Joseph to reign in peace. Although Joseph was in name commander-in-chief, he remained virtually powerless. Nevertheless, Napoleon continued to bombard him with letters criticizing his tactics. It was certainly not Joseph's fault that Napoleon's preparations for the new campaign, so carefully worked out in Paris, had not been followed, nor could he be held responsible for the breakdown in commissariat arrangements for which Napoleon blamed him. Instead of being kept near Vitoria, the left wing of the army under Suchet, contrary to Jourdan's orders, had advanced to Lérida, miles to the east on the borders of Catalonia, where some of the worst atrocities of an atrocious war were perpetrated;[5] while on the right wing, Marshals Lefebvre and Victor had marched westwards to attack the Spanish under General Blake and, after defeating him at Bilbao, had pushed on to Valmaseda. General Villate's division, part of Victor's corps, was at Valmaseda, when Lefebvre, for lack of supplies, fell back on Bilbao.[6] Victor, hearing of Napoleon's imminent arrival and anxious to return to headquarters where he would be under the Emperor's eye, marched back to Vitoria, leaving Villate exposed to superior forces. The army was dispersed and without proper leadership. 'Thus', wrote Thiers, 'began the series of faults, the result of the selfishness and jealousy of our own generals, which lost the cause of France in Spain and by losing it in Spain, lost it also in Europe.'[7]

On 5 November Napoleon, with a formidable advance guard, arrived at Vitoria. On the previous day he had written to Joseph from Tolosa, just across the border of the Bidassoa:

My brother – I reached Tolosa at six this afternoon. I start tomorrow at five and shall be at Vitoria at some time in the night. I wish to be lodged outside the town. I suppose that you have sent me escorts and above all relays of saddle horses . . . I shall, of course, ride the whole distance; nevertheless, a relay of carriage horses may be useful. I do not wish to ride the same horse for more than ten or twelve miles. I wish to enter the town incognito; indeed, even unsuspected. This is the reason why I shall arrive at night . . . I have just dictated to the Prince of Neufchâtel [Berthier] all the military instructions for Marshal Moncey and Marshal Ney. These will be sent off in a couple of hours . . .

With little consideration for Joseph's feelings, Napoleon had no intention of allowing his brother to take any active part in the direction of the campaign. When on 12 November Joseph made his entrance into Burgos, it was not as King, but 'in the baggage train of the conqueror'.[8] This despite Napoleon's assurance to him written two days earlier : '. . . I am as anxious that you should be treated with ceremony as I am careless about it myself; it does not suit the character of a soldier and I hate it. I think, however, that deputations from Burgos ought to meet you and receive you on arrival. [Signed] Your affectionate brother.'

Joseph was received with scant ceremony. By the time he arrived Napoleon had already left. Unable to intervene in any way, he was an unwilling witness to all the executions, pillage and arson which the Emperor encouraged to terrify the population into submission. Even the house next door to his lodgings had been set on fire. There was no excuse to sack the town as there had not been even a token resistance; Bessières had already cleared the road by defeating an inferior Spanish force at Gamonal, a village at some distance from Burgos itself.

It was in vain that Joseph tried to intercede on behalf of his unhappy 'subjects'. 'Yesterday and for the last four years', he wrote to his brother, 'I was able to command an army. Today, I haven't even the authority of a second lieutenant. Is my character such that I deserve to be the laughing-stock of the army in a country of which I shall be King?'

The short campaign met with only a few checks. Romana's and Blake's army had been routed by Soult and had dissolved into a mere mob and taken refuge in the Asturias; Castaños had been defeated by Lannes at Tudela. The Spanish had attempted to hold the pass of the Samosierra at a narrow defile on the road leading directly to Madrid. On the east of the Guadarramas it would have been easy to outflank the Spanish guns, but the Emperor, who took personal command, was impatient, and ordered his own escort of Polish hussars to charge the guns. Montbrun, at the moment in Napoleon's disfavour, was placed in command. With the exception of the charge of the Light Brigade, probably never has such a suicidal order been given to cavalry. By a miracle, Montbrun, like Lord Cardigan some forty years later, survived the hail of grapeshot and enfilading fire from either side of the narrow gorge, to gain the village beyond. But of the gallant Poles, scarcely a man survived. But what did this matter? *C'est la gloire.* What a wonderful episode to publish in army bulletins. Yet another myth had been added to the Emperor's renown. Half an hour later, the infantry, following, scrambled up the heights on either side of the gorge and turned the enemy position. The road to Madrid lay open. Over the corpses of his gallant escort, Napoleon rode triumphantly towards the Spanish capital. These were not even Frenchmen whose lives Napoleon had so uselessly thrown away, but Poles whom the Emperor had sworn to liberate from the yoke of Russia.

On 2 December, the anniversary of Napoleon's coronation and the Battle of Austerlitz, the two brothers were reunited at the Castillo de Chamartín on the outskirts of Madrid. At six o'clock on the morning of 4 December, Madrid capitulated. Although under the terms of the capitulation Napoleon guaranteed security of life and property, freedom from arrest and free exit to such persons as chose to remain in the capital, he immediately broke his word. The list of persons declared traitors and condemned to loss of life and goods was not very long; only ten were named, seven of whom were absent from Madrid, but three others, the Prince of Castelfranco, the Marquis of Santa-Cruz and the Count of Altamira, were seized and sent to France and condemned to life imprisonment. The arrests, however, were a much more serious matter. In flagrant contravention of the terms of surrender, Napoleon put under lock and key all members of the Council of the Inquisition on whom he could lay hands, irrespective of their conduct under the Junta. He also declared all senior Spanish officers resident in Madrid, even retired veterans, to be prisoners of war. The Council of Castile was abolished and its President Don Arias Mon and some thirty other notables were arrested. Some were sent away to France, others were set at liberty after swearing allegiance to Joseph.

All these measures were designed to strike terror in the hearts of the Spanish, but at the same time Napoleon promulgated a number of decrees which he hoped would conciliate the *liberales* and which would bestow tangible benefits on the country.

164

Many of these reforms were excellent – freedom of religious conscience, restriction of the powers of the Inquisition and abolition of torture and the removal of all manner of irritating local taxes, reduction of curtailed estates and of the number of monasteries, etc. Most of these reforming measures had already been included in the draft constitution drawn up at Bayonne with the complete approval of Joseph. There were many Spaniards who regarded these measures as beneficial, but who, like Jovellanos, did not wish them to be imposed on the country by foreigners. There was in fact a reaction in favour of the Church, and one of the first acts of the Central Junta, which had retired from Aranjuez to Seville as soon as it was obvious that the French would reoccupy Madrid, was to reinstate the Jesuits and appoint an Inquisitor-General. The Inquisition had long been moribund and the last *auto da fé* had taken place in 1777. Wherever it fell within the jurisdiction of the Inquisitorial Court to try a person charged with a crime which also fell within the jurisdiction of a civil court, the accused nearly always preferred the justice of the Inquisition. The days of Torquemada were long past.

Napoleon had not even bothered to inform Joseph of his actions. Not only was Joseph furious at the way his brother had broken his word and made arbitrary arrests, but also that the legislative measures had been signed in the name of the Emperor without even consulting him, the King, much less without consulting a popularly elected *Cortes.* On 8 December, Joseph wrote to the Emperor :

The legislative measures taken by Your Majesty have just been communicated to me . . . I blush with shame before my so-called subjects. I beg Your Majesty to accept the renunciation of all rights to the throne of Spain which you have given to me. I will always prefer honour and probity to power so dearly bought.

Despite everything, I remain always your affectionate brother and dearest of friends. I still remain your subject and will take my place wherever Your Majesty pleases to send me.

Joseph's abdication did not conform with Napoleon's policy. He was determined to have a Bonaparte on the Spanish throne, and since Lucien had refused, Joseph was the next best choice. Indeed, he had come to regard Joseph's weakness almost as an asset, since he believed that a man of Joseph's temperament would always be subservient to his will. He argued that it was he, Napoleon, who had placed Joseph on the throne and he was not going to allow him to forget it; he had no intention that his brother should be anything more than his puppet and that Spanish policy should be dictated by him, just as he intended to dictate the policies of his other royal brothers, Louis, King of Holland, and Jerome, King of Westphalia.

By cajolery and flattery he was determined that Joseph should retain the throne; he even paid an unofficial visit to Madrid with him (Napoleon was established at the Castillo de Chamartín, while Joseph was at Pardo, both in those days outside the capital) and visited the Royal Palace. No doubt thinking of the sombre walls of the Tuileries, the scene of so much drama, Napoleon remarked : 'You will be better lodged than I am.'

Spain as yet, however, was not entirely subdued. Palafox was still holding out in Saragossa, but now that 40,000 troops under Moncey had been sent to reinforce the besiegers Napoleon anticipated that within a week the city would be in French hands. Despite the news that Sir John Moore had entered Spain from Portugal and that Sir David Baird had landed a division at Corunna in October, it is clear that he expected no further trouble in Leon and Old Castile, since he left Soult there with only one corps. Catalonia, in the north-east, where Saint-Cyr and Duhesme were in command, was of little importance and could be dealt with later. His main preoccupation was the invasion of Portugal and the subjection of the south.

Despite Napoleon's almost bloodless re-entry into Madrid, the capital was not yet secure. It was not until Victor had decisively beaten General Venegas at Ucles and the Duque de Infantado had consequently retreated to Murcia that this was achieved, and then at a cost to Spanish lives which was never forgotten, since Victor ordered all enemy wounded and prisoners to be shot.[9] The war was still far from finished; Napoleon had not taken into account that the British under Sir John Moore, whom he believed to be retreating into Portugal, were in fact in Old Castile and in a position to cut his life-line with France. As soon as he learnt the truth

Napoleon acted with a sudden and spasmodic energy which was never surpassed in any of his earlier campaigns. He hurled on to Moore's track not only the central reserve at Madrid but troops gathered in from all directions, until he had at least 80,000 men on the march, to encompass the British corps which had so hardily thrown itself upon his communications. Moore had been perfectly right when he stated his belief that the sight of the redcoats within reach would stir the Emperor up to such wrath, that he would abandon every other enterprise and rush upon them with every available man.[10]

Moore, forewarned, was able to avoid what Napoleon had intended to be a vast encircling movement. On 7 December the Emperor had reached Valladolid. He was still certain that he could catch up with the British forces before they reached the mountains of Galicia. From Valladolid, where he had established his headquarters, he wrote to Joseph :

The English are running away as fast as they can . . . They have not only cut the bridges but have blown the arches; a barbarous and unusual use of the rights of war, as it ruins the country to no purpose; they are therefore abhorred by everybody. They have carried off everything, oxen, mattresses, blankets and then maltreated and beaten the inhabitants. There could not have been a better sedative for Spain than to send her an English army. Their robberies are indescribable.

It was unfortunately only too true that the retreating British army behaved abominably, but certainly no worse than the French. Napoleon's criticism that the English had blown up bridges contrary to the usages of war seems the height of absurdity, while to accuse the British army of theft is equally ridiculous in view of the atrocities already committed by the Imperial troops.

Apparently the Emperor saw nothing inconsequential in the fact that he should write to Joseph a fortnight later :

In Madrid you must hang a score of the worst characters. Tomorrow I intend to hang here [in Valladolid] seven notorious malefactors for their excesses. If Madrid is not delivered from at least one hundred of these firebrands you will be able to do nothing. Hang or shoot twelve or fifteen and send the rest to the galleys in France . . .

Nor did Napoleon seem to find it in the least incongruous to write a little further on : 'Desson [Director General of Museums] is anxious for some pictures. I wish you to seize all you can find from confiscated houses and suppressed convents and to make me a present of fifteen masterpieces . . .'

On 1 January a courier brought news to the Emperor that Austria was rearming, but even more important (although he did not admit this to Joseph) was the news that Talleyrand, Fouché and Murat were engaged in intrigues to overthrow his Imperial authority. Murat, King of Naples, had already earned Napoleon's displeasure for precisely the same reasons as had Joseph. Once King of the Two Sicilies, Murat wished to reign as a national monarch, not as the Emperor's puppet. He had issued a decree that all Frenchmen serving in his

167

government were to take Neapolitan nationality. His failure to conquer Sicily and drive out the English had given rise to rumours that he was putting himself under the protection of Lord William Bentinck, the virtual dictator of the island (he had originally come as official adviser to the exiled Ferdinand IV), who was hatching schemes to free Italy from French occupation and bring it under English protection. It was also rumoured that Italian priests were continually praising Murat in the hopes that he would re-establish the Pope in Rome and reunite the whole of Italy. Moreover, whereas previously diplomats accredited to the Neapolitan court were mainly French or Italian, and as such potential spies for the Emperor, Murat had now accredited an Austrian envoy, Graf von Mier, and a Russian, Prince Sergei Dolgorouki. Savary, who had replaced Fouché as head of police, further claimed that he had irrefutable proof that Fouché and Talleyrand were implicated in a plot to put Murat on the throne of France should Napoleon be killed.

The Emperor's presence in Paris was therefore essential. Confident that the English were now on the run, he decided to leave the command of his armies in Spain to Soult, who was already mopping up the Spanish armies in Old Castile.

There is no need to dwell on the story of Moore's gallant retreat to Corunna; of his final battle to fend off Soult's forces to allow the embarkation of his troops and of his own death. No greater homage could have been paid to an enemy than that accorded by Soult to Sir John Moore in erecting a memorial to him which stands in Corunna today. Moore had achieved what he had set out to do; he had successively diverted the whole of the Imperial forces from Portugal and the invasion of the south. It was a long time, however, before his achievement was recognized. When his half-starved ragamuffin army landed in England, the people were appalled. To the gentlemen in the Horse Guards it seemed a major defeat; in the long run he had saved the Peninsula.

Napoleon was to remain only two months in Madrid and never returned to Spain.

Before leaving for Paris, the Emperor had spent his last ten days (7 to 17 January) in Valladolid, drawing up a number of instructions for Joseph and his marshals. He was evidently anxious to leave an impression of terror behind him. He hectored and bullied in the most insulting fashion those unfortunate Spanish deputies who were forced to come before him. His harangues generally wound up with the declaration that if ever he was forced to return to Spain under arms, he would remove his brother from the throne and divide the realm into subject provinces, governed by martial law. Because some French soldiers had been killed by peasants for pillage or worse, he arrested and threatened to shoot the whole municipality of Valladolid until the murderers of the French soldiers had been named. In one of his last letters (written to Joseph on 14 January) he expressed his displeasure that thirty persons arrested in Madrid had been acquitted by the Civil Alcalde; he ordered them to be immediately re-arrested, tried(!) again before a court martial and shot. Nothing would keep the capital quiet but a dozen or more hangings.

His final legacy to his brother was a long despatch giving a complete plan of operations for the next campaign. After having destroyed Moore's army or forced it to embark, Soult was to march on Oporto (for which Napoleon allowed him a fortnight!). By 10 February the Marshal should be before Lisbon. Napoleon seemed unaware that some 10,000 British troops were still on the Tagus; as for the Portuguese levies, these he dismissed entirely.

With Soult well on his way to Lisbon, Marshal Victor was to strike at Estramadura; once Lisbon had been reduced, he was to join up with Soult on the Tagus. Victor, now reinforced by one of Soult's divisions, was next to march on Seville with 40,000 men. With such a force, Napoleon calculated, he would be able to subdue the whole of Andalusia with ease.

By this time, Saragossa would have fallen, leaving Lefebvre free to march on Valencia; Saint-Cyr would already have brought the Catalans to heel. Before the end of the summer of 1809, the whole Peninsula would be subdued. Such was Napoleon's plan. So confident was he, that he wrote to Joseph (11 January): 'Reserve yourself for the expedition to Andalusia, which may start in three weeks' time . . . this is an operation which will make an end to the war; *I leave the glory to you.*' To his brother Jerome he wrote a few days later : 'The Spanish affair is done with.'

All Joseph's warnings to the Emperor had been in vain. Napoleon was as much deluded now regarding the affairs in the Peninsula as he had been seven months previously. Apart from the fact that the 'greatest general of all time' allowed Soult only three weeks to expel the English, pacify Galicia, capture Oporto and march to Lisbon – and all this through some of the most mountainous country in Europe, over vile roads and in the midst of winter – Napoleon still completely misjudged the character of the Spanish people. In drawing up his plan of campaign he still imagined that in dealing with Spain he might act as if dealing with Austria or Prussia. By all the ordinary rules of warfare, a nation whose capital had been occupied, whose regular armies had been routed and half destroyed, should have laid down its arms. It was not until countless couriers had been captured or shot and innumerable small detachments had been destroyed that Napoleon ultimately came to realize that every foot of Spanish soil must not only be conquered, but held down. Three or four hundred thousand men seem a lot on paper, but when they have to garrison a country of almost as many square miles they are easily frittered away.

XI

The Intruder King

1809–1810

Joseph seemed pleased to see the back of Napoleon. On 18 January La Forest noted a complete change in the King's appearance and assumed that he must have received dispatches from the Emperor 'of an extremely agreeable nature'. Certainly, now that his brother had departed he felt himself at last to be *El Rey*.

On 22 January 1809, three weeks after the battle of Ucles, Joseph left the villa of Pardo to make his royal entry into Madrid. First he visited the church of San Isidoro where a Te Deum was sung, after which he delivered a speech, this time in the excellent Castilian he had had time to learn while in Vitoria. This speech was no less than a declaration of Spanish independence from France and that he was a Spanish King whose sole concern was the welfare of his subjects. One of his first acts was to order that only Castilian was to be spoken in his court, even by Frenchmen.

Joseph's happiness on being allowed to rule on his own, however, was marred by the fact that Napoleon refused to contribute to the maintenance of his armies or in any way to the Spanish Exchequer. In the disorganized state of the country it was impossible to raise money by taxation. 'Give me a million men and a million francs and I will restore peace to this country', Joseph wrote. Napoleon's reply was to withdraw his élite Imperial Guards from the country and, although promising to allow Jourdan to remain his brother's military adviser, he appointed Berthier as chief of staff in faraway Paris, often leaving Joseph in complete ignorance of the orders issued to his generals. Joseph's intention to appoint only Spanish ministers was also thwarted; instead Napoleon appointed his own choice of ministers, who only accepted orders from the Emperor and reported to him every movement made by the King.

171

Only a few weeks after his second entry to Madrid, Joseph, exasperated by the invidious position in which he was placed, wrote to his brother :

Sire – My misery is as much as I can bear. What I deserve from you is consolation and encouragement. Without these my burden becomes intolerable . . .

Again on 19 February, in a moment of despair, Joseph wrote another letter to his brother, in which he again threatened to abdicate and retire to Mortefontaine :

Sire – It grieves me to infer from your letter of 6 February that with respect to the affairs of Madrid you listen only to persons who are interested in deceiving you. I have not your entire confidence and yet without it my position is untenable. I shall not repeat all that I have written on the state of my finances. I devote to business all my faculties from seven in the morning until eleven at night. I have not got a farthing to give to anyone. I am in the fourth year of my reign and my guards are still wearing the same coats as I gave them four years ago . . . I have no real power beyond Madrid and even here I am frustrated by persons who are displeased that things are not managed in their own interests. It would be infamous if I were to leave them to be judges of the tribunals . . .

  If then, Sire, my whole life does not entitle me to your perfect confidence . . . If I must be insulted even in my own capital; If I am denied the right of nominating my own governors and commanders I am made contemptible in the eyes of the Spaniards and am power-less to do good . . . I am King of Spain only through the force of your arms; I could be king through the love of the Spanish people, but for that purpose I must govern them my own way . . . otherwise I shall return to Mortefontaine where I ask for no other happiness than to live without humiliation and die with a good conscience . . .

The Emperor ignored this pathetic letter.

A few weeks after Joseph had written this letter to the Emperor, Soult captured Oporto (weeks behind schedule) and was resting his tired army before his assault on Lisbon, made all the more difficult by the arrival of Wellesley's expeditionary force on 22 April. Victor had defeated Cuesta at Medellin; Corunna and Ferrel had capitu-lated to Ney; Saint Cyr had overwhelmed the Spanish at Vallas and made himself master of all Catalonia; Saragossa had been reduced to rubble. The campaign, however, was by no means over.

Although the north and centre of Spain were lost to the French, Andalusia was still unconquered and Lisbon still remained in British hands.

The whole of Galicia rose in revolt and everywhere the peasants formed bands of guerillas who pinned down the French forces. Napoleon's master plan had indeed broken down.

Although the timetable drawn up by Napoleon at Valladolid had long fallen in arrears, he still believed that he could master the whole of the Peninsula. His principal objective was, of course, to drive the English out of Portugal and seal off the whole of the Atlantic coastline from San Sebastian to Gibraltar. Joseph was not in the least interested in the Emperor's policy of incorporating Portugal in his dominions. He was only anxious to bring peace to Spain. He found himself nevertheless in an impossible situation. Armed opposition by the Spanish to the French occupation still required the presence of a large French army if he was to retain his throne. He could not survive without the French army, but nor could he rule with it. His attempts at administrative reforms were to show no signs of success except where French bayonets could enforce them. In those regions which were inadequately garrisoned he was to make no headway. Moreover, there was a conspicuous lack of unity between the French commanders which further delayed operations. He incessantly asked Napoleon to confirm his appointment as Commander-in-Chief with Jourdan as military adviser (which Napoleon had promised to do months previously), but the generals and marshals continued to pursue their own independent ways and pillage the provinces, of which they were the virtual rulers, to their own advantage.

In March 1809, the Spanish regular armies were in no position to launch a major offensive. The Central Junta, now established in Seville under the presidency of Jovellanos (he had succeeded the elderly Conde Floridebianco, who had died en route for Seville from Aranjuez) was divided among itself. On the one hand there were the *liberales*, men like Jovellanos himself, who were anxious to see reforms put into practice, but not by Frenchmen; on the other hand there were the diehard reactionaries supported by the Church who deplored any change in the social system. Furthermore, they quarrelled among themselves over the conduct of the war and brought ridiculous charges against those who had been in command of operations; there were even a number of political assassinations in the regions to which the French had not yet penetrated. It looked, indeed, as if the central government would be unable to organize any further resistance or establish any sort of order for a long while to come – if ever.

Although the abominable behaviour of the Imperial troops had generally exacerbated the Spanish people, in Madrid itself Joseph, despite his pathetic letter of 19 February, was gaining a degree of popularity and was able to devote his attention to the more congenial task of improving his capital. Just as he had done in Naples, so now in Madrid he engaged in plans for new squares (which earned him the nickname of *el Rey de los plazuelas*). He ordered the slums round the Royal Palace to be razed and terraces to be built along the banks of the Manzanares to provide some dignity to this miserable little stream. He designed and planned gardens and embellished the city with fountains and commissioned statues of Spain's greatest writers. These were grandiose schemes, but, alas, with an empty purse he destroyed more than he could rebuild. But there was nothing which endeared him so much to the Madrileños as his decision to re-establish the national pastime of bull-fighting, which had been banned by Godoy, and it was Joseph who, according to legend, appointed Goya to design the 'suit of lights' which has remained until today the traditional costume of the matador.

The Madrileños were agreeably surprised to find their new king so different from his brother, whose brief visit to the capital had filled them with terror, and quite unlike the ugly caricatures of the drunken, one-eyed Don Pepé which had been so widely circulated. On the contrary, Joseph, who regularly attended the theatre and *corridas*, presented a handsome figure as he entered the royal box, dressed in the green uniform with the yellow facings of his light cavalry regiment of the guard and preceded by torchbearers. Joseph indeed lost no opportunity of appearing in public. Early each morning he attended mass and was often to be seen riding in the many ceremonial processions in which Madrileños so delighted, accompanied by his staff and sporting the red cockade of the Spanish National Movement.

His greatest success, however, was with the intellectual élite, with whom he had much more in common than had had any of the Spanish Bourbon monarchs. He welcomed poets and artists to his palace and awarded them decorations and pensions. He was quick to recognize the genius of Goya, whom he persuaded to accept the directorship of the Prado museum and the *Légion d'honneur*.

At the same time, Joseph remained very much a lady's man and, despite his enduring affection for the Marquesa de Montehermoso, he still found opportunities to pay court to the well-known actresses he encouraged to visit his capital, in particular the delightful Italian, La Fineschi. It was also about this time too that he formed a tender attachment for the Countess Jarnuco, widow of the Governor-General

174

of Cuba.[1] But his amorous proclivities always went hand in hand with his love of the fine arts. He enjoyed organizing literary soirées in his palace, where, just as at Mortefontaine, his guests were invited to give readings from the French and (now) Spanish classics in which he himself at times participated. Little by little, some of Spain's most famous writers and artists were drawn into his circle, including Corisitza, the leading dramatist of the day, and two of the most distinguished poets, Leandro Moratín (whom he appointed Royal Librarian) and Meléndez Valdes, both of whom wrote odes in his honour.

Although many of the nobility who had sworn loyalty to him at Bayonne had deserted him after Baylen, there were others to take their place. Pablo de Arriba, former treasurer of the court of the Alcalde, was appointed Minister of Police; General Gonzalo O'Farril Minister of War; the Marqués de Azanza, former Viceroy of Peru, was created Duque de Santa Fé and given the portfolio of Foreign Affairs; the Marqués de Montehermoso, in addition to his other titles, was made Captain-General of the Civil Guard of Madrid. Four other grandees were pleased to accept important court appointments. Joseph also constituted a *corps de pages*, which not only included the sons of *afrancesados* but also relatives of rebels. Only one of his forty pages was French – Abel Hugo, the elder brother of Victor, the poet, and son of General Sigisbert Hugo (*Mon père, ce héros au regard si doux*), one of the few French generals to remain consistently on friendly terms with Joseph. Abel, who has left us many details of Joseph's reign, tells us that he treated all his pages with equal impartiality, and when out shooting, a sport of which he never tired, gave each in turn the privilege of acting as his loader.

'Collaboration' today is a dirty word, but the majority of Spaniards who collaborated with Joseph were enlightened bureaucrats who saw in the Napoleonic system a hope of ordered regeneration by modern laws and administrative practice. They sincerely believed that collaboration, not resistance, was the best way to protect national independence; allegiance to Joseph would, as they believed, at least save Spain from direct military rule from Paris and the division of the country by right of conquest as threatened by Napoleon before his departure for France. War, however, allowed little time for reforms. The regenerating constitution was never applied: ambitious schemes for a new educational system and a modern legal code, based on the *Code Napoléon*, remained on paper. The only decree to be implemented, the dissolution of monasteries, like the expropriation of ecclesiastical properties in France, was not so much a reforming measure as an expedient for raising ready money, an act which was frowned on by the Conservative opposition but when applied by the Central Junta of Seville was regarded as 'an act of patriotism'.

But much of the *afrancesado* collaboration must also be attributed to expediency and a desire to hold on to salaries and to keep families together. Loyalty in fact varied from region to region, even from town to town, depending on the stability of French rule.

Take for example the case of Gaspar de Jovellanos, a distinguished man of letters and, by Spanish standards, a liberal, and the equally distinguished poet, aforementioned Meléndez Valdes, once Minister of Marine. Before Joseph's second entry into Madrid (when Valdes was still writing patriotic odes against the French) there was not much to choose between the two friends, but whereas Jovellanos escaped from the capital to become a leader of the Central Junta in Seville, Valdes's plans for escape broke down and he remained behind to become one of Joseph's literary court circle and write odes in honour of the 'intruder king'. Valdes, of course, did have the excuse that he had nearly been lynched by a mob of patriots in his native Oviedo, for the same reasons as the people had threatened to hang Cuesta; reason enough, perhaps, to persuade anyone to become an *afrancesado*. Goya, too, whether from political motives or expediency, was also an *afrancesado* and accepted Joseph's patronage as willingly as he had accepted that of Charles IV. Certainly his opinion of war was shared by Joseph and although the King never saw the artist's series of prints – *Los desastres de la Guerra* and the *Caprichos*, attacking religious superstition and Godoy, which were only published posthumously in 1863 – he would have unreservedly approved of the sentiments Goya expressed therein.

In Andalusia little was to be gained by resistance at a time when French power looked invincibly stable; the intellectuals and nobility of Seville, Cordoba and elsewhere went over en bloc. Wherever qualified admiration for the French revolution went hand in hand with hatred of Godoy's 'tyranny', collaboration was inevitable.

In Barcelona active resistance ended with the plot of May 1809. As soon as the French government looked stable, theatres opened, social life picked up and émigrés returned.

Each stage of the occupation had its own specific brand of collaboration. When the uneasy co-operation of the authorities in Barcelona was broken by Saint Cyr's insistence on the oath of loyalty to Joseph (April 1809), Duhesme's corrupt military government was served by a certain Casanova, a profiteer in identity cards, ransoms and municipal marketing. An adventurer with a magnificent villa and a mistress, he became one of the richest and most powerful men in Barcelona. Suchet's enlightened rule in Valencia, and later over the whole of Aragon, made *afrancesados* of the majority of the population.

Less offensive than men like Casanova were those who could not face dismissal: 'He who won't take the oath will lose his job.' In Catalonia, Augereau, advised by sincere *afrancesados*, tried to get rid of these time-servers and appeal to enlightened opinion to convince local patriots of the positive advantages of French rule and a modern system of government. The moral conquest could not take root, if only because it meant efficient taxation. The new municipal councils worked only where troops were stationed, and with military defeat the system collapsed.[2]

By and large, it would be true to say that the propertied classes found it expedient to collaborate; if they assumed command of the rebels, as did Palafox in Saragossa and the Marqués de Santa Fé in Oviedo, it was often to channel the popular revolt into the Junta rather than to allow dangerous demagogues to usurp control of the mob.

Joseph had realized that however wise and moderate his policy might be it would always remain ineffective unless he could protect his exasperated subjects from the abuses committed by his generals and the troops under their command, but on whom, for the time being, he was dependent. Atrocity stories, the shootings of the Ninth of May, Dupont's sack of Córdoba and the horrors committed at Espinosa and elsewhere, fed xenophobic hatred of the French as heretics and vandals. A proclamation issued by the Valencian Junta in June 1809 before Suchet's advent, reads: '[The soldiers of the French Army] have behaved worse than Hottentots. They have profaned our temples, insulted our religion and raped our women.' The behaviour of the generals was not much better. In the same month, Joseph wrote to the Emperor from General Sebastiani's headquarters at Toledo: 'For the last weeks I have been sending detachments into the mountains to round up flocks of seven to eight thousand merino sheep, which have been in the charge of soldiers of the First Army Corps, acting as shepherds on behalf of a number of generals. I have deprived these of their commands and returned the sheep to their owners.'

To write this letter must have taken considerable courage as it was an indirect criticism of the Emperor himself. Joseph must have known that in the previous November, Napoleon himself had committed an equally barefaced robbery when he seized 20,000 bales of privately owned merino wool stored in Burgos, and gloatingly announced in an army bulletin that he would be able to sell them in France for more than fifteen million francs.

Napoleon was far from pleased with his brother's independent and moderate views and interpreted his clemency as weakness: he wanted a cipher on the Spanish throne obedient only to himself; Spain was to be a vassal state. He was furious when Joseph gave orders that none of his subjects taken under arms should be hanged (but we only have to look at Goya's etchings to see how ineffective these orders were) and even accepted captured guerilleros into his own army (though not with much success since most of them took the first opportunity to desert). 'These fanatical Spanish patriots would have preferred the reactionary rule of Ferdinand VII to that of the enlightened Joseph.'[3] On 24 April 1809, Jovellanos wrote an open letter to General Sebastiani in which he declared that he would be 'only too happy to show his respect and admiration for the philosophical principles of the king provided he exercised them elsewhere'.

Despite this hostility, Joseph still believed in the possibility of a negotiated settlement with the Junta, which by bringing resistance to an end would make the intervention of the French armies unnecessary. In some respects he was as blind as the Emperor; he neither appreciated how serious was the English threat, nor did he seem to realize that however excellent his rule might be, the very strong conservative elements which constituted the nerve of the resistance would always equate his decrees and his enlightened *afrancesado* ministers with 'liberalism', which conjured up in their minds the very worst aspects of the French Revolution. Mesonero Romanos, in his *Memoria de un seteton* (Memoirs of a Septuagenarian, 1881), recalls how, when a Josephite news sheet such as the *Gaceta de Madrid* or the *Diario* fell into the hands of his father, he would angrily cast it aside, exclaiming: 'Nothing but news of that *canaille*, Don José Napoleon, King of Spain by the grace of the Devil!' Never would they accept to be ruled by such a king.

In the summer of 1809, however, Joseph was suddenly confronted with reality when news arrived that the British expeditionary force which had landed in Portugal in April was on the offensive. There was now certainly no chance of a negotiated settlement while the Junta was supported by British arms, and however much he might

178

dislike his generals, Joseph was now more than ever dependent on them for his throne.

No sooner had Wellesley arrived in Portugal than he immediately set about strengthening the defences of Lisbon and then marched north to regain Oporto and drive Soult back into Spain. Soult, with 13,000 men at his disposal and a splendid position behind Douro, imagined with some justification that his army was unassailable. All boats on the south bank had either been scuttled or removed to the north bank, and the only danger that the Marshal feared was that Wellesley might cross the Douro by fishing boats at its lowest reach, just within the bar at its mouth; he therefore took no precautions to secure the immediate upper reaches of this broad and apparently impassable river. The story of Wellesley's capture of Oporto can only be compared with one of the daring commando raids of the Second World War. By a combination of luck and daring, Wellesley was able to sieze four wine barges from the northern reaches of the Douro and ferry more than a thousand men in broad daylight to the shelter of a massive building – the bishop's seminary – on the further bank. Not until an hour later was their presence made known to Soult. The French troops sent to dislodge them were met by a devastating artillery fire from the opposite bank. In desperation Soult now ordered up a further brigade which had hitherto been guarding the quays. But no sooner were the quays deserted than hundreds of citizens poured from their houses to the water's edge, where they launched all the boats that had been drawn ashore and took them to the southern bank. It was only a matter of hours before Wellesley's men were in complete command of the city.

Soult had no alternative but to withdraw. In fact, so precipitate was his retreat that Wellesley was able to sit down that same evening to enjoy the supper already prepared for the Duke of Dalmatia. Abandoning their cannon, the French retreated north-eastwards over the inhospitable Tras-os-Montes into Galicia. Soult's retreat, in bitterly cold, driving rain, has been compared with Moore's retreat to Corunna, but whereas Moore's troops reached Corunna with their arms intact, and were still able to fight a successful battle to cover their embarkment, Soult's troops, following mountain paths and goat tracks, were obliged to discard everything except what was needed for immediate survival. The pursuing British, burdened with knapsacks, rifles and ammunition and all the impedimenta of the early nineteenth-century infantryman, had no chance to catch up with the fleeing enemy. Nevertheless the rout of Soult's army gave Wellesley the opportunity to strike at Madrid in collaboration with Cuesta's freshly formed Spanish army.

Joseph was now to prove himself a man of action. If he was to be dependent on the army for his throne he would at least put himself at its head; never again, he promised himself, would he consent to be placed in the ignominious position of trailing in the rear, as Napoleon had obliged him to do during the latter's advance on Madrid in the preceding November, nor would he subject himself to the humiliation of being treated by his generals as a mere puppet. This time he was determined to show his military capacity.

As soon as Joseph heard of the danger threatening his capital he ordered Soult, with his now partly reorganized forces, to march south to Plasencia to cut off Wellesley in the rear, while he himself, leaving a small garrison to hold Madrid, marched south-east, with Jourdan as his military adviser, to place himself at the head of Marshal Victor's army.

On 27 July, on being informed of Joseph's advance, Wellesley withdrew his forces to Talavera de la Reina, a more suitable defensive position than that in which he found himself. The hard-fought battle which followed was by no means as simple as most history books would have us believe. Both French and British were to claim Talavera as a victory. The French because they had saved Madrid; the English because they had saved Portugal. The French losses were 7,268 men out of 46,000 present, the British 5,363 out of 20,641; the Spanish 1,200 out of 36,000. Joseph, determined to show his brother that he too was capable of winning victories, sent off a most mendacious report to Napoleon, by which the Emperor was not in the least bit taken in. Indeed, he sent a scathing rebuke to his brother for trying to hide the truth from him. The English history books, which claim that Wellesley counter-attacked with the Guards on the second day and drove the French from the field, are almost equally misleading.

Although technically master of the field, Wellesley (who for his handling of this campaign was created Viscount Wellington) with his exhausted and almost starving army, and without adequate reinforcements, was unable to continue his advance on Madrid and fell back into Portugal, recognizing that the present possibilities were limited to the defence of that country. Soult, perhaps through no fault of his own (the artillery promised him from Astorga had not materialized), arrived too late to cut off the British retreat, and Wellington spent the winter months secretly preparing the famous triple line of earthworks, the Lines of Torres Vedras, to cover his base at Lisbon.

Joseph may now have hoped to occupy himself with peaceful affairs. His capital was safe, the British were in retreat, while the Spanish army was, as he believed, in disorderly flight.[5] He was overwhelmed with congratulations on his generalship and was almost persuaded that Talavera had indeed been a great victory. It was therefore with mixed feelings that he learnt that Napoleon was once again thinking of returning to Spain to assume command of the armies. Rumours of his return continued to circulate, and Joseph even sent the Marqués de Casapalacio and his 'dear friend', Montehermoso, to the frontier in anticipation of the Emperor's arrival. But Napoleon was now preoccupied with arrangements for his second marriage, and had no intention of risking his military reputation in Spain in tiresome and costly engagements which would afford him no opportunity of adding to his laurels as the hero of great battles. If anything went wrong, Joseph was a convenient scapegoat; instead, the Emperor contented himself with conducting operations from Paris, where he was quite out of touch with events. The courier service between Paris and Madrid was slow and dispatches were frequently intercepted by guerilleros; when dispatches did arrive, they were already out of date, sometimes by as much as four months. Much to Joseph's chagrin Napoleon, without consulting him, now made several staff changes and appointed Soult to replace Jourdan, which prompted the King to write a sarcastic letter to Julie: 'If the Emperor's feelings towards me have changed, I would prefer to occupy a position where I would not be constantly the object of his affectionate goodwill. If it is his purpose to disgust me with Spain, he has fully succeeded.'

Soult and Joseph had never liked each other ever since the old Boulogne days. Furthermore, the Marshal was well aware that the King resented the fact that he had superseded his old friend Jourdan. But however much Joseph may have mistrusted and despised Soult as a man, he could not deny his military ability, which had already been so amply proven at Fleurus, Stockach, in the Swiss and Italian campaigns and on the field of Austerlitz, the loss of Oporto being his only failure. It was therefore with confidence that he faced a new offensive against Madrid by the Junta's newly-organized Army of La Mancha, under Carlos Areizaga, who had succeeded Cuesta as Commander-in-Chief.

The rapidity of the Spanish advance, however, took both Soult and Joseph by surprise. Areizaga had already come within some thirty-five miles of Madrid when a fatal and unnecessary delay on his part allowed the French time to concentrate. In a number of costly engagements with Areizaga's forward troops (including the largest cavalry action of the whole war, in which 8,000 horses were involved without support of infantry) the French further delayed the Spanish advance and gave time to Marshal Victor to cross the Tagus and threaten Areizaga's rear. It was not until ten days later, on 19 November 1809, that the two main armies confronted each other before the little town of Ocaña. From the very beginning, there was no doubt what the result of the battle would be. Areizaga's deployment of his troops was incredibly inept. Indeed, in its combination of rashness and vacillation his generalship throughout this campaign excelled that of any other Spanish general during the whole war. Brigade after brigade was rolled up, dispersed or captured. The remnants of Areizaga's routed army streamed wildly across the plain to the safety of the passes of the Sierra Morena, hotly pursued by Sebastiani's Polish cavalry.

Next morning, it was the turn of Victor's cavalry to take up the pursuit, capturing on the way the whole artillery and baggage train of the Spanish army. The Spanish losses were appalling – 4,000 killed and 14,000 prisoners; thirty regimental standards and fifty out of sixty guns captured. When the wreck of the army had been rallied in the Sierra Morena three weeks later, only some 21,000 infantry and 3,000 horse reported present.

While Areizaga was conducting his disastrous campaign, the Duque del Parque was carrying out his orders from the Junta to distract the attention of the enemy from the Army of La Mancha. In fact he did his job admirably, and but for Areizaga's incompetence the outcome might have been very different. Del Parque's army, after some initial success, was utterly routed at Alba de Tormes and fled in great confusion, though without much loss of life. Three thousand men were killed or captured, a further three thousand deserted – not a ruinous proportion out of 32,000. In addition, del Parque lost five standards, nine guns and most of his baggage. It was not until later, while his army was in winter cantonments, that his army suffered its most severe losses. Having only the ruined region round Coria, Plasencia and Ciudad Rodrigo to feed them, the troops suffered dreadful privation, living on half rations, eked out with edible acorns. By January 1811, del Parque had lost another 9,000 men from dysentery, fever and starvation.

The news of the disaster of Ocaña, so swiftly followed by the rout of Alba de Tormes, gave the death-blow to the Junta. Its attempt to win back its lost credit by an offensive campaign against Madrid having ended in such a lamentable fashion, there was nothing left for it but to agree in its own supersession by the often discussed National *Cortes* which was to meet four months hence, in March, in Seville. Meanwhile, Joseph had once again returned to Madrid triumphant. The volatile Madrileños gave their king a heart-warming reception; Joseph, in turn, responded with a splendid and magnanimous gesture. After parading some 18,000 prisoners through the streets of his capital, he unconditionally gave them their freedom, a quixotic gesture which was given great prominence in the royalist paper *Gaceta de Madrid*, copies of which were immediately forwarded to Paris.

Napoleon was furious; but was this gesture really so quixotic? As we have seen, Joseph wished to reign as a 'National' king with the consent of his subjects and without having to depend on the support of his brother's generals. To this end he tried to raise a large force of his own, which should be at his personal disposal. He formed cadres of regiment after regiment, and filled them with deserters from the foreign troops of the Junta and with any prisoners who could be induced to enlist under his banner to avoid transportation to France. He was lavish in awarding decorations and titles to any of the nobility who would accept his commission, and promised 500 *reals* to any mounted cavalryman who should desert to him from the Junta and 85 *reals* to any foot-soldier who brought with him a gun or pistol. But the recruits, when sent to join the new regiments, deserted within a few weeks. Joseph thought it was from lack of pay and was furious that but for want of money he might have had a formidable army of his own. However, he deceived himself. In the ranks of the Junta's army the soldier was even worse fed, clothed and paid than in that of Joseph. No amount of pampering would have turned the King's Spanish levies into loyal soldiers; after a few weeks the released prisoners too deserted to join their old colours – the real renegades were few.

All his efforts were in vain. Despite his good intentions, the peasants and guerilleros, encouraged by their priests, refused to believe that Joseph was genuinely interested in the welfare of their country: indeed how could they, while the French armies continued to plunder the countryside, pillage their churches and rape their women?

The peasants fled from villages occupied by the French troops and hid their daughters and wives, only returning reluctantly by day to cultivate their crops. In these circumstances, Joseph needed all his courage to persevere in his task; he certainly had his faults, but could never be accused of cowardice. He never despaired of ultimately winning the affection of his subjects, even when the Junta of Seville, after the disastrous defeat at Ocaña, published the most scurrilous and crude broadsheets inciting the people never to recognize 'this spoiled imbecile, sent to us by Bonaparte'.

But the Junta, after the disasters of Ocaña and Alba de Tormes, was in no position to dictate terms. Even in the unlikely case of its suing for peace or agreeing to a negotiated settlement (as Joseph and his *afrancesado* advisers desired), the Emperor would never have agreed to treat with an illegal assembly[6] – the only legitimate government in Spain was that which he had set up in Madrid. He had seen to that when he made Joseph King. It was quite clear that the Spanish would never submit of their own accord, and that the Junta was resolved to fight out the losing game to the end. Even Joseph realized he would never be King of Spain until every province was held down by French bayonets. Not only must each corner of the land be conquered, but after conquest it must be garrisoned. Then perhaps, and then only, would he be able to introduce the enlightened constitution he so desired for the country; only then could his fiscal system be successfully implemented to bring him in sufficient revenue to carry out the reforms he so earnestly desired.

In the later months of 1809, the only regular income he could procure was that which came in from the local taxes of Madrid and the few other larger towns which were in his secure possession. Elsewhere, the guerilleros were cutting off all his supplies; and even in those other areas securely held, his agents and intendants had the greatest difficulty in extracting even minor contributions from the military governors. Joseph could not even command a quarter of the sum required to pay the ordinary expenses of government, nor could he meet the cost of equipping and paying the Spanish army he was so anxious to form.

Apart from the confiscation of church property, Joseph's only other expedient for raising money, recommended by Napoleon, was to confiscate the property of all persons in the service of the Junta, an act which he deplored. This would have given him vast sums if only he could have found buyers, but who wanted to pay ready cash for properties already overrun by guerilleros? Property of immense value was sold for wholly inadequate sums. There still remained, however, the immensely rich province of Andalusia, as yet unoccupied, as a potential source of revenue. The Junta's armies after the defeats of

Ocaña and Alba de Tormes were in no position to put up any effective resistance to a French invasion, but before Joseph decided on this next move, he wished to make certain that Wellington had retired into Portugal and that there would be no danger from this quarter, and that he had sufficient troops to garrison the already occupied provinces. He had not therefore immediately followed up Areizaga's rout at Ocaña, but had waited until the new reinforcements from Germany had begun to pour across the Pyrenees into Biscaya and Navarre in enormous numbers. It was not until he knew that his rear was well guarded that Joseph felt safe to embark on his great offensive against Andalusia.

Why Soult should have agreed to the invasion is difficult to understand – as a strategist he should have envisaged the situation from the military rather than the political point of view. Had Jourdan still been Joseph's military adviser, he would almost certainly have advised against the expedition. In his memoirs he wrote:

The English army being now the only organized force in a state to face the Imperial troops, and its presence in the Peninsula being the only thing that sustained the Spanish government and gave confidence to the Spanish people, I believe that we ought to have set ourselves to destroy that army, rather than to have disseminated our troops in garrisoning the whole surface of Spain.[7]

XII

The Conquest of Andalusia and disillusion

1810–1811

It is easy to understand Joseph's point of view – he wished rather to complete the conquest of his own realm, by subduing its wealthiest and most populated province, than do his brother's work in Portugal. It was natural that he should be fascinated by the idea of conquering in person the one great province of Spain that still remained intact, and which Napoleon had foreseen would be his by the summer. A brilliant campaign, in which he would figure as commander-in-chief as well as King, might at last convince the Spaniards and his brother of his abilities. He was anxious to play the part of a merciful and generous conqueror; at the worst, the revenues of a wealthy Andalusia would be a godsend to his depleted treasury.

On 14 December 1809, Soult made a formal request in a dispatch to Berthier for leave to commence the march on Seville. No direct reply was received to this dispatch, or to several subsequent communications, in which Soult and Joseph set forth the arrangements they were making, always subject to the Emperor's approval. In fact it was not until January, when Joseph had already crossed the Sierra Morena, that Napoleon vouchsafed to answer him at all. Since no prohibition came, Joseph made up his mind to strike.

On 19 January 1810 Areizaga, who despite his incompetence was still in command of the Junta's army, learnt that the whole of his defensive line, from Villamanrique in the east to Almadén on the west, was about to be attacked by the enemy. His position was hopeless; his front extended over 150 miles and at no single point could he concentrate more than 15,000 men.

186

It has been said that Joseph's invasion of Andalusia was more like a royal progress than a military operation. This is an exaggeration. Areizaga's armies put up what resistance they could, but they were outnumbered and outmanoeuvred. While Joseph, Soult, Mortier and Sebastiani were forcing the defiles of the Sierra Morena, Victor's corps was making an outflanking movement to cut off the Spanish rear. By 24 January Victor was in Córdoba, which opened its gates without resistance.

The Córdoba–Seville road was now open to Joseph and Soult, with no enemy to bar their progress. On 21 January, Joseph had spent the night peacefully at Baylen, the scene of Dupont's disastrous defeat in 1808. Here he learnt that the central government had precipitately left Seville, taking with it both its executive committee and ministers of state.

The panic, in fact, had begun on the 18th when news was received that Victor was marching on Córdoba. The Junta appealed to the people of Andalusia to keep calm; they were informed that Albuquerque from Estramadura and del Parque from the mountains between Bejar and Ciudad Real had been summoned to fall on Victor's flank. But it was palpably obvious that the French would be at the gates of Seville long before either of these generals had even received their orders.

The ineptitude of the government and the imminent peril to which Seville was exposed gave a chance to local agitators, who had already twice prepared a *pronunciamento* against the Junta. Riots broke out and Seville fell into the hands of the mob, who, led by a Capuchin friar riding on a mule and brandishing a crucifix, broke open the prisons and the arsenal, armed themselves, and nominated a new Supreme National Council.

The discredited Junta fled to the safety of Cadiz, but on their flight many of its members were mobbed and arrested. Its new President, the Conde Altamira, and the War Minister, Cornel, were seized by the mob on their way through Jerez and narrowly escaped assassination. Twenty-three members reached Cadiz, where, by a proclamation dated 29 January, they renounced their authority and nominated a Council of Regency (presided over by the Bishop of Orense), to which they resigned their power until such time as the much-discussed National Cortes should meet.

Although Joseph would have preferred to have captured the whole of the Central Junta in Seville, it was gratifying to know that now it was dispersed he was unlikely to meet with any further organized resistance. Even the peasantry seemed amicably disposed, perhaps

187

because for once Joseph's stringent orders against pillage had been observed. When he entered Córdoba on 26 January, the horrors perpetrated by Dupont's troops three years earlier seemed to have been forgotten. The city was *en fête* and all the leading citizens, headed by the clergy and a bevy of girls scattering flowers, turned out to meet their King. Through cheering crowds and to the strains of martial music and the peal of bells, Joseph made his triumphant way to the episcopal palace, where apartments had been prepared for him. To what extent Victor had organized this demonstration of apparent loyalty is a matter of conjecture; certainly Joseph, and many of his staff, were persuaded that it was sincere.

On the day after his arrival, the cathedral chapter escorted the King in great pomp to the *Mezquita*, the famous mosque, with its hundred and fifty columns of jasper and marble, which after the expulsion of the Moors had been dedicated as a Christian place of worship. After the Te Deum, the Archbishop approached Joseph and humbly returned him the French colours captured at Baylen – an extraordinary and unexpected gesture of goodwill. Almost in tears, Joseph mounted the pulpit and in a moving speech called on all Spaniards to rally to him : 'May this day mark the beginning of a new era which will bring glory and happiness to the nation !'

With Areizaga's army now in full retreat to the south-east, Soult and Joseph had leisure to plan the rest of their campaign. The question of whether it was Soult or Joseph who decided to march first on Seville instead of Cadiz has often been disputed. Cadiz was obviously the more important objective now that the Council of Regency was established there. But apart from topographical considerations (the easiest route to Cadiz lay through Seville) a desire to seize the capital from which the Junta had so long defied him seems to have overridden all other considerations in Joseph's mind. The Council of Regency in Cadiz he believed to be impotent; the new Junta in Seville, which had quite illegally proclaimed itself the government of all Spain, could easily be disposed of. Then at last the provinces would submit, the regular armies would lay down their arms, the guerilla bands would disperse to their homes, and he might rule as a real king, not merely as the tool of his imperious brother. The capture of Seville would be the last act but one of the drama; after that, Joseph would become the national monarch of a submissive people and carry out all the benevolent schemes on which his mind dwelt during his more hopeful hours. That the resistance would continue, even if Seville were taken and the Junta scattered and discredited, he never dreamed; there would be time in plenty to

188

reduce Cadiz, which, although an island fortress of extreme strength, was panic-stricken and without an adequate garrison. On 25 January when the plan was drawn up no one realized that the Spanish Army of Estramadura, commanded by Albuquerque, whose presence in Andalusia was not even suspected, would deliberately leave Seville to its fate, as incapable of defence, and by forced marches hasten to occupy Cadiz, which was destined to become the new and impregnable capital of insurgent Spain and which was to hold out for three more years.

Anti-Josephite historians have always laid the blame on the King for making Seville his first goal; this is most unjust. Bigarré, his aide-de-camp, and Miot de Melito, who were present at the council of war when the plan was discussed, both mention in their memoirs that Joseph did in fact suggest that at least part of the army should be diverted to Cadiz, but was overruled by Soult and his other generals. In du Casse's *Mémoires et correspondance du roi Joseph*, the same story is given by the King himself.

On 25 January, therefore, Joseph, with all his army, with the exception of Sebastiani's corps which was sent to occupy Granada, marched on the Andalusian capital. The new revolutionary Junta now installed there had at its disposal an armed mob of 20,000 men and a mere handful of regular troops of the late Junta. On counting its resources it was realized that to man the defence lines which had hastily been thrown up by the people would require at least 50,000 men. Even if every man, woman and child in the city was in possession of a musket, the place could still not be held. The revolutionary Junta now copied the prudent and cowardly example set by the Central Junta, which they had been at such pains to denounce five days earlier, and ignominiously crept away by night without so much as bidding farewell to their followers. Nevertheless, although lacking coherent leadership, the mob, headed by fanatical friars, rushed to the improvised fortifications as soon as the first French dragoons appeared on the scene and let fly with muskets and cannon at every *vedette* who showed himself.

On 30 January Victor arrived with the infantry to reinforce the cavalry, with Joseph, Soult and Mortier not far behind. No further military operations were necessary however. On the 31st, the corporation of Seville sent a deputation to sue for peace. They offered to admit the enemy into the city if they were guaranteed security of life and property for all who would submit, and a promise that no extortionate war indemnity should be levied on the city. To this, Joseph, anxious as ever to appear the pacific conqueror, gave his willing consent. While these negotiations were in progress, those regular Spanish troops still in the town quietly made their escape to the borders of Portugal, and ultimately to Cadiz, to reinforce the garrison there.

On the afternoon of 1 February, Joseph, at the head of his guard and surrounded by a glittering escort of officers, made his official entry into Seville and installed himself in the Alcazar, the former palace of the Moorish emirs and residence of the kings of Spain. The impression made on the citizens by the conduct of the two Juntas and the turbulence of the mob which had ruled during the last week had been so deplorable that many Sevillians, despairing of the national cause, rushed to acknowledge the 'intruder king'. Indeed, there were more *Josefinos* to be found in this city than in any other corner of Spain.

General Bigarré, who has left a vivid account of Joseph's Andalusian expedition, tells us that the welcome he received in Seville surpassed even that given him by the people of Córdoba:

> From morning to night priests and monks came to kiss his hand, telling him that he had been sent by God. The Andalusian nobility, for their part, did everything in their power to please. One grandee presented him with twelve magnificent bulls, another with Andalusian horses, beautifully caparisoned. Others placed their wives or daughters at His Majesty's disposal. In the midst of scenes of indescribable enthusiasm, the populace, whenever they caught sight of the King, whether on horseback in the street, or on the balconies of the Alcazar, prostrated themselves before him.[1]

Even allowing for some slight exaggeration, there seems little doubt that Joseph was a 'success'. He spent twelve unforgettable days and nights in Seville. Every evening he gave a magnificent dinner party in the lovely gardens of his Moorish palace. Once his guests had departed, he amused himself by wandering incognito through the streets illuminated in his honour and mixing with the gay crowds. Bigarré also adds that he engaged the services of a pretty young flamenco dancer to perform for his private enjoyment.

On the day following their entry into Seville, Joseph and Soult, having learnt that Albuquerque's hitherto unsuspected army was marching on Cadiz, directed Victor to hasten in its pursuit, destroy it, and take possession of the town. But it was already too late. Albuquerque, with extraordinary expedition, had already reached the safety of the island fortress and had no intention of surrendering to

Victor or anyone else. Cadiz lies on a peninsula linked to the Isla de León by a narrow isthmus, which in those days was heavily fortified. The Isla itself is separated from the mainland of Andalusia by a shallow, marshy stretch of salt water, some four to five hundred yards wide. Albuquerque had destroyed the only bridge across this formidable barrier and had thus rendered the city virtually impregnable except from the sea. But so long as the British fleet remained paramount, any attack from that quarter was out of the question; nor could the city be reduced by starvation while British ships were free to come and go as they pleased. There was nothing Victor could do but contain the garrison.

On 13 February, Joseph tore himself away from the delights of Seville to inspect the situation for himself. On the 18th he was at Puerto Santa-Maria on the Bay of Cadiz, from where he had a clear view of the beleaguered city. Encouraged by his recent enthusiastic reception at Cordoba and Seville, he decided to send a delegation to the Council of Regency to negotiate, if possible, some sort of settlement.[2] It was a forlorn hope. The delegation was ignominiously forced to beat a retreat, without so much as a hearing.

Since there was nothing more to be achieved by his presence on the Atlantic seaboard, Joseph set out on 28 February for the Mediterranean on the last stage of his conquest of Andalusia. Only one more incident (and an ominous one, had he but realized it) marred his triumphal progress when, on 2 March, 1,500 guerilleros attempted to prevent his advance on Ronda. General Bigarré with the advance guard, after a sharp engagement, succeeded in routing the enemy, and Joseph was able to enter the city. But this was only a minor incident in an otherwise successful and comparatively peaceful campaign; Joseph had every reason to be proud of his achievement. Even in the countryside, apart from isolated incidents, the people had shown no overt hostility to his armies and indeed had often given proof of their loyalty and even affection for their king. Despite the presence of guerilla forces in the neighbourhood, Ronda, too, was to give Don José Primero a warm welcome. But the news which greeted Joseph on his arrival in the city was sufficient to dissipate all his complacency. He learnt to his mortification that without consulting him Napoleon on 8 February had issued decrees setting up independent military governments in the provinces north of the Ebro – in Catalonia, Aragon, Navarre and Biscaya – over which Joseph was to have no control. It was clear that this was the first step to total annexation, just as Napoleon had threatened before his departure from Valladolid in January of the previous year. Marshal Jourdan wrote in his memoirs: 'It seemed as though the Emperor wished to punish his brother for having found the way to the hearts of the people of the south.'³ Abel Hugo, who was with Joseph at the time, wrote later: 'If Napoleon had not himself become, to all intents and purposes, an accessory to English intrigues and Joseph's worst enemy, the pacification of the whole of Spain would have been simply a matter of time. The new state of affairs could not fail to destroy all the good that the wise and noble conduct of the King had achieved.'⁴

From a political point of view, Napoleon's policy was so unsound that one must ask oneself what prompted him to take such an obviously harmful decision. It was bound to exacerbate the Resistance still further; it would destroy Joseph's prestige for ever and ruin any hope he had had of one day being accepted as a national king. Unable to find any other plausible reason for the Emperor's course of action, pro-Bonapartist historians, including Frédéric Masson, claim that it was precisely in order to disgust Joseph with his position, and thereby force him to abdicate of his own free will, that Napoleon acted as he did.

This contention is ridiculous. As we know, Joseph had frequently expressed his wish to abdicate but had always been refused. He was to do so again later, but with no greater success. Jourdan's explanation is much more plausible; Napoleon may well have regarded Joseph's growing popularity in the Peninsula, and in particular his triumphant tour through Andalusia, as a threat to his own authority and prestige. Napoleon was never one to share glory – one only has to remember his jealousy of Moreau and his deliberate omission of any mention of the unfortunate Desaix's preponderant role in the victory of Marengo.

At the end of March 1810, Joseph left Ronda for Malaga. En route there occurred an incident which illustrates one side of Joseph's character and how successfully he could endear himself to his subjects by his personal charm. It was just the sort of incident to encourage his euphoric dreams and persuade him that all would be well in the end. Bigarré, who was present at the time, recounts:

> Observing a town a little distance away, where he proposed to halt, the King rode on ahead, alone except for one aide-de-camp. A short gallop brought him to the gates of the town, which he entered just as a guerilla band, under the command of the celebrated *contrabandista*, López Muñoz, was assembling in the main square. Boldly riding forward, Joseph gave the order: 'Commandant! Stand to your

arms! I will review your troops.' Although somewhat astonished to receive such a command, the worthy López, who had apparently heard of the favourable reputation enjoyed by Joseph among all enlightened Andalusians, promptly made up his mind and replied 'At your orders, Sire,' and then, mounting his horse, ordered his men to draw their sabres. Joseph was acclaimed with shouts of *'Viva el rey don José'* . . . [After inspecting the troop] the King informed the rebels that he was prepared to take them into his service as the nucleus of a regiment of Andalusian light cavalry. A quarter of an hour later, when the municipal council came to pay their respects to the King, they were astonished to find two fully armed *contrabandisti* guarding the door to his lodgings and the walls of the staircase already garlanded with flowers.[5]

The accounts of the King's progress through Andalusia, furnished by Miot, Bigarré and other trustworthy sources, make us realize that Joseph was not altogether unjustified in indulging in his pipedreams. A stronger-minded man than he might well have had his head turned.

General Bigarré tells us that at the entry to every village, the King was met by the head man and the curé, who knelt before him. Everywhere the people continued to demonstrate their loyalty and affection. Bigarré recounts that he himself saw women 'prostrate themselves before the King and entreat His Majesty to do them the honour of riding over their bodies'. In Malaga, the faithful General tells us, 'One of the most beautiful and highborn ladies of the city wrote to His Majesty soliciting the honour of spending the night with him.'[6] Joseph certainly would not have appreciated his aide-de-camp's revelations;[7] on the contrary, though one might think rather belatedly, he was anxious to avoid the reputation of a libertine, and it was perhaps for this reason that he wrote, while still in Malaga, to his Queen Julie, inviting her to join him with the children. But there was also another reason why he wanted Julie to be at his side; he was unwilling that she should attend the marriage of the Emperor to Marie-Louise of Austria. He feared that Napoleon would not accord her the honour due to her rank and thus strike yet another blow at his prestige as King. If, for some reason, she should be unable to come to Spain, he begged her to excuse herself from attending the wedding on the grounds of ill health. But Julie, the plain little daughter of a Marseilles merchant, preferring to risk a snub from her Imperial brother-in-law rather than incur his displeasure, remained in Paris for the ceremonies. Joseph sent d'Azanza, his Minister of Foreign Affairs, to whom he awarded the title of Knight of the Golden Fleece, to act as his representative with instructions to enlighten the Emperor on the true situation in Spain and endeavour to persuade him that the establishment of military governments was nothing less than disastrous.

After a delightful though anxious fortnight in Malaga, Joseph next proceeded to Granada, where he took up residence in the Alhambra. Here, once again, he was received like a caliph. But there was still no indication that Napoleon proposed to change his mind and, despite all the displays of loyalty and affection he had lately received, Joseph's thoughts inevitably returned to abdication. The only heartening news to reach him was that Masséna with an army of 65,000 men was preparing to invade Portugal and drive the English into the sea.

After a week in Granada, Joseph retraced his steps and, passing once more through Jaen, Andujar and Córdoba, reached Seville at the beginning of April. Here he called a meeting of his ministers to discuss the situation arising from Napoleon's draconian decrees. His faithful and sincere friend Miot de Melito advised him to abdicate. In a somewhat quaintly phrased speech, he told the King that 'Fortune itself seems to favour this happy issue. The conclusion of a brilliant campaign, the welcome you have received in Andalusia, your humanity and moderation, are all conducive to lending your abdication an air of respectability and good sense.'[8]

His Spanish ministers, however, supported by the Marquesa de Montehermoso, were of a different opinion and continued to remind the King that the future welfare of Spain lay in his hands and that he had promised that the territorial boundaries of Spain would never be violated. Joseph once again fell a victim to their blandishments and agreed, although unwillingly, to remain as king. However, if he was to retain any vestige of authority, he should have to counter Napoleon's decisions with decrees of his own. In his heart of hearts, he must have known that his brother would never agree to his enactments (promulgated on 17 and 23 April 1810) whereby, on the French system, he decided that Spain should be divided into thirty-eight departments and, in place of an army of occupation, a civil militia should be formed to keep the internal peace. It was a completely unrealistic scheme : he must have known that he could not dispense with the Imperial armies while Spain was still unsubdued. The Central Junta might have been dispersed and its army destroyed, but there were still other provincial Juntas and other armies quite apart from the bands of guerilleros roving the country. Moreover, there was still the British army strongly entrenched in Portugal. That Joseph should have ever contemplated such an idea is so inconceivable that one is forced to look for a rational explanation for his conduct.

Was it possible that he hoped to exasperate his brother to such an extent that the Emperor would recall him to France and demand his abdication? Certainly at that particular moment nothing would have pleased Joseph more. We know from his letters to Julie at this time that he certainly anticipated a violent reaction from his brother. Knowing that all his correspondence was intercepted by the Imperial police, he dispatched letter after letter to his wife in the hopes that one at least would reach her. He warned her that it might be essential for her to leave France at a moment's notice and instructed her to make all the necessary arrangements for the transfer of his personal fortune in case it became necessary for her to live with him in exile. But despite all his anxieties Joseph still continued to promote his own public image: he made a point of attending all the Holy Week religious ceremonies, which have always played such an important part in the life of Seville, and followed all the processions, candle in hand.

On 2 May 1810 he finally left for the north, journeying by easy stages, and only reached Madrid on the 15th. Rumour had been current for some time that Joseph was making Seville his permanent capital, and the relief of the Madrileños at seeing him again was the occasion for further outbursts of enthusiasm. His presence guaranteed that there would be no more mob risings like that of 2 May 1808, which had so terrified the bourgeoisie and which had been so ruthlessly repressed by Murat, and that the city would now be saved from the rapacity of the military authorities.

But apart from the gratifying news that his old friend Bernadotte had been elected Crown Prince of Sweden, there was little else to give Joseph cause for rejoicing. Now that he had left Andalusia, the Spanish officials whom he had appointed there were powerless against Sebastiani, 'the church plunderer', and Soult, 'the judicious art collector'. 'At the very moment when the King was lavishing assurances and promises,' writes Miot, 'and everywhere extolling the thorough disinterestedness of the French, severe and crushing exactions were being made in all the provinces in our occupation. An iron hand was grinding them to dust. The King was powerless to resist the open violation of promises which he was daily giving.'[9]

Open resistance, however, had ceased in Andalusia, save at Cadiz (where the Spanish garrison had been reinforced by 8,000 British troops) and in the inaccessible passes of the Sierra Nevada. Andalusia had been subdued from end to end, but neither Soult nor Joseph yet realized that a disastrous strategic mistake had been made. Seventy thousand Imperial troops were pinned down to garrison the newly conquered realm, while Portugal and Wellington's army remained untouched. In their opinion, as in Napoleon's, the conquest of Portugal was sufficiently provided for by the new reinforcements, numbering some 10,000 men, which were now pouring over the Ebro.

In July 1810 Joseph learnt that Louis, exasperated by the Emperor's demands on his subjects, had relinquished his throne of the Netherlands and fled to Germany. Joseph was strongly tempted to follow his young brother's example.

On 8 August, he sent the Marqués de Almenara, his Minister of the Interior, to Paris, to replace Ananza, who had failed to obtain an audience with the Emperor. Almenara was the bearer of a long letter[10] in which Joseph made it quite clear that so long as the Emperor endorsed the policy of allowing his generals to govern the provinces independently, his role as King was untenable and Spain would never see peace. 'My position in this country,' he wrote, 'always difficult, often deplorable, is now such that it cannot continue under the arrangements which have been made and are threatened.'

If Soult were now to be made Governor-General of Andalusia, Joseph's last source of revenue would be denied him. He would be confined to Madrid which barely provided him with a revenue of 80,000 francs per month with which to pay the salaries of his own guard, his government servants and ministers and contribute to the support of the hundreds of refugees who had flocked to the capital to escape the rapacity of the generals. 'If the army of Andalusia is taken from me, what shall I be?' he continues. 'The porter of the hospitals of Madrid and depots of the army and jailer of the prisoners?' In conclusion he boldly states:

> . . . I weep over the change of heart of my brother; over the gradual diminution of his great glory, which would have been better preserved by generosity and heroism than by any extension of power . . .

Napoleon never replied.

On 7 September he wrote to Julie from Madrid:

> Use all your charm, prudence and wisdom to find out how and when the Emperor wishes me to extricate myself from this position. I will never be able to thank you enough if you can get me out of here and any public office. You cannot imagine how happy I would be just

with you, my children and my conscience and surrounded by a few friends.

The popularity which Joseph had been at such pains to acquire was completely dissipated by Napoleon's decree of February. In the newly formed independent military governments, the generals were behaving with a ruthlessness unparalleled except by the German and Russian occupation of Poland in the last war. Everywhere and every day, the guerillero bands were becoming bolder. On 8 November Joseph wrote to Julie from Madrid :

> Day and night I must be ready to mount my horse and defend my life against the armed and infuriated bands that surround this city. At this very moment my own guard which has received no pay for six months, is out fighting these same bands. So long as this nation is unable to recognize that I am the protector of the people [*le pouvoir protecteur*] and their real king, it will never calm down . . . I try to be as patient as I can, but I will never condone the horrible treatment meted out to the people by the military governors.

A few days later, he sent his nephew Marius Clary to Paris, the third negotiator in three months. He also wrote to his uncle Fesch begging him to intervene with the Emperor on his behalf. But all to no avail. Uncle Fesch advised his nephew to remain in Madrid, while Napoleon, who was only too pleased to find in Joseph a scapegoat for his own mistakes, paid no attention to his complaints and sent back his negotiators without so much as a hearing.

The year 1811 opened inauspiciously. The French armies suffered defeat in Portugal, in Estramadura and in Andalusia itself. In Catalonia, the French had the humiliation of losing Figueras, on the frontier of the Pyrenees, to the organized guerillero army of Campoverde. Joseph would have liked to make himself useful, but what could he do? At one time he thought of leaving Madrid for Valencia, the only province still not in open rebellion and where, thanks to Suchet's wise rule, the people still expressed their loyalty to him. For this, however, he required permission from the Emperor. Napoleon had other things on his mind; Marie-Louise was expecting his child; war with Russia was imminent. Then suddenly, after virtually depriving Joseph of all power, Napoleon wrote to him in almost affectionate terms, to announce the birth of the King of Rome and inviting him to act as godfather to his son and heir.

This was an opportunity not to be missed. Napoleon expected Joseph to allow a proxy to stand in for him, but Joseph had no such intention; perhaps never again would he have such a good excuse to speak to his brother personally. Without waiting for official authority, Joseph set out for Paris on 23 April 1811, accompanied by Miot de Melito and three of his Spanish ministers. He had no idea how he would be received, but despite everything he had said, despite all his sufferings, he still held Spain too dear to renounce entirely all hopes of bringing peace and a liberal constitution to his long-suffering subjects.

On 10 May 1811, Joseph and his suite crossed the frontier into France.

XIII

Vitoria :

The End of a Reign

1811–1812

At Dax, where Joseph and his suite were to spend the night, he was met by an Imperial courier ordering him to return to Spain immediately. This time Joseph was undeterred. Julie, who had repeatedly but ineffectively attempted to intercede with Napoleon on behalf of her husband, had already warned Joseph as early as January that should he cross the frontier, the Comte de Champagny, Minister of Foreign Affairs, had orders to have him arrested at Bayonne.

Despite the Emperor's threats, however, Joseph was able to proceed unhindered across France. On 15 May he reached Paris and spent the night in the Luxembourg Palace, where he still retained his apartments as Grand Elector. Here Julie gave him all the latest news and informed him that his brother was expecting him at Rambouillet on the following day. Napoleon was now much more preoccupied with affairs in Russia than with those of Spain. Instead of bursting into one of those simulated rages at which he was so adept, he even gave Joseph a cordial welcome and apparently listened patiently to all his complaints. He could not blame him for the recent reverses in Spain, since he had long deprived him of any real military control. Not knowing how to extricate himself from the hornets' nest (to use Miot's terms) which he had stirred up in Spain, Napoleon had no intention of allowing Joseph to abdicate – he was too useful a scapegoat for all his own mistakes. Accordingly he appeared in one of his most magnanimous moods and in the course of the next few days promised to meet all Joseph's requirements. Napoleon never had the slightest difficulty in making promises; their implementation was a different matter. At this moment, too, he was anxious to maintain appearances and to pretend that Joseph's visit was solely at his own invitation. He was particularly anxious that the world should see no further rift in the Imperial family. It was bad enough that Lucien should have retired to Italy and that Louis had resigned the throne of Holland to live in Styria, where he had renounced his royal prerogatives and assumed the title of Comte de Saint-Leu.

On the afternoon of 9 June, Joseph, in his ridiculously theatrical costume of Grand Elector, surrounded by the diplomatic corps, bishops, marshals and princes, attended the christening of his nephew, the King of Rome, and then retired to Mortefontaine. Immediately after the ceremony Napoleon left for Normandy. Joseph took the occasion to invite his old friend Stanislas de Girardin to Mortefontaine. Girardin has left an account of this visit:

> I found an entirely different welcome and manners to those to which I had been accustomed. The King dined in private with his family and I only saw him when he entered his carriage to drive to Paris. After he had left, I saw the Queen with whom I had long conversations and who did not hide from me the fact that she was very disturbed by the extreme irresolution shown by the King . . . His attitude towards the Emperor was always very cold. The information which Miot (a fellow guest) provided me concerning Spain was far from optimistic. He was of the opinion that the French army would never take possession of Lisbon or Cadiz, and that it would soon have to evacuate the whole of Andalusia. Government employees were unpaid and the entire administration was in a state of chaos or lacking in initiative. The truth is that the King cannot positively make up his mind. *The intoxication of grandeur is not easily dispersed in the hearts of those who believe themselves capable of bearing its burden* [my italics; M.R.].[1]

Girod de l'Ain writes that it is in this respect that Joseph is most to be criticized, 'since his vacillation was due to vanity. The very fact that he had been "King of Spain, of the Indies, etc., etc." had turned his head, and if he hesitated to leave the "hornets' nest of Spain" it was because he believed that by becoming once again merely Grand Elector, his prestige would suffer.'[2]

On 12 June, Joseph had his last interview with Napoleon, when the Emperor renewed his promises: sufficient subsidies; authority over his generals, the right to accord pardons, a peaceful settlement of the annexation of the provinces north of the Ebro and of Portugal.

On 16 June, after touching farewells with his family, Joseph took his seat in his carriage, together with Jourdan (whom Napoleon had once more allowed Joseph to retain in his suite as chief-of-staff) and the faithful Miot.

On the 23rd he arrived at Bayonne, where he spent four days at the Château de Marrac. On 27 June he crossed the little frontier river of the Bidassoa. He was in no hurry to reach Madrid. He broke his journey at Vitoria, where he spent several days in the villa which he had bought from the Marquis of Montehermoso.[3] He stopped again at Burgos and then at Valladolid and only reached the capital on the evening of 15 July.

Ever since the early morning, the Madrileños, who had been alerted of the arrival of their king, thronged the streets. Joseph, instead of driving through the city, entered by the Puerto San Vincente, close to the Royal Palace, the entrance by which the Spanish kings had been accustomed to make their return from their *sitios*. As soon as his arrival was announced, an enormous crowd surrounded the palace, giving every demonstration of pleasure at his return, grateful to be spared from a military dictatorship and rule by martial law.

For several days, to celebrate his return, a succession of corridas, free to the public, were held in the capital. Although tired by his journey, Joseph never failed to make his appearance at the bull ring. He walked in the Prado and mixed with the crowd, talking familiarly with his subjects. On one occasion he was accosted by a woman who begged him to forgive a guerillero taken prisoner, to whom he immediately granted a pardon.

He had returned to his capital, to his people and to his delightful, now widowed, Marquesa de Montehermoso. But he was soon disenchanted. Napoleon's promises were not kept. No subsidies arrived, and all he had was 1,500,000 francs which Nicolas Clary had lent him against the Emperor's promises. The generals were no more obedient to him than before and all continued to rule like autocrats in their own conquered provinces. Fouché in his memoirs recalls: 'The generals, who were dependent on Paris and Madrid at the same time, so arranged matters that they were dependent on neither. Above all, they wished to be masters of the provinces they occupied.'

To add to Joseph's worries, the harvest that year was one of the worst for years, not only in Spain, but also in France. There was little the King could do to alleviate the miseries of his people. He despatched officials to collect what corn there was available and founded a bakery in the royal palace to distribute bread to the poor.

On 31 August the King wrote to Julie to intervene again on his behalf with the Emperor. Of the million francs the Emperor had promised him he had so far received only 500,000. He wanted Julie to come and join him, but warned her that she must persuade the Emperor to make regular payments and to obtain an advance to cover three or four months 'which you may bring with you in your convoy, otherwise I will find myself, with you and my children in an even more embarrassing situation than I am at present'.

It was always very difficult (and how much more difficult today) to unravel Joseph's financial situation. On instructions from the Emperor, the Comte François-Nicolas Mollient, Minister to the Treasury, attempted to balance his budget, but in vain: all that remained clear was that the war in Spain, between 1808 and 1810, had cost the French treasury 220 million francs. At the time when Napoleon persuaded Joseph to accept the throne of Spain, he believed he could get the Banque de France to advance him 25 millions with the diamonds of the Spanish throne as collateral. But in mysterious circumstances most of the jewels disappeared, and it was finally from contributions levied on Prussia that Joseph's treasury was reimbursed from time to time.

In 1814 after the defeat of the French at Vitoria the Spanish demanded to know what had happened to the crown jewels, of which a detailed inventory, now in the state archives, had been drawn up before Ferdinand VII's departure for Bayonne. There is no evidence that Murat had appropriated them for himself, as has been suggested. Ferdinand and his Minister accused Joseph of having sent, or taken, them to France, where he had sold them. The Baron du Casse explained to the Spanish treasury that, since the Spanish Government had been unable to pay Joseph out of the civil list, he had been given the equivalent in jewellery and it was the King's prerogative to sell or keep this jewellery as he wished. According to a letter written by La Forest, dated 22 September 1811, Joseph had admitted that the famous pearl known as La Pelegrina, featured in Velasquez's portrait of Philip III now in the Prado museum, was in his wife's possession. Enquiries instituted by Joseph himself, however, failed to show how this pearl came to be (if ever) in Julie's possession. There is no record in Julie's personal inventory of jewellery that she ever possessed it. The most probable hypothesis is that it was stolen by one of the five Spaniards placed in charge of the crown jewels between the departure of Ferdinand and the arrival of Joseph in Spain, and was sold in Paris. La Forest, who disliked Joseph, would have been only too ready to attribute the theft to the King. But it is almost certain that the pearl set in the ring purchased by the actor Richard Burton for his wife Elizabeth Taylor, at the Parke-Bernet Galleries of New York, on

23 January 1969, was none other than *La Famosa Pelegrina.* What happened to the twenty crown diamonds, originally valued at 19,640,779 *reales* but finally assessed at a sum of 4 million francs, which Joseph used as collateral, has never been established.

Julie's intervention on her husband's behalf met with no success and Joseph's personal letters to his brother continued to remain unanswered. He therefore addressed himself directly to Berthier; but Berthier himself was too preoccupied with the Emperor's forthcoming Russian campaign to pay much attention to Joseph's complaints. Undoubtedly the wisest course for Napoleon to have taken would have been to renounce the whole of his Peninsular campaign and allow Joseph to abdicate the throne, but for Napoleon the very idea of voluntarily abandoning conquered or occupied territory, even to obtain peace, as Joseph had so sensibly advised him, was inconceivable. To quote Girod de l'Ain: 'This pig-headed notion, which seems to us so puerile, but which to Napoleon's admirers spells glory, led him finally to lose all the conquests of the Revolution, even Nice and Savoy.'[4]

The result of this insensate desire for conquest was that Napoleon withdrew his finest troops from Spain to the Eastern front while still garrisoning the whole country with second-rate, reduced divisions. He needed 500,000 men on the banks of the Niemen. Spain counted for nothing. Soult had driven out the English from Sahagun over the mountains of Galicia; Wellington, the 'Indian' General, would surely never dare take the offensive. As for the Spanish generals, they had proved so incompetent that they could be dismissed as merely a nuisance. Talavera might not have been a victory, but it had proved that a combined British and Spanish army had been unable to drive out Imperial troops from Madrid.

Did Napoleon realize that even then Wellington had 60,000 perfectly equipped, trained men under his command and that every Spaniard was on his side, or that the Duke knew, even better than Joseph, the deployment of French forces? At the end of April there were theoretically 230,187 Imperial troops confronting the English, but already on 15 May, 20,000 men under Victor and Mortier were withdrawn for the Russian front. Cambacérès attempted to point out to his master the dangers of this policy, but with no success.

The year 1812 opened auspiciously for Joseph with the occupation of Valencia by Suchet on 9 January. In an article published in the *Moniteur* of May in the previous year, Suchet was reported to have said that Valencia was longing to be annexed by the French Empire – an article which had surprised both Suchet and the Valencians, for although, with the exception of Seville, Valencia was more Josephite than anywhere else in Spain, it had certainly no desire to become part of the French Empire.

That it was Josephite is hardly surprising, for if all Joseph's generals had been of Suchet's calibre, the whole of Spain might well have welcomed the King, for Suchet had shown himself to be not only an able and resolute soldier in the field (both in Spain and in the Italian campaigns) but a skilful and benevolent administrator. As soon as he was appointed Generalissimo of Aragon, he quickly cleared the province of brigands and guerillas. He suppressed corruption, re-organized the customs, protested vehemently against the Emperor's orders that all English produce should be burnt; he continued with the construction of the Imperial Canal of Charles V in order to create employment and at once started rebuilding Saragossa, destroyed by his colleague Lannes. He designed fountains, parks and a new water supply. He restored and endowed hospitals and orphanages; he restored the bull ring and started schools of drawing, architecture and mathematics; he even admitted Spaniards to a share of his government. He rigidly suppressed on looting and pillaging, and in 1811 the soldiers of the Army of Aragon were the only ones in all Spain who, although completely isolated from all other French armies as well as from France, were able to move about singly and freely and fraternize with the people. There even came the point when kindly peasants protected the French against marauding guerilleros.[5] Suchet was certainly marching in the footsteps of his uncle Joseph. He was married to a Mlle Clary, a niece of Julie.

The occupation of Valencia, however was offset in the following week by Wellington's capture of Ciudad Rodrigo.

Moreover, particularly in the north and south, the guerilleros, supported by British sea power, were every day becoming increasingly bold. 'Porlier, the guerilla chief, had surprised Santander in the previous August; Martínez, with 4,000 starving indomitables, had mobilized an entire French corps in front of Figueras during the whole summer; Ballasteros, with the end of British cruisers, kept descending and re-embarking at various points along the Andalusian coastline, sending Soult's harassed columns on a wild-goose chase through the mountains. Hardly a day passed without some foray against Napoleon's three-hundred-mile lifeline from Bayonne to Madrid.'[6]

Perhaps Napoleon's most extraordinarily oblique attitude towards the Spanish campaign is illustrated by the fact that, although furious that Spanish guerilleros had even crossed the Pyrenees and ravaged Rousillon and that the reinforcements which he had ordered to Spain were delayed on the road for weeks by guerilla attacks, and that almost every courier or *estafette* was waylaid, he still regarded Joseph's complaints as unjustified. Even if he himself had been in command, Spain under martial law would never have laid down her arms. It was a lesson he never learnt; what is even more inexplicable is that while continually condemning Joseph's moderation he fully recognized and appreciated Suchet's wise and benevolent rule in Aragon.

It was not until March 1812, realizing that he could not command his armies in Spain from the banks of the Niemen, that Napoleon wrote to Berthier: 'Inform the King of Spain by special courier that from this evening [16 March 1812], *I entrust him with command of all the armies in Spain.*' On 3 April he further delegated his powers to Joseph: 'Send word to the King of Spain – in cipher – *that I delegate to him the political and military control of all Spain.*'

But it was already too late.

On 27 February Joseph had written: 'I know nothing concerning the military operations; I only know of the miseries of the country.' In spite of everything, Joseph still had grandiose ideas for the pacification of his country. He still wished, as a Spanish king, to convene a Cortes and to make terms with the Regency of Cadiz, which he knew to be not only quarrelling among themselves but with their English supporters. None of these projects, however, could be realized without Napoleon's assent. On 23 March, shortly after Napoleon had dictated his despatches to Berthier, he wrote to Julie once more expressing his desire to abdicate, enclosing a letter which he desired her to deliver to the Emperor. He entrusted these to his confidential secretary Deslandes, with orders to convey them to Paris without delay. In his letter to Napoleon he wrote:

I beg your Majesty to allow me to leave in your hands the rights which you deigned to give me over the crown of Spain four years ago. I have never had any intention other than to bring happiness to this kingdom. This is now not within my power.

These letters never reached their destination. The story of their non-delivery was sufficiently romantic to become the subject of a number of popular prints and of a picture painted by Baron Lejeune, exhibited in the Salon of 1819. The facts were as follows:

One night Joseph was awakened by Rosita, a beautiful young Spanish girl, recently married to the King's private secretary Deslandes, who had just surprised her in gallant conversation with Colonel Clermont-Tonnerre. While the secretary and the colonel were angrily quarrelling, Rosita led the King to the scene of her indiscretion. With the utmost dignity, the King, although dressed only in his night attire, placed the colonel under arrest, reconciled the young married couple and suggested that they should undertake a mission to Paris. This suited them admirably since the young wife admitted that she was at the beginning of a pregnancy.

The King confided to his secretary his letters to Julie and Napoleon, in which once again he proposed to commit his crown into the hands of his brother. On 24 March M. and Mme Deslandes left Madrid with a convoy of almost 2,000 soldiers escorting 300 prisoners of war and numerous wagons. But on 9 April, while passing through the mountain passes of Aranzazu, between Vitoria and Tolosa, the convoy was ambushed by the redoubtable Mina, leader of a very considerable band of guerilleros. Deslandes, mad with helpless rage, cursed his assailants in such excellent Spanish that they took him to be a renegade compatriot and stabbed him to death. Rosita, terrified, was taken sobbing to Mina's headquarters, who exchanged her, together with two other prisoners, in return for his mother, whom the French had captured a short time previously.

All the despatches, of which Deslandes was the bearer, were published by the insurgents in their gazettes and it was thus that Spain learnt that their King's only thought was of abdication.[7]

The death of Deslandes affected Joseph and Julie very seriously; Deslandes, who had had Joseph's complete confidence, had managed all the King's financial affairs. It is not surprising that it is difficult to unravel Joseph's finances, for it was Deslandes, who under the fictitious name of J. Martin, had wisely placed most of the King's capital, amounting to £89,000, the equivalent today of four times that sum, with bankers in London[8] and a further 376,000 florins with Hope & Co. in Amsterdam, the latter sum deposited on the advice of Nicolas Clary, who feared that otherwise it might be confiscated by Napoleon. No one, neither Joseph nor Nicolas, had been given power of attorney by Deslandes, alias J. Martin. Deslandes's sudden death therefore put Joseph in a most embarrassing situation. Nicolas Clary, however, solved the problem by the simple expedient of forging 'J. Martin's' signature, giving him powers of attorney, to which Joseph gave his willing assent in a letter dated 23 February 1813.[9]

The Emperor had so often publicly voiced his opinion that Joseph was incapable of commanding an army, that it is hardly surprising that although the King had been officially nominated commander-in-chief, his generals still paid no attention to his orders. Even Suchet refused to send a division to Madrid on the grounds that he feared a British landing on the east coast.[10] But by far the most insolent was Soult, who, having failed to occupy Portugal (of which he had thought to become king), refused to leave the fleshpots of Andalusia, where he acted in every respect as though he were ruler of this rich province.

Wellington, marching northwards, captured Salamanca; Marmont's army of Portugal was threatened. On 6 July Joseph ordered the Duke of Dalmatia to evacuate Andalusia and come to Marmont's support. Soult refused. Joseph angrily wrote to the Emperor (via Clarke) voicing his suspicions that, since his generals systematically refused to obey him, they were receiving secret orders from the Emperor. Joseph himself, with the Army of the Centre, left Madrid to hurry to the aid of Marmont's threatened forces. But Marmont, learning of Joseph's approach, decided on no account to share what he considered certain victory with another, and decided to force the English into battle alone. On 22 July 1812, the French suffered the greatest defeat since Baylen. Marmont himself was seriously wounded. Joseph, with his small army of 15,000, was no match for Wellington, who had at his disposal not only his English troops, but German, Portuguese and Spanish levies. On 5 August, Joseph fell back on Madrid and prepared to evacuate his capital. On the 15th he left for Valencia at the head of an immense procession, including more than 20,000 civilians, both Spanish and French, and 2,500 carriages. Under a burning sun this hopelessly undisciplined endless procession wound its way across the plains of Cuenca, Joseph wearing a paper hat to protect him from the sun.

On 6 August he had ordered Soult to join him at Valencia. Soult once again refused; instead, he suggested that Joseph and his armies would be much more independent of Napoleon in Andalusia and, according to La Forest, advised him to 'cross the Rubicon'.

> He [Soult] assured His Catholic Majesty that it was in his best interests to come to him and dazzled him with prospects of the abundance and resources of the south. From beginning to end he used the most equivocal expressions . . . The messenger declared that M. le Duc de Dalmatie had expressed his most passionate devotion to the King with supplications and even tears in order that his invitation should be appreciated.[11]

This was so utterly absurd that Joseph suspected some trap, believing that Soult wished to take 'possession of his person and proclaim himself King'. Knowing Soult, he was quite aware that the Duke of Dalmatia was perfectly capable of doing such a thing.

On 31 August Joseph and his retinue arrived at Valencia, where he was soon to learn of Soult's perfidy. The Duke of Dalmatia, after receiving the sharpest orders from Clarke, Minister of War, had at last decided to leave Seville but, before doing so, he had summoned his six generals to whom he expressed his opinion that Joseph was betraying the Emperor to please the Spanish. He even wrote to the Emperor to inform him that his brother was a traitor. Soult based his accusations on the fact that the King had attempted to enter into peaceful negotiations with the Junta of Cadiz and had been in secret correspondence with his 'dear friend and brother-in-law', Bernadotte, now Crown Prince of Sweden. Ever since Imperial troops had invaded Swedish Pomerania, Bernadotte had openly declared himself against Napoleon, had entered into an alliance with England and Russia and was on friendly terms with the Junta of Cadiz, which in turn had shown its friendship by dispatching 250 Spanish soldiers to form part of Bernadotte's personal bodyguard.

The ship bearing Soult's despatches from Malaga was driven ashore at Valencia. The despatches were impounded by the police and handed to Joseph, who now learnt the full extent of Soult's treachery. Soult accused him of scheming to negotiate a separate peace with England and for the withdrawal of all Imperial troops from the Peninsula, and to rule entirely independently from France – in fact, to make Spain a kingdom as independent of the Emperor's rule as was Sweden. Soult also accused Joseph of entering into secret negotiations with his brother Lucien, who was known to have written to Lord Castlereagh at the beginning of August suggesting that he should sign a treaty with the Emperor, whereby all troops, both French and British, should be withdrawn from Spain and Portugal.

There may have been an element of truth in Soult's accusations, but there is no evidence that Joseph was in secret communication with Lucien or scheming to effect a separate peace with the British Government. Of course he attempted to negotiate with the Junta of Seville – or the *Cortes* of Cadiz as it had become – but this was with Napoleon's entire approval.

Joseph immediately demanded the dismissal of Soult and dispatched one of his aides-de-camp, Colonel Desprez, to the Emperor with Soult's accusations. In the incredibly short time of thirty-six days Desprez covered the distance from Paris to the Kremlin. Immediately on his return from Moscow, Desprez wrote to Joseph. Not only did his letter give a very gloomy picture of the military situation in Russia, it provided no satisfaction of Joseph's angry complaints about Soult's behaviour:

> The Emperor told me that a copy of the Duke of Dalmatia's letter had already reached him through another channel, however he could not attend to such trifles while he was at the head of 500,000 men and engaged on enormous undertakings – these were his expressions. However, the Duke of Dalmatia's suspicions did not surprise him: they were shared by many army generals belonging to the Army of Spain, who think that your Majesty prefers Spain to France; that he was convinced that you are French at heart, but that those who judged you by your public speeches might think otherwise.

On 12 August Wellington entered Madrid, 'with every bell pealing, palms waving, fountains flowing wine and women casting shawls before his horse. Everyone was shouting "Long live Wellington!" '[12] 'I am among a people mad with joy for their deliverance from their oppressors,' Wellington wrote to John Malcolm in India. 'God send that my good fortune may continue and that I may be the instrument for securing their independence and happiness.'

But although Wellington was master of Madrid, his position was extremely dangerous. He therefore only remained five days in the capital. With only 80,000 troops of mixed nationality, he had to face an attack before winter by two French armies from the north and two, or possibly three, from the south. To the disgust of his troops, Wellington was obliged to fall back once more on Portugal. The last British troops left Madrid on 31 October. On 22 November Joseph made his third entry into his capital. The Madrileños this time showed no enthusiasm. They feared reprisals for having collaborated with the English, and believing now that Joseph would soon again be driven out of his capital, they also feared that any collaboration with the French would meet with reprisals from the new Spanish rulers, of which they had already had a taste when, in the interim period between Wellington's departure and Joseph's return, the town had been governed by the famous guerillero leader El Empecinado ('Inky Face'). El Empecinado was an extraordinary adventurer (his real name was Juan-Martín Díaz) whose exploits were famous throughout Spain; a whole French division was required to combat him. No sooner were his guerilla forces defeated at the battle of Cifuentes by General Hugo than he formed another army. Joseph narrowly escaped capture at his hands while hunting on the outskirts

209

of Madrid. When Ferdinand returned to the throne, this one-time smuggler and innkeeper was made a general.

Although Wellington complained bitterly that, after his defeat of Marmont and his occupation of Madrid, there was no general rising throughout Spain, the guerilleros were in fact more active than ever. In the north, the bands of Mina, Longa and others, now well disciplined and organized, extended their authority over every town where there was no French garrison, and were constantly in communication with British cruisers which supplied them with arms and ammunition. Nevertheless they were unwilling to accept orders from Wellington. Every courier from France was intercepted and, even before Joseph was aware of the disaster which had overtaken the Imperial army in Russia, almost every town and village in Spain knew of the appalling retreat from Moscow. During the months of the spring of 1812 and the two and a half months of the winter of 1812 and 1813, the King received no courier from France. In consequence Clarke sent his orders direct to the Army of the North, where Clausel had replaced Cafarelli; to the Army of Portugal, where Cafarelli had replaced Clausel, and to Suchet, who was in command of Aragon. On 6 March 1813, Clarke wrote to Jourdan : 'It is now seventy-two days since I sent my first orders from His Imperial Majesty to the King and I am still awaiting an acknowledgement . . . The French departments are threatened at several points . . . The Army of Spain must cover the frontiers of the Empire; Mina is all-powerful in Aragon; the insurgents in Catalonia are threatening France.'

Soult, who despite his despicable behaviour was still recognized by Joseph to be an outstanding military commander, was summoned to Valencia. The Viceroy of Andalusia, shocked by the fall of Salamanca and Wellington's occupation of Madrid, reluctantly obeyed. It is safe to say that if any single man by his selfishness and personal ambition ruined the French chances of success in Spain, it was the Marshal-Duke of Dalmatia.

On 26 August 1812 Soult marched out of Seville for the last time with a vast train of waggons carrying the spoils of his viceroyalty, including pictures by Velasquez and Murillo. In a specially magnificent coach rode *'les Maréchales'*, two lovely sisters, the mistresses of Soult and Victor. But Soult was not to remain in Valencia for long. At the beginning of 1813, he was ordered to Saxony to assist the Emperor in reforming his shattered army. In order to replace the casualties suffered by the Grande Armée between Moscow and the Niemen, an army now reduced to a mere 50,000 men, the Emperor further depleted his armies in Spain by taking twenty-five men from each infantry battalion and cavalry regiment and ten from each artillery company, sometimes removing whole infantry companies, cavalry squadrons and even whole regiments.

On 16 February 1813 Joseph received orders from his brother to retire to Valladolid, leaving only a small garrison in Madrid under General Hugo, sufficient to hold the extremity of the line. Joseph only put this order into execution between 7 and 27 March. Not only had he to evacuate 9,000 sick from hospital, but to remove all his household and personal treasures, for this time he was convinced that he would never return. The only instructions he received from Clarke (written on 16 April) read : 'The Emperor has ordered me to instruct you to harass Wellington and to prevent an English landing on the coast of France.'

On 29 April Clarke wrote again : 'The Emperor has instructed me to make known to Your Majesty that you can expect nothing more from him due to the circumstances in which France now finds herself.' Joseph replied that with the means at his disposal he was quite incapable of any offensive action. He suggested that the three armies of Spain should be amalgamated under one command. Jourdan in turn wrote on 16 May to the Ministry of War, demanding more precise instructions should Wellington, now greatly reinforced, take the offensive. Neither Joseph nor Jourdan received replies.

It is difficult to know what passed through Joseph's mind between 22 November 1812 and 16 April 1813. It must be admitted that neither in Madrid nor in Valladolid did he do anything constructive. He fiddled while Rome burned. He still continued to entertain his court with literary entertainments and enjoy the favours of Daisy Derieux, with whom he had formed a liaison three years previously. In extenuation, it must be said, he had the excuse that he received no courier – no news of any sort. He believed that the fate of Spain was being decided in Saxony. Nor was he far wrong. Soult, in discussion with the Emperor, had nothing good to say of Joseph, and plans were afoot to marry Ferdinand VII to a Bonaparte princess and to restore him to the throne. To what extent was Joseph aware of the full disaster of the Russian campaign and that the Empire was already cracking? He was certainly unaware that Julie had been seriously ill until, thanks to the courtesy of Wellington, he learnt from intercepted letters forwarded to him by the Duke that she had for weeks been suffering from what had been diagnosed as erysipelas, and was convalescing at Aix. Her letters dated 20 August still show no hint of disaster. The Emperor was still marching on Moscow with no opposition – Borodino was as yet three weeks away.

Joseph still had no authority over his marshals and generals. The only bright spot during these gloomy days was the fact that the ambassador La Forest was recalled to Paris. 'We saw him leave without regret,' wrote Miot de Melito. 'No one could have contributed more to our difficulties at this time than La Forest, who consistently kept the Emperor in ignorance of the true situation in Spain.'[13]

Had Joseph and Jourdan fully realized the plight of Wellington, they might have been a little more optimistic. The Duke's siege of Burgos had proved disastrous and his subsequent retreat into Portugal a nightmare. The weather was appalling. 'Every stream and watercourse was a torrent and the roads rivers of icy mud which, rising to the men's ankles and sometimes to their knees, sucked the boots off their feet . . .'[14] The British commissariat had broken down and the soldiers were half starving and mutinous. 'It is impossible for any army to have given themselves up to more dissipation and everything as is bad as did our army [sic].' Thus wrote Private Wheeler of the 51st. 'The conduct of some men would have disgraced savages; drunkenness had prevailed to such a frightful extent that I have often wondered how a great part of our army was not cut off. It was no unfrequent thing to see a long train of mules carrying drunken soldiers to prevent them falling into the hands of the enemy.'[15]

In fact in those four disastrous days, the loss of men fallen by the way or captured by the enemy proved half again as great as the casualties sustained before Burgos.

Had Joseph been better informed of Wellington's difficulties, had his generals co-operated better, the English might well have been driven out of Spain and the nerve of Spanish resistance broken. Even so, unfounded rumours that the Regency of Cadiz had quarrelled with the English added to his euphoric belief that all was not lost. True, the Council of Regency was constantly at loggerheads, but when Wellington visited their impregnable fortress of Cadiz during the winter months he had received a rapturous welcome. He addressed the Cortes in Spanish and was invested with the command of the Spanish armies together with the dukedom of Ciudad Rodrigo in recognition of his liberation of Madrid; in addition he received the order of the Golden Fleece, the highest honour which Spain could confer, but which the self-elected Council of Regency was not legally entitled to bestow.[16]

During the winter months, while the French armies were fully occupied with the guerillero armies in the north, where Mina had forced Tafalla to surrender and where one of his detachments had stormed the fortress of Fuentarrabbia and where the British fleet had captured Santander, Wellington had had time to restore discipline and morale among his army. He had also received very considerable reinforcements – the 'Johnny newcomes' as the veterans called them, including glittering detachments of the household cavalry – and was preparing once again, in the greatest secrecy, to take the field.

By the end of April he was in command, not of 30,000 British troops as Napoleon and his advisers supposed, but of 52,000, in addition to which he had a further 29,000 well-disciplined British-trained Portuguese and (now that the council of Regency had appointed him generalissimo of Spanish armies) 21,000 Spanish, a total of 102,000 men, exclusive of the 50,000 irregulars operating independently. Now that Santander and Corunna had fallen into the hands of the British navy, his supply problems were greatly facilitated should he overrun the north-east. By advancing from Portugal into Spain by way of the seemingly impassible Tras-os-Montes, he planned to outflank the enemy and, instead of making a frontal attack against the easily defensible Douro (as in 1812), he now proposed to cross the Esla, its mountain tributary, and appear in the enemy's rear.

Wellington's movements were carried out in such secrecy that neither Joseph nor Jourdan had any idea to what extent they were threatened. To deceive the French further concerning his real intentions, Wellington advanced on Salamanca while his main force crossed the mountains to the north. A further diversion was made by a sea-borne attack under Lieutenant-General Sir John Murray against Suchet at Tarragona on the eastern front. Such unexpected tactics took Joseph and his staff completely by surprise. They were forced to retreat or be cut off. Joseph had no alternative but to evacuate Valladolid (2 June). On 13 June, Burgos too was abandoned and its citadel blown up. The French army, encumbered by hundreds of civilians and cartloads of plunder, not to mention 'ladies of pleasure' – 'a travelling brothel', as one French officer described the army – arrived at Vitoria on 19 June. Joseph was greeted by the Marquesa de Montehermoso and stayed in the villa which he had bought at such an exorbitant price five years previously. His happiness with his mistress was shortlived.

The King left all military operations in the hands of Jourdan. The latter vainly hoped that Clausel, labouring in Navarre, would arrive to his support before 70,000 Anglo-Portuguese with 7,000 Spaniards attacked. By four o'clock in the afternoon of 21 June the French were in rout. The victory, though the turning-point of the whole campaign and the dissolution of Joseph's empire, did not however bring French resistance to an end. The main body of the French army was able to escape to Pamplona, not only due to the ineffectiveness of the British cavalry, which for one reason or another was deprived of efficient command at this critical moment, but because Joseph's baggage train proved too much for the discipline of Wellington's men.[17]

On 29 June Wellington wrote to Earl Bathurst:

> The night of the battle instead of being passed in getting rest and food to prepare for the pursuit of the following day, was spent by the soldiers in looking for plunder. The consequence was that they were incapable of marching in pursuit of the enemy and were totally knocked up.

Wellington further cited the fact that, while before the battle the total of British and Portuguese in arms was 67,036 rank and file, twelve days later the 4,186 lost in battle was almost equalled by the 4,156 lost in plundering and desertion since.

Joseph escaped on horseback by side roads, leaving his coach and all his personal papers and treasures behind him. He was accompanied by General Jamin and a small escort of light cavalry. Twenty miles from Vitoria he halted at a little inn at Salvatierra, where he was joined by Jourdan, Miot and O'Farrill. On the following day they covered a further eighteen miles in appalling weather conditions and reached Irurzun on 23 June. From here, Joseph wrote to Julie:

> *Ma chère amie,* the day before yesterday . . . the army was attacked in its position at Vitoria, before General Clausel could join it with the troops from the army of Portugal and after it had been weakened by having to furnish escorts to two immense convoys. The battle was fierce, and lasted the whole day. The killed and wounded on each side were about equal, but the state of the roads occasioned us to lose all our baggage and artillery; the teams only were saved . . .
>
> If the Emperor has returned, tell him that as soon as I have placed my army on the frontier and united it to those of the North and of Aragon, I shall repair to Mortefontaine, as I told you, at the time, that I ought to have done after Salamanca. Let me have the Emperor's answer. Whatever it be, I shall go home. I can do no good here.
>
> Tell Clary to transmit, through James and Brocq, 100,000 francs to my secretary, M. Presle. Among the killed were M. Thibaud defending my treasure and poor Alphonse,[18] whom I loved, though I scolded him.

Send me back the courier. I shall not stop at Paris, but at Mortefontaine, whether you are there or at a watering place.

Kisses to you and to the children.

On the following day Joseph and his faithful Miot arrived at Pamplona, where he left a garrison of 4,000 men. At midnight on the 24th he resumed his journey and spent the night at the little Basque village of Elizondo, only a few miles from the frontier. As though unwilling to leave Spain, he did not immediately enter France but, retracing his steps, proceeded up the valley of Baztan to reach the Bidassoa by the Col de Echalar. At 8 o'clock in the evening of 27 June he was at Vera, still on Spanish soil. It was only on the following day that he finally left his kingdom for ever and established his headquarters at Saint-Jean-de-Luz. From here he wrote long letters to Julie, to Napoleon and to Clarke. He told the latter that orders from Paris had always paralysed military operations. 'The pacification of Spain by force of arms is an impossibility,' he wrote. 'I can only repeat today what I have always said.' One of his main concerns was the fate of the Spanish nobility who had followed him and were now dispossessed of everything. In each of his letters to the Emperor, he pleads their cause. In the meantime, the French army having regrouped, his intention was to secure Pamplona which was the key to all the main roads leading to France. He, or Jourdan, had enough military sense to know that Wellington would not attempt to drive into France with two major fortresses, San Sebastian and Pamplona, still in French hands in his rear.

Joseph still refused to believe that all was lost. Despite the fact that half a million men had perished in the Russian campaign between December and 14 April, when the last survivors of the Grande Armée had left the soil of Russia, the Emperor had still managed to raise another army. On 2 May, after a temporary truce, he had defeated a combined Russian and Prussian army at Lützen and had entered Dresden. On 21–22 May he had won another, though not decisive, victory at Bautzen. The possibility of another Continental peace was in everybody's mind. If Joseph could hold the frontier of the Pyrenees, he could well expect reinforcements. Despite Joseph's shattering defeat at Vitoria he was therefore not altogether in despair. Dispatches and letters from Paris were optimistic.

What he had not realized was Napoleon's reaction to the news of Vitoria. The Emperor was consumed with rage. In letters to Clarke, Savary and Cambacérès, he blaimed every single disaster in Spain during the last five years on the incompetence of his brother. He could scarcely have heaped more odium on wretched Joseph. Even more disgraceful was that Napoleon addressed these letters to his ministers and never to Joseph himself. All reference to the defeat was suppressed in his censored press. On 6 July, Cambacérès was ordered to send Roederer immediately to Joseph's headquarters and inform the King that he and Jourdan were to consider themselves under house arrest: Soult, whose disobedience had been the cause of half their troubles, was to take command of the armies of Portugal and Spain. 'It was not enough that the English army should chase the King of Spain from his realm, but now the Emperor himself declared war on him.'[19]

XIV

The Hundred Days:
Joseph as the Emperor's
right hand

1812–1814

Joseph's first thought was that this disgrace was due to the intrigues of Soult. Nor was he mistaken. Napoleon had been only too ready to listen to the Duke of Dalmatia. The Emperor, on the other hand, must have been perfectly well aware that it was largely his own fault that everything had been bungled in Spain but, unwilling to admit his mistakes, he wished to find a scapegoat. It had not been Joseph's idea to remove the Bourbons from the throne – the Spanish Bourbons who had been France's allies for almost two centuries – nor was it Joseph who was responsible that the Spanish fleet and army had allied themselves with the Coalition; nor was it he who was responsible for the French defeats at Baylen and Salamanca. Having made the grave mistake of driving the Bourbons out of Spain, Napoleon had chosen Joseph to abandon the throne of Naples to take their place. Certainly, he had made an excellent choice, for there can be little doubt that had the Emperor taken his brother's advice Spain would have accepted Joseph's rule, which, as time was to show, would certainly have been better than that of Ferdinand. The Spanish people were tired of war. Wellington could never have defeated the French armies without the help of the guerilleros, but the guerilleros had only risen against the French because of Napoleon's policy of terrorism. We have only to see how successful Joseph had been in Andalusia and Suchet in Valencia. Napoleon's greatest mistake had been the annexation of the northern provinces. Many years later,

217

while in America, Joseph admitted that when called to the throne of Spain he had never really discussed the policy to be followed in the Peninsula. While Napoleon only thought of the grandeur of his Empire, Joseph believed, according to the Revolutionary ideals on which he had been brought up, that the only justification for being a king – his only mission – was to promote the welfare of his subjects.

Joseph had never claimed to be a military man. True, he wished to be generalissimo of his armies, not only so that he could exercise authority over his generals and marshals and so prevent them from pillaging his country, but also to achieve some co-ordination between them. At least as King he was entitled to know what military strategy was being planned. In military matters he was always prepared to take the advice of Jourdan. On the few occasions when he took joint command, as at Talavera and prior to Arpiles (Salamanca), he had shown common sense. It was ridiculous for Napoleon to blame Joseph for the defeat of Vitoria. If anyone was to blame it was Jourdan and Clausel, particularly the latter.

Once Joseph's anger had cooled down, he acknowledged Soult's appointment in a letter to Clarke dated 22 July, which he concluded with the words :

> My sincerest wish is that a greater experience of war than I have ever been able to offer, will allow the Commander-in-Chief to re-establish affairs in the Peninsula. But this I fear is a vain hope. The enemy has twice as many troops as we have, and it would be impossible to advance into the country and pacify it without taking many other measures.

No one paid any attention to Joseph's warning.

On 15 July, Joseph left Bayonne. He had no clear idea as yet where he would fix his residence. He toyed with the idea of settling in Gascony. He finally stopped at Puyoo, on the border of Béarn and Gascony. As soon as Soult was informed of his departure from St-Jean-de-Luz, the Marshal was worried that Joseph might attempt to return to Spain and sent messengers in his pursuit, forbidding (!) him to take up residence too close to the Spanish frontier. Napoleon, on the other hand, was fearful that he might continue his journey to Paris, where, during his own absence in Dresden, Joseph might take the opportunity to claim his rights as Grand Elector and proclaim himself Regent.

When Napoleon had left for his ill-fated Russian campaign, he had thought that he was accomplishing a clever political stroke by bestowing the Regency of his Empire on the Empress Marie-Louise. The

Regency, by rights, should have been bestowed on the senior French prince, in fact on Joseph. During the Emperor's absence with his army he was constantly haunted by the idea that his brother might return to Paris and, at the head of his liberal friends, dispute the government of the royal princess who had given him an heir, a future king by Divine Right. This fear explains his strongly worded letters to his ministers and perhaps why, ever since 1808, he had refused to allow Joseph to abdicate and return to Paris.

Joseph, however, had never entertained any intention of usurping the Regency. Since he was forbidden to return to Mortefontaine, he was genuinely anxious to settle in Gascony where he had found the Château de Payonne for sale, halfway between Dax and Saint-Sever, large enough to house his suite, which included Spanish ministers, his aides-de-camp, his doctor Paroisse, his secretary Presle, and several other French and Spanish officers. But the negotiations for the sale of this property were never concluded. Thanks to the intercession of Julie and Roederer, Joseph was allowed to return to Mortefontaine, provided he took the name of Comte de Survilliers and that he on no account set foot in Paris.

On the morning of 24 July, the King left St Jean-de-Luz on horseback accompanied by Miot. Anxious that his departure should not be made public, he said farewell to no one. After crossing the Adour, he took a post-chaise outside Mont-de-Marsan, whence, without stopping, and unrecognized by anyone, he drove northwards through Périgueux, Limoges, Orleans and Croix-de-Berny.

On the night of 28 July he passed through Paris and arrived at Mortefontaine on the following morning. Julie, who was still in Vichy, joined him two days later, to be followed by his whole suite, including his Spanish court. Had the Emperor not ordered Savary and other ministers to put such restrictions on his freedom, Joseph might have continued to lead the agreeable life of former days. But Napoleon was still suspicious of his brother's liberal *philosophe* friends, and imagined that Mortefontaine was becoming a centre of intrigue. From Dresden the Emperor wrote to Savary and Roederer : 'Should he [Joseph] come to Paris or Saint-Cloud, you will arrange to have him arrested. He is to be informed of this. If you show any weakness, the King will begin to hold receptions which will become the centre of intrigues. There is absolutely no other means by which he can be restrained.'

Joseph, after all the disasters which he had suffered and all the obloquy to which he had already been subjected, was not too upset by his brother's orders. Although Mortefontaine was under surveillance by Savary's police, he still entertained his friends there. It was only when he visited Paris, where the Marquesa de Montehermoso was now living, that he had to take precautions, and where, to put the police off his track, he usually stayed with his faithful Uncle Fesch.

Napoleon was soon informed of Joseph's clandestine visits to Paris, but on being persuaded by Roederer and the always forgiving and loyal Julie that these visits were entirely devoted to pleasure, he wrote to Savary, whose gendarmes on several occasions had turned back the King's coach :

> The action you have taken against the King of Spain is unseemly from every point of view. Since you know the object of his visits to Paris, you should appear to ignore them. In all your conduct you have shown a lack of tact. The art of being a policeman is to disregard what it is unnecessary to see.

Poor Savary; after all he was only obeying orders.

What seems extraordinary is that Napoleon should have bothered to write this letter at all, for it was dated 'Erfurt, 24 October 1813', the same day as he published his official bulletin informing his subjects of his defeat at the battle of Leipzig, fought six days previously, and which he claimed would have been a glorious victory but for the treachery of the Saxons.

Napoleon returned to Saint-Cloud on 9 November, after one of the most shattering defeats he had ever suffered; after his army in Spain had been routed at Vitoria and with Wellington already on French soil,[1] it is incredible that Napoleon could still continue to concern himself with his brother's private affairs.

Roederer reports the following conversation he had with the Emperor on 12 November :

The Emperor	What is the King of Spain saying? What is he up to? Will he force me to have him arrested?
Roederer	It seems the King would be happy if his residence at Mortefontaine did not appear like an exile and were he free to come to Paris to enjoy himself.
The Emperor	Let him come to Paris when he wants to see some girls or Madame de M. [Montehermoso]. I reproved the Minister of Police for the obstacles he wished to put in his way. But apart from that, what does he want to do? Does he still think of ruling?
Roederer	I believe so.

The Emperor	It's just a dream. The Spanish don't want him. They think he's incapable. They don't want a King who spends all his time with women and playing hide and seek and blind man's buff. Ferdinand would be preferable to him.
Roederer	Sire, perhaps it is not precisely the Crown of Spain that he wants, but a crown nevertheless . . . It is necessary for the King to be occupied.
The Emperor	Occupied! That is just what he does *not* like. He doesn't know how to occupy himself. Shooting rabbits; playing hide and seek – that's what he enjoys. I could make him Governor of Rome. He loves the arts and women. Perhaps that would suit him.[2]

The post of Governor of Rome was a sinecure, largely reserved for those whose presence annoyed the Emperor. In 1809 he had unsuccessfully offered it to Bernadotte and, equally unsuccessfully, to Fouché in 1810.

Since his defeat at Leipzig on 18 October 1813, Napoleon had been forced to revise his whole political 'system'. Although the last campaign had cost Napoleon 45,000 men, besides 23,000 who were left behind in hospital, the Allies had suffered so severely – more, numerically, than the French – that they had been unable to carry on a pursuit, and for the time being there existed an uneasy truce. The Emperor was now determined to put into practice his scheme of marrying Ferdinand VII to a Bonaparte princess and restoring him to the throne of Spain. The most eligible Bonaparte princess was Zenaïde, Joseph's daughter. Although Ferdinand was twenty-nine and Zenaïde was only twelve, Napoleon did not seem to find this difference in ages excessive. 'The Princess Zenaïde is a plump little person, perfectly formed, who speaks with a great deal of good sense and aplomb. One can see no reason to put off finding her a husband.' So wrote Roederer to General Dumas in September. Zenaïde was a little southern beauty, half-Corsican, half-Marseillaise, who like most Mediterranean girls matured quickly.

Napoleon, on his return to Paris at the beginning of November, was determined to put his plan into action. He first approached Julie, who visited him at Saint-Cloud on the 10th, but Julie was not prepared to tell her husband of the Emperor's plans. Napoleon then proposed to Julie to speak to his brother himself. He was perfectly well aware that Joseph would raise objections. Without waiting to consult his brother, however, he ordered ex-Ambassador La Forest to enter immediately into negotiations with Ferdinand at Valençay. These negotiations, conducted in the greatest secrecy and without Joseph's knowledge, lasted until 11 December, when a treaty was signed 'affirming the Spanish princes' sympathy for France and their desire to drive the English out of the Peninsula'.[3]

The projected marriage ('very much to the prince's taste') was to be postponed until Ferdinand should enter his capital, lest his prior marriage to a Bonaparte might lose him the sympathy of those Spaniards who had been fighting for the restoration of the Desired One.

It was not until 28 November that Joseph was informed of these negotiations, when the Comte de Flahaut, Napoleon's aide-de-camp, brought the King to Roederer, who introduced him by a secret staircase to the Emperor's study. Joseph was not only naturally indignant when he learnt that, without consulting him, his crown was to be bestowed on Ferdinand, but also pointed out to his brother the unwisdom of such an act. Napoleon replied: 'I hope by making such a great concession to be able to remove, without danger, my army from the Pyrenees and transfer it to Italy against the Austrians. To achieve this, all is good.[4]

Joseph protested. He attempted to point out the folly of such ideas. But the Emperor, who believed Joseph to be entirely motivated by self-interest, refused to listen. Two days later, Joseph wrote: 'Sire, my first thoughts have only been the more strengthened by reflection. Prince Ferdinand on his arrival in Spain can do nothing for France: he can do everything against her.

Three days later, he gave his proposals for resolving his own situation. He suggested that Bernadotte should be invited to negotiate the question of Spain with the Allies. He himself was perfectly prepared to discuss the matter with his brother-in-law. Secondly, if he was asked to resign the throne of Spain, he demanded to know what compensation he would receive (obviously he would never be content with the governorship of Rome). Thirdly, some sort of protocol in interviews with the Emperor must be established; and fourthly, and most important in order to obtain world peace, he offered to conduct negotiations with the Allies as he had done so successfully twelve years earlier at the Treaty of Amiens.

Napoleon paid no attention to the last three paragraphs of Joseph's letter, but the very idea that Bernadotte should be consulted was anathema to him. 'As far as the Prince of Sweden is concerned, in the eyes of France he is in the . . . ["here", writes Roederer in his memoirs, "I omit the word used by the Emperor"], which prevents any French prince having contact with him . . . In short, the Emperor considers your renunciation, pure and simple, of the throne of Spain as the highest token that you can give of your love for France and of your affection for him.'

Joseph was not to be moved. He refused to abdicate his throne on his brother's terms with such firmness that the Emperor ceased to insist, but nevertheless did not repudiate his secret treaty with Ferdinand.

Once again this quarrel ended in total reconciliation between the two brothers. At the close of 1813, when the territory of France itself had to be defended foot by foot, Napoleon felt the need to leave behind him a man who was entirely devoted to him, who was loved and welcomed in all circles, and, who, as he himself admitted, was far more capable than he of manipulating the political stage. He even went to far as to suggest that, should universal peace be proclaimed on his terms, when Italy was divided, Joseph should be made King of Tuscany.

On 29 December Joseph wrote to the Emperor :

Sire, violation of Swiss territory has laid France open to the enemy.

In this state of affairs I am anxious that Your Majesty should be persuaded that my heart is wholly French. Recalled by circumstance to France, I should be glad to be of some use and am ready to undertake anything which may prove to you my devotion.

I am also aware, Sire, of what I owe Spain; I see my duties and wish to fulfil them. If I make claims, it is only for the purpose of sacrificing them to the general good of mankind, esteeming myself happy if by such sacrifices I can promote the peace of Europe.

I hope that Your Majesty may think fit to commission one of your ministers to come to an understanding on this subject with the Duke of Santa Fé [Ananza], my Minister for Foreign Affairs.

To his letter Napoleon replied :

My Brother – I have received your letter of 29 December. It is far too clever for the state of my affairs. I will explain it in two words. France is invaded, all Europe is in arms against France, and above all against me. You are no longer King of Spain. I don't want Spain either to keep or to give away. I will have nothing more to do with that country than to live in peace with it and have the use of my army. What will you do? Will you as a French Prince come to the support of my throne? You possess my friendship and your apanage and will be my subject as Prince of the Blood. In this case, you must act as I have done and announce the part which you are about to play. Write to me in simple terms a letter which I can print, receive the authorities and show yourself zealous for me, to the King of Rome and friendly to the Regency of the Empress. Are you unable to do this? Then retire to the obscurity of some country house some forty leagues from Paris. You will live there quietly if I live; you will be killed or arrested if I die. You will be useless to me, to our family, to your daughters and to France. But you will do me no harm, and will not be in my way. Choose quickly the line which you will take.

On receipt of this letter, which was conveyed to him by Berthier, Joseph hesitated. The situation was very serious. In view of his moral obligations to those Spaniards who had left their country to follow him, he was not prepared to make up his mind immediately. He first wished to consult his own ministers and Julie. In consequence of this meeting, Joseph wrote to the Emperor :

Sire – The invasion of France imposes on every Frenchman the obligation to fly to her defence. As senior French prince and as such your first subject, allow me, Sire, to ask you to accept the offer of my arm and advice. You will still serve France, Sire, if all Frenchmen place at the service of your throne the same devotion as that with which I offer you my services.

On 10 January 1814, the two brothers were to have another interview which finally brought an end to their differences. On 10 January 1814, Napoleon wrote to Joseph :

My Brother, – I have inserted in the regulations of the palace that you are in future to be announced under the title of *King Joseph*, and the Queen under the title of *Queen Julie*, with the honours due to a French Prince of the Blood . . . I authorize you to take the uniform of the grenadiers of my guard, which is what I wear myself. I don't think you ought to wear any foreign decoration; you should wear only the French order. Forward to me a list of the persons of whom you wish to compose your household as well as that of the Queen and tell me on what day you will receive the court and the authorities.

Time was pressing. Napoleon immediately called on the services of Joseph, whose presence he had so missed since that January of 1806 when he had sent him to Naples – Joseph, the only man who might have stood up to him and prevented him from committing so many grave errors. He immediately employed him on the most delicate and difficult of tasks – to rally to his cause those of his former adherents who, by his own behaviour, he had managed to estrange. Joseph's first task was to write to Murat, unaware that the King of Naples had already committed himself entirely to the Allied cause : 'The day you go over to the Allies there will be no future for you, because they will have no interest in keeping on good terms with you. Their promises mean nothing.'

It was too late for the King of Naples to listen to Joseph's prophetic advice. The situation regarding Bernadotte was very different. Victorious over the Imperial troops at Leipzig, the Crown Prince of Sweden was marching with the army of the North across Germany. Joseph knew his brother-in-law too well not to know that this astute Gascon had already carefully summed up his chances. Nevertheless, forgetting what he had written concerning his former Marshal when Joseph had suggested him as an intermediary, Napoleon now wrote to his brother : 'It is reported that the Crown Prince of Sweden is in Cologne. Could you not, as of your own accord, send someone to him to point out the folly of his ways and try to persuade him to change his views . . .?'

Joseph immediately contacted a Doctor Franzenberg, the secretary of Désirée, to whom he confided a long verbal message which the latter promised to convey to Bernadotte when they met a few days later in Liège. Bernadotte's answer was unequivocal : 'You can tell my brother-in-law, Joseph, that I know Napoleon too well to see anything but a snare in all that relates to him . . . My reply to his insidious demands is that he should make peace at the earliest.'

Napoleon, however, had no intention of making peace, for although the so-called Frankfurt declaration drawn up by the Allies on 1 December 1813 was extremely generous, it was too damaging to the Emperor's *amour propre* :

The Allied Powers are not at war with France but with that haughtily announced preponderance, a preponderance which, to the misfortune of Europe and France, the Emperor Napoleon has for too long a time exercised outside the boundaries of his Empire. Victory has led the allied armies to the Rhine. The first use which their Royal and Imperial Majesties have made of victory has been to offer peace to his Majesty, the Emperor of the French. The allied sovereigns desire that France should be strong, great, and happy . . . The Powers confirm to the French Empire an extent of territory which France never had under her kings, because a valiant nation should not lose rank for having in its turn experienced reverses in an obstinate and bloody conflict in which it has fought with its usual courage. But the Powers also wish to be free, happy and tranquil. They desire a state of peace, which, by wise distribution of power and just equilibrium, may

225

preserve henceforth their peoples from the innumerable calamities which for the last twenty years have weighed upon Europe.

In short, in exchange for peace, France was to be given her natural boundaries, even larger than today, from the Scheldt in the north to the Rhine in the west and the Pyrenees in the south.

What Napoleon hoped, and which to a large extent proved true, was that although the majority of French people were tired of war, should France be invaded by foreign troops – especially Russians – Frenchmen, from patriotic instinct, would rise to defend their native soil. When the Frankfurt declaration was communicated to the members of the *Corps législatif*, they sent an address to the Emperor declaring themselves in favour of accepting its terms, which to them seemed honourable and reasonable. 'Conscription has become for all French an outrageous scourge . . . a barbarous and aimless war has swallowed up youths, torn them away from education, agriculture, commerce and the arts . . . The genius of a true hero spurns glory at the expense of the blood and repose of the people, but finds true glory in the public weal which is his work.'

The Emperor dissolved the Chamber and forbade the publication of this address. The majority of French people never knew, or even today know, what generous terms the Allies had offered.

Franzenberg had also another and much more secret mission entrusted to him by an important group of politicians, men like Talleyrand, Jaucourt and those senators who still retained revolutionary memories and who, like the Tsar Alexander, would have been delighted if Bernadotte had proclaimed himself successor to the throne of France in place of Napoleon. Although we know that Bernadotte had already drawn up a new liberal constitution[5] to be implemented should he be elected King, he refused to commit himself. As usual, he sat on the fence. It has been suggested that Joseph was aware of this second mission and that he envisaged a sort of duumvirate, with himself as head of civil affairs and Bernadotte as military commander-in-chief, a duumvirate similar to that which he had been accused of plotting many years previously when in 1798 Bernadotte had first sought the hand of Julie. From Joseph's subsequent behaviour, this seems unlikely. On the contrary, from now onwards he developed a passionate loyalty to his brother which only became the more enhanced as the Emperor's fortunes declined.

On 21 January, before leaving to join his armies, Napoleon convened an extraordinary council, at which Joseph was present, in order to organize a Regency during his absence. Napoleon now took one of the most unprecedented decisions of his whole career. While confirming the Empress as Regent, he appointed two Grand Councillors to advise her; Cambacérès as civil adviser, Joseph as military. Even the greatest admirers of the Emperor have difficulty in explaining this choice. That Joseph, who had no military genius whatsoever and on whom Napoleon had laid the entire blame for the defeat of Vitoria (which thanks to the Emperor himself was known throughout Europe) and whose lack of military ability he had never ceased to stress before his generals, should be chosen as his lieutenant-general in command of the National Guard, which the Emperor had always reserved for himself, together with troops of the line and the National Guards of the 1st Military Division, the Imperial Guard and the defence of Paris, was nothing less than extraordinary.

Joseph, despite all the rebuffs and obloquy he had so recently received from his brother, nevertheless applied himself with the greatest zeal and loyalty to his new task. With the assistance of his chief-of-staff, Marshal Moncey (who although a marshal, held the rank of major-general), General Mathieu and other officers who had served with him in Spain, he performed unexpected wonders. He raised twelve companies of gunners from cadets of the Polytechnic college, and a corps of engineers from engineers in civil occupations; scratch cavalry from gendarmerie and game wardens; he requisitioned horses, shoes and sporting guns; built defences at the thirty *barrières* of Paris; attempted to arm the recruits who began to flood into the capital as the danger increased, and did all in his power to reassure the population, which was becoming more and more alarmed every day.[6]

Joseph was well aware of danger from within. On 6 February he wrote to Napoleon :

If Your Majesty should suffer serious defeats, what form of Government should be retained here to prevent the first schemers from putting themselves at the head of some movement or other? Louis and Jerome have asked me to remind Your Majesty that they are prepared to fulfil whatever role you should think fit to give them. In my personal opinion, I believe that if the worst comes to the worst, and the enemy should enter the capital, *it would be advisable that it should not be abandoned by all Your Majesty's brothers.* It seems to me that between the departure of the Empress and the entry of the enemy, there should be an interval during which a provisional Government commission should be established with a prince at its head.

On the following day Napoleon, now in Troyes, replied that in the event of Paris being occupied by the enemy, the only man to remain in the capital should be a *commissaire impérial.* 'Consider whom you believe to be the best choice . . . I think we should leave behind no minister; but I hope the necessity will never arise . . . should such an unforeseen event come to pass, the idea of appointing King Louis at the head of Paris seems to me very good.'

Joseph wrote again to the Emperor on 7 February to tell him that, should the Empress leave Paris, the population would immediately be thrown into a state of despair and would deliver the capital and the Empire into the hands of the Bourbons. On the 8th, Napoleon replied from Nogent-sur-Seine :

> . . . Paris will never be occupied so long as I live . . . If Talleyrand has anything to do with the idea of allowing the Empress to leave Paris in case of the approach of the enemy, it is treachery. He is certainly the greatest enemy of our House now that fortune has temporarily abandoned us. If we lose a battle[7] and I am killed, you will be first to learn of it, before any other member of my House. You will give instructions for the Empress and the King of Rome to be sent to Rambouillet and order the Senate and Council of State and all troops, to unite on the Loire. Leave a prefect or an Imperial commission or mayor in Paris.
>
> *Never let the Empress or the King of Rome fall into the hands of the enemy* . . . I would prefer to have my throat slit rather than see my son brought up in Vienna as an Austrian prince. I have a sufficiently high regard for the Empress to believe that she is of the same opinion . . . You don't know the French nation. What may happen in the course of these great events is incalculable. As far as Louis is concerned, I think he will be guided by you.

How often has Joseph been blamed by historians for deserting the capital with Marie-Louise! This was no cowardice; he was simply obeying his brother's orders.

In addition to all his other worries, Joseph's detractors now accused him of being the lover of the Empress. Napoleon, who had written to Joseph on 7 February *'tenez gaie l'Impératrice'*, was quick to learn of this tittle-tattle. Knowing how attractive Joseph was to women, and well aware of his wife's sensual nature, he was momentarily disturbed, but any suspicions he may have entertained were soon dissipated. From Joseph's daily letters to him, he realized that his brother had no time for love affairs. Indeed, this was true. He had ceased to visit his mistress the Marquesa de Montehermoso, and the

Comtesse Saint-Jean d'Angely, for now he was far too busy endeavouring to supply his brother with the *matériel* of war, holding reviews, reassuring the public and writing reports. With so much on his hands, he had little time to amuse the Empress.

Joseph's loyalty to his Imperial brother, however, did not blind him to the true facts. Despite Napoleon's astonishing victories of Champaubert, Montmirail, Vauchamps and Montereau and the fact that the Austrian general, Prince Schwartzenberg, demanded an armistice (which Napoleon haughtily declined to discuss until every Allied soldier had left French soil), Joseph was not in the least deluded. In an extremely tactful letter to his brother, Joseph wrote :

> I have received the letter in which Your Majesty informs me of the enemy's request for a suspension of hostilities and Your Majesty's determination to grant nothing until peace is signed. With respect to Your Majesty, it signifies little whether, at the time of signature, the enemy have recrossed the Rhine or not, if what he signed on this side of the river is what was proposed when he was on the other side [i.e. the Frankfurt Declaration, which Napoleon was belatedly willing to accept].

Realizing that Napoleon's phenomenal successes had gone to his head, that he refused to discuss any terms until the Austrians and Russians had retreated to the east of the Rhine and seemed quite unaware that, in spite of his temporary advantage, France was drained dry, Joseph again wrote to him : '*If you can make peace, do so at any price.* If you cannot, we must perish with resolution. Your Majesty can count on me to obey him in every respect and that I will never do anything unworthy of him or of myself.'

Although the Emperor was not prepared to follow Joseph's advice, he authorized him to summon a council, presided over by the Empress, to discuss armistice terms. The result of this meeting was immediately communicated to the Emperor. The consensus of opinion was that France should immediately accept the terms of the Frankfurt Declaration, sooner than expose the capital to occupation by the enemy. 'Whether or not Your Majesty wins a battle today is immaterial; you must still think of peace.'

On 9 March, he again wrote to his brother begging him to make peace :

> After your recent victory, you may honourably sign a peace based on the former frontier boundaries [i.e. those imposed by the Declaration of

Frankfurt]. Such a peace would restore the prosperity of France after the long struggle that began in 1792; and there could be nothing dishonourable to her in it, as she would lose no portion of her territory, and has arranged her affairs at home as she thought fit.

As for you, Sire, who have been so repeatedly victorious, I am convinced that you possess all the qualities which might make the French forget, or rather might recall to them, the best features of the reigns of Louis XII, Henri IV and Louis XIV, if you will make a lasting peace with Europe, and if, returning to your natural kindness, and, renouncing your assumed character and your perpetual efforts, you will at last consent to relinquish the role of superman for that of a great sovereign.

After having saved France from anarchy within, and from all Europe without, you will become the father of your people. You will be adored as much as Louis XII, admired more than Henri IV and Louis XIV; in order thus to accumulate every sort of glory, you have only to will your own happiness, as well as that of France.

Napoleon's only reply was: 'I am master here, just as I was at Austerlitz.'

Two days later, on 11 March, Joseph again wrote. After giving a long detailed exposé of the desperate situation of the country, he continued:

Individual distress is extreme; and on the day when it is believed that Your Majesty has preferred prolonging the war to making even a disadvantageous peace, there is no doubt that disgust will incline public opinion in another direction. If Toulouse or Bordeaux should set up a Bourbon, you will have civil war, and the immense population of Paris will support the side which promises to give them peace the soonest.

Such is the state of opinion that no one can change it. This being the case, the only way is to submit. If the peace be unfavourable, it will be no fault of yours, as all classes here insist upon it. I cannot be mistaken, as my view is the same as that of everybody else. We are on the eve of total destruction; our only hope is in peace . . .

Unfortunately, it was already too late. The Allies were no longer willing to discuss conditions. On 27 February Soissons had capitulated without firing a shot. Napoleon ordered the commandant to be executed in the Place de Grève with the utmost publicity. At the same time, Paris learnt with horror that Soult's Army of Spain had been driven across the Pyrenees, to be defeated at Orthez, and then had fallen back on Toulouse without even holding the line of the Garonne.

Masséna had retreated to Toulon, which had declared itself pro-Bourbon. The whole of the south-west of France lay open to the British forces. For some reason, Napoleon had never taken the threat to his southern frontier seriously. He had always had the greatest confidence in the Duke of Dalmatia and despite Joseph's warnings had always underrated Wellington. It came as a shock that, not only were the British firmly entrenched on French soil, but the population of the south-west greeted them almost as liberators. Much to Wellington's embarrassment, Toulouse hoisted the white banner of the Bourbons and gave the Duke a hero's welcome on his entry into the town.

The imminent arrival of the armies of the Coalition in Paris naturally provoked the most intense political intrigues. Talleyrand and his friend Jaucourt, who only a few days earlier would have been only too pleased to see Bernadotte on the throne, supported by Joseph, were now openly in favour of a Bourbon restoration.

On 28 March, Marmont and Mortier arrived from Provins, about fifty miles from Paris, pursued by an enemy against whom they could no longer put up further resistance. Apart from the National Guard, no troops were left in Paris itself. Joseph's conduct during these fateful days was above reproach. Despite the advice of the Council of Regency, he had sent the Empress and the King of Rome to Rambouillet. He did his best to galvanize the people of Paris into improving the defences, despite the lackadaisical and pessimistic attitude of many of the mayors of *arrondissements*, and to put spirit into the National Guards. At daybreak of 30 March, when he himself was in Montmartre on the Clignancourt road, surrounded by his staff, which was now augmented by his brother Jerome, Marshals Marmont, Mortier and Moncey, and Clarke, the Minister of War, the people of Paris were able to read a proclamation posted on the walls of the city :

Citizens of Paris – An enemy column is marching on Meaux [thirty miles to the east of Paris] advancing on the road from Germany. The Emperor is closely following it at the head of a victorious army.

The Council of Regency has provided for the safety of the Empress and the King of Rome. I remain with you.

Let us arm to defend this city, its monuments, its wealth, our women, our children and all that is dear to us. Let us preserve the honour of France.

(Signed) JOSEPH

When he published this proclamation, Joseph was not yet aware how pressing was the danger. On the same morning of 30 March he held a council of war. The Russian and Austrian armies were already investing the capital. All his marshals and generals agreed that it was impossible to hold the city. It was essential to fall back on the Loire. After several hours of deliberation, he gave the order to withdraw all troops. In the early afternoon, Joseph left on horseback accompanied by Jerome, his ministers and staff officers. He crossed the Bois de Boulogne and the Pont de Sèvres, a few moments before the bridge fell into the hands of a Cossack patrol, and passing through Versailles spent the night at Rambouillet with the Empress and the King of Rome.

Three days later he was at Blois. What could he have done, together with Marmont and Moncey, to save Paris? Napoleon's reputed statement that if only *he* had been there, Paris would have been saved, bears no relation to reality. There is no question but that Joseph acted wisely. Had Paris resisted, under the contemporary rules of war, the city would have been sacked. Chateaubriand later accused Joseph of deceiving the populace: 'Rostopshine [Governor of Moscow] never claimed to defend Moscow; he burnt it. Joseph announced that he would never desert the Parisians, but decamped silently, leaving his courage behind him placarded on the street corners.'[8] This is grossly unfair. At the time the proclamation was posted, Joseph still believed that the capital might be saved; nor as yet had the Emperor abdicated. He still believed that Napoleon might come to terms with the Allies. By leaving Paris with his Government, he was only obeying the Emperor's orders. To have made public announcement that he was leaving Paris would have thrown the city into a state of panic.

On his arrival at Blois, the town to which Napoleon had previously advised him to retire, Joseph's first intention was to join the Emperor at Fontainebleau and seek directives from him, but the road through Orleans was barred to him by the enemy.

On 7 April Napoleon signed his abdication. On the 8th Joseph wrote to Désirée, who had remained in Paris, awaiting the arrival of her husband :

My dear Désirée, – Julie has given me your letters to read and I am more touched than surprised by your sentiments for us. Since I am as anxious not to be parted from my wife as I am anxious for her not to be separated from you, I beg you to continue your efforts on our behalf. I am convinced that they will end happily because they are so right and their purpose is so legitimate. I send you a letter for the

Emperor Alexander – on several occasions he has shown me great consideration.

If Montefontaine is too close to Paris, we will choose a residence further away; at the very worst, in Switzerland.

Yesterday I wrote to Bernadotte. I won't say any more; to insist would be to doubt your true friendship.

I embrace you,

J.

This letter was delivered to Désirée by Miot. Miot in his memoirs writes that Désirée was to meet the Emperor of Russia on the following day. She hoped to obtain permission for Julie and her two daughters to remain in France. 'She asked me', writes Miot, 'not to compromise them when I made my request for passports which I would have to obtain from the provisional government. On 10 April, I learnt from the Princess of Sweden that the Emperor of Russia had graciously met with her request.'[9]

Unlike the Tsar, Talleyrand and Jaucourt, the one-time friend of Joseph, who were now members of the Provisional Government, both raised objections to supplying Joseph with passports. These ministers obviously feared the return to Paris of the ex-King of Spain and even considered banishing Joseph to Elba with his brother. Strangely enough, it was La Forest, the ex-French Ambassador to Madrid, who had never shown Joseph any sympathy in Spain, who finally agreed to issue him with a passport on condition he left France, never to return without permission of the Government. Joseph refused to accept such terms, which he regarded as equivalent to banishment; all he demanded were ordinary passports similar to those supplied to Jerome by the Tsar. Rather than accept La Forest's terms, Joseph, after ordering Julie and the children to remain with Désirée in the Bernadotte mansion in the rue d'Anjou,[10] immediately left Orleans without official papers in company with his aide-de-camp, General Espert, his secretary, Presle, and his personal doctor, Paroisse, under whose name he travelled, while the doctor took the name of Cesarini.

On 19 April, the fugitives arrived at Bourges, where they spent the night, whence they drove via Nevers to Autun, where they were welcomed by Joseph's former teacher, old Abbé Chardon, to whom he had awarded a pension. From here, the travellers continued their journey to the Swiss frontier, which they crossed without hindrance.

Unlike Jaucourt, Joseph did not forget faithful old friends. He was always worried for the future of the Spaniards who had followed him. Just before leaving Orleans, he wrote to O'Farrill, Azanza and others to ask them if they were in need of anything: 'The uncertainty of their position being not the least of my worries,' as he wrote later.

On 16 April, his former ministers replied :

We are Spaniards; Your Majesty too, was Spanish when he was in Spain. Like a Spanish prince he protected our integrity and national independence. We ask nothing of Your Majesty.

The recollection of the good intentions Your Majesty entertained for our country and his kindness to us, is all we need to keep your memory in our hearts.

XV

First Exile:
Switzerland

1814–1815

If Joseph expected to find a warm welcome among the liberal Swiss of the Canton of Vaud, he was to be disappointed. The very name of Bonaparte, now that Napoleon was no longer master of Europe, was execrated. Fortunately for Joseph, he still had a friend in the Comte de Sellons, a true *philosophe* and one of the first philanthropists to advocate the abolition of corporal punishment and the death penalty. The Comte de Sellons put his lovely lakeside château of Allaman, near Lausanne, at the disposal of the ex-king. Joseph found his new home so much to his liking that he offered to buy it, but when his offer was declined he looked for an equally delightful property in the neighbourhood. His choice fell on the Château de Prangins, an old building overlooking the lake of Geneva. It was a charming spot, with a large park surrounded by vineyards, altogether an estate after Joseph's heart. He settled here at the end of June 1814. He immediately began exercising his passion for enlarging and improving his property, just as he had done at Mortefontaine and was to do later at Point Breeze in the United States.

Little by little, he made additions to the property. He dammed a mountain stream to form a lake where he was able to indulge his passion for shooting snipe and wild duck. Here, under the title of Comte de Survilliers – the same incognito he had assumed on his flight from Spain – he settled down to what he hoped would be a life of pleasant exile. Already visitors flocked to visit him. He even received a visit from Julie and his daughters. Jerome and his family also came to visit him en route for Berne. There was also the great occasion when, dressed in all the splendour of his Spanish uniform, and covered with decorations, he went to meet Marie-Louise at Payern and escorted her back to spend the night at Prangins. Many of his old friends from Mortefontaine came to visit him, including Baron de Ménéval, who wrote in his memoirs: 'I was enchanted by the elegant hospitality which distinguished this delightful residence. I found the master of the house more preoccupied with his country life and the future of his brother, than with his own brilliant and stormy past.'[1]

The great actor Talma was also another visitor, as was his old friend, Napoleon's *bête noire* Madame de Staël, who lived close by at Coppet. Although Germaine de Staël had been bitterly opposed to Napoleon during his hours of glory, she was now filled with generosity towards the fallen idol and was devoting all her very considerable energies – to use Talleyrand's words – 'to fish back from the water those whom she had previously drowned'.[2]

Nothing that Madame de Staël said or did went unobserved by the chancelleries of Europe. She was a particular source of anxiety to the French ambassador in Berne, the Comte Auguste de Talleyrand, brother of the 'great' Talleyrand, who, having transferred his allegiance to the Bourbons, had set his spies to supervise every single action of Joseph ever since the ex-king had set foot on Swiss soil. The good-natured, intelligent Joseph soon accumulated a large circle of friends, innocent friendships which Talleyrand's over-zealous secret police interpreted to be the nucleus of a Bonapartist faction. Joseph's relations with women, platonic or not, were politically suspect, his banking account was carefully scrutinized and, whenever possible, his letters to France were intercepted and their contents carefully noted. Spies were posted among his domestic servants and even the mistresses of his secretaries were questioned. So great was the harassment to which he was subjected that Désirée Bernadotte personally intervened on her brother-in-law's behalf and tried to extract a promise from Louis XVIII that the French Government would never demand Joseph's extradition but leave him to enjoy his retreat in peace. The King's reply was courteous, but equivocal. He contented himself with promising Désirée that her sister Julie would never be put to an inconvenience – not a very satisfactory answer since Julie was hundreds of miles away from her husband, living quietly in Auteuil. Désirée's good intentions, in fact, had quite the opposite effect to what she had hoped. The spying and petty harassments, if anything, increased. In October the Canton of Vaud threatened the ex-King with expulsion. Joseph was furious. Forthwith he called on the Austrian and Russian ministers in Zurich. The Baron du Casse quotes him as addressing the ministers in the following terms : 'What have I ever done to harm France? Am I responsible for my brother's faults? I, who more than anyone else have been his victim. The King has assured the Princess of Sweden that he was pleased to see me happy in Switzerland.'[3]

This brief speech had, temporarily, the required effect. Baron von Schrand, the Austrian Minister, promised Joseph that he would look after his interests and that he could remain tranquilly at Prangins for at least the remainder of the year. It was not an entirely satisfactory reply : indeed, the truce was of only short duration. On 23 February 1815 he was informed by the representatives of the Canton of Vaud that M. le Ministre, the Comte Auguste de Talleyrand, had stated that 'it was absolutely essential not only in his own interests, but in those of the canton, that he should leave the country as soon as possible'.

No one at the time guessed that three days later Napoleon was to leave Elba secretly, and that after years of extraordinary adventures Joseph, ex-King of Naples and Spain, would find himself two months later domiciled in the United States.

At the beginning of March, Auguste Talleyrand left for Vienna.

Despite the warning given to him in February, Joseph had made no move to leave Prangins. He had even been able to outwit Talleyrand and von Schrand's spies and keep in touch with his brother in Elba, to whom he wrote that an attempt was to be made on his life, the news of which had been imparted to him by Germaine de Staël. Together with Talma, Germaine volunteered to leave for Elba to forewarn the Emperor (two more unlikely secret emissaries it would be hard to find). Joseph, however, wisely declined this generous offer from one of the most notorious women in all Europe and one of the world's greatest actors, and sent instead an obscure former *commissaire ordonnateur* of the Army of Italy, who was living in retirement near Prangins. Thanks to this man, the plot failed and the two conspirators were banished from Elba.

Joseph, too, was one of the first to receive news of Napoleon's landing at Fréjus; how, we don't know. He lost no time in sending his confidential *valet de chambre* Mailliard, who had so often been successful in eluding Talleyrand's spies and conveying his master's correspondence to friends and relatives in Paris, with a letter to his brother expressing his loyalty.

Mailliard safely crossed the Jura and was able to deliver Joseph's letter to Napoleon, who by this time had already reached Grenoble, where the garrisons, 'at the sight of the little man in the grey coat', had, to a man, declared themselves for the Emperor. On 12 March Napoleon wrote to Joseph from Lyon:

> . . . I have received your letter brought to me by your *valet de chambre*. Write all the news to the Empress under the cover of a business letter. I have already more than 30,000 men under my command. All the Lyonnais and Dauphinois are delirious with joy. I enclose all my proclamations and everything printed concerning current events. Have a great number of these printed and send them in all haste to Alsace and the Franche-Comté. I see no reason why you should not go to Zurich [to see the Austrian minister]. You will emphasize that the Empress and my son must be returned to me immediately and that Austria must send me a representative without delay and that I particularly desire peace for France. I would prefer it if the Austrian minister came to see you. Write to him to come; he cannot very well refuse. I hope to be in Paris on the 20th or 25th.

With that astonishing confidence in his star, which even after his defeats of 1813 and 1814 never seemed to have deserted him, Napoleon imagined himself once again to be not only master of France but also of Europe. He believed that Austria would bow to his slightest wish and that he could live at peace with the whole world.

The usually level-headed Joseph was so excited by his brother's return that he believed that the whole situation of Europe would be reversed in the twinkling of an eye. On 17 March he wrote to the Baron von Schrand, and he enclosed copies of Napoleon's proclamations.

> . . . The reign of the Bourbons was nothing but a bad dream . . . Napoleon only wants to assure peace and happiness to the whole world. Not being certain of my reception at Berne or Lucerne, it is only necessary for Your Excellency to arrange a meeting with me either at Prangins or Morat to contribute to this happy result.

Not only did von Schrand refuse to visit him, but after consulting with Metternich he requested the Swiss authorities to have Joseph immediately arrested and imprisoned in the fortress of Schaffenhausen, when he would be incapable of communicating with anyone and which was too far from the French frontier to allow his escape. Metternich would have been even more severe, and advocated his imprisonment in the grim fortress of Gratz.

Fortunately for Joseph, among his many friends was an officer of the Vaudoise gendarmerie, who warned him of his imminent arrest.

On the following day (20 March), when a Federal Commission arrived at Prangins with an escort of hussars, Joseph had already left the country. But before leaving he had taken the precaution of burying valuable documents, diamonds and other precious possessions in a very deep 'fox hole' which he had already secretly prepared in the grounds of his estate. At ten o'clock at night, accompanied by his daughter (Julie was in Aix), he left for France, crossing the frontier at the Fort de l'Écluse.

At Dijon, where he was recognized and given a warm reception, he received a message from the Emperor, requesting him to make all haste for Paris. At two o'clock in the afternoon of the 23rd he arrived in the capital, where, after greeting his brother, he took up his residence at the Élysée, where he stayed for a few days. Napoleon overwhelmed him with kindness and was lavish with his generosity. He immediately put forty carriage horses at his brother's disposal and, although no longer entitled to call himself King, Joseph was nevertheless officially endowed with the title of 'Prince' and was reinstated as Grand Elector, with a salary of one million livres per annum, to be doubled in 1816. Napoleon also presented him with the magnificently furnished Hotel Valentinois (today the Hôtel Matignon, seat of the Conseil d'État).

The services which Joseph could render the Emperor were invaluable. First, Napoleon desired him to reassemble around him his dispersed family. Joseph set about this business immediately. He wrote again to Marie-Louise and Murat in Naples. The Empress however returned no answer, not even after Julie had begged her to return – Julie, whose relations with Marie-Louise had always been most friendly. But Marie-Louise was far too much under her father's thumb and far too much in love with Count Neipergg to wish to exchange her placid life at the court of Vienna and travels with her gallant equerry in return for the uncertainty of once more becoming Empress of France. Napoleon was bitterly disappointed, for although he had never loved her as he had Josephine, nevertheless he was genuinely fond of her and particularly desired to have his son beside him. It had been one of his greatest regrets that she had not joined him while in Elba. Marie Walewska had visited him there and so had his sister Pauline, but not his wife.

Murat, on the other hand, responded cordially to Joseph's letter. At the end of May, Joseph succeeded in establishing an unexpected reconciliation between the 'rebel' Lucien and Napoleon, a reconciliation which pleased Napoleon much more than he was prepared to admit. He accorded Lucien the *grand cordon* of the Legion of

239

Honour and made him too a Prince of the Empire. Until the end of the Hundred Days, Lucien was to remain one of the most active supporters of his brother's regime.

These were not the only services that Joseph rendered his brother at this time. Napoleon, who was always in need of someone in whom he could confide, sought his elder brother's advice on innumerable questions. During his months in Elba, the Emperor had had time to look back over the last years and had undoubtedly revised his opinion of his elder brother. *Frivole et léger* he might be, but he was utterly trustworthy and his judgement had been invariably sound. It was to Joseph that he now turned for advice. It was Joseph whom he asked to draw up a list of a hundred and twenty names from among whom the new councillors of state were to be selected. Both Nicolas Clary and his old friend Jourdan were not forgotten. Joseph was also appointed President of the Council of Ministers, and when Napoleon left again for the armies in June, it was Joseph who was given plenipotentiary powers; it was he who opened all dispatches; it was to him that the ministers, of whom Davout and Fouché were the principles, made their daily reports.

On the day of Napoleon's departure, Joseph showed him the greatest sign of affection by handing over to him, in case the worst came to the worst, a fortune in diamonds, valued at 800,000 livres, which the Emperor took with him in his dispatch box together with the diamond necklace Pauline had given him in Elba. As soon as Napoleon left Paris, Joseph took up residence in the Tuileries to be at the centre of government. Even his detractor Frédéric Masson writes of him : 'In matters of finance, as in those of the police, he showed himself to be moderate, prudent and conscientious and an experienced business man; he never spoke without knowledge.'[4]

His reign was not to last long. On 16 June, Soult wrote to him from Ligny : 'Monseigneur, – The Emperor has just obtained a complete victory over the Prussian and British armies, united under the command of Lord Wellington and Marshal Blucher. The army is advancing through the village of Ligny beyond Fleurus. I hasten to announce this happy news to Your Imperial Highness.'

Joseph immediately ordered salvos to be fired to celebrate the event, but this was to be the last communiqué he received from the army. Two days later the Imperial army was utterly routed at Waterloo. The news of the defeat did not reach Joseph until the 20th. He immediately summoned the Council of Ministers to 'endeavour to save both France and the Empire'. But already intrigues were dividing the government. The situation was not improved by

Napoleon's return to Paris, leaving his routed army without their leader.

Napoleon's decision to return was one of his supreme mistakes. General Flahaut had strongly opposed the idea: 'The Emperor is lost if he sets foot in Paris. The chambers will think they can save themselves by sacrificing him. There is only one way of saving him and France: that is to negotiate with the allies and hand over the crown to his son.'[5]

Others declared that unless the Emperor went to Paris, the capital would surrender. 'When the Parisians see your Majesty, they will not hesitate to fight. If you stay away, a thousand rumours will be set in motion, it will be said that you have been killed, taken prisoner or wounded. The National Guard and the Federates will lose heart and, afraid of being abandoned as they were last year, will fight reluctantly, if at all.' 'Very well,' Napoleon agreed, 'I will go to Paris, but I am convinced you are making me do a foolish thing.'[6]

Napoleon and his suite arrived in Paris on 21 June at about 6 o'clock in the morning: Caulaincourt met him on the steps of the Elysée. The exhausted Emperor, who had not had his boots off since the battle, who had been in the saddle almost ten days without sleep, tormented by bladder trouble, ordered his valets to prepare him his bath. As he relaxed in the warm water, he sent for Joseph, Maret and Regnault de Saint-Jean d'Angely.

They disabused him of any hopes he might have entertained of the Chambers' supporting him: Fouché, the arch intriguer, and La Fayette would certainly demand his abdication, or, should he refuse, vote for his deposition. 'Return to your army,' was the advice of his faithful friends, 'while we fight it out with the Chambers.'

It was too late.

On the morning of 22 June, Napoleon fought his last battle – with his own parliament.

Lucien, who had returned on 8 May, used all his old eloquence to persuade the Chamber that all was not lost. But La Fayette demanded Napoleon's abdication. Leaping to his feet, he addressed Lucien:

'You accuse us of failing in our duty to our honour and to Napoleon,' he cried. 'Have you forgotten what we have done for him? Have you forgotten that the bones of our children and our brothers everywhere bear witness to our fidelity: in the African desert, on the banks of the

Guadalquivir, the Tagus and the Vistula, and on the frozen plains of Muscovy? During the last ten years and more, three million Frenchmen have perished for a man who still today wants to continue fighting against all Europe. We have done enough for him; our present duty is to save our country.[7]

On 22 June 1815 the Emperor resigned the throne in favour of his son. Everyone knew, and none better than Napoleon himself, that this was a mere formula, since the new Napoleon II, under the name of the Duke of Reichstadt, was in the hands of the Austrians who certainly had no intention of releasing him.

After a family meeting held on the 25th at which Napoleon, Joseph, Lucien and Jerome were all present, the brothers unanimously agreed to seek refuge in the United States. But how was this to be achieved? Napoleon had already asked Decrès, Minister of Marine, to put two frigates lying in the Garonne at his disposal, but Fouché had vetoed the idea. Fouché, now virtual ruler of France, wished to keep Napoleon, his trump card, in the country. Napoleon and Lucien thought the best and most dignified procedure was now to approach the English openly. Lucien volunteered to go to London himself. He left on 27 June but, on arrival at Boulogne, suddenly revised his plans and returned to Italy, where he was arrested – as he most certainly would have been had he gone to London – and imprisoned for some time in the citadel of Turin. Jerome, after some hesitation, decided to rejoin his wife and family in Württemberg. Joseph, the only one to keep his head, was of the opinion that it would be madness to trust the English and that any intention of crossing the Atlantic should be kept as quiet as possible. He tried to persuade Napoleon to forget his *amour propre* and that the best course would be to leave secretly, with the help of a small group of devoted persons, just as he himself had already done twice before when he had left France for Switzerland and, four months previously, when he had left Switzerland for France. This, he assured his brother, was the only way, but the Emperor remained irresolute. All he would agree on was to make for Rochefort, where Joseph was to join him later; here they could make a definite decision.

It would seem that for a year now Joseph had been considering exile in the United States, for in April 1814, during his brief stay in Blois, he had concluded a satisfactory business deal which assured him of the possession of very considerable property in the United States. The acquisition of this property had been largely a matter of luck. It belonged to a certain James le Ray, whose father, one of a wealthy shipping family in Nantes, had financed the American rebels at the time of the War of Independence, but who after the rebels' victory had not been repaid his loan.

At the age of twenty-four James (or Jacques, as he was then) had sailed for the United States, where he obtained a concession of 35,000 acres in Pennsylvania, became a naturalized American and was repaid one million of the two millions due to his father. He had married a Miss Grace Coxe, a young heiress from New Jersey, and had returned to France to live in the historic château of Chaumont, which he had inherited in 1803, and which at one time he had put at the disposal of Joseph's friend Germaine de Staël. Learning of Joseph's presence in Blois, James came to offer him his services should the former King consider making his home in the United States.

'You could not have arrived at a more appropriate moment,' Joseph told him. 'I have here with me seven van-loads of silver and valuable furniture. I run the risk of having them confiscated or stolen. I would willingly exchange them for property in the United States.'[8]

Le Ray agreed and at the same time introduced a young American named James Carret to the former King of Spain, who engaged him as secretary-interpreter.

When Joseph left Paris on 29 June for Rochefort, he was accompanied by this same Carret, together with his Spanish aide-de-camp Major Unzaga, his confidential valet Louis Mailliard and Mailliard's son Adolphe. This time he was supplied with blank French passports signed by Fouché as well as American passports, also blank, provided by the United States chargé d'affaires.

Joseph did not take a direct route to Rochefort, but approached the port from the south, via Saintes. Although taller and slimmer than his brother, he had put on weight in the last few years, and here, at Saintes, some royalists, mistaking him for the Emperor, stopped his coach and forced him to enter an inn : fortunately some National Guardsmen and local Bonapartists were on the spot to rescue him and allow him to continue his journey.

On the night of 4–5 July Joseph reached Rochefort, where Napoleon had preceded him. For three days the brothers discussed what action to take. According to several eyewitnesses, Napoleon seemed in a state of lethargy, brushing aside one suggestion after another proposed by his brother, or sometimes not listening to him at all. Las Cases was later to remark : 'Like a gambler who had truly lost all, he seemed almost relieved that he was now paying the penalty for his mad daring, for his most audacious coups, by suffering this miserable end.'

While Napoleon took refuge in the little island fortress of Aix, which lies between the Île d'Oléron and Rochefort, Joseph succeeded in chartering for 18,000 francs an American brig, the *Commerce*, 200 tons, whose master, a certain Captain Misservey, a Guernsey man by origin, was bound for Charlestown with a cargo consisting in part of cognac. Misservey, who had no idea of Joseph's true identity (Joseph had chartered the ship under the name of Bouchard), drove a hard bargain, for Joseph was obliged to purchase part of his cargo.

On 12 July, Joseph visited the Emperor on the Île d'Aix. This time he proposed that he should take Napoleon's place on the island and surrender his own berth on the brig to his brother. The mistake made at Saintes proved sufficiently that their resemblance was such that their identities could be confused. Joseph would pretend to be ill and not move from the Governor's house (where Napoleon was lodged) until the brig carrying the Emperor had safely passed through the British blockade.

Napoleon thanked Joseph, but refused to commit himself. On the following day Joseph sent Louis Mailliard, who had already rendered him so many services in the past, to obtain a definite answer from the Emperor. 'Tell King Joseph', said Napoleon, 'that I have given his proposal careful consideration. I cannot accept. It would be flight. I could not leave without my staff, all of whom are devoted to me. My brother may do so; he is not in my position. I cannot. Tell him to leave immediately. He will make a safe landing. Adieu!'[9]

For Napoleon the Great, Emperor of the French, to escape like a criminal under a false name, disguised, perhaps hidden in the hold of a ship, or even in a padded barrel (as had been proposed), was unthinkable. He still entertained ideas of grandeur and refused to be separated from his retinue, consisting of fifty persons, including the wives, children and servants of members of his staff.

Joseph, heartbroken, decided to remain a little while longer near Royan as the guest of Edouard Pelletreau, a fellow Freemason and wealthy Bordelais shipowner, while waiting anxiously for his brother's final decision. He had not long to wait. On the 14th, he received a message from Bertrand informing him that the Emperor had decided to accept the hospitality of Captain Maitland aboard the *Bellerophon*.

Joseph had no choice but to leave. He ordered James Carret to buy all necessities for his journey, including a quantity of books, and in order to put Louis XVIII's police off the scent Carret was to spread reports that he had been seen in the neighbourhood of the Swiss frontier.

Thanks to Carret, the vice-consul of the United States provided

Joseph (under the name of M. Bouchard) and his companions with visas. On the night of 24–5 July 1815, Captain Misservey took aboard his five passengers, 'M. Bouchard', Louis and Adolphe Mailliard, Mr Carret and a Spanish gentleman, Major Unzaga, of the medical corps, and set course for the United States.

XVI

Second Exile:
The Gentleman Farmer
of New Jersey, U.S.A.

1815–1830

While still within sight of the coast of France, the *Commerce* was hailed successively by two English frigates, *Bacchus* and *Endymion*, and ordered to heave to. The British officers who boarded her, already aware that the Emperor was aboard the *Bellerophon*, contented themselves with a cursory examination of the passports, while 'M. Bouchard' remained below 'suffering from seasickness'.

It was not until much later that Misservey learnt the true identity of his passengers. Although he guessed that M. Bouchard was no ordinary passenger, he convinced himself that he was Lazare Carnot and that Colonel Unzaga was General Clausel. When eventually he learnt that his passenger was none other than the brother of the Emperor he declared that he would sooner have blown up his ship than surrender his royal passenger. 'That's just what I wanted to avoid', observed Joseph drily.

The crossing of the Atlantic, which lasted thirty-two days, passed without incident. On 27 August, however, when the *Commerce* was approaching New York harbour, she was again intercepted by two English frigates; but this time she had a young American pilot aboard who brought the brig, under full sail, so close inshore that the English ships dared not follow.

It was still under the name of Bouchard that Joseph took up residence in a New York family boarding-house run by a Mrs Powell in Park Place. Meanwhile Misservey lost no time in letting everybody

246

know that he had brought the great Republican, the 'Organizer of Victories' and one-time member of the Directoire, Carnot, and General Clausel safely to the shores of America.

When the New York *Evening Post* published the news on 30 August, two days after Joseph's arrival, Jacob Radcliffe, mayor of New York and an ardent Republican, hurried to pay his respects. M. Bouchard was obliged to admit to the mayor that he was not Carnot, but that he had formerly belonged to the Imperial House – 'House' being a sufficiently vague term and not necessarily denoting that he was part of the family – and that he wished to remain incognito.

It was impossible, however, for Joseph to preserve his incognito for long. The United States harboured far too many French refugees for him to remain long unrecognized; indeed, the first person to recognize him was a Major Jacob Lewis, temporarily a fellow lodger in Mrs Powell's boarding-house, who had met Joseph in France some years previously. Lewis, however, faithfully promised to keep his secret and henceforth became Joseph's devoted guide and friend. He invited the King to spend some time with him at his home at Amboy in New Jersey, an invitation which Joseph readily accepted.

On his return to New York, on 6 September, while walking one afternoon with Mailliard down one of the streets off Broadway, he was accosted, as Mailliard recounts,

> by a big fellow with a military appearance, in the throes of a strong emotion. He was, as it happened, a former officer of the Royal Guard, who on recognizing the King, rushed towards him, knelt down, and seizing his hand, kissed it, and with tears pouring down his cheeks, called out in a voice, choked by sobs, 'Your Majesty! *Here!* Your Majesty!'
>
> A crowd, unused to such a sight, gathered round, curious to know to what king the veteran soldier was referring. In vain Joseph tried to calm the enthusiasm of his admirer who, deaf to all entreaties, was only too happy to shout at the top of his voice the identity of the successor to Charles Quint.[1]

On the following day, all the New York newspapers published the astonishing news that Joseph, ex-King of Naples and Spain, brother of the great Bonaparte, was living in their midst. Joseph was extremely worried. The European Powers – the so-called Holy Alliance – had determined on the residence of all the other members of the Bonaparte family, and since Joseph was considered the most dangerous, he feared, now that his identity was known, that he would be extradited and probably exiled to Russia. He therefore hastened to seek the advice of Jacob Radcliffe, the mayor who had shown such sympathy to him on his arrival. Radcliffe advised him to pay his respects to the President James Madison, the only man in the United States on equal footing with an ex-king, and to ask him to place him under the protection of the laws of his country.

On 10 September, in the company of his new friend Major Lewis, Joseph, now assuming the name of Comte de Survilliers, set out for Washington. He broke his journey at Philadelphia and again at Baltimore, where he was told that Madison refused to see him. Madison, the fourth President of the United States, who although no friend of Great Britain, with whom his country had been at war from 1811 to 1814, was also no friend of Napoleon and no lover of kings. He was therefore quite prepared to accept the advice of James Monroe, his Secretary of State and eventual successor, and promulgator of the famous Monroe Doctrine advocating non-interference in European affairs, who recommended to him that any meeting with Joseph would be politically unwise.

Joseph philosophically shrugged off this snub, which he attributed to bad manners rather than to political expediency. No objections, however, were raised to his remaining in the United States, and he was assured that there was no question of delivering his person to the European Powers; in brief, he could henceforth enjoy all the privileges of a citizen of the United States. Financially, he was not worried. He had made over Mortefontaine in name only to Julie's half-sister, Honorine, Madame de Villeneufve, to avoid its confiscation under the law passed by Louis XVIII, by which all property belonging to the Bonapartes was seized by the State, and had made similar provisions for his financial investments. His Swiss property of Prangins and all revenues from the estate were similarly made over to his banker Veret in Lyon. Furthermore, the investments in property he had made in the United States with the help of James le Ray now gave him additional security.

His first preoccupation was to find suitable homes, for he demanded for himself both a town and a country house. Under the name of Survilliers, the name which he was to retain for the remainder of his life, he rented a house in the centre of Philadelphia (260 South Ninth Street, still standing today)[2] and another, Lansdowne House, in Fairmount Park, to the west of the city, which was originally built by John Penn, the founder of Pennsylvania. He made many friends in the neighbourhood and often took a glass of cider with local farmers, but he could never quite accustom himself to the fact that he was merely a tenant. He had always liked large properties where he could indulge his passion for landscape gardening and buildings. With James Carret as interpreter, he explored the neighbourhood of Philadelphia for fifty miles around in search of a suitable estate. On 16 June 1816, on the road to Bordentown, he fell in with a certain Doctor William Burns who told him that one of his friends, a Mr Stephen Sayer, was putting up for sale just such a property as Joseph required, situated between the Delaware and Crosswick Creek. The name of this property was Point Breeze. By United States law, amended later, only naturalized American citizens were allowed to purchase property, but thanks to Carret, the purchase was made in the name of one of the latter's friends, John Reinhold. It was not until 22 January 1817 that the State of New Jersey passed a special law whereby the Comte de Survilliers could sign his own name to the title deeds. For this estate of 211 acres Joseph paid 17,500 dollars, but with successive alterations and additions it is estimated that he must finally have spent 300,000 dollars. It was an ideal situation, and the house Joseph proposed to build for himself was, as he said, only to be rivalled by the White House. Joseph spent his first winters in Philadelphia in a mansion which he rented from Stephen Girard, an immensely wealthy banker, an émigré from Bordeaux who became his financial adviser and one of his most intimate friends. In the 'season' he took the waters at Saratoga Springs.

It entirely suited the European Powers that Joseph should be on the other side of the Atlantic instead of living on the shores of Lake Leman, and therefore they took no steps to assign him a new place of residence. The only instructions given to Hyde de Neuville, who had replaced Sérurier as French Ambassador to Washington, were to keep a strict eye on Joseph and acquaint the French Government should he attempt to act as an intermediary between exiled French Bonapartists and the Emperor. Despite Joseph's quiet life, some perfectly groundless rumours were to centre round him. Grouchy's arrival at Baltimore on 27 January 1816 seems to have thoroughly alarmed Señor de Onis, the Spanish Ambassador to Washington, who communicated his fears (via Madrid) to Paris. He reported that Joseph, Grouchy, Clausel and others 'are gathering around them all banished Frenchmen and all the most turbulent spirits of this party; Joseph, whose wealth is immense, proposes to purchase a very considerable property; that a captain of an American privateer, a man named Carpenter, renowned for his enterprise and daring, has volunteered to abduct Napoleon from Saint Helena for the sum of 100,000 piastres.'

A few days after writing the above report, de Onis wrote again to say that the privateer had left for an unknown destination. As soon as the French Consul in Baltimore and Hyde de Neuville received copies of these communiqués, a careful watch was kept on all shipping. They reported the secret departure from Baltimore of sixteen to seventeen fast sailing ships, loaded with men and artillery, to abduct 'Buonaparte' [*sic*]³ from Saint Helena.

Hyde de Neuville wrote to his Government on 12 July 1816:

> The Spanish insurgents⁴ will neglect nothing in order to have Buonaparte as their leader. What they require of this man is his reputation; it cannot be denied that should he appear in South America, we will once again see him armed with formidable powers . . . They forget that this ogre is in the habit of always devouring his neighbour.

Obviously, it was believed that the Comte de Survilliers was financing the expedition. Hyde de Neuville went on to express his fear that 'these people [French refugees] are once again evincing the spirit of '93; in their eyes regicides are heroes.'

Joseph had no idea that he was an object of suspicion, nor had he an inkling that de Neuville and de Onis were reporting that he was engaged in what were entirely imaginary plots to rescue Napoleon. On the contrary, he was perfectly happy; for once in his life he had nothing to do with politics and was at peace with the world. He wrote to Presle, his former secretary:

> This country in which I live is very beautiful; the climate is good. Here one can enjoy perfect peace; there are no magistrates, no police, no malefactors. Everybody works, everyone respects his neighbour . . . There is perfect freedom. The people's way of life is perfect; the standard of craftsmanship is very high, though the fine arts are still in their infancy. The necessities of life are reasonably cheap; but the cost of *objets de luxe* is prohibitive. In Switzerland, one hides one's wealth, here you display it. Here you live by work and on credit; in Switzerland by work and saving . . . The American works and spends. The American is hospitable and kind. He is not as ceremonious as the Spanish, nor as polished as a Frenchman, but he is more cordially disposed to strangers.
>
> In general, this country and its inhabitants greatly please me, and so long as I am surrounded by people who interest me, I am content and much happier than I was in Switzerland.

By the same post (28 January 1816) he also wrote to Désirée expressing his wish that Julie should join him with the children. We know of no particular reason why Julie decided to remain in Europe, though we know she made constant approaches to the Allied Powers to allow Joseph to settle in Italy, where most of the Bonapartes were now living. But since Joseph was so happy in the United States, even had he been given permission he had no wish to change his place of residence. Julie's refusal to leave for America might be explained by her horror of the sea (her brother Nicolas had already gone so far as to book her a passage from Antwerp) and the fact that she was crippled by rheumatism but, although like other members of the Bonaparte family she was no longer permitted to live in France, her passport allowed her to make her home wherever else she liked in Europe – or America. Why she should have chosen to reside in Frankfurt remains a mystery. She wrote from here to Nicolas of her loneliness, of the weather, which was abominable, and that her house was flooded in winter. In 1820 she decided to leave for Brussels, complaining always that her itinerant life was costing her far beyond her means, which was not surprising in view of the entourage she insisted on maintaining, peculiar for a woman of such modest tastes as Julie.

Meanwhile, despite the fact that Joseph was consoling himself with a beautiful Creole, the wife of an accommodating Corsican officer named Sari whom he had appointed as his general factotum, he would have been genuinely happy to have his wife and family with him. If it was generally known in American circles that Mme Sari was his mistress, it seems to have made no difference to his popularity and the respect in which he was held. He was surrounded by many distinguished friends, including Daniel Webster, the celebrated jurist and congressman, and one of the greatest of all American orators; John Quincy Adams, later to become sixth President of the United States; Admiral Charles Stewart, the hero of the war of 1812; Judge Joseph Hopkinson, a former member of Congress and author of *Hail Columbia*; General Thomas Cadwallader; Doctor Nathaniel Chapman and two former diplomats to France, William Short and Charles J. Ingersoll (who was to be one of Joseph's memorialists); not to mention the banker Stephen Girard (to whom he tried unsuccessfully to sell Mortefontaine).

From time to time he also invited French refugees to Point Breeze; among these were Grouchy and Clausel, both of whom lived in Philadelphia; his old friend Regnault Saint-Jean d'Angely (whose wife at one time had been his mistress); General Vandamme (his former divisional commander at Boulogne); the Comte de Réal (former Jacobin and Napoleon's one-time chief of police) and the ex-*préfet*

Quinet, all of whom lived in New York. More rarely among his guests were Generals Lallemand, Bernard and Lefebvre-Desnouettes, the former Jacobin and hero of Bautzen and Waterloo. There were also many Spanish *afrancesados* welcomed at Point Breeze. Nearly all these refugees from Europe were continually sponging on the ex-king. When the Comte Saint-Jean d'Angely, reputed to be mad, uttered a number of worthless cheques, it was Joseph who got him out of trouble and paid his passage back to Antwerp. But the money he 'loaned' to his French and Spanish friends was nothing compared to the money he remitted, at Bertrand's request, to his brother in Saint Helena, who, before his exile on his rocky island, had left many debts unpaid, and whose devoted followers and servants felt it was their due to be paid as though they were still courtiers at the Tuileries. It can be said that Joseph was only paying back what he rightly owed to his brother, for, in addition to the millions stolen by Napoleon in Italy, which he had appropriated for himself and had entrusted to Joseph's care before leaving for his Egyptian campaign (monies which Joseph had never refunded, and which, to use Napoleon's own words, he would never so far 'demean himself as to reclaim'), the Emperor had also entrusted Joseph with a very large sum of money, variously estimated at anything between 20,000 and a million livres, when the brothers parted for the last time at Rochefort. The money Joseph now remitted to his brother's creditors was greatly in excess of this sum owing, discounting the 800,000 livres' worth of diamonds he had presented to Napoleon before the Waterloo campaign and which were mysteriously lost at Charleroi.[5]

We have already mentioned that de Onis and Hyde de Neuville suspected a plot to rescue Napoleon. Although in fact there was no such plot, there was a curious conspiracy in which the two brothers Lallemand, Generals Rigaud and d'Angen were implicated. In 1816, these former officers placed themselves at the head of a group of French refugees who had founded a small colony in Texas on the banks of Trinity River which they had named Champ d'Asyle. These rash exiles had the intention of raising the banner of revolt in Texas and, in alliance with the Mexican insurgents, of proclaiming Joseph Bonaparte 'King of Mexico'. Joseph received the French deputation with the usual courtesy he accorded to all visitors, but firmly declined their offer. In the following year, it was the Mexican rebels themselves who approached the Comte de Survilliers. The Mexican leader was the ex-Spanish general Xavier Mina, nephew of the celebrated Francisco Espoz y Mina, the most celebrated of all guerilla commanders. Xavier Mina, like his uncle, had fought against Don José

Primero in Spain. In 1810 he had been captured by the French and imprisoned in the fortress of Vincennes together with Palafox. Liberated in 1814, but disgusted with the reactionary rule of Ferdinand VII, he had embarked for Mexico with a band of determined Spaniards to seek freedom in the New World. It was this former adversary of Joseph and other rebels from all over Mexico who now came to Point Breeze to invite him once again to accept the crown of Mexico. Joseph thanked them for the honour, but once again declined. 'No greater recompense for my public life could be offered to me', he said, 'than to see men, who having refused to accept my authority in Madrid, come to me now that I am in exile. But every day I spend in this hospitable country proves to me more clearly how excellently a Republican form of government suits America. Preserve it in Mexico as a precious gift from Heaven . . .' The rebels departed extremely disappointed. For the moment there was no question of establishing a republic in Mexico, but only of achieving independence from the crown of Spain, and for this, in their opinion, the collaboration of the ex-king was indispensable.

Although Joseph had unequivocally twice refused to collaborate in any way with the insurgents, the very fact that Bonapartist officers and Spaniards had come to visit him at Point Breeze gave rise to the most extraordinary rumours. The Duc de Richelieu, Louis XVIII's *Président du Conseil*, who, as a close friend of Désirée, might have been thought to be well disposed towards Joseph, took these rumours seriously and wrote on 2 September 1816 to the Marquis d'Osmond : 'We have been assured today that Joseph Buonaparte, Grouchy and Clausel have left the United States for Mexico. I hope they will be captured and hanged which should cure them for ever of this mania for stirring up revolutions.' Even a year later, Hyde de Neuville was still writing of plots to liberate Napoleon and of the vast sums of money that Joseph was spending to equip Spanish and French rebels. It was quite true that Joseph was spending vast sums, but not for the purpose that Hyde de Neuville imagined. Just as at Mortefontaine, he spent thousands on his house and vast grounds of Point Breeze. Not for the first time in his life he dammed a river and constructed an artificial lake; he planted a variety of exotic trees and in front of the house created a huge lawn bordered with magnolias and rhododendrons. He laid out twenty kilometres of winding carriage roads, erected statues and little rustic cabins in which he organized picnics for his guests. At the same time he arranged to have sent from Europe some of his most valuable furniture, his library of 8,000 books, his collection of pictures and sculptures, his plate and porcelain. But in addition to the vast sums of money spent on Point Breeze, he was generous to a fault in assisting French and Spanish refugees, not to mention the huge sums of money he was remitting to Bertrand in Saint Helena.

To cover these enormous expenses, he dispatched Mailliard to Europe to recover the valuables he had buried in the grounds of the Château de Prangins. Mailliard, who by now was much more than a *valet de chambre* and was treated by Joseph as a friend and personal secretary (Joseph, like Napoleon, disliked writing and dictated nearly all his very considerable correspondence), arrived in Europe after an eventful journey in which he suffered shipwreck. He visited Julie in Frankfurt, and then proceeded to Prangins in the company of Veret, Joseph's banker from Nyon. It was with some difficulty that Mailliard and Veret found the cache, which was extremely deeply hidden, but after making a careful inventory Mailliard succeeded in avoiding customs and returned to Point Breeze with all his master's valuables intact, including his collection of uncut diamonds, valued at five million francs. Joseph found himself once more an extremely wealthy man.

In July 1818, he renewed his acquaintance with his old friend James le Ray, who was on a visit to the United States. With le Ray he visited the property he had acquired from him while staying in Blois. He now bought more land from him – 24,000 acres on the Black River, between Lake Ontario and the Adirondacks – property of immense prospective value, with vast virgin forests where Napoleon in distant Saint Helena dreamed of founding a Bonapartist colony. Joseph was too wise to risk the displeasure of the Americans and British by indulging in any such foolishness. Even the French Ambassador Hyde de Neuville had finally come to realize that Joseph was not dangerous, and went so far as to present him with a portrait of the Emperor painted by Gérard, which had hung in the Embassy and which Joseph later gave to the Academy of Fine Arts of Philadelphia. This Academy was one of many which were proud to include the Comte de Survilliers among their members.

The next four years were spent quietly perfecting his estate, entertaining his friends, attending meetings of learned societies and increasing his fortune by wise investments and developing his properties. On Sunday 4 January 1820, while visiting New York, he learnt to his horror that his beautiful country mansion had been burnt to the ground. The local volunteer fire brigade from Bordentown, equipped with neither pumps nor pipes and relying solely on bucket chains to quench the blaze, was quite inadequate. Fortunately, thanks to the efforts of Joseph's servants and neighbours, the most important items of furniture, books, objets d'art, silver and even his cellar were saved. On 8 January Joseph wrote a letter to the muncipality of Bordentown, expressing his gratitude for the rescue of his treasures and the return of the gold specie found in the house. Instead of being grateful for this letter, the citizens of Bordentown were temporarily angered that their honesty should ever have been impugned.

Joseph, who had inherited his mother's fatalism, accepted this disaster with his habitual stoicism. He apologized to the inhabitants of Bordentown for his unintentional gaffe and once again expressed his gratitude. He was soon forgiven. He immediately began the construction of a new and even more beautiful mansion in American colonial style on a site a little lower down than that of his former dwelling. It was certainly one of, if not the most, luxuriously furnished houses of the whole of the United States. He acquired more pictures from Europe and his collection now included paintings by Raphael, Titian, Correggio, Veronese, Murillo and (more dubiously) Leonardo, as well as contemporary sculpture, including a bust of Pauline by Canova.

Joseph continued to enlarge his grounds and imported from Europe pheasants, quails, hares and rabbits (which soon became a menace), and swans for his lakes. It is little wonder that the people of Bordentown soon forgave him, for with the work in hand there was employment for all.

Joseph's pleasure in building and landscape gardening was marred from time to time by letters from Saint Helena. The Irish doctor O'Meara, who for some years had been Napoleon's constant companion, wrote to Joseph on Napoleon's behalf, asking him to publish the originals of the Emperor's letters, which the Emperor claimed he had entrusted to his brother at Rochefort. In the bitterness of his captivity, Napoleon now wished to show the world with what servility the European heads of state had once addressed him in his hours of glory. Either due to lapse of memory, or for some other reason, Napoleon claimed that it was to his brother that he had handed over the originals, but he had in fact insisted on giving them to Maret, Duke of Bassano, his former Minister of Foreign Affairs. Joseph had only received copies and even these had now been mislaid. An acrimonious correspondence followed. Joseph hotly denied ever having received them and in turn was accused of keeping them to serve his own interests, on the assumption that he wished to sell them to the highest bidder. The English publisher John Murray claimed that a person who preferred to remain anonymous had approached him with a view to publication. The European press made a great fuss of all this, but it was all just a storm in a teacup.

In the following year, these petty annoyances were eclipsed by the news of Napoleon's death. This occurred on 5 May, but Joseph and the American people only learnt of it three months later. It has frequently been said that, on learning of his brother's death, Joseph was prostrated with grief and fell seriously ill. The truth is that in April 1821 Joseph was already suffering from a mild attack of nephritis and suffered another and more painful attack in the following June, before he ever learnt of his brother's death. By August he was completely cured, thanks, as he claimed, to the medicinal qualities of the waters of Bristol, a nearby town on the right bank of the Delaware. Although Joseph kept a magnificent cellar for his guests, it was no hardship for him to drink these waters in lieu of wine, since throughout his life he had been extremely abstemious, and, if we are to believe Miot de Melito, invariably mixed his wine – even his champagne! – with water. So much for the reputation as a drunkard which he had so unjustly earned in Spain.

Like all persons who are seldom ill, Joseph took these attacks of nephritis very seriously. Not content with consulting American doctors, he wrote to Julie asking her to seek medical advice in France, and once more invited her to come to Point Breeze with the children. Julie sought the advice of Baron Dubois, the doctor who had attended Marie-Louise during her confinement. The Baron made the following amusing reply:

> I have the honour, Madame la Comtesse, to inform you in all con-
> science that the greatest misfortune that can befall an invalid is to
> be extremely rich and in a position to consult many doctors. In this
> case, and it applies to your husband, he will find himself in the most
> deplorable state of perplexity, because I am absolutely certain that
> among all these consultants he will not find two opinions which
> coincide.

Although Julie did not come to America, pleading that her rheumatism prevented her from travelling, she felt she could no longer deprive Joseph of the comfort of at least one of his daughters. Zenaïde had just reached marriageable age, and Julie, in pursuance of Napoleon's own wishes, which he had stated clearly in his will, was anxious that she should marry one of her Bonaparte cousins. She had plans for Zenaïde to marry Charles, the natural son of Lucien and Madame Jouberthon, who had been legitimized when his father, much to Joseph's and Napoleon's disapproval, married his mistress. In the circumstances, Zenaïde could not leave Europe. It was therefore Charlotte who was sent to America in the care of a duenna and the English Dr Stockoe, surgeon of the *Bellerophon*, who had accompanied Napoleon to Saint Helena.

Charlotte arrived at Philadelphia on 21 December 1821. News of her arrival had already preceded her, and the quayside was crowded with curious people interested to witness the arrival of a 'real princess' on American shores.

The following months were probably some of the happiest that Joseph had ever spent at Point Breeze. Six years of separation from his brother had somewhat dimmed his affection for him, and he regarded the Emperor's death 'more as the end of a long martyrdom, than an inconsolable loss'.[6] Like Julie, Charlotte was dark-haired, petite, with a vivacity and turn of wit altogether Provençal, which delighted her father. She brought life and gaiety to Point Breeze and at last allowed Joseph to exercise his role as a father. He could not do enough to entertain his charming little daughter; he took her on long trips as far afield as his estates on the Black River and to admire the wonders of the Niagara Falls. He also encouraged her very real talent for painting (she had studied under the aged Louis David in Brussels) and even arranged for an exhibition of her best works to be held in Philadelphia.

There was only one cloud now on Joseph's horizon. He did not in the least approve of Julie's plan to marry off Zenaïde to Charles. Although Charles was reputed to be interested in the sciences, he had earned the reputation of a ne'er-do-well. Actually he was an ornithologist of distinction and wrote and illustrated a number of books on the subject. But more important in the eyes of Joseph was the fact that Lucien, now Prince of Canino (a papal title), had a very large family[7] and would be unable to make adequate provision for Charles and his wife. Lucien, on the other hand, was as anxious for his son to marry Zenaïde as Joseph was opposed to the match. Joseph was by far and away the richest of all the Bonapartes and his fortune would be divided between only two daughters. He was therefore in a position to provide Zenaïde with a very handsome dowry. In order to persuade Joseph that Charles would make a suitable husband, Lucien decided to visit America with his son, but got no further than Brussels where, although he received Julie's formal consent to the proposed marriage, he was unable to obtain the necessary passports for the United States. Like Napoleon, Joseph would have preferred Zenaïde to marry Napoleon-Louis, the elder son of Louis, ex-King of Holland and Hortense de Beauharnais, who after the King of Rome was next in line to the Imperial Crown. Since Joseph, however, had never given his official veto to Zenaïde's union with Charles, Lucien took the pretext of his brother's absence in faraway America to hurry through with the wedding.

Although Joseph was a reluctant king, it must not be forgotten that, ever since the days of the Consulate, he had always been obsessed with the concept of rights of succession. He had only accepted the throne of Naples on condition that, as senior member of the Bonaparte clan, he was entitled to succeed Napoleon in the event of his death. As King of Spain, he had renounced these pretensions and had recognized that the King of Rome was next in line to the throne of France; nor had he had any intention of usurping the Regency bestowed on Marie-Louise during Napoleon's absence with his armies during the Hundred Days, although this was only his right.

Now that Napoleon was dead and the French people were already disgusted with the rule of the Bourbon Charles X, there seemed every possibility of another coup d'état and that a Bonaparte would be recalled to the throne. In this event, the King of Rome – or the Duke of Reichstadt, as he was now called – would be the legitimate heir, and Joseph would be Regent. Should the King of Rome die, which seemed very likely, since it was recognized that he was already suffering from advanced pulmonary tuberculosis, Napoleon-Louis would assume the Emperor's mantle.

Joseph only learnt of Zenaïde's marriage to Charles at the end of June 1822, several months after its celebration in Brussels. Lucien had himself provided the dowry for Zenaïde by mortgaging his estates, the interest on which he knew he could never pay, but which he counted on his brother's generosity to meet, knowing full well that Joseph would never allow one of his brothers to disgrace the family by falling into debt.

Now that Zenaïde was married to Charles, it only remained for Charlotte to marry Louis's son, former Crown Prince of Holland.[8] In America, Charlotte had no lack of suitors. All her impecunious Bonaparte cousins visited Point Breeze to pay court to the charming daughter of the millionaire Comte de Survilliers. The first suitor was Jerome Paterson-Bonaparte, the son of Jerome and Betty, the Baltimore belle, whose marriage had been annulled on the orders of Napoleon. Betty's mother, Mrs Paterson, had taken her grandson, a most handsome young man, to Rome, to introduce him to the

Bonapartes living there, among them being Pauline, who in her usual frivolous way had immediately promised to support his suit; this however in no way prevented her from using her influence to persuade Charlotte to marry Louis-Napoleon, her favourite nephew.

A little later Achille, the elder of the Murat boys, received permission from the Allied Powers to visit America, provided he signed a declaration that he would not return to Europe without prior authorization from them. He arrived in America on 11 July 1823. To Joseph's relief he showed no inclination to marry Charlotte and, after staying some little while with his hospitable uncle, took himself off to Florida, where he bought an estate at Tallahassee and started farming. He married Catherine Bird-Willis, a great-niece of General George Washington. The marriage was not a success.

In 1825, Lucien, the younger Murat, arrived at Point Breeze, but by this time Joseph had already sent Charlotte back to her mother, now living in Florence. It was not until two years later, however, that Charlotte married Louis-Napoleon, on 16 July 1824. As for Lucien Murat, he married a Miss Caroline Frazer, daughter of a retired English officer living in Bordentown, and thenceforth lived the life of a complete wastrel, continually sponging on his mother and uncle.

To console Joseph for the loss of Charlotte, Zenaïde and her husband came to stay with him on 9 September 1823. The first of her thirteen or fourteen children, most of whom died at birth, was born in Philadelphia on 13 February 1824 and christened, with extraordinary lack of originality, Lucien-Charles-Napoleon; he was to become the principal inheritor of Joseph's fortune.

Joseph gave a splendid fête to celebrate the birth of his grandson, and gave the Archbishop of Philadelphia, who officiated at the baptism of the child, a magnificent ring, once in the possession of Cardinal Ximenes, which he had acquired in Spain.

In the same year of 1824, a few days after Charlotte's departure for Florence, Joseph received a visit from La Fayette, now in his sixties, who was making a triumphal tour of the United States. In the old days, La Fayette had been one of Joseph's most intimate friends at Mortefontaine, but after Waterloo their relations had become strained. Now, however, their differences were forgotten and their meeting was most cordial. How much had happened since 1792!

La Fayette stayed almost a year in the United States. On 16 July 1825 he made a return visit to Point Breeze, where a huge crowd gathered to meet 'the Patriarch of Liberty'. La Fayette apologized to Joseph for this invasion of his privacy. 'I'm not worried,' Joseph replied. 'I am used to seeing just as many people every year on 4 July when we all celebrate the anniversary of American independence.'[9]

La Fayette's political opinions had considerably changed since the advent of Charles X, whose dictatorial and priest-ridden rule was hateful to this son of liberty. He had ambitions to stage a coup d'état and drive the King from the throne, substituting Napoleon II in his place. For this he needed money, but Joseph, still a little suspicious of La Fayette, whose behaviour after Waterloo he could never quite condone, was not prepared to finance the coup.

La Fayette's visit and that of his old friend Miot de Melito, which followed shortly after, filled Joseph with a longing to return to Europe together with Charles and Zenaïde, who after a miscarriage had given birth to another child, Alexandrine Gertrude, born at Point Breeze on 9 June 1826. Joseph's relations with Charles, while the latter was his guest, had been most friendly. Charles shared many of his uncle's tastes and spent his time completing Webster's book, *The Ornithology of America*, illustrated from life and translated into several languages. In 1825, Joseph's lovely, giddy sister Pauline had died in exile and he himself in the same year had had a serious coach accident in which he nearly lost his life. He was now more than ever determined to spend his last days in Europe. He therefore addressed himself to Bernadotte to say that he would be content to reside in Brussels until the repeal of the law forbidding members of the Bonaparte family to live in France, which he believed to be imminent. Despite Bernadotte's genuine affection for Joseph, he was unable to obtain permission from the French Government for Joseph's return. 'I do not know', wrote Joseph, 'if I will ever see my friends again. Those who preside over the destinies of Europe must accept me as I am. It is too much to expect me to be perfect.'[10]

On 23 February 1828 Zenaïde and Charles left for Italy alone in the *Delaware*, an American warship, put at their disposal by the courtesy of John Quincy Adams, now President.

Joseph was certainly a man of consequence in the United States.

During the following years, he maintained a constant correspondence with old friends living in France – with Roederer and his former Spanish Minister, O'Farrill,[11] Azanza and Almanera. There were many others who wrote to him, asking him his advice on the memoirs they were compiling – Thibaudaut, Méneval, Jourdan, etc. He also now embarked on dictating his own memoirs (a task for which he had little inclination) and visited his properties on the Black River, where he hunted and indulged in his passion for building by constructing a hunting lodge in the wilds. He was also constantly engaged in financial deals, buying and selling property; he brought a successful action against a railroad company which was proposing to build a track through Point Breeze, linking New York with Philadelphia. He founded a French language newspaper in New York, *Le Courrier des États Unis*, and was a well-known and respected figure in scientific and artistic circles. He also founded a theatre in Philadelphia and introduced the first ballet company ever to be seen in the United States. The ladies of New Jersey were deeply shocked by the sight of the ballerinas' legs and boycotted the performance, while the gentlemen regarded the spectacle as a huge joke. Joseph was deeply disappointed.

In 1829, Joseph was very affected by the news of the death of his 'best friend', Stanislas de Girardin, but not too pleased to read his *Mémoires*, which revealed a little too much of his love affairs with the Duchessa d'Atri and the Marquesa de Montehermoso.

Whenever anyone spoke to Joseph about politics at this time, he always claimed that he had no further interest in the subject, but this is certainly belied by his correspondence and his disappointment that Zenaïde had not married Louis's son. Once again, rumours were current of Bonapartist plots in the United States, and once again Joseph was said to be the instigator. Certainly a flood of Bonapartist propaganda was emanating from America, much of it in the *Courrier des États Unis*. The French Consul-General in New York wrote to the Prince de Polignac, Minister of Foreign Affairs: 'This newspaper is not written for the United States, where is has few subscribers, but for France. A very large number of copies are carried there by every packet boat.'

Although Hyde de Neuville for some time had ceased to consider Joseph as a potential threat, recent events in France and the ever-increasing unpopularity of Charles X had led to a resurgence of the Bonaparte faction. Attention was once more focused on the Comte de Survilliers. Naturally La Fayette's visit to Point Breeze could not pass unnoticed by French agents in the States, but apart from financing the *Courrier des États Unis*, there was still no concrete evidence to link Joseph with any political activities. There was nothing for which he could be reproached except a certain laxity of morals : in the salons of Paris it was constantly rumoured that he was still a *coureur de filles comme il l'était à Madrid*. Bourbon agents were obviously anxious to disparage his name in the eyes of the French public – utter hypocrisy, considering the private life of Charles X.

Second Exile

A man of Joseph's temperament, separated for years from his wife, could hardly have been expected to remain chaste, though to call him a *coureur de filles* was an exaggeration. Nevertheless, as we know, Madame Sari had for a time been his mistress and there were others whose presence could not have remained a secret in a small provincial town such as Bordentown. It seems strange that in puritanical States like New Jersey and New York, he still remained a respected figure.

As far back as 25 January 1825, La Forest (a relative of the former ambassador to Madrid), the French Consul in Philadelphia, wrote that these rumours concerning Joseph's immoral behaviour were entirely justified. 'He has several known mistresses,' he wrote, 'and keeps one openly at Bordentown. He has given her a sufficiently fine house and has had several children by her.'[12]

All American and French historians agree that the 'kept mistress' was a certain Annette Savage, the daughter of a Quaker family, by whom Joseph was captivated, not only because of her beauty, but because she wrote and spoke French impeccably. In order to legitimize the two daughters she bore him in 1821 and 1822 (the first was killed when a flowerpot fell on her head) he found a complacent husband for her, named Delafolie. By 1827, Joseph had already tired of her. After the death of Delafolie in 1840, Annette threatened to publish her intimate memoirs unless her former royal lover paid her the sum of 20,000 dollars. The indispensable Mailliard was able somehow to dissuade her from her purpose. That she was paid 20,000 dollars is improbable, since in the previous year, when Caroline, her surviving daughter by Joseph, had married at the age of seventeen Colonel Zebulon Howell Benton, a highly respected citizen, her royal father had provided her with a most handsome dowry. Perhaps Mailliard was able to persuade Annette that the publication of her memoirs could only damage her daughter's future. At all events, Annette remarried a short time later and left America. Her life thereafter remains unknown.[13]

Meanwhile Joseph had fallen in love with a beautiful Creole, Madame Lacoste, whose husband, a former officer in the Imperial army, had business interests in San Domingo. During her husband's absence on business affairs, which Joseph helped to finance, Emilie Lacoste stayed at Point Breeze in the ostensible capacity of companion to the Princess Charlotte. When Charlotte left for Florence, Emilie still remained at Point Breeze to comfort the lonely ex-king. On 22 March she gave birth to a boy, christened Félix-Joseph. But there was no scandal. As soon as Emilie had realized she was pregnant, she had summoned her husband to Point Breeze on the pretext that

Joseph wished to discuss business with him. In due course, Joseph was proclaimed godfather. This time it was Emilie who left her lover to return to Paris, where she engaged in a tempestuous love affair with the poet Prosper Mérimée which ended in a somewhat farcical duel between the poet and the outraged Lacoste, who was now separated from his wife. In April 1828, Emilie wrote a long and touching letter to Joseph: 'Everybody in Paris is persuaded that I was your mistress. They say my husband sold me to you and, today, now that I am worthless, he has taken the first pretext to get rid of me . . .'

Although she did not ask Joseph for financial help in so many words, it is obvious from her letter that she expected some assistance from her formal royal lover. She made no mention of Prosper Mérimée. Joseph answered her politely, expressing surprise at her separation from her husband. 'I knew you so united during the four years that you spent here with your children [Emilie had had a son, Léon, by her husband] that nothing can equal the surprise with which I learn of your present circumstances and the sorrow it causes me . . .' It would seem that Lacoste never realized that little Félix-Joseph was other than his own son. Joseph did nothing to disabuse him and remained in friendly correspondence with him; indeed, appointed him editor of the *Courrier des États Unis*, but did nothing to help his former mistress.

From none of his love affairs does Joseph emerge with any credit, but, strange as it may seem, his private life in no way affected the respect and popularity which he enjoyed in American society; nor does his popularity seem to have suffered to any great extent among the citizens of Bordentown: if anything it was the unfortunate Annette who was castigated and known as the 'Mad Savage', while in all probability his affair with Madame Lacoste remained unsuspected.

XVII

The Last Years

1830–1844

The Revolution of 1830, which brought an end to the reign of Charles X and substituted Louis-Philippe of Orleans on the throne of France, proved a bitter disappointment to Joseph, as it did to all other Bonapartists. Stirred to indignation, Joseph now showed a rare flash of his brother's spirit, and issued a manifesto to the Chambre des Députés which he ensured would receive maximum publicity:

> Banished as I am, far from my native soil, I myself would have come before you no less speedily than this letter, if among all the names available to a proud nation, I had not read that of a Bourbon prince. When princes are born with the presumption of a divine right to rule their people, it is impossible for them to rise above the prejudices of their birth.
>
> It is of no avail that the Duc d'Orléans should disclaim his heritage in the hour of misfortune which has befallen his House – does this make him any the less a Bourbon? No, Gentlemen, there can be no legitimate rulers save those whom their subjects have acknowledged. It is the people who make and break their rulers as their needs dictate . . .
>
> Three million, five hundred thousand voters called for a return of a Napoleon . . . In 1815, Napoleon II was acclaimed as sovereign. I have good reason to believe that Napoleon II would show himself worthy of France . . .
>
> While France waits for Austria to restore him to us, I offer myself [as Regent] to share your perils, your efforts, and at his coming, to pass on to him the goodwill, the example and dying wishes of his father.

Many of Joseph's friends wrote assuring him that the moment had arrived for him to return to Europe and overthrow the régime of Louis-Philippe. An American diplomat named Poinsett, recently returned from a mission to France, told him that the Old World was impatiently awaiting his return. The young poet Victor Hugo, the son of one of Joseph's best and most loyal generals, wrote him letter after letter, addressing him as 'Sire', begging him to leave America. But equally there were also many friends who wrote to him pointing out that his Bonapartist pretensions were quite unrealistic. La Fayette, who since his visit to America five years previously had once again revised his political opinions, now wrote to Joseph that he considered that it was more in conformity with the interests of France to establish a liberal and constitutional monarchy under the Duke of Orleans than to proclaim the Duke of Reichstadt as Emperor Napoleon II. 'I could content myself', he wrote,

> by pointing out to you that your dynasty is dispersed, that some are in Rome, that you yourself are in America and that the Duke of Reichstadt is in the hands of the Austrians; but in the name of friendship, I must tell you my true thoughts. The Napoleonic system was resplendent with glory, but stamped with despotism, aristocratic pretensions and servitude . . . Moreover, the son of your immortal brother is now an Austrian prince, and you know full well what the Austrian Cabinet is like. These, therefore, my dear Count, are the reasons, why, despite my personal regard for you, I could not lend my support to the re-establishment of the Imperial throne; the Hundred Days had already shown me that the unremittent errors of the past would only be repeated.

When La Fayette wrote 'you know full well what the Austrian Cabinet is like' this was precisely what, after seventeen years in America, Joseph did not know. In September he wrote to Marie-Louise, to the Emperor Francis I and to Metternich, asserting that if he could only 'show the Duke of Reichstadt to the French people, his presence alone would establish him on the throne of France', and that this solution would be most welcome to Britain, Russia, Prussia, Spain and Naples.

Joseph received no replies. Far from helping his cause, these letters only strengthened the determination of the Great Powers to exclude the Bonaparte family from French soil, and served to irritate his family, Lucien in particular, who had anticipated an early permission to return to France. Only Napoleon-Louis, Charlotte's husband, and his younger brother Louis-Napoleon (the future Napoleon III) were ambitious enough to support their uncle. Both claimed that the

Emperor had been the champion of European liberty; both had engaged in the carbonari revolt in Romagna, aimed at overthrowing the despotic rule of the Pope and Italian princes – the same carbonari who, ironically enough, had been so ruthlessly suppressed by Napoleon and Murat.

To Charlotte's and Joseph's great sorrow, Napoleon-Louis died very suddenly, officially from measles, at Forli on 17 March 1831. There were very strong suspicions, however, that he had been stabbed or shot by the carbonari for his refusal to obey orders to march on Rome.

When asked about his brother's death, Louis-Napoleon invariably evaded the question, because it was 'too sad a subject to discuss'. How he extricated himself from the ranks of the carbonari to return to his mother at Arenenberg in Switzerland, without being accused of contumacy, remains problematical. His own story was that he was stricken with fever and 'excused further duties'.

These subversive activities on the part of his nephew infuriated Joseph, whose sole aim now was to placate Austria and the other Powers in order that the Bonaparte family should be allowed to live in France. His nephews' quixotic behaviour had made the chances of abrogating the law of exile more remote than ever. Louis-Napoleon explained later that their action had been motivated by his brother's belief that 'the time had come to show the world that the family of Napoleon, not content with living in the reflected glory of its illustrious leader, also wished to show itself worthy of him and as deserving of a civil crown as of a royal diadem. As soon as we heard the cry of "Liberty" in Italy, our only thought was to embrace a just and noble cause.'[1]

As though Joseph had not already enough troubles on his hands, he learnt from Zenaïde that, although her husband Charles had proved himself a scholar (he had published his *Iconografia della fauna Italica* and had been elected a member of various learned societies), he had drifted into a life of dissipation, and, in her own words, was a debauchee who was making her life a misery.

Joseph's manifesto, although not read to the Chamber, was widely circulated throughout France. His friends, in particular the Comte de Ménéval and the Comte de Flahaut (the lover of Queen Hortense and the father of the Duc de Morny) were tireless in spreading Bonapartist propaganda and circulating the *Courrier des États Unis*, in which its editor Lacoste emphasized all the advantages that the

Emperor's rule had brought to France – the great public works he had initiated, freedom of worship and the pacification of the West, the implementation of the Code Napoléon, his encouragement of scientific inventions, etc., etc.; but the suppression of the press, the millions of lives he had uselessly sacrificed in megalomaniac wars, the wholesale deportation and imprisonment of innocent people, his reintroduction of slavery in the colonies, his complete abnegation of Revolutionary ideals – all these were forgotten.

In a long letter addressed to the Duke of Reichstadt, Joseph wrote on 15 February 1832 :

A Government which has usurped the rights of the Nation has once again condemned us to exile; but the voice of the people calls for you – I know this of a certainty. If only His Majesty would be good enough to send me a passport allowing me to meet both him and you and permit you to be confided to my care, I would honour his confidence by leaving my retreat, and in obedience to the dictates of my heart, spare nothing to render to the loving care of Frenchmen the son of the man, whom, above all others, I have loved most in the world. . . .

Time has now allowed us to see the fruits of his labours. Nations are more enlightened; they are aware that the most privileged nation is that where the majority of men enjoy the benefit of a supreme ruler loved by all – a ruler, who, himself has not the fatal power to abuse the lives, property or liberty of his subjects, but whose unique role is to preserve the rights entrusted to him by his people.

Tout pour le peuple, such were your father's thoughts. Alas, he did not live long enough.

Joseph went on to interpret the Emperor's foreign policy in just as tendentious and inaccurate a manner as he had interpreted his internal policy. Could Joseph have been sincere? Joseph, who had so often criticized his brother? As Girod de l'Ain writes : 'At certain moments Joseph had the same aptitude as Napoleon for presenting facts to others, not as they really were, but as they suited himself.'[2]

It was not until June 1832, when Joseph first learnt from a Colonel Collins, a former aide-de-camp to Marshal Exelmans, that the Duke of Reichstadt was seriously ill, that he finally decided to leave America for England, where he had obtained permission to reside.

In view of all the kindness and hospitality he had received at the hands of the American authorities, he decided before leaving to say farewell to the President in Washington. On 3 July 1832 the National Gazette of Philadelphia published the following:

> Count Survilliers was received by the President and other members of the Government with the utmost courtesy . . . He was received not as a political personage but as a gentleman of elevated ideas and perfect rectitude. The behaviour of the Count during the seventeen years in this country has earned him the esteem and affection of all American citizens.

Perfect rectitude! Annette Savage and Emilie Lacoste must have given a wry laugh if ever this article met their eyes.

A week later Joseph embarked on the *Alexander* with Colonel Collins, M. and Mme Sari, Louis Mailliard and five domestic servants.

On 16 August Joseph and his party disembarked at Liverpool. The first news to greet him was that the Duke of Reichstadt was dead.[3] The news came as a deep shock to Joseph. All his propaganda, all his efforts to restore a Napoleonic dynasty, his very visit to Europe, now seemed to have been in vain. The heir to the Imperial throne, whom the faithful already referred to as Napoleon II, and the heir apparent, Napoleon-Louis, were both dead. Joseph himself was now too old to entertain any personal ambitions; he was left with only two purposes in life; to obtain permission for his scattered family to live in France and to re-establish, not the Empire, but the reputation of the Emperor in the eyes of the world.

From Liverpool, Joseph journeyed to London. We know nothing of his movements or whom he met in the immediate following weeks. Perhaps he renewed acquaintance with some of the Englishmen he had met thirty years previously at Amiens. We do know that Joseph, who never liked cities, rented a house near Godstone, Surrey. Here, in November, Louis-Napoleon came from Arenenberg to visit him. Joseph gave him a cold welcome. 'You received me like a stranger rather than a nephew, summing me up without any warmth of feeling' – thus wrote Louis-Napoleon to his uncle later. The arrival of Joseph's dear daughter Charlotte a week later considerably helped to improve relations, at least for the time being, between uncle and nephew, for we find Joseph writing to Hortense: 'My dear sister, Louis has arrived here . . . He seems to me to be quiet and studious, full of honourable intentions and sensibility.'

Louis-Napoleon spent six months with his uncle, quite long enough for Joseph radically to change his mind concerning his nephew's character. This presumptuous young man was continually proffering his uncle gratuitous advice and expounding nebulous ideas on politics and the future of the world, whereas he would have done better to listen to Joseph.

Joseph continued to write articles for the *Courrier des États Unis* and for various French newspapers which he subsidized. In a letter of 18 August 1833, in reply to a virulent attack on Napoleon's policies, he wrote : 'My brother was neither a parricide, despot nor a tyrant. In his day, whatever he did, either for good or ill, he was always supported by a great accomplice, the people of France.'

Gradually Joseph's adroit propaganda to re-establish his brother in the eyes of France began to show results. On 28 July 1833 a statue of the Emperor was erected with great ceremony on the summit of the column of the Place Vendôme. But still the government of Louis-Philippe refused to rescind the law of exile. In October, Joseph appealed to La Fayette, with whom, despite his letter, quoted above, he remained on friendly terms. La Fayette responded cordially, but explained that he was merely a deputy with no influence; moreover, the *Chambre* did not meet again until 19 November. For better or for worse, Joseph had to remain patient and attempt to reconcile his family to the idea of further exile. Lucien and Jerome came to visit him; Lucien, who loved him dearly, spent some time with him, but it was with increasing annoyance that Joseph noted the growing divergence of opinion within his family, and tried his best to restore harmony within the clan. Furthermore, he was continually worried by his family over money matters. With the exception of Désirée, now living as Queen of Sweden in Stockholm, and Madame mère, living economically in Rome with Uncle Fesch, the family was generally in debt. Joseph himself, although still a very rich man, had nearly all his money invested in the United States, where he was still expending vast sums on the upkeep of Point Breeze. He would now have preferred to leave England and live in Italy, but the Austrian and Italian rulers were still too suspicious, too timid, to allow the head of the Bonaparte family to take up residence in the peninsula.

Many friends and acquaintances and even persons whom he had never known personally, came to pay their respects to the former king. Many made the journey to England for no other purpose than to visit him. O'Meara, Napoleon's Irish doctor in Saint Helena, was a constant and favourite visitor. Perhaps of all the visits he received, that of General Espoz y Mina[4] was the most gratifying. Mina, who had been one of Joseph's most bitter enemies in Spain, now expressed his regret that Joseph was no longer king. During the years 1834 and

269

1835, this old and noble enemy was a frequent visitor. Mina admitted that in 1812 nearly all the guerillero generals – even the great El Empecinado himself – would have gladly accepted José as king had he dismissed his generals and French troops. Mina further confirmed that he had been betrayed by his own generals, by Soult in particular, whose name was still execrated in Spain; Soult, who had made himself a fortune from the mines of Almaden and stolen the pictures from the Alcazar, but who was now overwhelmed with honours by Louis-Philippe, having been made not only a *maréchal-général* of France but *Président du Conseil*; and who, as such, was responsible for the prolonged exile of the Bonaparte family.

In February 1834, a petition signed by 30,000 people had been presented to the *Chambre* demanding that French territory should be reopened to all members of the Bonaparte family; but had been rejected by the old marshal. When Joseph learnt that it was Soult who was responsible for his and his family's continued exile, he wrote a vehement letter to his old enemy. On 20 March, conjointly with Lucien, he addressed another petition to the *Chambre*, in which he wrote :

> Napoleon's prolonged dictatorship has caused him to be misunderstood . . . In addition to a general peace, Napoleon's intention to introduce universal suffrage, freedom of the press, and guarantees of prosperity to a great Nation, would ultimately have been revealed to all France and would have made him the greatest man in all history . . .

'After reading such an assertion,' writes Girod de l'Ain, 'one wonders whether Joseph, after seventeen years' exile in the United States, was not confusing Napoleon with George Washington.'[5]

Agreeable as were the visits, confidence and compliments which Joseph received, they were not sufficient to dispel his sorrow at the news he continued to receive from his dear daughters. Zenaïde, who although once again pregnant – her eighth pregnancy – continued to complain of her husband's 'debaucheries', while Charlotte was perhaps even more unhappy than her sister.

After the death of her husband, Charlotte had become extremely friendly with a young artist named Léopold Robert, an old friend of Napoleon-Louis. They shared the same tastes, the same love of art, but Charlotte was much more of a Clary than a Bonaparte, and although attached to Robert was never in love with him and would certainly never have consented to become his mistress. Robert, on the other hand, adored the young widow and, unable to obtain the object of his passion, committed suicide in Venice in 1835. His tragic death caused some stir at the time – it must not be forgotten that his suicide occurred at the height of the Romantic movement, at the same time as Berlioz had also attempted to commit suicide for love and was writing his *Symphonie Fantastique*. Charlotte's and Leopold's 'love affair' even became the subject of a five-act drama.[6]

Joseph, unable to visit either France or Italy to comfort his daughters or his aged mother in Rome, decided to return to Point Breeze. He was not to stay there long. In the winter of 1835–6 he was inundated with letters from his family requesting him to return to Europe. Joseph's presence was needed not only to continue his propaganda, but to settle the inheritance of Madame mère, who had died on 2 February 1836 at the age of eighty-six. Joseph was deeply moved by the news of her death; he had always loved and admired his mother. He had never been ashamed of her simple peasant ways and had always maintained a correspondence with her. *Pourvou que ça doure*, she had said in her strongly accented French, almost forty years ago. Well, it had not lasted. She had seen her children become kings and queens, she had seen her Nabulio become Emperor and master of half Europe. Madame mère had remained the simple, honest Corsican woman she had always been. She had earned the respect of the French people.

The death of this great matriarch had considerable repercussions in Paris. A wave of Bonapartist sympathy swept over the capital; wreaths were laid at the foot of the Colonne Vendôme and more petitions for the abrogation of the law of exile were submitted to the *Chambre*.

In answer to the annoying letters he received from his family begging him to come back to Europe, Joseph promised that, no matter what loss he might suffer by leaving a country which had become his second home, he would nevertheless return. He was in no hurry however to face the worries which he knew awaited him on the other side of the Atlantic, and it was not until the end of August 1836 that he once again set foot in London.

Worries he found in plenty. Madame mère's inheritance could have been easily settled if only Caroline had not protested when asked to return a large sum of money lent to her by her mother. Since such undignified behaviour (which was widely known) could only damage the Bonapartist cause, Joseph sacrificed his own interests to silence his sister. Louis, too, was not prepared to settle accounts. Sooner than indulge in undignified family bickering, Joseph wrote to Uncle Fesch to tell him to give to Louis all he claimed – silver, porcelain and anything else he demanded.

All these petty annoyances, however, were suddenly to become of secondary importance. Two months after Joseph's return to London, there occurred an event which was seriously to undermine the situation of the Bonaparte family.

On 30 October 1836, Joseph's egregious young nephew, Louis-Napoleon, of whom he had written too hastily four years previously 'he seems full of honourable intentions and sensibility', arrived in Strasbourg, sporting the uniform of a colonel and wearing a general's hat, and attempted to induce the garrison of the town to mutiny. His coup failed. He was arrested, but Louis-Philippe's government, considering that banishment was more expedient than imprisonment, banished him to the United States.

From this absurd charade the whole family emerged humiliated and slightly ridiculous. Hortense, the only member of the family to regard her son's futile action with some favour, nevertheless took to her bed and never left it again. Lucien and Jerome both publicly disowned any previous knowledge of Louis-Napoleon's plans. Louis, his heart-broken father, wrote that every time he received a letter from his 'wretched son' or any correspondence relative to him, he burned it unread. As for Joseph, he was stupefied that this nephew had not recognized him as head of the family. 'No true Corsican could ever behave like this. There is not a drop of Bonaparte blood in him,' he wrote later. How right he was! To Felix Lacoste he wrote on 16 November, 'You will have already learnt of Louis-Napoleon's act of folly at Strasbourg. Nothing could have been more underhand; he behaved as though his father and uncles were already dead.'

As Joseph was the first to appreciate, the immediate result of this attempted coup was, of course, that the law of exile imposed on the Bonaparte family would never be abrogated during the reign of a Bourbon. The whole of Joseph's long campaign had been rendered completely ineffective by this 'young and unfortunate man', as Joseph always referred to him. Although Joseph considered it beneath his dignity to disown him publicly, he forbade him to make Point Breeze his home and wrote to him :

My nephew, – By thinking that during my lifetime and that of your father, you could assume our place, you have broken the ties which attach me to you. You are separated from the four brothers of the Emperor. *As from today*, I demand that you leave me in peace in my retirement. You have already caused enough bitter feelings to upset your whole family.

In September 1837 Louis-Napoleon returned to Switzerland to be at his mother's bedside when she died on 5 October. He took the opportunity of once more trying to ingratiate himself with his family. It was Charlotte who acted as an advocate and effected some sort of reconciliation. Her father grudgingly agreed to meet him in London.

On 23 August Joseph again left for America on the *Philadelphia*, one of the first steam packets ever to cross the Atlantic. But, back at Point Breeze, he could no longer enjoy the tranquil life of former days. Old friends had passed away; even Point Breeze was not the same. The company which had planned to build a railway through his estates, against which he had brought an injunction, had appealed and won its case. Now his beautiful grounds were invaded by smoking, noisy locomotives. It was no longer a pleasure to drive along his twenty kilometres of winding roads or to go out with his gun and dog and shoot quail or hare. He suddenly felt an old man. What he had described as a second homeland now seemed alien to him.

In the spring of 1839 he received news which almost prostrated him. On 18 April his beloved Charlotte had died of a haemorrhage on her way from Florence to Genoa to seek medical advice. She had died in Sarzane, where so many years ago Joseph and his father, the small town lawyer from Ajaccio, had tried to trace the problematical noble lineage of the Bonaparte family. Joseph did not know that his chaste and darling daughter had at last fallen in love with a Polish nobleman (perhaps Count Potocki) and it was by him that she was pregnant of the child which her husband had never been able to give her. It was after a caesarean operation resulting in a stillborn child that Charlotte died. Julie was told the facts but, fearing the effect on Joseph, never divulged the real cause of her death to him. Until his dying day he continued to believe the official version, according to which Charlotte had died of an aneurism. Julie was probably right to hide the truth, for when Joseph returned to London in the autumn of 1839 he was already an old man. Henceforth, although he still had all his wits about him, he took no further interest in events. He accepted the death of Lucien at Viterbo on 29 June 1840 with calm resignation; Louis-Napoleon's second attempt to effect a coup d'état at Boulogne no longer roused him to the same anger as had the farce of 1836. He noted with a degree of contempt his nephew's speech when arraigned before the *Chambre des Pairs*: 'It is my right to re-awake the glorious memories of the Empire and to speak of the Emperor's elder brother, that virtuous man, who, before me, is worthy of succeed him.' Joseph was never to see the future Napoleon III after his imprisonment at Ham.

With this last futile attempt by Louis-Napoleon to seize power, Joseph resigned himself never to see France again, but he had the gratification of learning that Louis-Philippe had authorized Napoleon's body to be brought from Saint Helena to the Invalides.[7] Joseph, however, was still not allowed to set foot on the Continent. It was not until May 1841 that the King of Sardinia gave him permission to reside in Genoa, where, as a young married man, he had set up in business forty-six years ago with Nicolas Clary. He left England by steamship, accompanied by Charles, Prince of Canino.[8]

After several weeks spent in Genoa, Joseph received permission from the Grand Duke of Tuscany, more generous and less timid than other Italian princes, to reside in Florence with Julie in the Serrestori palace in Florence.

Twenty-six years had passed since the now elderly couple had been united. Joseph was seventy-three, Julie was seventy. Although they had lived so little together, mutual esteem, the love they shared for their daughters, common political and financial interests had all helped to maintain ties of affection between them which had never been severed.

Joseph had already had a slight stroke on 14 July 1840 while in London. Now on 19 October 1843 Julie wrote to her nephew Joachim Clary: 'Your uncle has once again been afflicted with one of those serious attacks which are so alarming.' Two days later she wrote: 'I have left your uncle for a few moments to dictate these lines. His condition remains most alarming. He does not give me a moment's rest. He is extremely weak.'

During the winter his health improved a little. On sunny days he was to be seen driving out in his coach. He seemed scarcely moved when he learnt of the death of his old friend Bernadotte, King of Sweden and Norway, but it was forty years since the two had met, and time makes strangers of us all.

On 28 May 1844 Julie again wrote to her nephew Joachim: 'Your uncle suffers greatly, he is still very weak and cannot leave his bed . . .' Joseph's condition worsened rapidly.

On 19 July 1844 Julie dictated a brief and identical note to all members of the family:

A sad duty obliges me to inform you of another sorrow which has afflicted me in the person of my well-beloved husband, who expired in my arms yesterday morning at 9 hrs 16 mins, in his seventy-seventh year after a long illness.

Julie survived her husband little more than a year, 'dying as quietly and discreetly as she had always lived'[9] on 9 April 1845 at the age of seventy-three. She was buried in Florence beside her husband and her daughter Charlotte in the chapel of the church of Santa Croce.

Epilogue

It was shortly after he had suffered his first mild stroke in England that Joseph had made his will. Apart from the many generous legacies to relatives, friends and employees, he bequeathed the bulk of his very considerable fortune, including properties in France and America and his house near Godstone, England, to Julie in trust for his dear daughter Zenaïde. To his faithful Louis Mailliard, who had served him with such devotion for thirty-six years, he bequeathed his prosperous farm of Groveville, near the village of that name in Pennsylvania, as well as his shares in the Pennsylvania Union Canal. Mailliard was also to be entrusted with 10,000 dollars, for discreet disbursement to the King's ex-mistresses and illegitimate offspring, and for which no account need be rendered to the executors. Further, Mailliard was to remain in residence at Point Breeze (suitably indemnified for running expenses) until such time as Joseph's grandson Joseph Lucien Charles Napoleon, son of Zenaïde and Charles, should be of age to inherit the property.

On the death of her mother, Zenaïde inherited an annuity of nearly £130,000, to which, under Italian law, Charles had no claim. It is difficult to believe that Charles was altogether the complete ne'er-do-well Zenaïde had represented him to be. True, he was a compulsive gambler and Zenaïde was obliged to pay enormous gambling debts, but by 1850 he was also a world-famous naturalist, a scholar of great distinction whose many works were to be found in every natural history museum and in many universities of the Old and New Worlds.

On Julie's death, the twenty-one-year-old Joseph took possession of his inheritance of Point Breeze. Although the American way of life was by no means displeasing to the young man, he found his occupancy of his grandfather's mansion intolerably lonely. He shared neither Joseph's love of shooting and country pursuits nor his passion for landscape gardening, while the house itself was altogether too big, too grand, for a young man of his age. In 1847 he decided to sell the property and return to Rome to be beside the mother he adored. The house and grounds were acquired by a Mr Thomas Richards of Philadelphia, who in turn sold them to a naturalized American Englishman, Henry Beckett, the son of the British Consul in Philadelphia.

Beckett, too, found the mansion, with its vast reception rooms, rather grander than he liked. He had the house razed to the ground and in its place built an elegant colonial-style residence, with an Italian terrazzo and a colonnaded portico, approached by a flight of steps flanked by two large, neatly trimmed bushes.

In the course of years the estate was to change hands many times, and each time part of the grounds was sold in lots and modifications were made to buildings. For a time the former Beckett mansion was occupied by the Congregational Mission of Saint Vincent de Paul, but by the beginning of the First World War it was untenanted and unfurnished. The elegant colonial house no longer possessed its green shutters, its rough-cast walls had lost their pristine whiteness, the topiary bushes had long disappeared and what remained of the once lovely park had fallen into decay. Only the splendid staircase and the rose marble baths and Carrara marble mantelpieces – a gift from Uncle Fesch – transferred from Joseph's original residence, remained of the former regal splendour.

In 1939 the Point Breeze estate, now heavily mortgaged and owing 135,000 dollars in unpaid tax, was put up for compulsory sale by order of the Court of New Jersey. Today [1970] the house and out-buildings, renovated and enlarged, are occupied by the Divine World Seminary. The Mobiloil Guide accords only three lines to the 'Bonaparte Park' under the heading of Bordentown : 'Only 242 acres remain of the Bonaparte estate. The only original structure is the gardener's lodge at the entrance to Park Street.'[9]

Sic transit gloria mundi.

Ironically, it was Louis-Napoleon, the nephew of whom Joseph had so bitterly disapproved for his foolhardy escapades at Strasbourg and Boulogne and whom he blamed for the persistent implementation of the decree exiling all Bonapartes from France, who was to fulfil Joseph's dearest wish when, as Napoleon III, he ordered his uncle's remains to be transferred to France and laid beside the tomb of the Emperor in Les Invalides on 14 June 1862.

After thirty-seven years, the Reluctant King had at last returned from exile.

Notes

MC = *Mémoires et correspondance du roi Joseph*, ed. Baron du Casse, 10 vols., Paris 1855–8.

Chapter I: Childhood and Youth, 1767–93

1. *Napoléon et sa famille*, 13 vols. (Paris 1897–1900).
2. Vol. 1 (Paris 1897), p. 19.
3. They were married on 2 June 1764.
4. This was not equivalent to French nobility. It gave him neither the entrée to Versailles nor all the privileges granted to the French *noblesse*.
5. *MC*, vol. 1, pp. 26–7.
6. *MC*, vol. 1, p. 98.
7. Th. Jung, *Lucien Bonaparte et ses mémoires 1775–1840*, 3 vols., vol. 1 (Paris 1882), pp. 11–16.
8. *MC*, vol. 1, p. 28.
9. *MC*, vol. 1, p. 29.
10. R. F. Delderfield, *The Golden Milestones* (London 1964).
11. *MC*, vol. 1, p. 40.
12. Il Babbo (Grandad) was the name affectionately given to Paoli by his followers.
13. Charles had even claimed a pope and a saint among his ancestors.
14. These eleven letters are to be found in Giovanni Sforza's *Miscellanea Napoleonica*, ed. Alberto Lumbroso (Rome 1899), p. 250, cited by Bernard Nabonne in his *Joseph Bonaparte, le roi philosophe* (Paris 1949).
15. See also *Le Temps* of 7 July 1899.
16. *MC*, vol. 1, pp. 39–41.
17. *MC*, vol. 1, p. 43.
18. See Louis de Villefosse and Janine Bouissounouse, *L'Opposition à Napoléon* (Paris 1969), pp. 16–17.
19. Vol. 1 (Paris 1821).
20. Published as *pièce justicative* No. 3 in *MC*, vol. 1, pp. 117–18.

21. Villefosse and Bouissounance, op. cit.
22. 'Prepare yourself, this country is not for us.' Villefosse and Bouissounouse, op cit.

Chapter II: Marriage and Napoleon's Rise to Power, 1793–6

1. *MC*, vol. 1, p. 54.
2. This, of course, was the occasion when Napoleon who, thanks to Saliceti, had been appointed commander of the siege artillery on 12 or 16 September, first established his name as a brilliant soldier. Under the admiring eyes of Saliceti, Barras, Fréron, Augustin Robespierre (the brother of Maximilien) and Fouché, Napoleon had systematically bombarded the enemy's key positions and then carried them by assault. Hood's squadron, raked by cannon, was forced to abandon its blazing anchorage, alight with the flames of the French Royalist ships, to which the English had set fire, rather than let them fall into the hands of the enemy.
3. See A. Chuquet's 'La Mission de Joseph Bonaparte en 1783', *Annales révolutionnaires* (Paris 1908).
4. To a Mlle Fléchon.
5. Baron Hochschild, *Désirée, reine de Suède et de Norvège* (Paris and Stockholm 1888), pp. 3–6.
6. Victor Somis, brother-in-law of François Clary. François Clary had been twice married and had thirteen children in all, of which several were dead at the time of Joseph's first acquaintance with the family. From François's first marriage there still survived Jeanne and Catherine (who married the brothers Le Jeans), Rose (who married a rich merchant, Antoine Anthoine; he was created Baron de Saint-Joseph under the Empire), and Honorine (who in 1791 married the Sieur Blait de Villeneufve; during the Terror Villeneufve called himself Blait *tout court* and later emigrated to Spain). In addition to these surviving daughters, François had three sons by his first marriage: Étienne (whom Joseph helped to release from prison), Justinien (who was murdered in mysterious circumstance, almost certainly political), and Nicolas (who assumed his father's business when the latter died in 1794). The two daughters by the second marriage were Marie-Julie (b. 26 December 1771; she was to marry Joseph) and Bernadine-Eugénie-Désirée (b. 8 November 1777; she was to marry Bernadotte). A complication arises from the fact that Julie was wont to address her half-brother Nicolas as 'uncle'.
7. op. cit.
8. Duchesse d'Abrantès, née Laurette de Saint-Martin-Permon, wife of Marshal Junot. Her very unreliable *Mémoires*, published in 18 volumes between 1831 and 1835, gained her a reputation in the literary world.

9. See note 6 to this chapter, p. 36.
10. Both were executed on 9 Thermidor.
11. This pamphlet was written in the form of an imaginary conversation conducted between a military officer (obviously Napoleon himself) and three Girondist merchants from Marseilles, Montpellier and Nîmes, who meet by chance over supper at a hostelry in Beaucaire.
12. Th. Jung, *Lucien Bonaparte et ses mémoires 1775–1840*, vol. 1 (Paris 1882), p. 94.
13. *MC*, vol. 1, p. 99.
14. Genoa had remained neutral during France's war with Austria and Piedmont and was thus free from the British blockade.
15. See Michael Ross, *Banners of the King: The War in the Vendée, 1793* (London 1975).
16. In his correspondence Napoleon always referred to Désirée as Eugénie, her second given name.
17. As originally drafted (by Paul-Jean-François Daunou, one of the founders of the Institut), there was to have been only one Director, or rather President, like that of the United States, or alternatively, two Consuls, taking office turn and turn about.

Chapter III: Napoleon's Marriage–First Italian Campaign, 1796–7

1. Carnot, Barras, Rewbell, Letourneur and La Réveillère-Lepeaux.
2. Actually it was not Rewbell but Barras who was responsible for Napoleon's appointments. An interesting sidelight on this promotion is provided in a letter written by Josephine: 'Barras promised that if I marry the General he will give him command of the Army of Italy. Yesterday, when speaking to me of this favour (which is already making his brother officers grumble) Bonaparte said: "What! Do they imagine I need Barras' protection to succeed? Some day they'll be only too happy if I give them my own. I have my sword at my side, and with its help I'll go far." '
3 *MC*, vol. 1, p. 61.
4. Joseph still employs the word *louis* although it was banned from the Republican vocabulary. Three years later, one *livre d'or* was worth 60,000 *assignats*!
5. Sir James Marshall-Cornwall, *Napoleon as a Military Commander* (London and Princeton, N.J., 1967).
6. Las Cases, *Mémorial de Sainte-Hélène*, 8 vols. (Paris 1821–3).
7. It was here that Napoleon was to add further lustre to his legend. One of the many bridges spanning the canals which threaded the surrounding rice fields was strongly contested by the Austrians. Several attempts to storm the bridge having failed, Napoleon,

seizing a regimental colour and accompanied by his brother Louis and two other aides-de-camp, personally led the troops forward to the attack. Before he ever reached the bridge, however, he was forcibly dragged back by another officer who told him that he was facing certain death. In the ensuing confusion, Napoleon, violently protesting, accidentally slipped from the canal embankment and fell into the muddy waters, from which he was rescued by two soldiers. The news of his gallant example soon spread through the army, adding further to the prestige and popularity of the 'Little Corporal'.

Chapter IV: Corsican Deputy and Ambassador to Rome, 1797–8

1. This was important due to the constant depreciation of *assignats*.
2. It will be recollected that Louis had originally been trained as a gunner and had served in an artillery regiment.
3. Some historians maintain that Joseph first returned to Parma and that it was only in July that he received his letters of appointment to the Holy See. Joseph in his memoirs constantly confuses dates.
4. Bernard Nabonne (*Joseph Bonaparte, le roi philosophe*, Paris 1949) gives the date as 28 September.
5. Nabonne, op. cit.
6. Provera was the Austrian general who was defeated at La Favorita in his attempt to relieve Mantua on 16 January.
7. Ceracchi was involved in a plot, known as the Arena-Ceracchi plot, to assassinate Napoleon during a performance at the Opera on 10 October 1800.
8. Baron Hochschild, *Désirée, reine de Suède et de Norvège* (Paris and Stockholm 1888).
9. General Desaix, who joined the Army of Italy from the Rhine in 1797, wrote of Napoleon: 'He is proud, dissimulating, vindictive and never forgives . . . and is a great intriguer. He has plenty of money; naturally, since he receives the revenue of a whole country and *never presents accounts.*'
10. *Mémoires de Barras*, edited with a general introduction, prefaces and appendices by G. Duruy, vol. 3 (Paris 1895), p. 381.

Chapter V: Joseph, Député, Philosophe and Man of the World, 1798–1800

1. The letters of marque, allowing him to practise 'legitimate piracy', had provided him with handsome profits. (cf. G. P. Garnier, *L'Extraordinaire destin des Bonapartes*, Paris 1968.)

2. Bernadotte was by no means unique in this respect. Although popular with his men, Bonaparte failed, with few exceptions, to win the affection of his senior officers, frequently belittling their achievements in official bulletins. Another habit of Bonaparte's which did not endear him to his divisional commanders was his trick of sending forward his own favourite staff officers at the climax of a battle, and then giving them credit which was really due to those who had borne the brunt of the fighting. (cf. Sir James Marshall-Cornwall, *Napoleon as a Military Commander*, London and Princeton, N.J., 1967.)

3. cf. Marshall-Cornwall, op. cit.

4. An unconfirmed story, but one which later Bernadotte himself liked to tell, was that while in Marseilles he presented himself at the Clary house with a billeting order. Madame Clary, however, had protested to the military authorities that she wanted no common soldiers in her house; she would accept only officers.

5. Napoleon had just learnt from the indiscreet Junot that Josephine was still continuing her liaison with Hippolyte Charles.

6. This theory, as Bernard Nabonne points out in *Joseph Bonaparte, le roi philosophe* (Paris 1949), is quite absurd. Bernadotte, a convinced Jacobin, was absolutely opposed to any form of dictatorial government. Neither he nor Joseph ever had the slightest intention of establishing an autocracy.

7. *Mémoires de Barras*, ed. G. Duruy (Paris 1895).

8. Lucien at the time was only twenty-four, and, strictly speaking, ineligible for election; by law, no person under twenty-five was permitted to stand as a candidate.

9. A. Castelot, *Bonaparte* (Paris 1968).

10. ibid.

11. The Republican Army in Holland was under the command of General Brune, probably the most incompetent of all French generals. Fortunately for Brune, he had as his adversary the Duke of York, the son of George III, 'probably the only commander in the world whom he could have defeated and defeat him he did at the battles of Bergen and Kastricum' (A. G. Macdonnell, *Napoleon and his Marshals*, London 1934).

12. Joseph Fouché, *Mémoires*, with an introduction and notes by Louis Madelin (Paris 1945).

13. ibid.

14. It was Sieyès who, when asked what he had done during the Reign of Terror, replied with the famous *mot* : *'J'ai vécu'* (I survived).

15. op. cit.

16. op. cit.

17. Th. Jung, *Lucien et ses mémoires 1775–1840*, 3 vols. (Paris 1882–3).

18. cf. Richard Cobb's *The Police and the People: French Popular Protest 1789–1820* (Oxford 1970), and his *Paris and its Provinces* (Oxford 1975).
19. Fouché, op. cit.
20. On 25 September Masséna defeated Souvoroff at Zürich, three weeks before Napoleon disembarked at Fréjus.
21. According to A.-F. Miot, Comte de Melito (*Mémoires*, ed. General W. A. von Fleischmann, Paris 1893, p. 240), Bourbakis was paid 24,000 francs to undertake this mission. One of his two sons was to command a French division at the battle of Alma during the Crimean War.
22. *MC*, vol. 1, pp. 74–5.
23. A. Vandal, *Avènement de Bonaparte*, 6th edn, vol. 1 (Paris 1903), pp. 251–5.
24. P.-L. Roederer, *Mémoires* (Paris 1942).
25. *MC*, vol. 1, pp. 74, 75, 76.
26. op. cit.
27. *MC*, vol. 1, p. 80.
28. ibid.
29. Louis de Villefosse and Janine Bouissounance, *L'Opposition à Napoléon* (Paris 1969).

Chapter VI: The Peacemaker, 1800–2

1. He was misled by his commissaries in this respect and believed the armies to be much better equipped than in fact they were, despite Bernadotte's hard work.
2. *Napoleon as a Military Commander* (London and Princeton, N.J., 1967).
3. Sir James Marshall-Cornwall, op. cit.
4. *MC*, vol. 1, pp. 84–5.
5. Joseph Fouché, *Mémoires*, with an introduction and notes by Louis Madelin (Paris 1945), p. 161.
6. Scarcely any highway was safe for travellers without an escort. The prevalence of marauding armed bands throughout the length and breadth of France since 1794 had become a national threat. cf. Richard Cobb, *Paris and its Provinces* (Oxford 1975).
7. Either Joseph or a copyist is in error here. For Georgetown read Yorktown. It was at Yorktown that Washington's American army, in conjunction with the French forces under La Fayette and Rochambeau, surrounded the British under Cornwallis and forced him to surrender on 19 October 1781, thus bringing the War of American Independence to a conclusion.
8. *MC*, vol. 1, pp. 85–6.
9. *MC*, vol. 1, p. 91.

Chapter VII: Imperial Highness, Heir Presumptive, and Colonel of the 4th Regiment of the Line, 1802–5

1. François Pietri, *Lucien Bonaparte* (Paris 1930).
2. Th. Jung, *Lucien et ses mémoires 1775–1840*, vol. 2 (Paris 1882), pp. 107–8.
3. Louis believed, as did many other people, that Louis-Napoleon was the son of the Dutch Admiral van Werhuel. General Flahaut de la Billarderie was openly acknowledged to be the father of Hortense's fourth son, the future Duc de Morny (b. 1811). Flahaut himself was the natural son of Talleyrand.
4. Madame de Staël goes further and claims that Bernadotte was the instigator of the plot. See Christopher Herold, *Mistress of an Age* (London 1959), p. 226.
5. Jung, op. cit., vol. 2, pp. 107–8.
6. ibid, vol. 2, p. 373, note 2.
7. ibid, vol. 2.
8. A.-F. Miot, Comte de Melito, *Mémoires*, ed. General W. A. von Fleischmann (Paris 1893).
9. *Journal du Comte Roederer* (Paris 1909), p. 44.
10. Jung, op. cit.
11. Melito, op. cit.
12. Quoted by Sir Arthur Bryant in *The Great Duke* (London 1971).
13. P.-L. Roederer, *Mémoires* (Paris 1942), pp. 206–11.
14. *MC*, vol. 1, pp. 122, 123.
15. *MC*, vol. 1, pp. 9–10; 'the consequent annoyance resulting from disappointed hopes' – '*l'ennui résultant d'une espérance deçue*' in the original.
16. *MC*, vol. 1, pp. 122–3; '. . . during the first Italian campaign' : one can only assume that Joseph regarded his short visit to Napoleon's headquarters as 'military service'. He was certainly never in action.
17. Constant, (extracts from) *Mémoires intimes de Napoléon I*, published by Maurice Dernelle in *Mercure de France* (Paris 1967), pp. 125–7. The first edition of Constant's complete work in 6 vols. was published in 1830. See also André Gavoty, *Les drames inconnus de la cour de Napoléon* (Paris 1962), p. 212.
18. Gabriel Girod de l'Ain, *Joseph Bonaparte, le roi malgré lui* (Paris 1970).
19. One is reminded of Louis XV's insistence that Mlle Poisson should become the Marquise de Pompadour and that the milliner Jeanne Becu should marry the Marquis du Barry before being officially received at Court and acknowledged as *Maîtresses en titre*.
20. Flame-coloured for Napoleon's brother. Each dignitary had his own colour. cf. Frédéric Masson, *Le sacre de Napoléon* (Paris 1907).

21. In David's famous picture all the family is present. This is entirely inaccurate.
22. For a detailed description see Masson, op cit.
23. 'The same warmth of heart': the population of the newly acquired departments of the north were far from grateful for being made subjects of France, under whose rule they suffered not only economically but also a loss of liberty much worse than under their former Austrian rulers. Joseph was surely hoodwinked. See Richard Cobb, *Paris and its Provinces* (Oxford 1975).

Chapter VIII: King of the Two Sicilies, 1805–8

1. He was made a marshal in 1813.
2. P.-L. Roederer, *Mémoires* (Paris 1942).
3. Sir Sidney Smith garrisoned Capri with Royal Corsican Rangers under the command of Colonel Hudson Lowe, the same who was to be Napoleon's 'gaoler' in Saint Helena.
4. *Mémoires du Général Bigarré, aide de camp du roi* (Paris 1893).
5. One child by Mme Lamy who died in infancy and another by the Duchessa d'Atri.
6. *Joseph Bonaparte, le roi malgré lui* (Paris 1970).
7. Roederer, op. cit.
8. *Mémoires, journal et souvenirs*, vol. 1 (Paris 1829), pp. 336, 369.
9. A.-F. Miot, Comte de Melito, *Mémoires*, ed. General W. A. von Fleischmann (Paris 1893).
10. cf. Sir Arthur Bryant, *The Great Duke* (London 1971).
11. ibid.
12. Felix Markham, *The Napoleonic Adventure* (Cambridge 1965).
13. Which Goya executed, contrary to popular belief, after the restoration of the Bourbons.
14. In fact he did leave, but his ship was intercepted by a British frigate. Lucien and Alexandrine were taken back to England. He was treated generously and lived quietly in the West Country. Only one official 'guard' was placed in his house. It was here that his eldest son Charles was born.
15. 'The King arrived like a sovereign and left like a brigand/The Queen arrived in rags and left like a sovereign.'

Chapter IX: From Naples to Madrid, 1808

1. *MC*, vol. 4, pp. 228, 229.
2. *MC*, vol. 10, pp. 296, 300.
3. *MC*, vol. 10, pp. 296, 300.
4. Sir Arthur Bryant, *The Great Duke* (London 1971).
5. *Joseph Bonaparte, le roi malgré lui* (Paris 1970).

6. See *MC*, vol. 4, pp. 245–8.
7. Together with his uncle Don Carlos and his young brother. The Château of Valençay was the property of Talleyrand, on whom Napoleon had thrust, much to Talleyrand's annoyance, these thoroughly unwelcome guests.
8. *Mémoires, journal et souvenirs*, vol. 2 (Paris 1829), p. 130.
9. Stanislas de Girardin, op. cit., vol. 2, p. 132.
10. Wellington to the Hon. William Wellesley-Pole; see Sir Arthur Bryant, op. cit.
11. Jovellanos was later executed by his own Junta of Cadiz for his liberal views.
12. *Correspondance 1808–1813*, ed. G. de Grandmaison, vol. 5 (Paris 1905).
13. A. G. Macdonell, *Napoleon and his Marshals* (London 1934).
14. ibid.

Chapter X: King of Spain and the Indies, 1808–9

1. *Revue des deux mondes*, vol. 2 (Paris 1883), p. 322. Abel Hugo, elder brother of Victor, was the son of General Sigisbert Hugo, whose *Mémoires militaires* were published and edited by his son, and are included in *Revue des deux mondes*.
2. *Mémoires de M. de Bourienne, ministre d'état, sur Napoléon, le directoire, le consulat, l'empire et la restauration*, ed. M. de Villemarest, 10 vols. (Paris 1829). Another edition was reprinted in 5 vols. by Désiré Lacroix in Paris in 1899.
3. *Mémoires, journal et souvenirs* (Paris 1829).
4. ibid.
5. The dichotomy in Suchet's character (i.e. his benevolent rule once the Spanish people were subjugated) is admirably explained by Sir Arthur Bryant in *The Great Duke* (London 1971).
6. He was captured later by English cavalry at Benevento.
7. L. A. Thiers, *History of the Consulate and Empire* (Paris 1861).
8. Sir Arthur Bryant, op. cit.
9. See Albert-Jean-Michel de Rocca, *Mémoires sur la guerre des Français en Espagne* (Paris 1817).
10. Sir Charles W. C. Oman, *History of the Peninsular War*, 10 vols. (Oxford 1902–30).

Chapter XI: 'The Intruder King', 1809–10

1. The last records of Joseph's correspondence with the Duchessa d'Atri date from this time.
2. See Raymond Carr, *Spain 1808–1939* (Oxford 1966).

3. A.-F. Miot, Comte to Melito, *Mémoires*, ed. General W. A. von Fleischmann (Paris 1893).
4. cf. Sir Charles W. C. Oman, *History of the Peninsular War*, vol. 1 (Oxford 1902), p. 475.
5. Venegas' Army of La Mancha, which had attempted to intercept the French withdrawal from Madrid, had been routed by Joseph and Sebastiani at Almonacid on 12 August, an additional reason for Joseph to indulge in a feeling of security.
6. Though later he was prepared to negotiate a peaceful settlement with the Junta of Cadiz.
7. Marshal Jourdan, *Mémoires militaires* (Paris 1893), p. 303.

Chapter XII: The Conquest of Andalusia and Disillusion, 1810–11

1. *Mémoires du Général Bigarré, aide de camp du roi* (Paris 1893), p. 270.
2. Although Napoleon criticized Joseph for not making Cadiz his first objective instead of Seville, he now approved of his attempt to enter into negotiations with the Junta in Cadiz.
3. Marshal Jourdan, *Mémoires militaires* (Paris 1893).
4. Abel Hugo, *Revue des deux mondes*, vol. 1 (Paris 1883), p. 303 : 'L'entière pacification de l'Espagne n'aurait été qu'ajournée si Napoleon lui même, par un décret inopportun et impolitique, ne fût devenu en quelque sorte l'auxiliare des intrigues brittaniques et l'ennemi le plus réel du trone et son frère. Le nouvel état de choses ne pouvait manquer de detruire tout le bien que la conduite noble et mesurée du roi avait produit.'
5. Quoted by Abel Hugo, op. cit.
6. *Mémoires du Général Bigarré.*
7. Just as he resented Stanislas de Girardin's revelations concerning his first meeting with the Marquesa de Montehermoso.
8. See Bernard Nabonne, *Joseph Bonaparte, le roi philosophe* (Paris 1949).
9. A.-F. Miot, Comte de Melito, *Mémoires*, ed. General W. A. von Fleischmann (Paris 1893).
10. Quoted in *MC*.

Chapter XIII: Vitoria: The End of a Reign, 1811–12

1. Stanislas de Girardin, *Mémoires, journal et souvenirs* (Paris 1829).
2. Gabriel Girod de l'Ain, *Joseph Bonaparte, le roi malgré lui* (Paris 1970), p. 263.

3. The Marquis, who had accompanied Joseph to Paris, had fallen ill en route and had died at Mortefontaine on the eve of the King's departure for Spain.
4. Girod de l'Ain, op. cit.
5. Raymond Carr, *Spain 1808–1939* (Oxford 1966).
6. Sir Arthur Bryant, *The Great Duke* (London 1971).
7. Girod de l'Ain, op. cit.
8. Baring Bros and Co. and Rougemont and Verhend.
9. All these details are to be found in Nicolas Clary's papers, now in the possession of G. Girod de l'Ain.
10. With some justification. The British had already made several tip-and-run raids for this very purpose.
11. Comte de la Forest, *Correspondance 1808–1813*, ed. G. de Grand-maison (Paris 1905).
12. See Sir Arthur Bryant, op. cit.
13. Bryant, op. cit.
14. A.-F. Miot, Comte de Melito, *Mémoires*, ed. General W. A. von Fleischmann (Paris 1893).
15. *The Letters of Private Wheeler*, ed. B. H. Liddell Hart (London 1951).
16. Bryant, op cit.
17. There are innumerable accounts of this battle. I refer the reader to Sir Arthur Bryant again for a splendid résumé and bibliography.
18. He was left on the field for dead, and taken prisoner. He afterwards joined Joseph in America.
19. Bernard Nabonne, *Joseph Bonaparte, le roi philosophe* (Paris 1949).

Chapter XIV: The Hundred Days: Joseph as the Emperor's Right Hand, 1812–14

1. Wellington forced the Nivelle on 10 November 1813.
2. *Journal du Comte Roederer* (Paris 1909), pp. 322–3.
3. Comte de la Forest, *Correspondance 1808–1813*, ed. G. de Grand-maison (Paris 1905).
4. *Journal du Comte Roederer*, p. 271
5. With the assistance of Benjamin Constant. cf. Christopher Herold, *Mistress to an Age* (London 1959).
6. During the 1814 campaign, Joseph and the Emperor corresponded almost daily, sometimes twice daily. The courier service was excellent.
7. Napoleon often used the word *Bataille*, meaning campaign.
8. Chateaubriand, *Mémoires d'outre tombe* (Paris 1845).
9. A.-F. Miot, Comte de Melito, *Mémoires*, ed. General W. A. von Fleischmann (Paris 1893).
10. Désirée later rented a modest villa in Auteuil for Joseph's family.

Chapter XV: First Exile: Switzerland, 1814–15

1. Baron C.-F. de Méneval, *Mémoires*, vol. 3 (Paris 1894), p. 357.
2. See Christopher Herold, *Mistress to an Age* (London 1959), p. 226.
3. *MC*.
4. Frédéric Masson, *Napoléon et sa famille*, 13 vols. (Paris 1897–1900).
5. Fleur de Chaboulan, *Mémoires* (Paris 1901).
6. A. de Vaulabelle, *Histoire des deux restaurations* (Paris 1855).
7. Quoted by Gilbert Martineau in *Napoleon Surrenders*, trans. from the French by Frances Partridge (London 1971).
8. Wander Vuliez, '*Une Dynastie française aux Etats Unis*', in *Miroir de l'Histoire* (April 1967), quoted by Girod de l'Ain in *Joseph Bonaparte, le roi malgré lui* (Paris 1970).
9. Gérard Pesme, *Les dernières heures de Napoléon a l'île d'Aix* (Paris 1954).

Chapter XVI: Second Exile: The Gentleman Farmer of New Jersey, U.S.A., 1815–30

1. G. Bertin, *Joseph Bonaparte en Amérique* (Paris 1893).
2. See Gabriel Girod de l'Ain, *Joseph Bonaparte, le roi malgré lui* (Paris 1970).
3. Derisively, during the reign of Louis XVIII and Charles X, the name Bonaparte was always spelt in its original Italian form.
4. De Neuville is referring to the South American and, in particular, Mexican insurgents fighting for independence.
5. For Joseph's extremely complicated financial transactions, which were to make him a multimillionaire, see Girod de l'Ain, op. cit.
6. Bernard Nabonne, *Joseph Bonaparte, le roi philosophe* (Paris 1949).
7. Four sons and six daughters by Alexandrine and two daughters by his first wife, Christine Boyer.
8. Natural confusion arises from the fact that so many of the cousins bore similar names. Louis' three (putative) children were respectively Napoleon-Louis-Charles, b. 1803, d. 1807; Louis-Napoleon, b. 1804, d. 1831, the one who concerns us here; and Charles-Louis-Napoleon, b. 1808, d. 1873, who became Emperor Napoleon III in 1852.
9. A. Levasseur, Secretary of General La Fayette, *La Fayette in America in 1824 and 1825*, or *Journals of Travels in the United States*, trans. from the French, 2 vols. (New York 1829).
10. Quoted in Georges Bertin, *Joseph Bonaparte en Amérique* (Paris 1893), pp. 193–4.
11. In contemporary documents, the name of Gonzalo O'Farrill is spelt inconsistently, sometimes with two l's and sometimes with one.

12. See Owen Connelly, *The Gentle Bonaparte* (New York and London 1968).
13. In 1859 Caroline Benton obtained an audience with Napoleon III, who immediately recognized her resemblance to Joseph. He accorded her a pension and appointed her lady-in-waiting to the Empress. After 1870 Caroline was forced to return to the U.S., where she died in misery.

Chapter XVII: The Last Years, 1830–44

1. Hector Fleischmann, *Lettres d'exile du roi Joseph 1825–1844* (Paris 1912).
2. Gabriel Girod de l'Ain, *Joseph Bonaparte, le roi malgré lui* (Paris 1970).
3. The Duke of Reichstadt died at five o'clock in the morning of 22 July.
4. Whose nephew had invited Joseph to assume the crown of Mexico.
5. Girod de l'Ain, op. cit.
6. This drama was not produced until 1855 in Lausanne. The Robert family seem to have possessed a morbid streak; several other members of the family also committed suicide. cf. F. Feuillet de Conches, *Léopold Robert* (Paris 1854) and Dorette Berthoud, *Vie du peintre Léopold Robert* (Neufchâtel 1934).
7. Joseph presented Napoleon's regalia of the Legion d'Honneur, to which were added his sword and hat as soon as the tomb was completed.
8. Joseph's relations with Charles, despite Zenaïde's censures, seem to have remained good. In a letter Emilie Lacoste wrote to him in December 1842, she said : 'I hear that the Prince of Canino has returned to Rome, which must afford you great peace of mind.' Joseph also left him a considerable sum of money in his will.
9. Girod de l'Ain, op. cit.

Bibliography

Bertin, G., *Joseph Bonaparte en Amérique*, Paris 1893.
Bryant, Sir Arthur, *The Great Duke*, London 1971.
Castelot, André, *Bonaparte*, Paris 1967.
Connelly, Owen, *The Gentle Bonaparte*, New York and London 1968.
Correspondance de Napoléon Ier, compiled under the auspices of Napoleon III, Paris 1858–69.
de Budé, Eugène, *Les Bonaparte en Suisse*, Paris 1905.
du Casse, Baron, ed., *Mémoires et correspondance du roi Joseph*, 10 vols., Paris 1855–8.

—*Les rois frères de Napoléon Ier*, Paris 1883.

Fleischmann, Hector, *Lettres d'exil inédites du roi Joseph*, Paris 1912.

Garnier, Jean-Paul, *L'extraordinaire destin des Bonaparte*, Paris 1968.

Gavoty, André, *Amours et aventures au temps de Napoléon*, Paris 1969.

— *Les drames inconnus de la cour de Napoléon*, Paris 1962.

Girod de l'Ain, Gabriel, *Joseph Bonaparte, le roi malgré lui*, Paris 1970.

Herold, Christopher, *Mistress to an Age: A Life of Madame Staël*, London 1959.

Macartney, C. E., and Dorrance, Gordon, *The Bonapartes in America*, Philadelphia 1939.

Masson, Frédéric, *Napoléon et sa famille*, Paris 1897–1900.

— *Napoléon inconnu*, Paris 1895.

Nabonne, Bernard, *Joseph Bonaparte, le roi philosophe*, Paris 1949.

Rambaud, J., *Lettres inédites ou éparses de Joseph Bonaparte à Naples*, Paris 1914.

— *Naples sous Joseph Bonaparte*, Paris 1911.

Woodward, Major, *Bonaparte's Park and the Murats*, Trenton 1879.

Sforza, Giovanni, *Miscellanea Napoleonica*, ed. Alberto Lumbroso, Rome 1899.

Index

Abercromby, General Sir John, 94
Abrantès, Duchess of, 37, 43
Abu Qir, battle of, 82
Adams, John Quincy, 251, 260
Ajaccio, 12, 15, 20, 22, 23, 25–31, 57–8, 59
Alba de Tormes, battle at, 182–5 *passim*
Albani, Cardinal, 63
Albitte, 33, 35
Albuquerque, Duke of, Spanish general, 189, 190
Alessandria, Convention of, 92
Alexander I, Tsar, 147, 154, 226, 233
Allvintzy, Field Marshal, 55, 56
Almenara, Marques de, 196, 260
Almonacid, battle, 287
Alps, crossing of, 90
Altamira, Count of, 164, 187
Amiens, Peace of, 97, 108, 109, 222
Ananza, Duke of Santa Fé, 196, 223
Ancona, 56, 62, 63, 65, 66
Andalusia, 184, 185, 186–98, 207, 217
Andréossy, General, 113
Andrieux, François, 81
Angelini, Minister to Tuscany, 66
Angen, General d', 252
Angiolini, Cavaliere, 106
Anthoine, Antoine (m. Rose Clary), 35, 279
Arcola, battle of, 55, 56, 71
Areizaga, Juan Carlos de, Spanish general, 181, 182, 185, 186–8 *passim*
Arena-Ceracchi plot, 281
Armies, French: Grande Armée, 210, 215; of Aragon, 204; of Italy, 32, 33, 38, 46, 48, 89; of Observation, 75; of Portugal, 207, 210; of Naples, 123; of Spain, 155, 230; of Reserve, 90; of the Centre, 207; of the Danube, 89; of the North, 210; of the Orient, 92; of the Rhine, 89, 101; of the West, 102
Armies, Spanish: of Estramadura, 189; of La Mancha, 181, 182, 287

Arriba, Pablo de, 175
Atri, Maria-Giulia Colonna, Duchessa d', 130, 131, 133, 134, 140, 144, 146, 147, 159, 261, 286
Aubry, General, 42–3
Augereau, Marshal Pierre-François-Charles, Duc de Castiglione, 55, 70, 72, 80, 177
Austerlitz, battle of, 122, 124, 151, 164, 181, 230
Austro-Russian coalition (1805), 119, 121
Auteuil, 236, 288
Autun, 16, 17, 18
Azanza, Duque de Santa Fé, Marques de, 175, 193, 233, 260
Azara, Spanish ambassador to Rome, 66, 97

Bacciochi, Félix, created Prince of Lucca and Piombino (m. Élise Bonaparte), 59
Baird, Sir David, 166
Bâle, Treaty of, 138
Ballasteros, Spanish guerillero, 204
ballet company, 261
Banque de France, 202
Baring Bros and Co., bankers, 288
Barras, P. J. F. N., Comte de, 36, 43, 45, 46, 47, 51, 52–3, 65, 67, 71, 72, 76, 78, 79, 81, 82, 83, 107, 280
Barthélémy, François, 72
Bathurst, Earl, 214
Bautzen, battle of, 215
Baylen, battle of, 149, 150, 151, 152, 154, 156, 188, 207, 217
Bayonne, 218
Bayonne, Junta of, 149
Beauharnais, Eugène de, 50, 61, 119
Beauharnais, Hortense de (m. Louis Bonaparte), *see* Bonaparte, Hortense
Beauharnais, Josephine de (m. Napoleon Bonaparte), *see* Bonaparte, Josephine
Becket, Henry, 277
Bentinck, Lord William, 168

293

Benton, Caroline, 262, 290
Benton, Zebulon Howell, 262
Berlioz, Hector, 271
Bernadotte, Désirée (née Clary, Berna-dine-Eugene-Désirée; Queen of Sweden), 35–7, 40, 42, 46, 47, 50, 61–2, 64, 65, 86, 120, 225, 232–3, 236, 237, 250, 269, 279; marriage, 70–1, 73
Bernadotte, Jean-Baptiste-Jules (King Charles XIV of Sweden), 57, 69–71, 73, 75, 78, 79, 85–6, 87, 101, 102, 156, 208, 221, 222, 225–6, 231, 233, 260, 274, 282, 284; elected Crown Prince of Sweden, 196
Bernard, General, 252
Bernier, Abbé, 95
Berthier, L.-A., Prince of Neuchâtel and Wagram, 53, 67, 69, 82, 85, 90, 154, 163, 171, 186, 203, 205, 224
Berthollet, Comte Claude Louis, 82
Bertrand, Comte Henri Gratien, General, 244, 254
Bessières, Duc d'Istrie, Jean-Baptiste, Marshal, 143, 150, 153, 155, 163
Bigarré, General, 11, 113, 130, 155, 189–93 *passim*
Bird-Willis, Catherine, 259
Blake, Spanish general, 143, 162, 163
Blouin, Louis, 96
Blücher, G. L. von, Prussian field-marshal, 240
Bolgarde, Mme, 117
Bonaparte (Buonaparte) family: aristo-cratic status of, 12–13, 14, 18, 23, 24–5, 273; reunion (1797), 59; exiled, 272
Bonaparte, Alexandrine, *see* Jouberthon, Alexandrine
Bonaparte, Alexandrine Gertrude (daughter of Charles and Zenaïde), 260
Bonaparte, Caroline (Maria-Annur-ziada), 14, 30, 59, 61, 118, 119, 271; m. Joachim Murat, 86–7, 100
Bonaparte, Charles (father), 12–16 *passim*, 18, 19, 20, 26
Bonaparte, Charles (son of Lucien), 257, 258, 259, 260, 266, 285, 290
Bonaparte, Charles-Louis-Napoleon (b. 1808, later Napoleon III), 100, 105, 125, 289
Bonaparte, Charlotte, 105, 130, 134, 257, 258, 259, 262, 266, 270–1, 273, 275
Bonaparte, Christine, *see* Boyer, Charlotte
Bonaparte, Élise (Maria-Anna-Eliza; m. Félix Bacciochi), 14, 16, 18, 21, 28, 30, 34, 59, 118
Bonaparte, Hortense (*née* de Beau-harnais), 100, 118, 132, 258, 266, 268, 272, 284

Bonaparte, Jerome (brother; King of Westphalia), 14, 30, 42, 43, 50, 59, 115, 118, 119, 166, 227, 231, 235, 242, 269, 272
Bonaparte, Joseph (J.B.)
  affairs with women, 113–15, 130–1, 144, 159, 174–5, 211, 220, 228–9, 251, 261, 262–3, 268
  as head of family, 20–1, 32–3, 70, 91, 99, 105–8, 110, 258
  appointments: to Directoire of Ajaccio, 25, 27–31; Commissaire des Guerres, 33; to Executive Council, Corsica, 34; Inspector of Hospitals, 41; Deputy for Liamone, Corsica, 58; Minister to Parma, 58; Minister Plenipotentiary to Holy See, 58–9; Corsican deputy, 68; to Council of State, 86; Col. Commandant, 4th Regiment of the Line, 111, 120; Grand Elector, 112, 115, 200, 239; to Senatorerie de Bruxelles, 112; Grand Officer of the Legion of Honour, 112; Serene Imperial Royal Highness, 112, 116; Regent (1805), 121; C. in C. Army of Naples, 123; King of the Two Sicilies, 127–41, 142, 145–6; King of Spain, 132, 133, 139, 140, 142–216, 223, 234, 258; Regent for Napoleon (1814), 226; Grand Coun-cillor (military), 227; President of Council of Ministers, 240
  children by Julie, 49 (died), 97 (Zenaïde), 105 (Charlotte)
  children, illegitimate, 131, 134, 144 (Giulio d'Atri); 262 (Caroline Savage); 262 (Félix-Joseph Lacoste, *q.v.*)
  claim to succeed Napoleon, 91, 105, 109–12, 258
  collection of works of art, 255
  costume, 116, 118, 235
  education, 15–17
  events: birth, 11, 14; elected Free-mason, 34–5; meets Désirée Clary, 35; expedition to Corsica, 38; marries Julie Clary, 39; return to Corsica (1796), 57–8; in Rome, 59; military service, 112–15; entries into Madrid, 149, 171, 201, 209; proclaimed King of Spain, 150; in exile, Switzerland, 235–9; in U.S.A., 242, 244–5, 245–68 *passim*; death, 274; *see also* appoint-ments
  finances and wealth, 48, 201–2, 252, 289
  flair for diplomacy, 88
  health, 17, 256
  houses and properties: Department of La Marne, 52; Palazzo Orsini 'alla Longhara', Rome, 59; rue de Saints-Pères, Paris, 68; rue des Errancis,

Index

Reichstadt, Duke of, *see* Bonaparte, Napoleon II
Reinhold, John, 249
Rewbell, Jean-François, President of the Directoire, 48, 65, 71, 72, 76, 81, 82, 280
Reynier, General Ebenezer, 125, 126, 128–9
Richards, Thomas, 277
Richelieu, Duc de, 253
Rigaud, General, 252
Rivoli, battle of, 55, 71
Robert, Léopold, 270–1
Robespierre, Augustin, 39, 40
Robespierre, Maximilien, 17, 33, 39, 42
Rocca, Colonna de Cesare, 25
Rochambeau, Marshal Jean-Baptiste, 283
Roederer, Comte Pierre-Louis, 78, 81, 85, 89, 105, 110, 127, 133–4, 216, 219, 220, 221, 222, 260
Roger-Ducos, Conventionnel, member of the Directoire, and Consul after 18 Brumaire, 78, 79, 84, 85
Romana, Marques de la, 156, 163
Romanos, Mesonero, 178
Rome : declared Republic, 67 ; Governor of, 221, 222 ; King of, *see* Bonaparte, Napoleon II
Rossi, General, 25
Rossignol, General, 70
Rostopshine, Governor of Moscow, 232
Rougemont and Verhend, bankers, 288
Ruffo, Cardinal, 125, 126
Rusca, Cardinal, 63
Russia, French campaign in, 203, 210, 212, 215, 218, 242

Saint-Cyr, General Laurent, Comte (later Marquis) de Gouvion-Saint-Cyr, 123, 125, 166, 169, 172, 176
Saint-Cyr, Maison Royale de, 16, 18
St Helena, 252 ; Napoleon leaves for, 244
Saint-Hilary, General, 113
Saint-Jean-d'Angely, Comte Regnault de, 85, 241, 251, 252
Saint-Jean-d'Angely, Mme Regnault de, 114, 251
Saint-Leu, Comte de (Lucien Bonaparte), 200
Saint-Pierre, J. H. Bernardin de, 81
Salamanca, battle of, 217, 218
Saliceti, Antoine, 23, 25, 29, 30, 32, 33, 34, 37, 40, 48, 49, 58, 62, 86, 127, 279
Salligny, General, 120, 147, 149
Salligny, Rose, 134
San Domingo, 101
San' Ildefonso, Treaty of, 98, 107, 138
Santa-Cruz, Duque de, 143, 152, 164
Santa Fé, Marques de, 177
Saragossa, 159, 204
Saratoga Springs, 249

Sarazin, General, 86
Sardinia, 50, 53, 62, 109
Sari, Corsican officer, 251
Sari, Mme, 251, 262, 268
Sarzane, 23, 24, 273
Savage, Annette, 262, 268
Savary, Duc de Rovigo, Anne-Jean-Marie-René, 148, 149, 154, 215, 219, 220
Sayer, Stephen, 249
Scherer, 48, 75
Schimmelpenninck, Dutch envoy, 97
Schrand, Baron von, 237, 238
Schwartzenberg, Prince, 229
Sebastiani, General, 177, 178, 187, 189, 195, 287
Ségur, Marquis de, 18
Sellons, Comte de, 235
Sellons, Comte de, 235
54, 55
Seville, J.B.'s entry, 190 ; as capital under J.B., 194, 195
Seville, Junta of, 151
Sherlock, General, 61, 64
Short, William, 251
Sieyès, Emmanuel J. C., 43, 77–81, 83–4, 85, 90, 282
Smith, Sir Sidney, 82, 128
Somis, Victor, 36, 70
Soult, Duc de Dalmatie, Marshal Nicolas-Jean de Dieu, 111, 113, 114, 163, 166, 168, 169, 172, 179–82 *passim*, 185, 186–90 *passim*, 195, 196, 203, 204, 207–11 *passim*, 216, 217, 218, 230–1, 240, 270
Souvoroff, General, 75, 80
Spanish National Movement, 174
Spira, Cardinal, 95
Staël, Anne Louise Germaine, Mme de, 44, 69, 77, 81, 87, 99, 102, 236, 237, 243, 284
Stendhal (Marie Henri Beyle), 130
Stewart, Admiral Charles, 251
Stockoe, Dr, 257
Stroltz, General, 155
Stuart, Major-General Sir John, 128
Suchet, Duc d'Albufera, Louis-Gabriel, 162, 177, 197, 203–4, 205, 207, 210, 213, 217
Survilliers, 74
'Survilliers, Comte de', J.B.'s incognito title, 219, 248, 252, 268
Sweden, King, Queen of, *see* Bernadotte
Switzerland (Helvetian Republic), 75, 109

Tafalla, city of Navarre, 213
Talavera, battle of, 180, 203, 218
Talleyrand, Comte Auguste de, 236, 237

301